Modern Cryptography

Applied Mathematics for Encryption and Information Security

Chuck Easttom

Mc
Graw
Hill
Education

New York   Chicago   San Francisco
Athens   London   Madrid   Mexico City
Milan   New Delhi   Singapore   Sydney   Toronto

Library of Congress Cataloging-in-Publication Data

Names: Easttom, Chuck, author.
Title: Modern cryptography : applied mathematics for encryption and
   information security / Chuck Easttom.
Description: New York : McGraw-Hill Education, [2016] | Includes
   bibliographical references and index.
Identifiers: LCCN 2015033200 | ISBN 9781259588082 (alk. paper) | ISBN
   1259588084 (alk. paper)
Subjects: LCSH: Data encryption (Computer science) | Information
   networks—Security measures—Mathematics. | Computer networks—Security
   measures—Mathematics. | Computer security—Mathematics.
Classification: LCC TK5102.94 .E225 2016 | DDC 005.8/2—dc23 LC record available at http://lccn.loc.gov/2015033200

McGraw-Hill Education books are available at special quantity discounts to use as premiums and sales promotions, or for use in corporate training programs. To contact a representative, please visit the Contact Us pages at www.mhprofessional.com.

Modern Cryptography: Applied Mathematics for Encryption and Information Security

3 4 5 6 7 8   QVS/QVS   21 20 19 18 17

ISBN   978-1-25-958808-2
MHID   1-25-958808-4

Sponsoring Editor	**Proofreader**	**Art Director, Cover**
Meghan Manfre	Paul Tyler	Jeff Weeks
Editorial Supervisor	**Indexer**	**Cover Designer**
Janet Walden	Rebecca Plunkett	Jeff Weeks
Project Editor	**Production Supervisor**	
LeeAnn Pickrell	James Kussow	
Acquisitions Coordinator	**Composition**	
Amy Stonebraker	Cenveo® Publisher Services	
Copy Editor	**Illustration**	
Lisa Theobald	Cenveo Publisher Services	

*This book is dedicated to the men and women working
in military and intelligence agencies who implement cryptography,
work with cryptanalysis, and apply cryptography to computer security.*

About the Author

Chuck Easttom has more than 20 years of experience working in various aspects of the computer industry. For the past 15 years, he has focused primarily on computer security. He has wide experience in security, penetration testing, and forensics, but his favorite security topic is cryptography. Easttom has taught cryptography to U.S. government personnel, Department of Defense–related personnel, and friendly foreign governments. Of his six computer science patents, one is a method of distributed steganography. He has published papers on cryptography, and his various computer security books always include chapters on cryptography. He is a frequent speaker on cryptographic topics including RSA encryption, cryptographic backdoors, and cryptanalysis.

Easttom's security-related background includes 30 industry certifications, work with various vendors in the creation or revision of their certification tests, years of hands-on direct experience, and extensive teaching experience.

Contents at a Glance

Contents

Acknowledgments

Writing a book is an arduous task. It is always my goal to make each book better than the last. I have to thank several people for aiding me in this ask. First, the very helpful editorial staff at McGraw-Hill Professional. They were simply wonderful to work with! And their commitment to quality is unsurpassed in the publishing world. The team included a copy editor and technical editor, both working to make sure no mistakes crept into the book. The McGraw-Hill Professional team included Meghan Manfre, Amy Stonebraker, and LeeAnn Pickrell. The technical editor did an excellent job of ensuring that all the details were technically correct, and nothing was overlooked. Without all their help, I could not have written this book. Finally, I must thank my wife, Teresa, who was so patient when I spent long hours working on this book.

Introduction

There are a number of cryptography books on the market today. Many are very well written. I would know; I have an extensive cryptography library and have read most of the books on the market. However, most of these books suffer from one common issue: they assume the reader has a solid mathematical background and approach cryptography from that perspective. It is also sometimes the case that cryptography authors write as if they were speaking to experienced cryptographers, or at least to those with a basic working knowledge.

This book was designed to bring cryptography to the general security community. You need not have any mathematics background beyond basic secondary school algebra. The book will cover the math you need. Furthermore, the book includes chapters on topics rarely covered in cryptography texts: cryptographic backdoors, military cryptography, and applied cryptography.

This book makes an excellent Introduction to Cryptography textbook for students taking a first course in cryptography. It is also appropriate for computer security professionals who wish to self-study and gain a working knowledge of cryptography. If you are reading this as self-study, pause at the end of each chapter, use the review questions, and ensure that you fully mastered the critical topics before proceeding.

The book is really a journey through cryptography, starting with historical cryptography and then moving into the mathematical foundations necessary to understand modern cryptography. The book then moves on to the symmetric and asymmetric algorithms used today. It also includes chapters on Secure Sockets Layer (SSL), cryptanalysis, military applications for cryptography, and the future of cryptography.

The book is replete with links to external sources where you can get additional information, particularly in the chapters on mathematics and number theory. Each chapter ends with a series of questions to test your knowledge. The Appendix includes a set of tutorials for using some cryptography tools. These make excellent labs if this book is used as a textbook. Also, instructors and professors can download slides from the publisher. The accompanying slides make this an excellent choice for teaching an introductory cryptography course.

1

History of Cryptography to the 1800s

In this chapter we will cover the following:

- Single substitution ciphers
- Multi-alphabet substitution
- Devices
- Transposition ciphers

The desire to send secret communications is almost as old as written communication itself. For centuries, it often involved military secrets or political intrigue. Generals needed to communicate about troop movements to ensure that if a message was intercepted it wouldn't be intelligible to the enemy. Political intrigue, such as a palace coup, required surreptitious communications.

Modern cryptography still includes military communications as well as political scheming, but it has expanded into more mundane areas as well. Online banking and shopping, for example, have made cryptography a part of most people's daily lives, whether they are aware of it or not. Many people also choose to encrypt their computer hard drives or files. Others encrypt their e-mail transmissions. Today, cryptography permeates our lives.

> **Note** The release of Apple's iOS 6.0 was interesting because it changed how the iPhone would implement cryptography.

Why Study Cryptography?

It is an unfortunate fact that most people have almost no knowledge of cryptography. Even within the discipline of computer science, and more specifically the profession of computer security, a dearth of cryptographic knowledge plagues the industry. Most computer security professionals have only the most basic understanding of cryptography. Some would even argue that a deeper knowledge of cryptography is unnecessary. It can be assumed that since you are reading this book, you feel a need to deepen and broaden your knowledge of cryptography, and there are clearly practical reasons to do so, particularly for those in the computer security profession.

By understanding cryptology, you can select the most appropriate cryptographic implementations to suit your needs. Even if you have no desire to be a cryptographer, you still have to choose which tool to use to encrypt a hard drive, for example. Should you use the Data Encryption Standard (DES)? Triple DES (3DES)? Blowfish? The Advanced Encryption Standard (AES)? If you use AES, then what key size do you use, and why? If you are interested in message integrity for e-mail, should you use the Secure Hash Algorithm (SHA-2)? Perhaps a message authentication code (MAC) or hash message authentication code (HMAC)? Which will provide the most appropriate solution to your particular problem, and why?

In addition, knowing about cryptology helps you understand issues that occur when cryptographic incidents broadly impact computer security. A good example occurred in 2013, when the *New York Times* reported that among the documents released by National Security Agency subcontractor Edward Snowden was evidence that the NSA had placed a cryptographic backdoor in the random number generator known as *Dual_EC_DRBG (Elliptic Curve Deterministic Random Bit Generator)*. This news story generated a flurry of activity in the computer security community. But what is a cryptographic backdoor? What does this mean for privacy and security? Does this mean that the NSA could read anyone's e-mail as if it were published on a billboard?

We will be examining these very issues as well as random number generators and cryptographic backdoors later in this book. For now, it is enough for you to realize that you cannot answer any questions about this particular news story without having some knowledge of cryptography. This story, in fact, was not news to the informed cryptographic community. As early as 2006, papers had been published that suggested the possibility of a backdoor in this random number generator. Well-known and respected cryptographer Bruce Schneier, for example, blogged about this issue in 2007.[1] Had the security community a deeper knowledge of cryptography, this backdoor would have been a non-story.

I could continue with other reasons—very practical reasons—why learning cryptography is important, and you will see some of those reasons in later chapters. Cryptography is not merely a mathematical endeavor to be engaged in by a select few mathematicians and cryptologists. In this chapter, you will begin your journey into the world of cryptography by learning some essential terms and then exploring some historical ciphers.

What Is Cryptography?

Before you can begin studying cryptography, you need to know what exactly cryptography is. A number of people seem to have some misconceptions about what *cryptography* and related terms actually mean. The Merriam-Webster online dictionary defines cryptography as follows: "1) secret writing 2) the enciphering and deciphering of messages in secret code or cipher; also: the computerized encoding and decoding of information."[2] This definition does not seem overly helpful and may not provide you with much insight into the topic. Columbia University provides a slightly better definition in its "Introduction to Cryptography" course: to "process data into unintelligible form, reversibly, without data loss—typically digitally."[3]

The Columbia University definition adds the important element of not losing information, certainly a critical component in secure communications. However, I cannot help but think that the definition could be a bit clearer on the issue of exactly what cryptography is. So allow me to try my hand at defining cryptography:

> Cryptography is the study of how to alter a message so that someone intercepting it cannot read it without the appropriate algorithm and key.

This definition is certainly not radically different from that of either Merriam-Webster or Columbia University. However, I think it is a good, concise definition, and one we will use throughout this book.

Note that *cryptography* and *cryptology* are not synonyms, though many people mistakenly use the terms as if they were. I'll define and differentiate these two terms, as well as some other common terms you will need throughout your study of cryptography. These terms are used in both ancient and modern cryptography.

- **Cipher**   A synonym for the algorithm used in transforming plain text to cipher text.
- **Cipher text**   The coded or encrypted message. If your encryption is sufficiently strong, your cipher text should be secure.
- **Cryptanalysis**   Also known as code breaking; the study of principles and methods of deciphering cipher text without knowing the key. This is more difficult than movies or television would indicate, as you will see in Chapter 17.
- **Cryptography**   The study of how to alter a message so that someone intercepting it cannot read it without the appropriate algorithm and key.
- **Cryptology**   Although some people, including more than a few computer security books, use the terms *cryptography* and *cryptology* interchangeably, that is inaccurate. Cryptology is more comprehensive and includes both cryptography and cryptanalysis.
- **Decipher (decrypt)**   *Decipher* and *decrypt* are synonyms. Both terms mean to convert the cipher text to plain text.
- **Encipher (encrypt)**   *Encipher* and *encrypt* are synonyms. Both words mean to convert the plain text into cipher text.
- **Key**   The information, usually some sort of number, used with the algorithm to encrypt or decrypt the message. Think of the key as the fuel the algorithm requires in order to function.
- **Key space**   The total number of possible keys that could be used. For example, DES uses a 56-bit key; thus the total number of possible keys, or the key space, is 2^{56}.
- **Plain text**   The original message—the information you want to secure.

These are some of the most basic terms that permeate the study of cryptology and cryptography. In any discipline, it is important that you know, understand, and use the correct vocabulary of that field of study. These terms are essential for your understanding.

If you suppose that you cannot study cryptography without a good understanding of mathematics, to some extent you are correct. Modern methods of cryptography, particularly asymmetric cryptography, depend on mathematics. We will examine those algorithms later in this book, along with the mathematics you need to understand modern cryptography. It is often easier for students first to grasp the concepts of cryptography within the context of simpler historical ciphers, however. These ciphers don't require any substantive mathematics at all, but they do use the same concepts you will encounter later in this book. It is also good to have an historical perspective on any topic before you delve deeper into it. In this chapter we will examine a history of cryptography, looking at specific ciphers that have been used from the earliest days of cryptography to the 1800s.

Let us begin our study of historical cryptography by examining the most common historical ciphers. These are fascinating to study and illustrate the fundamental concepts you need in order to understand cryptography. Each one will demonstrate an algorithm, plain text, cipher text, and a key. The implementations, however, are far simpler than those of modern methods and make it relatively easy for you to master these ancient methods. Keep in mind that these ciphers are totally inadequate for modern security methods. They would be cracked extremely quickly with a modern computer, and many can be analyzed and cracked with a pen, paper, and the application of relatively simple cryptanalysis legerdemain.

Substitution Ciphers

The first ciphers in recorded history are *substitution ciphers*. With this method, each letter of plain text is substituted for some letter of cipher text according to some algorithm. There are two types of substitution ciphers: single-alphabet (or mono-alphabet) and multi-alphabet (or poly-alphabet). In a single-alphabet substitution cipher, a given letter of plain text is always substituted for the corresponding letter of cipher text. For example, an *a* in the plain text would always be a *k* in the cipher text. Multi-alphabet substitution uses multiple substitutions, so that, for example, an *a* in the plain text is sometimes a *k* and sometimes a *j* in the cipher text. You will see examples of both in this section.

The Caesar Cipher

One of the most widely known historical encryption methods is the *Caesar cipher*. According to the Roman historian Gaius Suetonius Tranquillus (c. 70–130 CE), Julius Caesar used this cipher to encrypt military messages, shifting all letters of the plain text three places to the right. So, for example, the message

```
Attack at dawn
```

becomes

```
Dwwdfn dw gdzq
```

As you can see, the *a* in the plain text is shifted to the right three letters to become a *d* in the cipher text. Then the *t* in the plain text is shifted three letters to the right to become a *w* in the cipher text. This process continues for all the letters in the plain text. In our example, none of the shifts went beyond the letter *z*. What would happen if we shifted the letter *y* to the right three? The process would wrap around the alphabet, starting back at letter *a*. So the letter *y* would be shifted to a letter *b* in the cipher text.

Note   Decryption is trivial if the recipient knows the shift that was used and reverses it. For example, if the sender shifts three to the right to encrypt the message, the recipient can shift three to the left to decrypt the message.

Although Caesar was reputed to have used a shift of three to the right, any shifting pattern will work with this method, shifting either to the right or left by any number of spaces. Because this is a very simple method to understand, it's a good place to start our study of encryption. It is, however, extremely easy to crack. You see, any language has a certain letter and word *frequency*, meaning that some letters are used more frequently than others. In the English language, the most common single-letter word is *a*, followed closely by the word *I*. The most common three-letter word is *the*, followed closely by the word *and*. Those two facts alone could help you decrypt a Caesar cipher. However, you can apply additional rules. For example, in the English language, the most common two letter sequences are *oo* and *ee*.[4] Examining the frequency of letter and letter combination occurrences is called *frequency analysis*.

It is claimed that other Caesars, such as Augustus, used variations of the Caesar cipher, such as one shift to the right. It should be obvious that any shift, left or right, of more than 26 (at least in English) would simply loop around the alphabet. So a shift to the right of 27 is really just a shift of one.

Although the Caesar cipher is certainly not appropriate for modern cryptographic needs, it does contain all the items needed for a cryptography algorithm. First, we have the plain text message—in our current example, *Attack at dawn*. Then we have an algorithm—shift every letter. And then a key, in this case *+3*, or three to the right (*−3* would be three to the left). And finally we have cipher text, *Dwwdfn dw gdzq*. This is, essentially, the same structure used by all modern symmetric algorithms. The only differences between the Caesar cipher and modern symmetric ciphers are the complexity of the algorithm and the size of the key.

The size of the key brings us to one significant problem with the Caesar cipher—its small key space. Recall that key space is the total number of possible keys. Because there are only 26 letters in the English alphabet, the key space is *26* (that is, +−26). It would be relatively easy for a person working with pen and paper to check all possible keys, and it would be ridiculously trivial for a computer to do so. In the cyber security world, a malicious person who checks all possible keys to decipher an encrypted message is conducting what is called a *brute-force attack*. The smaller the key space, the easier a brute-force attack will be. Compare the Caesar cipher, with a key space of 26, to AES 128-bit, with a key space of 2^{128}, or about 3.4×10^{38}. Clearly, the larger key space makes a cipher more resistant to brute-force attacks. Note, however, that simply having a long key is not sufficient for security. You will learn more about this when we discuss cryptanalysis in Chapter 17.

Mathematical Notation of the Caesar Cipher

With the various ancient ciphers we will be using, the math is trivial. However, it is a good idea for you to become accustomed to mathematical notation, at least with those algorithms where such notation is appropriate. It is common to use a capital letter *P* to represent plain text and a capital letter *C* to represent cipher text. We can also use a capital letter *K* to represent the key. This gives us the following mathematical representation of a Caesar cipher:

$$C \equiv P + K \ (\mathrm{mod}\ 26)$$

Don't be overly concerned about the mod 26. We will explore modulus operations in detail in Chapter 4. For now, I just use the modulus operation to denote dividing by a given number (in this case, 26, because there are 26 letters in the alphabet) and listing only the remainder.

Decryption can also be represented via mathematical symbols:

$$P \equiv C - K \ (\text{mod } 26)$$

The mathematical representation of Caesar's method of shifting three to the right is

$$C \equiv P + 3 \ (\text{mod } 26)$$

According to the book *The Lives of the Caesars*, written by Suetonius, Julius Caesar used this cipher extensively:

> There are also the letters of his to Cicero, as well as to his intimates on private affairs, and in the latter, if he had anything confidential to say, he wrote it in cipher, that is by so changing the order of the letters of the alphabet, that not a word could be made out. If anyone wishes to decipher these, and get at their meaning, he must substitute the fourth letter of the alphabet, namely D, for A, and so with the others.[5]

If the plain text is the 24th letter of the alphabet (which is the letter *X*), then the cipher text is (24 + 3)/26, listing only the remainder. Thus, 27/26 = 1, or the letter *A*.

> **Note**   We cannot know how effective the Caesar cipher was at concealing messages. However, at the time of Julius Caesar, illiteracy was widespread and cryptography was not widely known. So what may seem a trivial cipher today—in fact, child's play—may well have been effective enough more than 2000 years ago.

The Caesar cipher is probably the most widely known substitution cipher, but it is not the only one. All substitution ciphers operate the same way: by substituting each letter in the plain text for some letter in the cipher text, with a one-to-one relationship between the plain text and cipher text. Let's look at a few other substitution ciphers.

Atbash Cipher

Hebrew scribes copying the biblical book of Jeremiah used the *Atbash substitution cipher*. Applying the Atbash cipher is fairly simple: just reverse the order of the letters of the alphabet. This is, by modern standards, a very primitive cipher that is easy to break. For example, in English, *a* becomes *z*, *b* becomes *y*, *c* becomes *x*, and so on. Of course, the Hebrews used the Hebrew alphabet, with *aleph* being the first letter and *tav* the last letter. However, I will use English examples to demonstrate the cipher:

```
Attack at dawn
```

becomes

```
Zggzxp zg wzdm
```

As you can see, the *A* (the first letter in the alphabet) is switched with *Z* (the last letter), and the *t* is the 19th letter (or 7th from the end) and gets swapped with *g*, the 7th letter from the beginning. This process is continued until the entire message is enciphered.

To decrypt the message, you simply reverse the process so that *z* becomes *a*, *b* becomes *y*, and so on. This is obviously a simple cipher and is not used in modern times. However, like the Caesar cipher example, it illustrates the basic concept of cryptography—to perform some permutation on the plain text to render it difficult to read by those who don't have the key to "unscramble" the cipher text. The Atbash cipher, like the Caesar cipher, is a single-substitution cipher (each letter in the plain text has a direct, one-to-one relationship with each letter in the cipher text). The same letter and word frequency issues that can be used to crack the Caesar cipher can be used to crack the Atbash cipher.

Affine Ciphers

Affine ciphers are any single-substitution alphabet ciphers (also called *mono-alphabet substitution*) in which each letter in the alphabet is mapped to some numeric value, permuted with some relatively simple mathematical function, and then converted back to a letter. For example, using the Caesar cipher, each letter is converted to a number, shifted by some amount, and then converted back to a letter.

The basic formula for any affine cipher is

$$ax + b \pmod{m}$$

M is the size of the alphabet—so in English that would be 26. The *x* represents the plain text letter's numeric equivalent, and the *b* is the amount to shift. The letter *a* is some multiple—in the case of the Caesar cipher, *a* is 1. So the Caesar cipher would be

$$1x + 3 \pmod{26}$$

You could obviously use any shift amount you want, as well as any multiplier. The *ax* value could be $1x$, as with Caesar, or it could be $2x$, $3x$, or any other value. For example, let's create a simple affine cipher:

$$2x + 4 \pmod{26}$$

To encrypt the phrase *Attack at dawn*, we first convert each letter to a number, then multiply that number by 2 and calculate that result mod 26. So *A* is *1*, 2 multiplied by 1 is 2, add 4, gives us 6 mod 26 yielding 6, or *F*.

Then we have *t*, which is 20, and 2 multiplied by 20 is 40, add 4, which gives us 44, and 44 mod 26 yields 18, or *r*. Ultimately we get this:

```
Attack at dawn
Frrfjo fr lfxf
```

Notice that the letter *k* did not convert to a letter; instead, a 0 (zero) appears. *K* is the 11th letter of the alphabet, and $2x + 4$, where $x = 11$, equals 26. And 26 mod 26 is 0.

This is one example of an affine cipher, and there are quite a few others. As you have just seen, you can easily create one of your own. You would want to limit your selection of *a* to values that produce only integer results, rather than decimals. A value of $1.3x$, for example, would lead to decimal values, which could not easily be converted to letters. We know that *1* is *a* and 2 is *b*, but what letter is *1.3*?

All affine ciphers have the same weaknesses as any single-substitution cipher. They all preserve the letter and word frequencies found in the underlying language and are thus susceptible to frequency analysis. In fact, no matter how complex you make the permutation, any single-substitution cipher is going to be vulnerable to frequency analysis.

ROT 13

ROT 13 is a trivial single-substitution cipher that also happens to be an affine cipher. *ROT* is short for *rotate*: each letter is rotated to the right by 13. So the affine representation of the ROT 13 (in English) is

$$1x + 13 \ (\mathrm{mod}\ 26)$$

Since the Latin alphabet has 26 letters, simply applying ROT 13 a second time will decrypt the message. As you can probably guess, this is not at all secure by modern standards. However, it is actually used in some situations. For example, some of the keys in the Microsoft Windows Registry are encrypted using ROT 13.[6] In this case, the reasoning is likely to be that, first and foremost, you need access to the system before you can explore the Windows Registry, and second, most people are not well versed in the Windows Registry and would have difficulty finding specific items there even if they were not encrypted at all, so ROT 13 may be secure enough for this scenario. I am not necessarily in agreement with that outlook, but it is a fact that the Windows Registry uses ROT 13.

> **Note** ROT 13 has been used in online forums and web pages to obfuscate the answer to some quiz, so that it is not readily apparent without applying ROT 13 to the answer. Some people have chosen to publish their e-mail encoded with ROT 13 so that it is easy for a human to decrypt, but difficult for an automated spam bot to decrypt and send spam e-mail.

It has also been reported that in the late 1990s Netscape Communicator used ROT 13 to store e-mail passwords. ROT 13 has actually become somewhat of a joke in the cryptology community. For example, cryptologists will jokingly refer to "ROT 26," which would effectively be no encryption at all. Another common joke is to refer to "triple ROT 13." Just a brief reflection should demonstrate to you that the second application of ROT 13 returns to the original plain text, and the third application of ROT 13 is just the same as the first.

Homophonic Substitution

Over time, the flaws in single-substitution ciphers became more apparent. *Homophonic substitution* was one of the earlier attempts to make substitution ciphers more robust by masking the letter frequencies, as plain text letters were mapped to more than one cipher text symbol, and usually the higher frequency plain text letters were given more cipher text equivalents. For example, *a* might map either to *x* or *y*. This had the effect of disrupting frequencies, making analysis more difficult. It was also possible to use invented symbols in the cipher text and to have a variety of mappings. For example, *a* maps to *x*, but *z* maps to ¥.

Tip	Having a single character of plain text map to more than one character of cipher text makes homophonic substitution ciphers more difficult to analyze. Using symbols other than characters can make them even more challenging to analyze.

There are variations of this cipher, and one of the most notable versions is called the *nomenclator cipher*, which used a codebook with a table of homophonic substitutions. Originally the codebook used only the names of people, thus the term nomenclator. So, for example, Mr. Smith might be *XX* and Mr. Jones would be *XYZ*. Eventually, nomenclators were created that used a variety of words rather than just names. The codes could be random letters, such as those already described, or code words. Thus, Mr. Jones might be enciphered as *poodle* and Mr. Smith enciphered as *catfish*. Such codebooks with nomenclator substitutions where quite popular in espionage for a number of years. The advantage of a nomenclator is that it does not provide any frequencies to analyze. However, should the codebook become compromised, all messages encoded with it will also be compromised.

The Great Cipher

The *Great Cipher* is one famous nomenclator used by the French government until the early 1800s. This cipher was invented by the Rossignol family, a French family with several generations of cryptographers, all of whom served the French court. The first, a 26-year-old Rossignol mathematician, served under Louis XIII, creating secure codes.

The Great Cipher used 587 different numbers that stood for syllables (note that there where variations on this theme, some with a different number of codes). To help prevent frequency analysis, the cipher text would include nulls, or numbers that meant nothing. There were also traps, or codes that indicated the recipient should ignore the previous coded message.

Polybius Cipher

The *Polybius cipher* (also known as the Polybius square) was invented by the Greek historian Polybius (c. 200–118 B.C.E.). Obviously, his work used the Greek alphabet, but we will use it with English here. As shown in the following grid, in the Polybius cipher, each letter is represented by two numbers. Those two numbers being the x and y coordinates of that letter on the grid. For example, *A* is 1 1, *T* is 4 4, *C* is 1 3, and *K* is 2 5. So to encrypt the word *attack*, you would use 114444111325.

Despite the use of two numbers to represent a single letter, this is a substitution cipher and still maintains the letter and word frequencies found in the underlying language of

	1	2	3	4	5
1	A	B	C	D	E
2	F	G	H	I/J	K
3	L	M	N	O	P
4	Q	R	S	T	U
5	V	W	X	Y	Z

the plain text. If you used the standard Polybius square, which is a widely known cipher, it would be easily cracked, even without any frequency analysis. If you wanted to use a different encoding for letters in the square, that would require the sending and receiving parties share the particular Polybius square in advance, so that they could send and read messages.

It is interesting to note that the historian Polybius actually established this cipher as a means of sending codes via torches. Messengers standing on hilltops could hold up torches to represent letters, and thus send messages. Establishing a series of such messengers on hilltops, each relaying the message to the next, allowed communications over a significant distance, much faster than any messenger on foot or horseback could travel.

Ancient Cryptography in Modern Wars

Here is a very interesting story that does not necessarily fit with the timeline of this chapter (pre-20th century), but it does concern the Polybius square. The Polybius square was used by prisoners of war in Vietnam, who communicated via tapping on a wall to signal letters. So, for example, four taps, a pause, and then two taps would be the letter *R*. When used in this fashion, it is referred to as a *tap code*.[7] This cipher was introduced into the POW camps in 1965 by Captain Carlyle Harris, Lieutenant Phillip Butler, Lieutenant Robert Peel, and Lieutenant Commander Robert Shumaker, all imprisoned at the Hoa Lo prisoner of war camp. It is reported that Harris recalled being introduced to the Polybius square by an instructor during his training. He then applied the Polybius square to a tap code so that he and his fellow prisoners could communicate. This technique was taught to new prisoners and became widespread in the POW camp. Vice Admiral James Stockdale wrote about using the tap code, stating, "Our tapping ceased to be just an exchange of letters and words; it became conversation. Elation, sadness, humor, sarcasm, excitement, depression—all came through."[8] This is a poignant example of cryptography being applied to very practical purposes.

Null Cipher

The *null cipher* is a very old cipher—in fact, by today's standards, it might be considered more steganography than cipher (you'll read about steganography in Chapter 16). Essentially, the message is hidden in unrelated text. So, in a message such as

We **a**re having breakfas**t** a**t** noon **at** the **c**afe, would that be o**k**ay?

the sender and recipient have prearranged to use some pattern, taking certain letters from the message. So, for example, the numbers

3 20 22 27 32 48

would signify the letters in the sentence and provide the message

attack

The pattern can be complex or simple—such as always using the second letter of each word or any other pattern. In addition, punctuation and spaces could be counted as characters (our example ignored punctuation and spaces).

Multi-Alphabet Substitution

As you know, any single-alphabet substitution cipher is susceptible to frequency analysis. The most obvious way to improve such ciphers would be to find some mechanism whereby the frequency of letters and words could be disrupted. Eventually, a slight improvement on the single-substitution cipher was developed, called *multi-alphabet substitution*. In this scheme, you select multiple numbers by which to shift letters (that is, multiple substitution alphabets). For example, if you select three substitution alphabets (+1, +2, and +3), then

```
Attack at dawn
```

becomes

```
Bvwbenbvgbxo
```

In this example, the first letter was shifted forward by one, so *A* became *B*; the second letter was shifted forward by two, so *t* became *v*; the third letter was shifted forward by three, so in this case *t* became *w*. Then you start over with one shift forward. As you can see, the use of multiple alphabets changes letter and word frequency. The first letter *t* became *v*, but the second letter *t* became *w*. This disrupts the letter and word frequency of the underlying plain text. The more alphabets you use, the more disruption there will be to the letter and word frequency of the plain text. This disruption of the letter and word frequency overcomes the weaknesses of traditional single-substitution ciphers. There are a variety of methods for making a multi-alphabet substitution cipher. We will examine a few of the most common multi-alphabet ciphers in the following sections.

Tabula Recta

Tabula recta is one of the earliest major multi-alphabet substitution ciphers. It was invented in the 16th century by Johannes Trithemius. A tabula recta is a square table of alphabets made by shifting the previous alphabet to the right, as shown in Figure 1-1.

This essentially creates 26 different Caesar ciphers. Trithemius described this in his book *Polygraphia*, which is presumed to be the first published book on cryptology. To encrypt a message using this cipher, you substitute the plain text letter for the letter that appears beneath it in the table. Basically, the first letter of the plain text (denoting the row) is matched with the first letter of the keyword (denoting the column), and the intersection of the two forms the cipher text. This is repeated with each letter. When the end of the keyword is reached, you start over at the beginning of the keyword. Trithemius used a fixed keyword, so although this did change the frequency distributions found in single-substitution ciphers, it still had a significant flaw when compared to later developments such as Vigenère.

```
  A B C D E F G H I J K L M N O P Q R S T U V W X Y Z
A A B C D E F G H I J K L M N O P Q R S T U V W X Y Z
B B C D E F G H I J K L M N O P Q R S T U V W X Y Z A
C C D E F G H I J K L M N O P Q R S T U V W X Y Z A B
D D E F G H I J K L M N O P Q R S T U V W X Y Z A B C
E E F G H I J K L M N O P Q R S T U V W X Y Z A B C D
F F G H I J K L M N O P Q R S T U V W X Y Z A B C D E
G G H I J K L M N O P Q R S T U V W X Y Z A B C D E F
H H I J K L M N O P Q R S T U V W X Y Z A B C D E F G
I I J K L M N O P Q R S T U V W X Y Z A B C D E F G H
J J K L M N O P Q R S T U V W X Y Z A B C D E F G H I
K K L M N O P Q R S T U V W X Y Z A B C D E F G H I J
L L M N O P Q R S T U V W X Y Z A B C D E F G H I J K
M M N O P Q R S T U V W X Y Z A B C D E F G H I J K L
N N O P Q R S T U V W X Y Z A B C D E F G H I J K L M
O O P Q R S T U V W X Y Z A B C D E F G H I J K L M N
P P Q R S T U V W X Y Z A B C D E F G H I J K L M N O
Q Q R S T U V W X Y Z A B C D E F G H I J K L M N O P
R R S T U V W X Y Z A B C D E F G H I J K L M N O P Q
S S T U V W X Y Z A B C D E F G H I J K L M N O P Q R
T T U V W X Y Z A B C D E F G H I J K L M N O P Q R S
U U V W X Y Z A B C D E F G H I J K L M N O P Q R S T
V V W X Y Z A B C D E F G H I J K L M N O P Q R S T U
W W X Y Z A B C D E F G H I J K L M N O P Q R S T U V
X X Y Z A B C D E F G H I J K L M N O P Q R S T U V W
Y Y Z A B C D E F G H I J K L M N O P Q R S T U V W X
Z Z A B C D E F G H I J K L M N O P Q R S T U V W X Y
```

FIGURE 1-1   Tabula recta

Vigenère

Perhaps the most widely known multi-alphabet cipher is the *Vigenère cipher*. This cipher was first described in 1553 by Giovan Battista Bellaso, though it is misattributed to 19th-century cryptographer Blaise de Vigenère. It is a method of encrypting alphabetic text by using a series of different mono-alphabet ciphers selected based on the letters of a keyword. Bellaso also added the concept of using any keyword, thereby making the choice of substitution alphabets difficult to calculate.

Note   For many years, Vigenère was considered very strong—even unbreakable. However, in the 19th century, Friedrich Kasiski published a technique for breaking the Vigenère cipher. We will revisit that when we discuss cryptanalysis later in this book.

It is important that you get accustomed to mathematical notation. Here, using *P* for plain text, *C* for cipher text, and *K* for key, we can view Vigenère very similarly to Caesar, with one important difference: the value *K* changes.

$$C_i \equiv P_i + K_i \pmod{26}$$

The *i* denotes the current key with the current letter of plain text and the current letter of cipher text. Note that many sources use *M* (for message) rather than *P* (for plain text) in this notation.

A variation of the Vigenère, the *running key cipher*, simply uses a long string of random characters as the key, which makes it even more difficult to decipher.

The Beaufort Cipher

The *Beaufort cipher* uses a tabula recta to encipher the plain text. A keyword is preselected by the involved parties. This cipher was created by Sir Francis Beaufort (1774–1857) and is very similar to the Vigenère cipher. A typical tabula recta was shown earlier in this chapter in Figure 1-1.

When using the Beaufort cipher, you select a keyword, except unlike Vigenère, you locate the plain text in the top row, move down until you find the matching letter of the keyword, and then choose the letter farthest to the left in the row as the cipher text.

For example, using the tabula recta in Figure 1-1, and the keyword *falcon*, you would encrypt the message *Attack at dawn* in the following manner:

1. Find the letter *A* on the top row.
2. Go straight down that column until you find the letter *F* (the first letter of the keyword).
3. Use the letter in the far left column as the cipher text letter. In this case, that would be *F*.
4. Repeat this, except this time use the next letter of the keyword, *a*. Locate the second letter of the plain text *t* in the top row.
5. Move down that column until you find an *a*, and then we select the letter on the far left of that row, which would be *h*.
6. When you reach the last letter of the keyword, you start over at the first letter of the keyword, so that

    Attack at dawn

    becomes

    Fhscmdfhicsa

Devices

In modern times, devices are almost always used with cryptography. For example, computers are used to encrypt e-mail, web traffic, and so on. In ancient times, there were also ciphers based on the use of specific devices to encrypt and decrypt messages.

Scytale Cipher

The *Scytale cipher* is one such ancient cipher. Often mispronounced (it actually rhymes with "Italy"), this cipher used a cylinder with a strip of parchment wrapped around it. If you had the correct diameter cylinder, then when the parchment was wrapped around it, the message could be read. You can see the concept shown in Figure 1-2.

If you did not have the correct size of cylinder, however, or if you simply found the parchment and no cylinder, the message would appear to be a random string of letters. This method was first used by the Spartans and later throughout Greece. The earliest mention of Scytale was by the Greek poet Archilochus in the seventh century B.C.E. However, the first

FIGURE 1-2   Scytale

mention of how it actually worked was by Plutarch in the first century B.C.E., in his work *Parallel Lives*:

> The dispatch-scroll is of the following character. When the ephors send out an admiral or a general, they make two round pieces of wood exactly alike in length and thickness, so that each corresponds to the other in its dimensions, and keep one themselves, while they give the other to their envoy. These pieces of wood they call "scytalae." Whenever, then, they wish to send some secret and important message, they make a scroll of parchment long and narrow, like a leathern strap, and wind it round their "scytale," leaving no vacant space thereon, but covering its surface all round with the parchment. After doing this, they write what they wish on the parchment, just as it lies wrapped about the "scytale"; and when they have written their message, they take the parchment off, and send it, without the piece of wood, to the commander. He, when he has received it, cannot other get any meaning of it—since the letters have no connection, but are disarranged—unless he takes his own "scytale" and winds the strip of parchment about it, so that, when its spiral course is restored perfectly, and that which follows is joined to that which precedes, he reads around the staff, and so discovers the continuity of the message. And the parchment, like the staff, is called "scytale," as the thing measured bears the name of the measure.[9]

Alberti Cipher Disk

The Alberti *cipher disk*, created by Leon Battista Alberti, is an example of a multi-alphabet substitution. Alberti wrote about this cipher in 1467 in his book *De Cifris*. It is said to be the first multi-alphabet cipher. It consists of two disks attached in the center with a common pin. Each disk had 24 equal cells. The larger, outer disk, called the *stabilis*, displayed an uppercase Latin alphabet used for the plain text. The smaller, inner disk, called the *mobilis*, displayed a lowercase alphabet for the cipher text.

To encrypt a message, a letter on the inner disk was lined up with a letter on the outer disk as a key. If you knew what letter to line up with, you would know which key to use. This has the effect of offering multiple substitution alphabets. You can see an example of the cipher disk, with the English alphabet, in Figure 1-3.

In Alberti's original cipher disk, he used the Latin alphabet. So the outer disk had the Latin alphabet minus a few English letters, as well as numbers 1 through 4 for use with a codebook that had phrases and words assigned four-digit values.

The Jefferson Disk

The *Jefferson disk*, which was called a "wheel cipher" by its inventor, Thomas Jefferson, is a rather complex device, at least for its time. Invented in 1795, the disk is a set of wheels or disks,

FIGURE 1-3   Cipher disk

each displaying the 26 letters of the English alphabet. The disks are all on a central axle and can be rotated about the axle. The order of the disks is the key, and both sender and receiver had to order their disks according to the key. An example of the Jefferson disk is shown in Figure 1-4.

When using the Jefferson disk, the sender would rotate the letters on the disks until the message was spelled out in a single row. The sender would then copy down any row of text on the disks other than the one that contained the plain text message. That enciphered message would then be sent to the recipient. The recipient then arranged the disk letters according to the predefined order and then rotated the disk until the message was displayed.

Note   This device was independently invented by Étienne Bazeries (1846–1931), a French cryptographer, although Jefferson improved on the disk in his version. Bazeries was known for being a very skilled cryptographer and cryptanalyst. After he broke several transposition systems used by the French military, the French government hired him to work for the Ministry of Foreign Affairs. During World War I, he worked on breaking German ciphers.

Stories such as this are not uncommon in cryptography. Two different parties may independently invent the same or remarkably similar ciphers. This often occurs from time to time in modern times, when at least some work in cryptography is classified by various governments. You will see other examples of this in later chapters on modern ciphers.

FIGURE 1-4   Jefferson disk

Book Ciphers

Book ciphers have probably been around for as long as books have been available. Essentially, the sender and receiver agree to use a particular book as its basis. The simplest implementation is to send coordinates for words. So, for example, *3 3 10* means "go to page 3, line 3, tenth word." In this way, the sender can specify words with coordinates and write out entire sentences. There are numerous variations of this cipher. For example you could combine book ciphers with Vigenère and use the book coordinates to denote the keyword for Vigenère.

Beale Ciphers

In 1885, a pamphlet was published describing treasure buried in the 1820s by one Thomas J. Beale in Virginia. The *Beale ciphers* are three cipher texts that allegedly give the location, contents, and names of the owners of the buried treasure. The first Beale cipher, which has not been solved, provides the location. The second cipher provides details of the contents of the treasure and has been solved. The second cipher was a book cipher that used the US Declaration of Independence as the book. Each number in the cipher represents a word in the document. They are presented here simply as an example of a book cipher.

Transposition Ciphers

So far, we have looked at ciphers in which some sort of substitution is performed. However, this is not the only way to encrypt a message. It is also possible to transpose parts of a message. Transposition ciphers provide yet another avenue for encryption.

Reverse Order

The simplest implementation of a transposition cipher is to reverse the plain text. In this way

```
Attack at dawn
```

becomes

```
Nwadtakcatta
```

Obviously, this is not a particularly difficult cipher to break, but it demonstrates a simple transposition.

Rail Fence Cipher

The *rail fence cipher* may be the most widely known transposition cipher. You encrypt the message by alternating each letter on a different row. So

```
Attack at dawn
```

is written like this:

```
A    t    c    a    d    w
     t    a    k    t    a    n
```

Next you write down the text on both lines, reading from left to right, as you normally would, thus producing

```
Atcadwtaktan
```

To decrypt the message, the recipient must write it out on rows:

```
A    t    c    a    d    w
     t    a    k    t    a    n
```

Then the recipient reconstructs the original message. Most texts use two rows as examples, but any number of rows can be used.

Geometric Shape Cipher

In the *geometric shape cipher*, the sender writes out the plain text in rows and then maps a path (that is, a shape) through it to create the cipher text. So if the plain text is

```
Attack the beach at sunrise
```

this message would be written in rows like this:

```
A    t    t    a    c    k    t
h    e    b    e    a    c    h
a    t    s    u    n    r    i    s    e
```

Then the sender chooses some path through the message to create the cipher text, as shown in Figure 1-5.

Using the path depicted in Figure 1-5, the cipher text reads

```
Ahatettbsueacanrckthise
```

For this example, I used a very simple geometric path through the plain text, but you could use other, more complex patterns as well. This method is sometimes called a route cipher, as it is encrypted using a specific route through the plain text.

FIGURE 1-5 Geometric shape cipher

Columnar Cipher

The *columnar cipher* is an intriguing type of transposition cipher. In this cipher, the text you want to encrypt is written in rows usually of a specific length and determined by some keyword. For example, if the keyword is *falcon*, which is six characters long, you would write out your messages in rows of six characters each. So you would write out

```
A   t   t   a   c   k
t   h   e   b   e   a
c   h   a   t   s   u
n   r   i   s   e   q
```

Notice the added *q* at the end. That was added because the last row is only five characters long. In a regular columnar cipher, you pad the last row so that all rows are of equal length.

If you leave the blank spaces intact, this would be an irregular columnar cipher, and the order of columns would be based on the letters in the keyword as they appear in the alphabet. So if the keyword is *falcon*, the order is 3 1 4 2 6 5 as *f* is the third lowest letter in the alphabet, *a* is the lowest, *l* is the fourth lowest, and so on. So if we apply 3 1 4 2 6 5 to encrypt the message, we first write out the letters down column 3, then column 1, then column 4, then column 2, then column 6, and then column 5. So the message

```
a   t   t   a   c   k
t   h   e   b   e   a
c   h   a   t   s   u
n   r   i   s   e   q
```

is encrypted like so:

```
teaiatcnabtskauqcese
```

Many variations of the columnar cipher, such as the Myskowski variation, have been created over the years, each adding some subtle twist to the concept.

Myskowski Variation

When using a columnar cipher, what happens if the keyword includes the same letter twice? Normally, you treat the second occurrence as if it were the next letter. For example, if *babe* is the keyword, the second *b* is treated as if it were a *c*, so the order would be 2 1 3 4.

In 1902, Emile Myskowski proposed a variation that did something different. The repeated letters were numbered identically, so *babe* would be 2 1 2 3. Any plain text columns that had unique numbers (in this case 1 and 3) would be transcribed downward as usual. However, the recurring numbers (in this case 2) would be transcribed left to right.

Combinations

One of the first thoughts that may occur when you're first learning cryptography is to combine two or more of the classic ciphers, such as those covered in this chapter. For example, you might use a Vigenère cipher first, and then put the message through a columnar transposition or a rail fence cipher. Combining some substitution cipher with a transposition cipher would increase the difficulty a human would have in breaking the cipher. You can think of this in mathematical terms as a function of a function:

$$f(g(x))$$

Where g is the first cipher, x is the plain text, and f is the second cipher. And you could apply them in any order—first a substitution and then a transposition, or vice versa.

When you're exploring this train of thought, be aware that if you simply apply two mono-alphabet substitution ciphers, you have not improved secrecy at all. The cipher text will still preserve the same letter and word frequencies. In fact, the best improvement will come from combining transposition and substitution ciphers. As you will see beginning in Chapter 6, modern block ciphers combine substitution and transposition, albeit in a more complex fashion. Don't think, however, that such innovations will lead to ciphers that are sufficient for modern security needs. Performing such combinations is an intriguing intellectual exercise and will hone your cryptography knowledge, but these methods would not provide much security against modern computerized cryptanalysis.

Conclusions

In this chapter, you have been exposed to a variety of historical ciphers. You were shown single-substitution ciphers such as Caesar and Atbash and multi-alphabet ciphers such as Vigenère. You learned about the weaknesses of mono-alphabet substitution ciphers and how multi-alphabet methods attempt to overcome those issues. You were introduced to a variety of transposition ciphers, including the rail fence and columnar ciphers. This chapter also introduced you to devices such as Scytale and the Jefferson disk. It is important that you get very comfortable with these ciphers before proceeding on.

You were also introduced to some basic mathematical notation to symbolize some of the ciphers in this chapter as well as some general cryptographic terminology such as *cipher text* and *key space*. That notation and those terms should be very familiar to you because they will help form the basis for modern symmetric ciphers you'll read about, beginning in Chapter 6.

Test Your Knowledge

A few questions are provided here to aid you in testing your knowledge before you proceed.

1. What is the most obvious weakness in a mono-alphabet cipher?
    A. It preserves word frequency.
    B. It can be cracked with modern computers.
    C. It is actually quite strong.
    D. It doesn't use complex mathematics.
2. The total number of possible keys for a given cipher is referred to as the _____.
    A. key group
    B. key domain
    C. key space
    D. key range

3. Which of the following methods used a cylinder with text wrapped around it?
   A. Vigenère cipher
   B. Jefferson disk
   C. Cipher disk
   D. Scytale
4. What is an affine cipher?
   A. Any cipher of the form ax + b (mod m)
   B. Only single substitution ciphers
   C. Any single substitution cipher
   D. A multi-alphabet cipher
5. What is the key feature of homophonic substitution?
   A. Multiple substitution alphabets are used.
   B. A single plain text letter may have several cipher text representations.
   C. The cipher text is phonically similar to the plain text.
   D. It combines substitution with transposition.

Answers

1. A
2. C
3. D
4. A
5. B

Endnotes

1. Bruce Schneier, "The Strange Story of DUAL_EC_DRBG," www.schneier.com/blog/archives/2007/11/the_strange_sto.html.
2. Merriam-Webster Dictionary, www.merriam-webster.com/dictionary/cryptography.
3. Columbia University "Introduction to Cryptography" course, www.cs.columbia.edu/~hgs/teaching/security/slides/crypto2.pdf.
4. For more about word and letter frequencies, see "Puzzle Barron's Cryptograms," www.cryptograms.org/letter-frequencies.php; "Cornell University Letter Frequency," www.math.cornell.edu/~mec/2003-2004/cryptography/subs/frequencies.html; and "Letter Frequencies in English," www.letterfrequency.org/.
5. Suetonius, *Lives of the Caesars* (Oxford University Press, 2009).
6. Ken Harthun discusses the use of ROT 13 in the Windows Registry in "How to Use the Windows Registry for Cyber Forensics: Part 2," at http://itknowledgeexchange.techtarget.com/security-corner/how-to-use-the-windows-registry-for-cyber-forensics-part-2/.
7. Tap codes were discussed in "Return with Honor," an episode of *American Experience* on PBS television. For information on the POWs' use of the tap code, see www.pbs.org/wgbh/amex/honor/sfeature/sf_tap.html.
8. Jim and Sybil Stockdale, *In Love and War: The Story of a Family's Ordeal and Sacrifice During the Vietnam Years* (Harper & Row, 1984).
9. From Plutarch's *Parallel Lives*, "The Life of Lysander": http://penelope.uchicago.edu/Thayer/E/Roman/Texts/Plutarch/Lives/Lysander*.html.

2

History of Cryptography from the 1800s

In this chapter we will cover the following:

- Playfair cipher
- Two-square and four-square ciphers
- Hill cipher
- ADFGX and ADFGVX ciphers
- Bifid ciphers
- Gronsfeld cipher
- Vernam cipher
- Enigma
- Historical figures in cryptography

I n Chapter 1, you were introduced to several relatively simple ciphers that were widely used for many centuries. Beginning in the 1800s, the art of cryptography entered an age of growth as more complex ciphers were developed. In this chapter we will look at the end of the classical (pre-computer) days of cryptography and continue on to the 20th century. The ciphers in this chapter are, for the most part, more complex than those of Chapter 1. You may find yourself having to reread the descriptions of some. If you have any difficulty with a cipher, I urge you to take a pencil and paper and experiment with it until you are comfortable.

Cryptography Marches On

Although these ciphers are more complex than those in Chapter 1, they are still not adequate for the modern computer age, so it would be an egregious mistake to attempt to implement one of these, perhaps via computer code, and then presume your data is secure. Modern computers can utilize brute-force methods, and, in fact, noncomputerized cryptanalysis methods have been developed to attack many of these ciphers. I examine those methods in Chapter 17, when we explore cryptanalysis in general.

Tip	Most people have some level of difficulty with cryptography when they first encounter it. In this chapter, as well as the rest of this book, keep in mind that some topics will require some hands-on practice and others will require reading the text more than once. But make sure you fully understand a topic before moving on to the next topic.

Playfair Cipher

The *Playfair cipher* was invented in 1854 by Charles Wheatstone, but it was popularized by Scottish politician and scientist Lord Playfair, thus it bears his name. This cipher works by encrypting pairs of letters, also called *digraphs*, at a time. Although it was first rejected by the British government as being too complex, it was actually used by the British military in World War I and to some extent in World War II. It was also used by the government of New Zealand as late as the early 1940s for non-military communications.

Note	Charles Wheatstone (1802–1875) was an accomplished inventor and scientist. Among his various contributions to science was the Wheatstone bridge, an electrical circuit that is used to measure electrical resistance. The original bridge was invented by Samuel Hunter Christie, but Wheatstone improved it. Wheatstone also made a number of contributions to our knowledge and application of electricity.

The Playfair cipher depends on a 5-by-5 table, or matrix, that contains a keyword or key phrase. To use the Playfair cipher, you need to memorize that keyword and four rules. Any square of 5-by-5 letters can be used. You first fill in the keyword, and then start, in order, adding in letters that did not appear in the keyword. Note that the letters *I* and *J* are combined. You can see this in the table below. In this example the keyword is *falcon*.

F	A	L	C	O
N	B	D	E	G
H	I/J	K	M	P
Q	R	S	T	U
V	W	X	Y	Z

Since the 5-by-5 matrix is created by starting with a keyword, and then filling in letters that did not appear in the keyword, the matrix will be different when different keywords are used.

The next step is to divide the plain text into digraphs (combinations of two letters). In this case, *Attack at dawn* becomes *At ta ck at da wn*. If the final digraph is incomplete (a single letter), you can pad it with a letter *z*. If there are any duplicate letters, replace the second letter with an *x*. For example, *puppet* would be *pu px et*. Playfair does not account for numbers or punctuation marks, so you must remove any punctuation from the plain text and spell out any numbers.

Next, you look at the plain text digraph—in our case *At ta ck at da wn*—and find the pairs of letters in the table. Look to the rectangle formed by those letters. In our example, the first two letters, *AT*, form the rectangle in the table as shown next, with *A* in the upper-left corner and *T* in the lower-right corner.

A	L	C
B	D	E
I/J	K	M
R	S	T

Use the letters at the opposite ends of the rectangle to create the cipher text. The letter *A* is in the upper-left corner, so you replace it with whatever appears in the upper-right corner, which in this case is the letter *C*. The letter *T* is in the lower-right corner, so you replace it with the letter in the lower-left corner, which is *R*. So the letters *AT* are enciphered as *CR*.

Just to make sure you're clear, let's continue with a few more examples. The next digraph is *TA* and will form the same rectangle in the table. However, since *T* is the first letter of the plain text, *R* will be the first letter of the cipher text, yielding *RC*. Next we have *CK*. Those letters form the rectangle shown here:

L	C
D	E
K	M

C becomes *L*, and *K* becomes *M*, so the enciphered letters are *LM*. If you continue this process to the end of the plain text,

`Attack at dawn`

is encrypted to yield

`CRRCLMCRBLVB`

Yes, this cipher does take some practice to master.

Note that the cipher disrupts the letter and word frequencies found in single-substitution ciphers, merely by encrypting digraphs instead of single letters.

Two-Square Cipher

The *two-square cipher* is also often referred to as a double Playfair, for reasons that will soon become clear. Like the Playfair, it works on digraphs. There are two variations of the two-square cipher, the horizontal and the vertical, which refer to how the table's squares are arranged. In the horizontal method, they are side-by-side, and in the vertical, the squares are arranged one on top of the other. Each square requires its own keyword, so the two-square cipher is based on using two keywords as well as two matrices.

Let's consider an example of a vertical two-square cipher with the keywords *falcon* and *osprey*, shown here:

F	A	L	C	O
N	B	D	E	G
H	I/J	K	M	P
Q	R	S	T	U
V	W	X	Y	Z

O	S	P	R	E
Y	A	B	C	D
F	G	H	I/J	K
L	M	N	Q	T
U	V	W	X	Z

As with the Playfair, you divide the plain text into digraphs. So *Attack at dawn* becomes *At ta ck at da wn.*

Next, you form a rectangle, as with Playfair, but the rectangle bridges both tables. Find the first letter of plain text in the top table and the second letter in the bottom table. In this case, *A* in the top table and *T* in the bottom forms the rectangle shown here:

A	L	C	O
B	D	E	G
I/J	K	M	P
R	S	T	U
W	X	Y	Z

S	P	R	E
A	B	C	D
G	H	I/J	K
M	N	Q	**T**

The letter *A* is in the upper-left corner, so you replace it with the letter in the upper-right corner, which is the letter *O*. The letter *T* is in the lower-right corner, so you replace it with the letter in the lower-left corner, *M*, providing the cipher text *OM*.

If you continue this process through the entire plain text, you will generate the cipher text shown here:

```
At   ta   ck   at   da   wn
OM   RC   OI   OM   BB   XM
```

Note that if the two letters in the digraph line up (that is, they appear in the same column in the two tables), the cipher text is the same as the plain text. If you are using the horizontal two-square cipher, the same rule applies if the two plain text characters are in the same row.

Four-Square Cipher

As you can probably surmise, the *four-square cipher* takes the Playfair concept and expands it to use four squares. This cipher was invented by Félix Marie Delastelle

(1840–1902), a Frenchman who invented several ciphers including the bifid, trifid, and four-square ciphers.

Delastelle's contributions to cryptography during the 1800s are numerous. He finished work on a book on cryptography, *Traité Élémentaire de Cryptographie* (*Elementary Treatise on Cryptography*) just 11 months before he died in April 1902, and the book was published 3 months after his death. Most notable is that Delastelle was an amateur cryptographer with no formal training in math.

To create a four-square cipher, you first create four matrices of 5-by-5 letters; usually, either the *Q* is omitted or the letters *I* and *J* are combined to account for all 26 letters in the alphabet. Notice that in the matrices shown next, in some cases I omitted the *Q*, and in others I combined *I* and *J*. Also note that the letters may, or may not, be in alphabetical order. In this cipher, the *two uppercase matrices are for the cipher text*, and the *two lowercase matrices are for the plain text*. This is why the two uppercase matrices are not in alphabetical order.

```
a  b  c  d  e        E  D  A  R  P
f  g  h  i  j        L  B  C  X  F
k  l  m  n  o        G  H  I  J  K
p  r  s  t  u        N  O  M  S  T
v  w  x  y  z        U  V  W  Y  Z


D  E  Y  W  O        a  b  c  d  e
R  K  A  B  C        f  g  h  i/j  k
F  G  H  I  J        l  m  n  o  p
L  S  N  P  M        q  r  s  t  u
T  U  V  X  Z        v  w  x  y  z
```

You then split the message into digraphs, so that *Attack at dawn* becomes *at ta ck at da wn*.

The next part may seem a bit complex, so follow along carefully. First, find the first letter in the upper-left plain text matrix. In this case, the letter *a* is in the first row. Then find the second letter of the digraph in the lower-right plain text matrix. The letter *t* is in the fourth column. These two letters are in boldface and underlined here:

```
a  b  c  d  e        E  D  A  R  P
f  g  h  i  j        L  B  C  X  F
k  l  m  n  o        G  H  I  J  K
p  r  s  t  u        N  O  M  S  T
v  w  x  y  z        U  V  W  Y  Z


D  E  Y  W  O        a  b  c  d  e
R  K  A  B  C        f  g  h  i/j  k
F  G  H  I  J        l  m  n  o  p
L  S  N  P  M        q  r  s  t  u
T  U  V  X  Z        v  w  x  y  z
```

Because we are dealing with a digraph, we need to encrypt both the *a* and the *t*. To find the first letter of the cipher text, use the upper-left matrix's row of the first letter of plain text— in this case, *a* is in *row 1*—and the lower-right matrix's column of the second letter of cipher text—*t* is in *column 4*. Look in the upper-right cipher text matrix and find that letter—row 1, column 4 is *R*. This is the first letter of the cipher text.

Then, to find the second letter of the cipher text, use the row of the second letter of plain text—in this case, *t* is in *row 4*—and the column of the first letter—*a* is in *column 1*. Then find that letter in the lower-left cipher text matrix—row 4, column 1 is the letter *L*. You can see this in the next four matrices, where the plain text letters are in boldface and the cipher text letters are in boldface and underlined.

```
a   b   c   d   e        E   D   A   R   P
f   g   h   i   j        L   B   C   X   F
k   l   m   n   o        G   H   I   J   K
p   r   s   t   u        N   O   M   S   T
v   w   x   y   z        U   V   W   Y   Z


D   E   Y   W   O        a   b   c   d   e
R   K   A   B   C        f   g   h   i/j k
F   G   H   I   J        l   m   n   o   p
L   S   N   P   M        q   r   s   t   u
T   U   V   X   Z        v   w   x   y   z
```

So, the first two letters, *at*, in plain text become *RL* in cipher text. You'd continue this process throughout the entire plain text phrase, yielding

```
at   ta   ck   at   da   wn
RL   NW   PA   RL   EW   WG
```

Hill Cipher

The *Hill cipher* was invented by mathematician Lester S. Hill in 1929. It is a bit more complex than other ciphers we have studied thus far. It is based in linear algebra and uses matrix mathematics. To encrypt a message, you break the plain text into a block of *n* letters (called an *n*-component vector). Each letter is represented by a number (a = 1, b = 2, c = 3, and so on); note that the number assignment is not critical—for example, some implementations start with a = 0. That block of numbers representing the block of plain text forms a matrix that is multiplied by some invertible *n*-by-*n* matrix, mod 26. (If you don't have some math background, this may seem rather intimidating—not to worry, it will all be made clear.)

> **Note**
>
> Lester Hill was a mathematician who received his bachelor's degree from Columbia in 1911 and his Ph.D. from Yale in 1926. He was a professor at several colleges including Princeton and Yale. His research interest included application of mathematics to communications, as evidenced by the Hill cipher. He also worked on methods to find errors in telegraph communications.

The matrix used is the key for this cipher. It should be selected randomly and be mod 26 (26 for the letters of the English alphabet; other alphabets would require a different mod). For our discussions on this cipher, we will use the following matrix as a key:

$$\begin{pmatrix} 4 & 5 & 10 \\ 3 & 8 & 19 \\ 21 & 5 & 14 \end{pmatrix}$$

> **Note**
>
> Although I am showing you a 3-by-3 matrix, you can use any size as long as it is a square.

For those readers not familiar with matrix math, I will show you just enough to allow you to understand the Hill cipher. Chapters 4 and 5 will give you a better introduction to mathematics for cryptography. To understand multiplying a matrix by a vector, examine this example using letters:

$$\begin{pmatrix} a & b & c \\ d & e & f \\ g & h & i \end{pmatrix} \times \begin{matrix} x \\ y \\ z \end{matrix} = \begin{pmatrix} ax & by & cz \\ dx & ey & fz \\ gx & hy & iz \end{pmatrix}$$

Each row of the original matrix is multiplied by each item in the vector to provide a resulting matrix.

In the case of the Hill cipher, the vector is simply numbers representing a block of text. Note that this conversion assumes 1 = a, 2 = b, and so on:

```
Attack at dawn
```

is

```
1202013 111204 1 23 14
```

Now let's break this down into three-character blocks:

```
 1  20  20
 1   3  11
11   1  20
 4   1  23
 4
```

We multiply each vector times the numbers in the key. So the first line goes like this:

$$\begin{pmatrix} 4 & 5 & 10 \\ 3 & 8 & 19 \\ 21 & 5 & 14 \end{pmatrix} \times \begin{array}{c} 1 \\ 20 \\ 20 \end{array} = \begin{pmatrix} 4\,(4\times1) & 100\,(5\times20) & 200\,(10\times20) \\ 3\,(3\times1) & 160\,(8\times20) & 380\,(19\times20) \\ 21\,(21\times1) & 100\,(5\times20) & 280\,(14\times20) \end{pmatrix} = \begin{array}{c} 304 \\ 543 \\ 401 \end{array}$$

That resulting vector (304, 543, 401) has to be mod 26, which produces

```
18 22 11
```

Next, you convert these numbers back to letters. The letters *ATT* in plain text encrypts to *TXM* (if we assume a = 1). Repeat this process for each block of letters until the entire message is encrypted. To decrypt a message, you need to convert the letters of the cipher text back to numbers, and then, taking blocks of cipher text, multiply them by the inverse of the key matrix.

ADFGX and ADFGVX Ciphers

The *ADFGVX cipher* is an improvement on a previous cipher, the *ADFGX*. We will look at both ciphers.

ADFGVX was invented by Colonel Fritz Nebel in 1918 and was used by the German Army during World War I. It is essentially a modified Polybius square combined with a columnar transposition. (Recall from Chapter 1 that you can combine ciphers to create a new cipher.) It is interesting to note that ADFGVX was designed to work well when transmitted by Morse code.

Let us start by examining the first cipher, the ADFGX cipher.

First, create a modified Polybius square. Rather than number coordinates, however, the letters *A*, *D*, *F*, *G*, and *X* are used (the letter *V* is not used to create the modified Polybius square).

	A	D	F	G	X
A	B	T	A	L	P
D	D	H	O	Z	K
F	Q	F	V	S	N
G	G	I/J	C	U	X
X	M	R	E	W	Y

Notice that the letters are not in alphabetic order in the Polybius square. This is a common variation to help make the cipher more secure. Again, the letters *I* and *J* are combined in one square.

The next step is to encrypt the message using this modified Polybius square. Let's assume the message is *Attack at dawn*. As with the traditional Polybius square, each letter is represented by its coordinates, in this case by two letters:

```
AF AD AD AF GF DX AF AD DA AF XG FX
```

Next, you write out the message in columns under some keyword; let's again use *falcon* as our keyword:

```
F  A  L  C  O  N
A  F  A  D  A  D
A  F  G  F  D  X
A  F  A  D  D  A
A  F  X  G  F  X
```

Next, we re-sort the columns after rearranging the letters of the keyword in alphabetic order, so *FALCON* becomes *ACFLNO*, like so:

```
A  C  F  L  N  O
F  D  A  A  D  A
F  F  A  G  X  D
F  D  A  A  A  D
C  G  A  X  X  F
```

To create cipher text, write down each column in sequence:

```
FFFC DFDG AAAA AGAX DXAX ADDF
```

Obviously, you can use any transposition keyword of any size. In practice, longer keywords were frequently used to make the ciphers more secure.

In 1918, the ADFGX cipher was expanded to add the letter *V*, making a 6-by-6 cipher, which allowed for all 26 letters of the English alphabet (no need to combine *I* and *J*) and the digits *0* to *9*. Otherwise, the ADFGVX works exactly the same as the ADFGX cipher.

	A	D	F	G	V	X
A	B	T	2	L	P	H
D	D	7	O	Z	1	K
F	3	F	V	S	4	B
G	0	IJ	C	U	X	8
V	G	A	0	J	Q	5
X	M	R	E	W	Y	9

Compared to various classical ciphers, and prior to the computer age, the ADFGVX was a very strong cipher and difficult to break. A French army officer, Lieutenant Georges Painvin, worked on analyzing this cipher and was eventually able to break it. However, his method required large amounts of cipher text to cryptanalyze. This was a forerunner to modern cipher text–only attacks that we will examine in Chapter 17.

Bifid Cipher

The *bifid cipher* is another cipher that combines the Polybius square with a transposition cipher. It was invented in 1901 by Félix Delastelle (who also created the four-square cipher, discussed earlier in the chapter).

The first step is, of course, to create a Polybius square, as shown here:

	1	2	3	4	5
1	B	G	W	K	Z
2	P	D	S	N	Q
3	I/J	A	L	X	E
4	O	F	C	U	M
5	T	H	Y	V	R

As you can see, the letters in the square are not necessarily in alphabetical order.

The coordinates are written down, as with the traditional Polybius cipher, except each coordinate is written vertically in a column. With this cipher, the phrase *Attack at dawn* is written in 12 columns in two rows, like so:

```
3 5 5 3 4 1 3 5 2 3 1 2
2 1 1 2 3 4 2 1 2 2 3 4
```

When the numbers are spread out, much like a rail fence cipher, you create the following stream of numbers:

```
3 5 5 3 4 1 3 5 2 3 1 2 2 1 1 2 3 4 2 1 2 2 3 4
```

Next, those numbers are paired and converted back to letters:

```
EYOESGPGXPDX
```

To decrypt a message, the process is reversed.

Gronsfeld Cipher

The *Gronsfeld cipher* is a variant of the Vigenère cipher discussed in Chapter 1. It uses 10 different alphabet orderings that correspond to the numbers *0* to *9*. The numbers can be picked at random, which is more secure but more difficult to remember, unless the numbers had some significance to the sender and recipient.

```
  ABCDEFGHIJKLMNOPQRSTUVWXYZ
0 ABCDEFGHIJKLMNOPQRSTUVWXYZ
1 BCDEFGHIJKLMNOPQRSTUVWXYZA
2 CDEFGHIJKLMNOPQRSTUVWXYZAB
3 DEFGHIJKLMNOPQRSTUVWXYZABC
4 EFGHIJKLMNOPQRSTUVWXYZABCD
5 FGHIJKLMNOPQRSTUVWXYZABCDE
6 GHIJKLMNOPQRSTUVWXYZABCDEF
7 HIJKLMNOPQRSTUVWXYZABCDEFG
8 IJKLMNOPQRSTUVWXYZABCDEFGH
9 JKLMNOPQRSTUVWXYZABCDEFGHI
```

For this cipher, you select each letter of plain text and substitute it for the cipher text corresponding to the appropriate alphabet. So you'd use alphabet 0 for the first letter, then alphabet 1 for the next letter, then alphabet 2, and so on. After you use alphabet 9, you start over with alphabet 0.

To encrypt the plain text *Attack at dawn*, you find the letter corresponding to *A* in alphabet 0, yielding *A* as the cipher text. Then you find the letter corresponding to *T* in alphabet 1, yielding *U* as the cipher text. Then you find the second *T*, and the third alphabet (alphabet 2) yields *V*. Continuing this process move down the rows of alphabets until

```
ATTACK AT DAWN
```

is encrypted as

```
AUVDGP GZ LJWO
```

As an interesting historical note, as late as 1892, the Gronsfeld cipher was still being used: the French government arrested several anarchists who were using it for communications.

Vernam Cipher

The *Vernam cipher* is a one-time pad cipher, in which the plain text is somehow altered by a random string of data so that the resulting cipher text is truly random. Gilbert Vernam (1890–1960) first proposed a stream cipher that would be used with teleprinters (teletype machines). It would combine character-by-character a prepared key that was stored on a paper tape, with the characters of the plain text used to produce the cipher text. The recipient would apply the same key to read the plain text.

In 1919, Vernam patented his idea (U.S. Patent 1,310,719). In Vernam's method he used the binary XOR (exclusive OR) operation applied to the bits of the message. (We will be examining binary operations, including XOR, in Chapter 3.) (Note that Vernam also patented three other cryptographic inventions: U.S. Patent 1,416,765; U.S. Patent 1,584,749; and U.S. Patent 1,613,686.)

To be a true one-time pad, by modern standards, a cipher needs two properties. The first is suggested by the name: the key is used only once. After a message is enciphered with a particular key, that key is never used again. This makes the one-time pad quite secure, but it is also very impractical for ongoing communications, such as those encountered in modern e-commerce. The second property is that the key be as long as the message, which prevents any patterns from emerging in the cipher text.

Note	One-time pads are used for communications today, but only for the most sensitive communications. The keys must be stored in a secure location, such as a safe, and used only once for very critical messages. The keys for modern one-time pads are simply strings of random numbers sufficiently large enough to account for whatever message might be sent.

Edgar Allen Poe

Although Edgar Allen Poe is most known for his literary works, he also was an accomplished amateur cryptographer. In 1841, Poe wrote an essay entitled "A Few Words on Secret Writing" that was published in *Graham's Magazine*. In addition, in his short story "The Gold-Bug," cryptography plays a central role in the plot. Poe is not known to have researched cryptography, nor did he create any ciphers, but he did play a key role in increasing public interest in the field of cryptography. In fact, cryptographer William Friedman (1891–1969) credited his interest in cryptography to Poe's "The Gold-Bug." Friedman was the director of research for the Army Signals Intelligence Service in the 1930s and is credited with coining the term *cryptanalysis*.

In December 1839, Poe published a challenge in the Philadelphia periodical *Alexander's Weekly Messenger*. In that challenge, he stated that he could solve any single-substitution cipher than readers could submit. His challenge stated

> It would be by no means a labor lost to show how great a degree of rigid method enters into enigma-guessing. This may sound oddly; but it is not more strange than the well known fact that rules really exist, by means of which it is easy to decipher any species of hieroglyphical writing—that is to say writing where, in place of alphabetical letters, any kind of marks are made use of at random. For example, in place of A put % or any other arbitrary character—in place of B, a *, etc., etc. Let an entire alphabet be made in this manner, and then let this alphabet be used in any piece of writing. This writing can be read by means of a proper method. Let this be put to the test. Let any one address us a letter in this way, and we pledge ourselves to read it forthwith—however unusual or arbitrary may be the characters employed.[1]

From December 1839 to May 1840, Poe was able to solve all the ciphers that readers submitted—except one. Since that time, however, various analysts have determined that this cipher was simply a set of random characters and not a legitimate example of cipher text.

Cryptography Comes of Age

The various ciphers used in the 19th through the early 20th centuries were certainly more complex than the ciphers of earlier times. However, they were still ciphers that could be decrypted manually, with pencil and paper. The 20th century moved cryptography toward encryption related to devices and alternative methods of encryption.

Enigma

Contrary to popular misconceptions, the *Enigma* is not a single machine, but a family of machines. The first version was invented by German engineer Arthur Scherbius near the end of World War I. It was also used by several different militaries, not only the Nazi Germans.

Some military texts encrypted using a version of Enigma were broken by Polish cryptanalysts Marian Rejewski, Jerzy Różycki, and Henryk Zygalski. The three basically reverse-engineered a working Enigma machine and then developed tools for breaking Enigma ciphers, including one tool called the *cryptologic bomb*.

The *rotors* were the core of the Enigma machine—disks that included 26 letters arranged in a circle, with several rotors aligned with one another. Essentially, each rotor represented a different single-substitution cipher—you can think of the Enigma as a sort of mechanical poly-alphabet cipher. After the operator was given a message in plain text, he typed the message into the Enigma. For each letter that was typed in, Enigma would provide a different cipher text based on a different substitution alphabet. The recipient would type in the cipher text to retrieve the plain text, but only if both Enigma machines had the same rotor settings. Figure 2-1 shows an Enigma machine.

FIGURE 2-1   An Enigma machine

Enigma Variations

The Enigma models included several variations:

- Enigma A, the first public Enigma
- Enigma B
- Enigma C
- Enigma B, used by United Kingdom, Japan, Sweden, and others
- Navy Cipher D, used by the Italian Navy
- Funkschlüssel C, used by the German Navy beginning in 1926
- Enigma G, used by the German Army
- Wehrmacht Enigma I, a modification to the Enigma G, used extensively by the German military
- M3, an improved Enigma introduced in 1930 for the German military

Other systems were either derived from Enigma or were similar in concept, including the Japanese system codenamed GREEN by American cryptographers, the SIGABA system, NEMA, and others.

Alan Turing

I cannot tell the story of Enigma without at least mentioning Alan Turing, who is famous for leading the team that was able to crack the Enigma version used by the German Navy during World War II—a story that has been immortalized in the book *Alan Turing: The Enigma* and the movie *The Imitation Game*. During World War II, Turing worked for the Government Code and Cipher School that operated out of Bletchley Park, located 50 miles northwest of London. The mansion and 58 acres were purchased by MI6 (British Intelligence) for use by the Code and Cipher School. A number of prominent people worked at Bletchley Park, including mathematicians Derek Taunt and Max Newman, and chess champion Hugh Alexander.

Turing's impact on the field of cryptography is profound. He led the British team responsible for attempting to break the German naval Enigma. He worked to improve the pre-war Polish machine that would find Enigma settings. He was successful, and MI6 was able to decipher German naval messages. This work was considered highly classified. They feared that if the Germans realized that the Enigma had been compromised, they would change how they communicated. So intelligence gathered via Turing's team was kept a closely guarded secret, and when it needed to be shared with others (such as military commanders), a cover story was given to account for the source of the information. Many sources claim that Turing's work at Bletchley Park shortened the war by at least two years, saving millions of lives.

Note   Alan Turing was a mathematician and an accomplished marathon runner as well. He also was a key figure in the development of computer science. Among his most notable achievements, he developed a test to determine if a machine was indeed sentient—that test is known as the Turing Test.

The work at Bletchley Park was kept in strict secrecy, but in the decades since the war, many details have been declassified and are now available to the public. Turing's team was by no means the only team working at Bletchley Park. Various "huts," or buildings, on the grounds were used for various purposes. Turing and his team worked on the Naval Enigma in Hut 8. In Hut 6, a team worked on the Army and Air Force Enigmas. Hut 7 concentrated on Japanese codes and intelligence. Other huts were used for intelligence work and support work (such as communications and engineering), and Hut 2 was a recreational hut where the workers at Bletchley could enjoy beer, tea, and relaxation.

The work at Hut 8 centered on use of a *bombe*, an electromechanical device that helped to determine what settings the Enigma machine was using. The initial design used at Bletchley was created by Turing and later refined by others such as Gordon Welchman, a British mathematician.

The work at Bletchley was kept top secret, and much of the equipment and documents were destroyed at the end of the war. Even close relatives did not know what their family at Bletchley worked on. Today it is home to a museum with extensive displays of cryptography history, including Enigma machines.

SIGABA

SIGABA was an encryption machine used by the U.S. military from World War II through the 1950s. The machine, a joint effort of the U.S. Army and Navy, was developed specifically to overcome weaknesses found in other rotor systems, such as Enigma. You can find detailed specifications for this machine today, but some of the operating principles remained classified until the year 2000. SIGABA was patented (6,175,625), filed on December 15, 1944, but the patent remained classified until 2001. Figure 2-2 shows a picture of a SIGABA machine.

Several similar devices were used during the mid-20th century, including the British Air Ministry device *Mercury*, used in the early 1960s. Mercury was designed by E.W. Smith and F. Rudd and was in wide use in the British military by 1950. Other rotor-based machines were in wide use, including the M-325, or SIGFOY (U.S. Patent 2,877,565), which was used in the early 1940s by the U.S. Foreign Service. The French government also used a rotor

FIGURE 2-2   **SIGABA machine**

machine in the 1950s, the HX-63, which was designed by a Swiss communications equipment manufacturer, Crypto AG. In the 1940s the U.S. Army used a device known as M-228, or SIGCUM, to encrypt communications. This device was designed by William Friedman, who later served as director of research for the Army Signals Intelligence Service.

Lorenz Cipher

The *Lorenz cipher* is actually a group of three machines—SZ40, SZ42A, and SZ42B—that were used by the German Army during World War II. These machines were rotor stream cipher machines. They were attached to standard teleprinters to encrypt and decrypt messages sent via teleprinter.

Navajo Code Talkers

Although code talkers are not considered ciphers, they are important to include in any history of cryptography. Phillip Johnston was raised on a Navajo reservation and was one of the few non-Navajo people who spoke the Navajo language. At the beginning of World War II, he proposed to the U.S. Marine Corps that the Navajo language be used to encode important tactical messages—very few non-Navajo knew the language, and it was an unwritten language, making it difficult for someone to learn it.

Johnston's system was tested and proved that Navajo men could encode, transmit, and decode a three-line message in 20 seconds or less. Time was a critical factor—the machines being used at the time required 30 seconds for the same steps to be accomplished, and in the heat of battle, time is of the essence.

In both World Wars I and II, hundreds of Navajo code talkers were used for secure communications by the U.S. military, specifically by the Marines in World War I. Indigenous code talking was pioneered by Cherokee and Choctaw code talkers during World War I.

IFF Systems

Identify Friend or Foe, or *IFF*, was developed during World War II. These systems allowed a friendly aircraft to be identified and thus differentiated from an enemy, or foe. As aircraft have become faster and missile systems reach further, waiting for visual confirmation of friend or foe status is no longer feasible. Most modern systems use cryptographic functions to identify friendly aircraft.

Britain was the first to work out an IFF system. The most primitive of these systems simply sent a prearranged signal at specific intervals. With the advent of radar, it was important to identify what aircraft the radar system had detected. The IFF Mark I was first used in 1939. It was an active transponder that would receive a query (called an interrogation) from the radar system. The query consisted of a distinctive pulse using a specific frequency. The transponder would then respond with a signal that used a steadily increasing amplitude, thus identifying the aircraft as friendly.

By 1940, the Mark III was in use by Western Allies and continued to be used throughout World War II. The Mark III expanded the types of communications that could be accomplished, including a coded Mayday response.

In Germany, IFF systems were also being developed. The first widely implemented system was the FuG 25a. Before a plane took off, two mechanical keys were inserted, each with 10 bits. These provided the keys to encode the IFF transmissions. British scientists, however, were able to build a device that would trigger a response from any FuG 25a system within range, thus revealing the position of German planes flying at night.

Since World War II, IFF systems have been used for a variety of purposes, operating in four primary modes:

- Mode 1 is not secure and is used to track the position of aircraft and ships.
- Mode 2 is used for landings on aircraft carriers.
- Mode 3 is a standard system used by commercial (non-military) aircraft around the world to communicate their position for air traffic control.
- Mode 4 is encrypted and thus secure.

In modern times, secure IFF systems are a part of military air defense operations. Cryptography is critical in ensuring that these systems are secure and reliable.[2] In some cases, the cryptographic key used is changed daily. These systems represent one very practical application of cryptography, whose primary goal is to ensure that friendly aircraft are not shot down.

The NSA: The Early Years

It is impossible to discuss the history of cryptography without including the history of the U.S. National Security Agency (NSA). A large organization, the NSA is often reported to be the single largest employer of mathematicians in the world. The history of cryptography in the latter half of the 20th century, and beyond, is closely intertwined with the history of the NSA.

Although the NSA formally was founded in 1952, it had many precursors. As early as 1919, the U.S. Department of State created the Cipher Bureau, often simply called the "Black Chamber," which operated in an office in Manhattan. Its main purpose was to crack communications of foreign governments. The operation persuaded Western Union to allow it to monitor telegraphs transmitted by Western Union customers. Although the group had significant initial successes, it was shut down in 1929 by Secretary of State Henry Stimson, who felt that spying was not a gentlemanly or honorable activity.

In 1924, the U.S. Navy formed its Radio Intelligence office with the purpose of developing intelligence from monitoring radio communications. By 1942, the U.S. Army renamed its Signal Intelligence Service to Signal Security Service. At this time, each military branch had its own initiatives on communications, radio intelligence, and cryptography, and cooperation was at a minimum.

In 1949, various military agencies coordinated cryptology activities with a new, centralized organization named the Armed Forces Security Agency, which was part of the Department of Defense rather than a specific branch of the military. In 1951, President Harry Truman set up a panel to investigate the shortcomings of the AFSA, including its failure to predict the outbreak of the Korean War. From this investigation came the National Security Agency. President Truman issued a classified directive entitled "Communications Intelligence Activities" that, among other things, established the NSA.

For much of its early history, the existence of the NSA was not acknowledged, and those who did know of it jokingly referred to the NSA as "No Such Agency." Obviously, the history of any intelligence agency is not completely public, but let's examine some highlights that are.

After World War II, Soviet encryption was unbreakable and thus posed a significant issue for U.S. intelligence agencies. This fact, coupled with the discovery of Soviet spies in various western governments, led to a renewed emphasis on signals intelligence (SIGINT) and cryptanalysis.

The NSA had two primary roles, the first being to monitor and decipher the communications of other nations to gather important intelligence. The second role was the protection of U.S. communications from other eavesdropping nations. This led the NSA to develop a standard now known as TEMPEST, an acronym for Transient Electromagnetic Pulse Emanation Standard. This standard applies both to equipment used and deployment and configuration of communications equipment.

During the Cold War, the NSA grew and had some significant successes. As one prominent example, in 1964 the NSA intercepted and decrypted communications regarding China's first nuclear weapons test. There were many other important communications captured by the NSA, and some are still classified today. In 2013, the *Washington Times* reported that NSA programs have foiled terrorist plots in more than 20 different countries.[3]

We will revisit the NSA in later chapters, particularly when we study modern cryptographic ciphers such as DES and AES in Chapters 6 and 7, and then when we discuss cryptographic backdoors in Chapter 18.

Conclusions

In this chapter you were introduced to more complex ciphers, many of which used tables and matrices to encrypt and decrypt text. You saw variations of the Polybius square you learned about in Chapter 1. The Hill cipher introduced you to the basics of matrix algebra, which you will see more of in Chapter 5. You also learned about contributions to cryptography made by historical figures such as Edgar Allen Poe and Allen Turing.

We examined some significant developments in the history of cryptography, including the famous Navajo code talkers and IFF systems that are critical to air traffic control and air defense. We ended the chapter with a discussion of the history of the National Security Agency and its impact on the history of cryptography.

Test Your Knowledge

A few questions are provided here to aid you in testing your knowledge before you proceed.

1. The _____ is based on using a matrix as the key and using *n*-letter groups.
2. Which of the following is a variation of Vigenère that uses ten alphabets, one for each decimal numeral 0 through 9?
   A. Playfair
   B. Hill
   C. Bifid
   D. Gronsfeld
3. What was Edgar Allen Poe's main contribution to cryptography?
   A. Popularizing cryptography
   B. Creating the Hill cipher
   C. Creating SIGABA
   D. Breaking the Hill cipher
4. What did Alan Turing work on?
   A. Breaking the German Naval Enigma
   B. Breaking the German Army Enigma
   C. Breaking all Enigma variations
   D. Breaking the SIGABA system
5. The _____ cipher works by modifying a Polybius square. Rather than number coordinates, letters are used.

Answers

1. Hill cipher
2. D
3. A
4. A
5. ADFGVX

Endnotes

1. This citation was included in the article "Edgar Allen Poe and Cryptography," by R. Morelli, at www.cs.trincoll.edu/~crypto/historical/poe.html.
2. In 2009, General Dynamics awarded a $37 million contract for a modern IFF system: www.generaldynamics.com/news/press-releases/detail.cfm?customel_dataPageID_1811=6123. In addition, a paper written in 2010 by E.A. El-Badawy, W.A. El-Masry, M.A Mokhtar, and A.S. Hafez, "A secured chaos encrypted mode-S aircraft identification friend or foe (IFF) system" (DOI 10.1109/ICSPCS.2010.5709756), discussed a new technique for IFF.
3. Kimberly Dozier, "NSA programs broke plots in 20 nations," www.washingtontimes.com/news/2013/jun/16/nsa-programs-broke-plots-20-nations-officials/.

3 Basic Information Theory

In this chapter we will cover the following:

- Information theory basics
- Claude Shannon's theorems
- Information entropy
- Confusing and diffusion
- Hamming distance and hamming weight
- Scientific and mathematical theories
- Binary math

In this chapter we are going to explore the fundamentals of information theory, which is very important to modern cryptography. Of course, entire books have been written on the topic, so in this chapter we'll provide just enough information to help you understand the cryptography we will discuss in subsequent chapters. For some readers, this will be a review. We will also explore the essentials of mathematical and scientific theories. This chapter also provides an introduction to basic binary mathematics, which should be a review for most readers.

Although information theory is relevant to cryptography, that is not the only application of information theory. At its core, information theory is about quantifying information. This will involve understanding how to code information, information compression, information transmission, and information security (that is, cryptography).

The Information Age

It is often stated that we live in the "information age." This would clearly make information theory pertinent not only to understanding cryptography, but also to understanding modern society. First, however, we must be clear on what is meant by the phrase "information age." To a great extent, the information age and the digital age go hand-in-hand. Some might argue the degree of overlap, but it is definitely the case that without modern computers, the information age would be significantly stifled. Claude Shannon, who is considered the father of information theory, wrote his famous paper, "A Mathematical Theory of Communication," in 1948—long before digital computers even existed.

From one perspective, the information age is marked by the information itself, which has become a primary commodity. Obviously, information has always been of value, but it was historically just a means to a more concrete end. For example, even prehistoric people needed information, such as locations for finding food and game. However, that information was peripheral to the tangible commodity of food. In this example, the food was the goal—the actual commodity. In the information age, the information itself is the commodity.

If you reflect on this even briefly, I think you will concur that in modern times information itself is a product. Consider, for example, this book you now hold in your hands. Certainly the paper and ink used was not worth the price of the book. It is the information encoded on the pages that you pay for. In fact, you may have an electronic copy and not actually have purchased any pages and ink at all. If you are reading this book as part of a class, you paid tuition for the class. The commodity you purchased was the information transmitted to you by the professor or instructor (and, of course, augmented by the information in this book). So, clearly, information as a commodity can exist separately from computer technology. The efficient and effective transmission and storage of information, however, requires computer technology.

Yet another perspective on the information age is the proliferation of information. Just a few decades ago, news meant a daily paper, or perhaps a 30-minute evening news broadcast. Now news is 24 hours a day on several cable channels and on various Internet sites. In my own childhood, research meant going to the local library and consulting a limited number of books that were, hopefully, not more than ten years out of date. Now, with the click of a mouse button, you have access to scholarly journals, research web sites, almanacs, dictionaries, encyclopedias—an avalanche of information. So we could view the information age as the age in which most people have ready access to a wide range of information.

Younger readers who have grown up with the Internet and cell phones and who have been immersed in a sea of instant information may not fully comprehend how much information has exploded. Once you appreciate the magnitude of the information explosion, the more you can fully appreciate the need for information theory. To give you some perspective on just how much information is being transmitted and consumed in our modern civilization, consider the following facts: As early as 2003, experts estimated that humanity had accumulated a little over 12 exabytes of data during the entire course of human history. Modern media, such as magnetic storage, print, and film, had produced 5 exabytes in just the first two years of the 21st century. In 2009, researchers claim that in a single year, Americans consumed more than 3 zettabytes of information.[1] As of 2013, the World Wide Web is said to hold 4 zettabytes, or 4,000 exabytes, of data.

Measuring Data

Such large numbers can be difficult to comprehend. Most readers understand kilobytes, megabytes, and gigabytes, but you may not be as familiar with larger sizes. Here are the various sizes of data:

Kilobyte = 1000 bytes
Megabyte = 1,000,000 bytes
Gigabyte = 1,000,000,000 bytes
Terabyte = 1,000,000,000,000 bytes
Petabyte = 1,000,000,000,000,000 bytes
Exabyte = 1,000,000,000,000,000,000 bytes
Zettabyte = 1,000,000,000,000,000,000,000 bytes

These incredible scales of data can be daunting to grasp but should give you an idea as to why information theory is so important. It should also clearly demonstrate that whether you measure data by the amount of information we access, or the fact that we value information itself as a commodity, we are truly in the Information Age.

Claude Shannon

It is impossible to discuss information theory thoroughly without including Claude Shannon, who is often called the "father of information theory." He was a mathematician and engineer who lived from April 30, 1916, until February, 24, 2001. He did a lot of work on electrical applications of mathematics and on cryptanalysis. His research interests included using Boolean algebra (we will discuss various algebras at length in Chapter 5) and binary math (which we will introduce you to later in this chapter) in conjunction with electrical relays. This use of electrical switches working with binary numbers and Boolean algebra is the basis of digital computers.

Note	During World War II, Shannon worked for Bell Labs on defense applications. Part of his work involved cryptography and cryptanalysis. It should be no surprise that his most famous work, information theory, has been applied to modern developments in cryptography. In 1943, Shannon became acquainted with Alan Turing, whom we discussed in Chapter 2. Turing was in the United States to work with the U.S. Navy's cryptanalysis efforts, sharing with the United States some of the methods that the British had developed.

Information theory was introduced by Shannon in 1948 with the publication of his article "A Mathematical Theory of Communication." He was interested in information, specifically in relation to signal processing operations. Information theory now encompasses the entire field of quantifying, storing, transmitting, and securing information. Shannon's landmark paper was expanded into a book entitled *The Mathematical Theory of Communication*, which he co-authored with Warren Weaver.

In his original paper, Shannon laid out some basic concepts that might seem very elementary today, particularly for those readers with engineering or mathematics backgrounds. At the time, however, no one had ever attempted to quantify information or the process of communicating information. The relevant concepts he outlined are provided here with a brief explanation of their significance to cryptography:

- An *information source* produces a message. This is perhaps the most elementary concept Shannon developed. There must be some source that produces a given message. In reference to cryptography, that source takes plain text and applies some cipher to create cipher text.
- A *transmitter* operates on the message to create a signal that can be sent through a *channel*. A great deal of Shannon's work was about the transmitter and channel, the mechanisms that send a message—in our case an encrypted message—to its destination.
- A *channel* is the medium over which the signal carrying the information that composes the message is sent. Modern cryptographic communications often take place over the Internet. However, encrypted radio and voice transmissions are often used. In Chapter 2, you were introduced to Identify Friend or Foe (IFF) systems.

- A *receiver* transforms the signal back into the message intended for delivery. For our purposes, the receiver will also decrypt the message, producing plain text from the cipher text that is received.
- A *destination* can be a person or a machine for whom or which the message is intended. This is relatively straightforward. As you might suspect, sometimes the receiver and destination are one and the same.
- *Information entropy* is a concept that was very new with Shannon's paper, and it's one we delve into in a separate section of this chapter.

In addition to these concepts, Shannon also developed some general theorems that are important to communicating information. Some of this information applies primarily to electronic communications, but it does have relevance to cryptography.

Theorem 1: Shannon's Source Coding Theorem

It is impossible to compress the data such that the code rate is less than the Shannon entropy of the source, without it being virtually certain that information will be lost.

In information theory, entropy is a measure of the uncertainty associated with a random variable. We will discuss this in detail later in this chapter. This theorem states that if you compress data in a way that the rate of coding is less than the information content, then it is very likely that you will lose some information. It is frequently the case that messages are both encrypted and compressed. Compression is used to reduce transmission time and bandwidth. Shannon's coding theorem is important when compressing data.

Theorem 2: Noisy Channel Theorem

For any given degree of noise contamination of a communication channel, it is possible to communicate discrete data (digital information) nearly error-free up to a computable maximum rate through the channel.

This theorem addresses the issue of noise on a given channel. Whether it be a radio signal or a network signal traveling through a twisted pair cable, noise is usually involved in signal transmission. This theorem essentially states that even if there is noise, you can communicate digital information. However, there is some maximum rate at which you can compute information, and that rate is computable and is related to how much noise there is in the channel.

Core Concepts of Cryptography

Some key concepts of information theory are absolutely pivotal in your study of cryptography. You been given a brief overview of information theory and those concepts have some relevance to cryptography. In this section, you will learn core concepts that are essential to cryptography.

Information Entropy

Shannon thought information entropy was a critical topic in information theory. His landmark paper included an entire section entitled "Choice, Uncertainty and Entropy" that rigorously explored this topic. Here we'll cover just enough about information entropy for you to move forward in your study of cryptography.

Entropy has a different meaning in information theory than it does in physics. In the context of information, entropy is a way of measuring information content. People often encounter two difficulties in mastering this concept. The first difficulty lies in confusing *information entropy* with the *thermodynamic entropy* that you may have encountered in elementary physics courses. In such courses, entropy is often described as "the measure of disorder in a system." This is usually followed by a discussion of the second law of thermodynamics, which states that "in a closed system, entropy tends to increase." In other words, without the addition of energy, a close system will become more disordered over time. Before you can understand information entropy, however, you need to firmly understand that information entropy and thermodynamic entropy are not the same thing. So you can take the entropy definition you received in freshman physics courses and put it out of your mind—at least for the time being.

The second problem you might have with understanding information theory is that many references define the concept in different ways, some of which can seem contradictory. In this section, I will demonstrate some of the common ways that information entropy is described so that you can gain a complete understanding of these seemingly disparate explanations.

In information theory, *entropy* is the amount of information in a given message. This is simple, easy to understand, and, as you will see, essentially synonymous with other definitions you may encounter. Information entropy is sometimes described as "the number of bits required to communicate information." So if you wish to communicate a message that contains information, if you represent the information in binary format, entropy is how many bits of information the message contains. It is entirely possible that a message might contain some redundancy, or even data you already have (which, by definition, would not be information); thus the number of bits required to communicate information could be less than the total bits in the message.

Note This is actually the basis for lossless data compression. Lossless data compression seeks to remove redundancy in a message to compress the message. The first step is to determine the minimum number of bits required to communicate the information in the message—or, put another way, to calculate the information entropy.

Many texts describe entropy as "the measure of uncertainty in a message." You may be wondering, how can both of these definitions be true? Actually, they are both saying the same thing, as I'll explain.

Let's examine the definition that is most likely causing you some consternation: entropy as a measure of uncertainty. It might help you to think of it in the following manner: only uncertainty can provide information. For example, if I tell you that right now you are reading this book, this does not provide you with any new information. You already knew that, and there was absolutely zero uncertainty regarding that issue. However, the content you are about to read in remaining chapters is uncertain, and you don't know what you will encounter—at least, not exactly. There is, therefore, some level of uncertainty, and thus information content. Put even more directly, *uncertainty is information*. If you are already certain about a given fact, no information is communicated to you. New information clearly requires uncertainty that the information you received cleared up. Thus, the measure of uncertainty in a message is the measure of information in a message.

Now let's move to a more mathematical expression of this concept. Let's assume X is some random variable. The amount of entropy measured in bits that X is associated with is usually denoted by H(X). We'll further assume that X is the answer to a simple yes or no question. If you already know the answer, then there is no information. It is the uncertainty of the value of X that provides information. Put mathematically, if you already know the outcome, then H(X) = 0. If you do not know the outcome, you will get 1 bit of information from this variable X. That bit could be a 1 (a yes) or a 0 (a no) so H(X) = 1.

Hopefully, you now have a good grasp of the concept of information entropy, so let's try to make it more formal and include the concept of probability.

Note I am purposefully avoiding a rigorous discussion of probability here. At some point in your cryptographic studies, you'll find it wise to take a rigorous statistics course. However, that is not necessary to understand the fundamentals of cryptography.

What is the information content of a variable X? First, we know X has some number of possible values; we will call that number n. With a binary variable that is 1 single bit, then n = 2 (values 0 or 1). However, if you have more than 1 bit, then you have n > 2. For example, 2 bits has n = 2^2. Let's consider each possible value of X to be i. Of course, all possible values of X might not have the same probability, and some might be more likely than others. For example, if X is a variable giving the height of your next-door neighbor in inches, a value of 69 (5 feet 9 inches) is a lot more probable than a value of 89 (7 feet 5 inches). So consider the probability of each given i to be P_i. Now we can write an equation that will provide the entropy (that is, the information contained) in the variable X, taking into account the probabilities of individual values of X. That equation is shown in Figure 3-1.

As stated earlier in this chapter, we won't be examining proofs in this text. In fact, for our purposes, you can simply accept the math as a given. A number of excellent mathematics books and courses delve into the proofs for these topics. The equation shown in Figure 3-1 provides a way of calculating the information contained in (that is, the information entropy) of some variable X, assuming you know the probabilities of each possible value of X. If you do not know those probabilities, you can still get at least a range for the information contained in X with the equation shown in Figure 3-2.

$$H(X) = -\sum_{i=1}^{n} p_i \log_2 p_i$$

FIGURE 3-1   The information entropy of X

$$0 \le H(X) \le \log_2 n$$

FIGURE 3-2   Range of information contained in X

This equation assumes that there is some information, or some level of uncertainty, so we set the lower range at greater than zero. Hopefully, this gives you a clear understanding of the concept of information entropy.

In addition to information entropy are a few closely related concepts that you should understand:

- **Joint entropy**   This is the entropy of two variables or two messages. If the two messages are truly independent, their joint entropy is just the sum of the two entropies. Here is the equation:

$$\sum_{x,y} p(x,y) \log p(x,y)$$

Joint entropy of X and Y

- **Conditional entropy**   If the two variables are not independent, but rather variable Y depends on variable X, then instead of joint entropy you have *conditional entropy*.
- **Differential entropy**   This is a more complex topic and involves extending Shannon's concept of entropy to cover continuous random variables, rather than discrete random variables. The equation for differential entropy is shown next:

$$h(X) = -\int_s f(x) \log f(x)\, dx$$

Differential entropy of X and Y

The basic concept of information entropy, often called *Shannon entropy*, is essential to cryptography, and you will encounter it later in this book. Joint entropy and differential entropy are more advanced topics and are introduced here for readers who want to delve deeper, beyond the scope of this book.

Quantifying Information

Understanding information entropy is essential to your understanding of how we quantify information. If you have any doubts about your understanding of entropy, please reread the preceding section before moving on. Quantifying information can be a difficult task. For those new to information theory, even understanding what is meant by "quantifying information" can be daunting. Usually it is done in the context of binary information (bits). In fact, although you can find many different definitions for what *information* is, within the context of *information theory*, we look at information as *bits of data*. This works nicely with computer science, since computers store data as bits. A bit can have only one of two values: 0 or 1, which can be equivalent to yes or no. Of course, several bits together can contain several yes or no values, thus accumulating more information.

Once we have defined information as a single bit of data, the next issue becomes quantifying that data. One method often used to explain the concept is to imagine how many guesses it would take to ascertain the contents of a sealed envelope. Let me walk you through this helpful thought experiment.

Suppose someone hands you a sealed envelope that contains a message. You are not allowed to open the envelope. Instead, you have to ascertain the contents merely by asking a series of yes or no questions (binary information: 1 being yes, 0 being no). What is the smallest number of questions required to identify the contents of the enclosed message accurately?

Notice that the scenario is "how many questions, on average, will it take?" Clearly, if you try the same scenario with different people posing the queries, even with the same message, you will get a different number of questions needed. The game could be repeated with different messages. We can enumerate messages, with any given message as M_i and the probability of getting that particular message as P_i. This leaves us with the question of what, exactly, is the probability of guessing a specific message. The actual equation takes us back to Figure 3-1. Computing the entropy of a given message is quantifying the information content of that message.

Confusion and Diffusion

The concept of confusion, as relates to cryptography, was outlined in Shannon's 1948 paper. In general, this concept attempts to make the relationship between the statistical frequencies of the cipher text and the actual key as complex as possible. Put another way, the relationship between the plain text, cipher text, and the key should be complex enough that it is not easy to determine what that relationship is.

If you don't have sufficient confusion, then someone could simply examine a copy of plain text and the associated cipher text and determine what the key is. This would allow the person to decipher all other messages that are encrypted with that same key.

Diffusion literally means "having changes to one character in the plain text affect multiple characters in the cipher text." This is unlike historical algorithms (such as the Caesar cipher, Atbash, and Vigenère), where each plain text character affected only one cipher text character.

Shannon thought the related concepts of confusion and diffusion were both needed to create an effective cipher:

> Two methods (other than recourse to ideal systems) suggest themselves for frustrating a statistical analysis. These we may call the methods of diffusion and confusion. In the method of diffusion the statistical structure of M which leads to its redundancy is "dissipated" into long range statistics—i.e., into statistical structure involving long combinations of letters in the cryptogram. The effect here is that the enemy must intercept a tremendous amount of material to tie down this structure, since the structure is evident only in blocks of very small individual probability. Furthermore, even when he has sufficient material, the analytical work required is much greater since the redundancy has been diffused over a large number of individual statistics.[2]

These two goals are achieved through a complex series of substitution and permutation. Although the historic ciphers you studied in Chapters 1 and 2 are not secure enough to withstand modern cryptanalysis, we can make an example using them. Let's assume you have a simple Caesar cipher in which you shift each letter three to the right. This will provide a small degree of confusion, but no diffusion. Now assume you swap every three letters. This transposition will provide another small degree of confusion. Next, let's apply a second substitution—this time two letters to the right. The two substitutions, separated by a transposition, provide minimal diffusion. Consider the following example:

Plain text: `Attack at dawn`
Step 1 (shift right 3)   `dwwdfndwgdzq`
Step 2 (swap 3 letter blocks)   `dfndwwdzqdw`
Step 3 (shift right 2)   `fhpfyy fbsfy`

Let's try changing just one letter of plain text (though it will make for a misspelled plain text word). Change *attack at dawn* to *attack an dawn*:

Plain text: `Attack an dawn`
Step 1 (shift right 3)   `Dwwdfndqgdzq`
Step 2 (swap 3 letter blocks)   `dfndwwdzqdq`
Step 3 (shift right 2)   `fhpfyy fbsfs`

Now compare this cipher text to the one originally produced. You can see that only one letter has changed—the last letter—and instead of *sfy* you now have *sfs*. This provides only minimal confusion and still no diffusion! What is missing? Two things: The first is that, at least by modern standards, this simply is not complex enough. It is certainly an improvement on the basic Caesar cipher, but still it is not enough. The second problem is that there is no mechanism to have a change in one character of plain text change multiple characters in the cipher text. In modern ciphers, operations are at the bit level, not the character level. Furthermore, in modern ciphers, there are mechanisms to propagate a change, and we will see those beginning in Chapter 6. However, this example should give you the general idea of combining substitution and permutation.

Avalanche

A small change can yield a large effect in the output, like an avalanche. This is Horst Fiestel's variation on Shannon's concept of diffusion. Fiestel's ideas are used in many of the block ciphers we explore in Chapter 6. Obviously, a high avalanche impact is desirable in any cryptographic algorithm. Ideally, a change in 1 bit in the plain text would affect all the bits of the cipher text. This would be considered a *complete avalanche*, but that has not been achieved in any current algorithm.

Hamming Distance

The Hamming distance is the number of characters that are different between two strings. This can be expressed mathematically as follows:

$$h(x, y)$$

Hamming distance is used to measure the number of substitutions that would be required to turn one string into another. In modern cryptography, we usually deal with binary representations rather than text. In that context, Hamming distance can be defined as the number of 1's if you exclusive or (XOR) two strings.

> **Note** The concept of Hamming distance was developed by Richard Hamming, who first described the concept in his paper "Error Detecting and Error Correcting Codes." The concept is used widely in telecommunications, information theory, and cryptography.

Hamming distance works only when the strings being compared are of the same length. One application is to compare plain text to cipher text to determine how much has changed. However, if two strings of different lengths are compared, another metric must be used. One such metric is the *Levenshtein distance*, a measurement of the number of single-character edits required to change one word into another. Edits can include substitutions (as with Hamming distance) but can also include insertions and deletions. The Levenshtein distance was first described by Vladimir Levenshtein in 1965.

Hamming Weight

The concept of Hamming weight is closely related to Hamming distance. It is essentially comparing the string to a string of all 0's. Put more simply, it is how many 1's are in the binary representation of a message. Some sources call this the *population count*, or *pop count*. There are actually many applications for Hamming weight both within cryptography and in other fields. For example, the number of modular multiplications required for some exponent e is computed by log2 e + hamming weight (e). (You will see modular arithmetic in Chapter 4. Later in this book, when the RSA algorithm is examined at length, you will find that the e value in RSA is chosen due to low Hamming weight.)

> **Note** Richard Hamming was not the first to describe the concept of Hamming weight. The concept was first introduced by Irving S. Reed, though he used a different name. Hamming later described an almost identical concept to the one Reed had described, and this latter description was more widely known, thus the term Hamming weight.

Kerckhoffs's Principle/Shannon's Maxim

Kerckhoffs's principle is an important concept in cryptography. Auguste Kerckhoffs's first articulated this in the 1800s, stating that "the security of a cipher depends only on the secrecy of the key, not the secrecy of the algorithm." Shannon rephrased this, stating that "One ought to design systems under the assumption that the enemy will ultimately gain full familiarity with them."[3] This is referred to as *Shannon's maxim* and states essentially the same thing Kerckhoffs's principle states.

Let me attempt to restate and expound this in terms you might find more verbose, but hopefully easier to understand. Both Kerckhoffs's principle and Shannon's maxim state that the only thing that you must keep secret is the key. You don't need to keep the algorithm secret. In fact, in subsequent chapters, this book will provide intimate details of most modern algorithms, and that in no way compromises their security. As long as you keep your key secret, it does not matter that I know you are using AES 256 bit, or Serpent, or Blowfish, or any other algorithm you could think of.

I would add to Kerckhoffs's principle/Shannon's maxim something I will humbly call *Easttom's corollary*:

> You should be very wary of any cryptographic algorithm that has not been published and thoroughly reviewed. Only after extensive peer review should you consider the use of any cryptographic algorithm.

Consider that you have just created your own new algorithm. I mean no offense, but the most likely scenario is that you have mistaken ignorance for fresh perspective, and your algorithm has some serious flaw. You can find many examples on the Internet of amateur cryptographers believing they have invented some amazing new algorithm. Often their "discovery" is merely some permutation on the polyalphabetic ciphers you studied in Chapter 1. But even if you are an accomplished cryptographic researcher with a proven track record, it is still possible you could make an error.

To demonstrate this fact, consider Ron Rivest. You will hear a great deal about Dr. Rivest in coming chapters. His name is the R in RSA and he has been involved in other significant cryptographic developments. He submitted an algorithm to the SHA-3 competition (which we will discuss in detail in Chapter 9); however, after several months of additional analysis, a flaw was found and he withdrew his algorithm from consideration. If such a cryptographic luminary as Ron Rivest can make a mistake, certainly you can, too.

The purpose of publishing an algorithm is so that experts in the field can review it, examine it, and analyze it. This is the heart of the peer review process. Once an algorithm is published, other cryptographers get to examine it. If it withstands a significant amount of time (usually years) of such analysis, then and only then should it be considered for use.

Note   This issue has serious practical implications. In September 2011, I was interviewed by *CNN Money* reporter David Goldman regarding a company that claimed to have an "unbreakable code." The reporter also interviewed cryptography experts from Symantec and Kaspersky labs. All of us agreed that the claim was nonsense. The algorithm was being kept "secret" and not open to peer review.

There is, of course one, very glaring exception to publishing an algorithm. The United States National Security Agency (NSA) organizes algorithms into two groups. The suite B group algorithms are published, which includes algorithms such as Advanced Encryption Standard (AES). You can find the complete details of that algorithm in many sources, including Chapter 7 of this book. The second group, the suite A algorithms, are classified and not published. This seems to violate the spirit of Kerckhoffs's principle and peer review. However, keep in mind that the NSA is the single largest employer of mathematicians in the world, and this means that they can subject an algorithm to a thorough peer review entirely via their own internal staff, all of whom have clearance to view classified material.

Scientific and Mathematical Theories

We have discussed information theory, but we have not discussed what constitutes a theory within the scientific and mathematical world. Mathematics and science are closely related, but the processes are slightly different. We will examine and compare both in this section.

Many words can mean different things in specific situations. For example the word "bug" usually refers to an insect, but in computer programming it refers to a flaw in a program. Even a simple and common word such as "love" can mean different things in different situations. For example, you may "love" your favorite TV show, "love" your spouse, and "love" chocolate ice cream, but you probably don't mean the same thing in each case. When you are attempting to define a term, it is important that you consider the context in which it is being used.

This is even truer when a word is being used in a specific technical or professional context. Various professions use very specific definitions for certain words. Consider the legal community, for example. Many words have very specific meanings within the context of law that might not exactly match their ordinary daily use.

It is also true that scientists as well as mathematicians have some very specific meanings for words they use. The term *theory* is such a word. This word has a very different meaning in a scientific context than it does in everyday language. In the day-to-day vernacular, a theory is often synonymous with a guess. For example, if your favorite sports team is on a losing streak, you might have a theory about why they are losing. And in this case, by *theory* you probably mean just a guess. You may or may not have a shred of data to support your theory. In fact it may be little more than a "gut feeling."

In science and mathematics, however, a theory is not a guess or gut feeling—it is not even an educated guess. Theories in mathematics and science are actually closely related, as you will see.

What Is a Mathematical Theory?

Theories in math flow from axioms. An *axiom* is a single fact that is assumed to be true without proof. I think it should be obvious to all readers that only the most basic facts can be taken on an a priori basis as axioms.

There are a number of interesting math theories. For example, graph theory studies mathematical structures that represent objects and the relationships between them. It does this by using vertices (the objects) and edges (the connections between objects). Set theory studies collections of objects or sets. It governs combining sets, overlapping sets, subsets, and related topics.

Unlike science, mathematics deals with proofs rather than experiments. So the hypothesis that applies in the scientific process (discussed next) is not strictly applicable to mathematics. That is why we begin with axioms. The statements are derived from those axioms, and the veracity of those statements can be objectively determined. This is sometimes taught using truth tables.

Individual mathematical theories address a particular system. They begin with a foundation that is simply the data describing what is known or what is assumed (that is, axioms). New concepts are logically derived from this foundation and are (eventually) proven mathematically.

Formal mathematics courses will discuss *first-order theories, syntactically consistent theories, deductive theories,* and other nuances of mathematical theory. However, this book is focused on applied mathematics, and more narrowly on a single narrow subtopic in applied mathematics: cryptography. We won't be delving into the subtleties of mathematical theory, and you won't be exposed to proofs in this book. We will simply apply mathematics that others have rigorously proven.

The Scientific Process

The scientific process is primarily about experimentation. Nothing is really considered "true" until some experiment proves it is true. Usually, multiple experiments are needed to confirm that something is indeed true. The first step is to create a *hypothesis*—an educated guess that can be tested. Then facts are developed from that. The key part is that a hypothesis is a *testable* guess. In fact, a guess that is untestable has no place in science at all. Once you have tested your hypothesis you have a *fact*. The fact may be that the test results confirm or reject your hypothesis. Usually, you repeat the test several times to make sure the results were not an error. But even a hypothesis is more than a wild guess or a hunch. It is an educated estimate that must be testable. If it is not testable it is not even a hypothesis.

Testing, experimentation, and forming hypotheses are all important parts of the scientific process. However, the pinnacle of the scientific process is the *theory*.

Note This was not always the case. In ancient times, it was far more common for philosophers to simply formulate compelling arguments for their ideas, without any experimentation. Ptolemy, in the 2nd century, was one of the early proponents of experimentation and what is today known as the "scientific method." Roger Bacon, who lived in the 13th century, is often considered the father of the modern scientific method. His experimentation in optics was a framework for the modern approach to science.

A Scientific Theory

You know that a hypothesis is a testable guess. You also know that after conducting a number of tests, one or more facts will be confirmed. Eventually, a number of facts are collected, requiring some explanation. The explanation of those facts is called a *theory*. Or put another way,

> A theory is an explanation of a set of related observations or events based upon proven hypotheses and verified multiple times by detached groups of researchers. How does a scientific theory compare to a scientific law? In general, both a scientific theory and a scientific law are accepted to be true by the scientific community as a whole. Both are used to make predictions of events. Both are used to advance technology.[4]

Now think about this definition for the word *theory* for just a moment. "A theory is an explanation." That is the key part of this definition. After you have accumulated data, you must have some sort of explanation. A string of facts with no connection, no explanation, is of little use. This is not only true in science, but in other fields as well. Think about how a detective works, for example. Anyone can notice a string of facts, but the detective's job is to put those facts together in a manner that is consistent with all the facts. This is very similar to what scientists do when trying to formulate a theory. With both the scientist and the detective, the theory must match all the facts.

It is sometimes difficult for non-scientists to become accustomed to this use of the word *theory*. A basic dictionary usually includes multiple definitions, and some of those are synonymous with *guess*. However, even a standard dictionary such as Merriam-Webster online offers alternative definitions for the word *theory*. Those applicable to science's use of the word *theory* follow:

> 1: the analysis of a set of facts in their relation to one another
> 3: the general or abstract principles of a body of fact, a science, or an art <music *theory*>
> 5: a plausible or scientifically acceptable general principle or body of principles offered to explain phenomena <wave *theory* of light>[5]

As you can see, these three definitions are not synonymous with *guess* or *gut feeling*. An even better explanation of theory was provided by *Scientific American* magazine:

> Many people learned in elementary school that a theory falls in the middle of a hierarchy of certainty—above a mere hypothesis but below a law. Scientists do not use the terms that way, however. According to the National Academy of Sciences (NAS), a scientific theory is "a well-substantiated explanation of some aspect of the natural world that can incorporate facts, laws, inferences, and tested hypotheses." No amount of validation changes a theory into a law, which is a descriptive generalization about nature. So when scientists talk about the theory of evolution—or the atomic theory or the theory of relativity, for that matter—they are not expressing reservations about its truth.[6]

The point to keep in mind is that a theory is an explanatory model. It explains the facts we know and gives us context for expanding our knowledge base. Although scientific theories are based on experimentation and mathematical theories are based on proofs and axioms, the issue of being an explanatory model is the same for a scientific theory and a mathematical theory. Putting it in the context of information theory, a theory provides a conceptual model of information and provides the framework to continue adding to our knowledge of information.

A Look at Successful Scientific Theories

Examining in general terms what a theory is and is not may not provide an adequate explanation for all readers. So let's look at a concrete example of a very well-accepted theory, the theory of gravity, and how it relates to specific facts. Sir Isaac Newton observed that things tend to fall. In a very general way, this is the essence of his law of gravity: Gravity makes things fall downward. Of course, he expressed that law mathematically with this equation:

$$F = Gm_1m_2/d^2$$

In this equation, F is the force of gravity, G is a constant (the Gravitational Constant) that can be measured, m_1 and m_2 are the masses of the two objects (such as the Earth and a falling apple), and d is the distance between them. This law of gravity can be measured and verified thousands of times, and in fact it has been.

But this law, by itself, is incomplete. It does not provide an adequate explanation for why this occurs. We know there is gravity and we all feel its pull, but what is it? Why does gravity work according to this formula? Einstein's Theory of General Relativity was an explanation for why gravity exists. He proposed that matter causes time and space to curve, much like a ball sitting on a stretched-out sheet causes a curve in the sheet. Objects that get close enough to the ball will tend to fall toward it because of this curvature.

Clearly Einstein's theory explains all the observed facts. But there is still yet another component to qualify it as a scientific theory: It must make some predictions. By *predictions*, I don't mean that it foretells the future. What I mean is that if this theory is valid, then you would expect other things also to be true. If those predictions turn out not to be true, then Einstein's theory must either be modified or rejected. Whether you choose to modify a theory or reject it depends on how well its predictions work out. If it is 90 percent accurate, then you would probably just look to adjust the theory so it matched the facts. However, if it was accurate less than half the time, you would probably consider rejecting the theory outright.

So what predictions can we make from the Theory of General Relativity?

- *Gravity can bend light.* This has been reconfirmed literally hundreds of times with more precision each time. In 2003, the Cassini Satellite once again confirmed this prediction—and this 2003 test was just one among many that all confirmed that gravity can bend light.
- *Light loses energy escaping from a gravitational field.* Because the energy of light is proportional to its frequency, a shift toward lower energy means a shift to lower frequency and longer wavelength. This causes a "red shift," or shift toward the red end of the visible spectrum. This was experimentally verified on Earth using gamma-rays at the Jefferson Tower Physics Laboratories.
- *Light is deflected by gravity.* General relativity predicts that light should be deflected, or bent, by gravity. This was first confirmed by observations and measurements of a solar eclipse in 1919. It has since been confirmed by hundreds of experiments over decades.

Other predictions relating to the General Theory of Relativity have been confirmed by dozens, and in some cases hundreds, of independent experiments. Note the word *independent*. These experiments were carried out by people with no particular vested interest in proving Einstein correct. And in a few cases, they really wanted to prove him wrong. Yet in every case the data confirmed Einstein's theory. You would be hard put to find any physicist who does not agree that the General Theory of Relativity is valid and is true. Some may argue it is not yet complete, but none will argue that it is not true. Hundreds of experiments spanning many decades and literally thousands of scientists have confirmed every aspect of general relativity. Now that this theory is well established, it can be used to guide future experiments and a deeper understanding of gravity as well as related topics.

Binary Math

Binary math is not actually a part of information theory, but it is critical information you will need to be able to understand cryptography in later chapters. Many readers will already be familiar with binary math, and this will be a review for you. However, if your background does not include binary math, this section will teach you the essentials you need.

Defining binary math is actually rather simple: It is mathematics that uses a base 2 rather than the more familiar base 10. The only reason you find base 10 (that is, the decimal number system) to be more "natural" is because most of us have 10 fingers and 10 toes. (As least most people have 10 fingers and toes—but even if you have a different number of fingers and toes, you understand that 10 is normal for humans.)

Once we introduce the concept of 0, we have 10 digits in the base 10 system: 0, 1, 2, 3, 4, 5, 6, 7, 8, and 9. Keep in mind there is not really a number 10 in the base 10 system. There is a 1 in the 10's place and a 0 in the 1's place. The same thing is true with binary, or base 2 numbers. There is not actually a number 2. There is a 1 in the 2's place and a 0 in the 1's place. This chart comparing the two might be helpful:

Number in Base 10 (decimal)	Number in Base 2 (binary)
0	0
1	1
2	10
3	11
4	100
5	101
6	110
7	111
8	1000

Binary numbers are important because that is, ultimately, what computers understand. You can, of course, represent numbers in any system you wish. And a number system can be based on any integer value. Historically, a few have been widely used. Hexadecimal (base 16) and octal (base 8) are sometimes used in computer science because they are both powers of 2 (2^4 and 2^3, respectively) and thus are easily converted to and from binary. The Babylonians used a base 60 number system, which you still see today in representation of degrees in a geographic coordinate system. For example, 60 seconds makes a minute and 60 minutes makes a degree, so you can designate direction by stating "45 degrees, 15 minutes, and 4 seconds."

Note The modern concept of binary numbers traces back to Gottfried Leibniz, who wrote an article entitled "Explanation of the Binary Arithmetic." Leibniz noted that the Chinese I Ching hexagrams correspond to binary numbers ranging from 0 to 1111111 (or 0 to 63 in decimal numbers).

Converting

Because humans tend to be more comfortable with decimal numbers, you will frequently want to convert from binary to decimal, and you may need to make the inverse conversion as well. You can use many methods to do this, and a common one takes advantage of the fact that the various "places" in a binary number are powers of 2. So consider for a moment a binary number 10111001 and break it down into the powers of 2. If there is a 1 in a given place, then you have that value. If not, you have a 0. For example, if there is a 1 in the 2^7 place, then you have 128; if not, you have a 0.

Power of 2	2^7	2^6	2^5	2^4	2^3	2^2	2^1	2^0
Value of That Place	128	64	32	16	8	4	2	1
Binary Numeral	1	0	1	1	1	0	0	1
	128	0	32	16	8	0	0	1

Now just add the values you have: $128 + 32 + 16 + 8 + 1 = 185$.

This may not be the fastest method, but it works and it is easy to understand.

Binary Operations

You can do all the mathematical operations with binary that you can do with decimal numbers. Fortunately, with cryptography you will be primarily concerned with three operations, AND, OR, and XOR, and these are relatively easy to understand. For all of our examples, we will consider two 4-bit binary numbers: 1101 and 1100. We will examine how the AND, OR, and XOR operations work on these two numbers.

Binary AND

The binary AND operation combines two binary numbers, 1 bit at a time. It asks, "Is there a 1 in the same place in both numbers?" If the answer is yes, then the resulting number is a 1. If no, then the resulting number is a 0. Here, you can see the comparison of the rightmost digit in two 4-digit binary numbers:

Binary AND for rightmost digit

Because the first number has a 1 in this place and the second has a 0, the resultant number is a 0. You continue this process from right to left. Remember that if both numbers have a 1, then the resulting number is a 1. Otherwise, the resulting number is a 0. You can see this here:

```
1101
1100
1100
```

Binary AND for two numbers

Binary OR

The binary OR operation is just a little different. It is asking the question, "Is there a 1 in the first number or the second number, or even in both numbers?" In other words, "Is there a 1 in the first number *and/or* the second number?" So, basically, if either number has a 1, then the result is a 1. The result will be a 0 only if both numbers are a zero. You can see this here:

```
1101
1100
1101
```

Binary OR operation

Binary XOR

The binary XOR is the one that really matters for cryptography. This is the operation that provides us with interesting results we can use as part of cryptographic algorithms. With the binary exclusive or (usually denoted XOR), we ask the question, "Is there a 1 in the first number or second number, but not in both?" In other words, we are exclusively asking the "OR" question, rather than asking the "AND/OR" question that the OR operation asks. You can see this operation next:

```
1101
1100
0001
```

A "1" in both numbers
yields a "0"

Binary XOR operation

What makes this operation particularly interesting is that it is reversible. If you perform the XOR operation again, this time taking the result of the first operation and XOR'ing it with the second number, you will get back the first number. You can see this here:

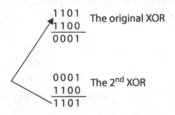

```
1101
1100
0001
```
The original XOR

```
0001
1100
1101
```
The 2nd XOR

Reversing the binary XOR operation

This is particularly useful in cryptographic algorithms. Our example used 4-bit numbers, but extrapolate from that. Assume instead of 4 bits, the first number was a lengthy message of, for example, 768 bits. And the second number was a randomly generated 128-bit number that we use as the key. You could then break the 768-bit plain text into blocks of 128 bits each (that would produce six blocks). Then you XOR the 128-bit key with each 128-bit block of plain text, producing a block of cipher text. The recipient could then XOR each 128-bit block of cipher text with the 128-bit key and get back the plain text.

Before you become overly excited with this demonstration, this simple XOR process is not robust enough for real cryptography. However, you will see, beginning in Chapter 6, that the XOR operation is a part of most modern symmetric ciphers. It cannot be overly stressed, however, that it is only a *part* of modern ciphers. The XOR operation is not, in and of itself, sufficient.

Conclusions

In this chapter you were introduced to a number of concepts that will be critical for your understanding of modern ciphers, particularly symmetric ciphers, which we begin studying in Chapter 6. Information entropy is a critical concept that you must understand. You were also introduced to confusion and diffusion, Hamming distance, and Hamming weight. These concepts are frequently used in later chapters. You also learned about mathematical and scientific theory. The chapter ended with a basic coverage of binary math.

Test Your Knowledge

1. The difference in bits between two strings X and Y is called _____.
2. If you take 1110 XOR 0101, the answer is _____.
3. A change in 1 bit of plain text leading to changes in multiple bits of cipher text is called _____.
4. The amount of information that a given message or variable contains is referred to as _____.
5. _____ refers to significant differences between plain text, key, and cipher text that make cryptanalysis more difficult.

Answers

1. Hamming distance
2. 1011
3. diffusion
4. information entropy
5. Diffusion

Endnotes

1. Roger Bohn and James Short, "How Much Information?" http://hmi.ucsd.edu/pdf/ HMI_2009_ConsumerReport_Dec9_2009.pdf.
2. Claude Shannon, "Communication Theory of Secrecy Systems," http://netlab.cs.ucla .edu/wiki/files/shannon1949.pdf.
3. Kerckhoffs's principle is discussed at Crytpo-IT, http://www.crypto-it.net/eng/theory/ kerckhoffs.html.
4. Bohn and Short, "How Much Information?"
5. Merriam-Webster, http://www.merriam-webster.com/.
6. John Rennie, "Answers to Creationist Nonsense," *Scientific American*, June 2002.

4 Essential Number Theory and Discrete Math

In this chapter we will cover the following:

- Number systems
- Prime numbers
- Important number theory questions
- Modulus arithmetic
- Set theory
- Logic
- Combinatorics

Number theory is an exciting and broad area of mathematics. Although it is considered pure mathematics, there are applications for number theory in many fields. When you read Chapters 10 and 11 concerning asymmetric cryptography, you will find that all asymmetric algorithms are simply applications of some facet of number theory. This leads us to the question, What is number theory? Traditionally, *number theory* is defined as the study of positive, whole numbers. The study of prime numbers is a particularly important aspect of number theory. The Wolfram MathWorld web site (http://mathworld.wolfram.com /NumberTheory.html) describes number theory as follows:

> Number theory is a vast and fascinating field of mathematics, sometimes called "higher arithmetic," consisting of the study of the properties of whole numbers. Primes and prime factorization are especially important in number theory, as are a number of functions such as the divisor function, Riemann zeta function, and totient function.

If you already have a solid background in mathematics, you may be asking yourself how well this topic can be covered in a single chapter. After all, entire textbooks have been written on number theory and discrete mathematics. In fact, entire books have been written on just the subtopics, such as prime numbers, set theory, logic, combinatorics, and so on. How, then, can I hope to cover these topics in a single chapter? Allow me to set your mind at ease. First, keep in mind that the goal of this chapter is not to make you a mathematician (though I certainly would not be disappointed if after reading this you feel motivated to read more on mathematics, or perhaps take math courses at a university). Rather, the goal is to give you just enough number theory and information to help you understand the modern cryptographic algorithms we will be discussing in later chapters. For that reason, I have not included discussions on some items that would normally be covered when discussing number theory. The most obvious of these are proofs—you won't see coverage of mathematical proofs in this chapter. There are countless books with very good coverage of proofs, including proofs of the very concepts and statements covered in this chapter. If you want to explore these mathematical proofs, you will have no trouble locating resources.

> **Note** Any one of these topics could certainly be explored in more depth, and I certainly encourage you to do so. For example if you are reading this book as part of a college course, I would hope it would motivate you to take a course in basic number theory or discrete math (if you haven't done so already).

If you have a solid foundation in mathematics, this chapter provides a brief review. If you lack such a foundation, as famed author Douglas Adams once said, "Don't panic." You will be able to understand the material in this chapter. Furthermore, this chapter will be sufficient for you to continue your study of cryptography. If these topics are new to you, however, this chapter (along with Chapter 5) might be the most difficult chapters to understand. You might need to read the chapters more than once.

> **Note** I provide some study tips throughout this chapter, directing you to some external sources that offer more coverage of a particular topic, including books and web sites. Although all the web sites may not always be up and available, they are easy and free for you to access. If a URL is no longer available, I suggest you use your favorite search engine to search the topic.

Number Systems

The first step in examining number theory is to get a firm understanding of number systems. Although number theory is concerned with positive integers, some of the number sets include additional numbers. I mention all the number sets here, but the rest of the chapter will focus on those relevant to number theory. You probably had some exposure to number systems even in primary school.

Natural Numbers

Natural numbers, also called counting numbers, are so called because they come naturally— that is, this is how children first learn to think of numbers. If, for example, you look on your desk and count how many pencils you have, you can use natural numbers to accomplish this task. Many sources count only the positive integers: 1, 2, 3, 4, …, without including 0; other sources include 0. I do not normally include 0 as a natural number, though not everyone agrees with me. (For example, in *The Nature and Growth of Modern Mathematics*,[1] author Edna Kramer argues that 0 should be included in the natural numbers. And despite this rather trivial difference of opinion with that esteemed author, I highly recommend that book as a journey through the history of mathematics.)

Note	The number 0 (zero) has an interesting history. Although to our modern minds, the concept of zero may seem obvious, it actually was a significant development in mathematics. Some indications point to the Babylonians, who may have had some concept of zero, but it is usually attributed to ninth-century India, where they were carrying out calculations using 0. If you reflect on that for a moment, you will realize that 0 as a number, rather than just a placeholder, was not known to ancient Egyptians and Greeks.

Negative Numbers

Eventually the natural numbers required expansion. Although negative numbers may seem perfectly reasonable to you and me, they were unknown in ancient times. Negative numbers first appeared in a book dating from the Han Dynasty in China (c. 260). In this book, the mathematician Liu Hui (c. 225–295) described basic rules for adding and subtracting negative numbers. In India, negative numbers first appeared in the fourth century and were routinely used to represent debts in financial matters by the seventh century.

The knowledge of negative numbers spread to Arab nations, and by at least the tenth century, Arab mathematicians where familiar with and using negative numbers. The famed book *Kitab al-jabr wa l-muqabala*, written by Al-Khwarizmi in about 825, from which we derive the word "algebra," did not include any negative numbers at all (www.maa.org /publications/periodicals/convergence/mathematical-treasures-al-khwarizmis-algebra).

Rational and Irrational Numbers

Number systems have evolved in response to a need produced by some mathematical problem. Negative numbers, discussed in the preceding section, were developed in response to subtracting a larger integer from a smaller integer (3 − 5). A *rational number* is any number that can be expressed as the quotient of two integers. Like many early advances in mathematics, the formalization of rational numbers was driven by practical issues. Rational numbers were first noticed as the result of division (4/2 = 2, or 4 ÷ 2 = 2). (Note the two symbols most of us learn for division in modern primary and secondary school: ÷ and /. Now that is not a mathematically rigorous definition, nor is it meant to be.)

Eventually, the division of numbers led to results that could not be expressed as the quotient of two integers. The classic example comes from geometry. If you try to express the ratio of a circle's circumference to its radius, for example, the result is an infinite number. It is often approximated as 3.14159, but the decimals continue on and no pattern repeats. If a real number cannot be expressed as the quotient of two integers, it is classified as an *irrational number*.

Real Numbers

Real numbers is the superset of all rational and irrational numbers. The set of real numbers is infinite. It is likely that all the numbers you encounter on a regular basis are real numbers, unless of course you work in certain fields of mathematics or physics. For quite a long time, real numbers were considered to be the only numbers that existed.

Imaginary Numbers

Imaginary numbers developed in response to a specific problem. As you undoubtedly know, if you multiple a negative with a negative you get a positive ($-1 \times -1 = 1$). This becomes a problem, however, if you consider the square root of a negative number. Clearly, the square root of a positive number is also positive ($\sqrt{4} = 2$, $\sqrt{1} = 1$, and so on). But what is the square root of a negative 1? If you answer negative 1, that won't work, because when you multiply two negative 1's, the answer is a positive 1. This conundrum led to the development of *imaginary numbers*, which are defined as follows: $i^2 = -1$ (or conversely $\sqrt{-1} = i$). So the square root of any negative number can be expressed as some integer multiplied by i. A real number combined with an imaginary number is referred to as a *complex number*.

Note	As far back as the ancient Greeks, there seems to have been some concept of needing a number system to account for the square root of a negative number. But it wasn't until 1572 that Rafael Bombelli first established formal rules for multiplying complex numbers.

Prime Numbers

Although the various numbers discussed in the preceding sections are interesting from a cryptography perspective, it is difficult to find a set of numbers that is more relevant than prime numbers. A *prime number* is a natural number greater than 1 that has no positive divisors other than itself and 1. (Note that the number 1 itself is not considered prime.) Many facts, conjectures, and theorems in number theory are related to prime numbers.

The fundamental theorem of arithmetic states that every positive integer can be written uniquely as the product of primes, where the prime factors are written in order of increasing size. Basically this means that any integer can be factored into its prime factors. This is probably a task you had to do in primary school, albeit with small integers. If you consider the fundamental theorem of arithmetic for just a moment, you can see that it is one (of many) indications of how important prime numbers are.

As first proven by Euclid (328–283 B.C.E.), an infinite number of primes exist. (Many other proofs of this have been constructed later by mathematicians such as Leonhard Euler [1707–1783] and Christian Goldbach [1690–1765], both of whom we will discuss later in this chapter.) How many primes are found in a given range of numbers is a more difficult problem. For example, there are four primes between 1 and 10 (2, 3, 5, 7). Then, between 11 and 20, there are four more (11, 13, 17, 19). However, there are only two primes between 30 and 40 (31, 37). In fact, as we progress through the positive integers, prime numbers become more sparse. (It has been determined that "the number of prime numbers less than x is approximately x/ln(x)." Consider the number 10, for example. The natural logarithm of 10 is approximately 2.302, 10/2.302 = 4.34, and we have already seen there are four primes between 1 and 10.)

Note	Euclid's famous work, *Elements*, written around 300 B.C.E., contains a significant discussion of prime numbers, including theorems regarding there being an infinite number of primes.

Finding Prime Numbers

As you will discover later in this book, prime numbers are a key part of cryptographic algorithms such as RSA. How do you generate a prime number? An obvious first thought is to think of a number and then check to see if it has any factors. If it has no factors, it is prime. You can check by simply trying to divide that random number n by every number up to the square root of n. So, if I ask you if 67 is prime, you first try to divide it by 2, then by 3, then by 4, and so forth. In just a few steps, you will determine that 67 is a prime number. (That wasn't so hard.) Using a computer, you could determine this much faster.

Unfortunately, for cryptographic algorithms such as RSA, we need much larger prime numbers. Modern RSA keys are a minimum of 2048 bits long and need two prime numbers to generate, and those prime numbers need to be very large. So simply generating a random number and checking it by hand is impossible to do and could take quite some time even with a computer. For this reason, there have been numerous attempts to formulate some algorithm that would consistently and efficiently generate prime numbers. Let's look at just a few of those algorithms.

Mersenne Prime

French theologian Marin Mersenne (1588–1648) made significant contributions to acoustics and music theory as well as mathematics. He posited that the formula $2^p - 1$ would produce prime numbers. Investigation has shown that this formula will produce prime numbers for p = 2, 3, 5, 7, 13, 17, 19, 31, 67, 127, and 257, but not for many other numbers such as p = 4, 6, 8, 9, 10, 11, and so on. His conjecture resulted in a prime of the form $2^p - 1$ being named a *Mersenne prime*. By 1996, there were 34 known Mersenne primes, with the last eight discoveries made on supercomputers. Clearly, the formula can generate primes, but frequently it does not. Any number of the format $2^p - 1$ is considered a Mersenne number. It so happens that if p is a composite number, then so is $2^p - 1$. If p is a prime number, $2^p - 1$ *might* be prime. Mersenne originally thought all numbers of that form *would* be prime numbers.

Fermat Prime

Mathematician Pierre de Fermat (1601–1665) made many significant contributions to number theory. He also proposed a formula that he believed could be used to generate prime numbers:

$$2^{(2^n)} + 1$$

Several such numbers—particularly the first few powers of 2—are indeed prime, as you can see here:

$2^1 + 1 = 3$	prime
$2^2 + 1 = 5$	prime
$2^4 + 1 = 17$	prime
$2^8 + 1 = 257$	prime
$2^{16} + 1 = 65537$	prime

Unfortunately, as with Mersenne primes, not all Fermat numbers are prime.

Sieve of Eratosthenes

In some cases, the goal is not to generate a prime, but to find out if a known number is a prime. To determine whether a number is prime, we need some method(s) that are faster than simply trying to divide by every integer up to the square root of the integer in question. The Eratosthenes sieve is one such method. Eratosthenes (c. 276–195 B.C.E.) served as the librarian at the Library of Alexandria, and he was also quite the mathematician and astronomer. He invented a method for finding prime numbers that is still used today, called the sieve of Eratosthenes. It essentially filters out composite integers to leave only the prime numbers. The method is actually rather simple. To find all the prime numbers less than or equal to a given integer n by Eratosthenes's method, you'd do the following:

1. Create a list of consecutive integers from 2 to n: (2, 3, 4, . . . , n).
2. Initially, let p equal 2, the first prime number.
3. Starting from p, count up in increments of p and mark each of these numbers greater than p itself in the list. These will be multiples of p: 2p, 3p, 4p, and so on. Note that some of them may have already been marked.
4. Find the first number greater than p in the list that is *not* marked. If there is no such number, stop. Otherwise, let p now equal this number (this is the next prime), and repeat from step 3.

To illustrate, you can do this with a chart, such as the one shown next. For the purposes of demonstrating this concept we are concerning ourselves only with numbers through 100.

1	2	3	4	5	6	7	8	9	10
11	12	13	14	15	16	17	18	19	20
21	22	23	24	25	26	27	28	29	30
31	32	33	34	35	36	37	38	39	40
41	42	43	44	45	46	47	48	49	50
51	52	53	54	55	56	57	58	59	60
61	62	63	64	65	66	67	68	69	70
71	72	73	74	75	76	77	78	79	80
81	82	83	84	85	86	87	88	89	90
91	92	93	94	95	96	97	98	99	100

Numbers through 100

First, cross out the number 2, because it is prime, and then cross out all multiples of 2, since they are, by definition, composite numbers, as shown here:

1	2̶	3	4̶	5	6̶	7	8̶	9	1̶0̶
11	1̶2̶	13	1̶4̶	15	1̶6̶	17	1̶8̶	19	2̶0̶
21	2̶2̶	23	2̶4̶	25	2̶6̶	27	2̶8̶	29	3̶0̶
31	3̶2̶	33	3̶4̶	35	3̶6̶	37	3̶8̶	39	4̶0̶
41	4̶2̶	43	4̶4̶	45	4̶6̶	47	4̶8̶	49	5̶0̶
51	5̶2̶	53	5̶4̶	55	5̶6̶	57	5̶8̶	59	6̶0̶
61	6̶2̶	63	6̶4̶	65	6̶6̶	67	6̶8̶	69	7̶0̶
71	7̶2̶	73	7̶4̶	75	7̶6̶	77	7̶8̶	79	8̶0̶
81	8̶2̶	83	8̶4̶	85	8̶6̶	87	8̶8̶	89	9̶0̶
91	9̶2̶	93	9̶4̶	95	9̶6̶	97	9̶8̶	99	1̶0̶0̶

Eliminating multiples of 2

Next, do the same thing with 3 (since it is also a prime number) and for all multiples of 3, as shown here:

1	~~2~~	~~3~~	~~4~~	5	~~6~~	7	~~8~~	~~9~~	~~10~~
11	~~12~~	13	~~14~~	~~15~~	~~16~~	17	~~18~~	19	~~20~~
~~21~~	~~22~~	23	~~24~~	25	~~26~~	~~27~~	~~28~~	29	~~30~~
31	~~32~~	~~33~~	~~34~~	35	~~36~~	37	~~38~~	~~39~~	~~40~~
41	~~42~~	43	~~44~~	~~45~~	~~46~~	47	~~48~~	49	~~50~~
~~51~~	~~52~~	53	~~54~~	55	~~56~~	~~57~~	~~58~~	59	~~60~~
61	~~62~~	~~63~~	~~64~~	65	~~66~~	67	~~68~~	~~69~~	~~70~~
71	~~72~~	73	~~74~~	~~75~~	~~76~~	77	~~78~~	79	~~80~~
~~81~~	~~82~~	83	~~84~~	85	~~86~~	~~87~~	~~88~~	89	~~90~~
91	~~92~~	~~93~~	~~94~~	95	~~96~~	97	~~98~~	~~99~~	~~100~~

Eliminating multiples of 3

Notice that you've already crossed out many of those numbers, because they are also multiples of 2. You can skip 4, since it is a multiple of 2, and go straight to 5 and multiples of 5. Some of those (such as 15) are also multiples of 3 or multiples of 2 (such as 10, 20, and so on) and are already crossed out. You can skip 6, 8, and 9, since they are multiples of numbers that have already been used, and that leaves 7 and multiples of 7. Given that we are stopping at 100, you will find if you use 11 and multiples of 11, that will finish your application of the sieve of Eratosthenes. After you have crossed out multiples of 5, 7, and 11, only prime numbers remain. (Remember 1 is not prime.) You can see this here:

(1)	~~2~~	~~3~~	~~4~~	~~5~~	~~6~~	~~7~~	~~8~~	~~9~~	~~10~~
~~11~~	~~12~~	13	~~14~~	~~15~~	~~16~~	17	~~18~~	19	~~20~~
~~21~~	~~22~~	23	~~24~~	~~25~~	~~26~~	~~27~~	~~28~~	29	~~30~~
31	~~32~~	~~33~~	~~34~~	~~35~~	~~36~~	37	~~38~~	~~39~~	~~40~~
41	~~42~~	43	~~44~~	~~45~~	~~46~~	47	~~48~~	~~49~~	~~50~~
~~51~~	~~52~~	53	~~54~~	~~55~~	~~56~~	~~57~~	~~58~~	59	~~60~~
61	~~62~~	~~63~~	~~64~~	~~65~~	~~66~~	67	~~68~~	~~69~~	~~70~~
71	~~72~~	73	~~74~~	~~75~~	~~76~~	~~77~~	~~78~~	79	~~80~~
~~81~~	~~82~~	83	~~84~~	~~85~~	~~86~~	~~87~~	~~88~~	89	~~90~~
~~91~~	~~92~~	~~93~~	~~94~~	~~95~~	~~96~~	97	~~98~~	~~99~~	~~100~~

The prime numbers that are left

This can be a tedious process and is often implemented via a computer program. If you are going past 100, you just keep using the next prime number and multiples of it (13, 17, and so on).

Other Sieves

A number of more modern sieve systems have been developed, including the sieve of Atkin, developed in 2003 by Arthur O.L. Atkin and Daniel J. Bernstein, and the sieve of Sundaram, developed in the 1930s by mathematician S.P. Sundaram.

Like the sieve of Eratosthenes, the sieve of Sundaram operates by removing composite numbers, leaving behind only the prime numbers. It is relatively simple:

1. Start with a list of integers from 1 to some number n.
2. Remove all numbers of the form i + j + 2ij. The numbers i and j are both integers with $1 \leq i < j$ and $i + j + 2ij \leq n$.
3. Double the remaining numbers and increment by 1 to create a list of the odd prime numbers below 2n + 2.

Lucas-Lehmer Test

The Lucas-Lehmer test is used to determine whether a given number n is a prime number. This deterministic test of primality works on Mersenne numbers—that means it is effective only for finding out if a given Mersenne number is prime. (Remember a Mersenne number is one of the form $2^p - 1$.) In 1856, French mathematician Édouard Lucas developed a primality test that he subsequently improved in 1878; then in the 1930s, American mathematician Derrick Lehmer provided a proof of the test.

> **Note** Throughout the study of cryptography you will encounter the terms "probabilistic" and "deterministic" in reference to primality tests, pseudo-random number generators, and other algorithms. The meanings of these two terms is fairly simple: A probabilistic algorithm has a *probability* of giving the desired result, and a deterministic algorithm *will* give the desired result. In reference to primality testing, a probabilistic test can tell you that a given number is probably prime, but a deterministic test will tell you that it is or is not definitely prime.

A Lucas-Lehmer number is part of a sequence of numbers in which each number is the previous number squared minus 2. So, for example, if you start with 4, you would get the sequence shown here:

$$S_1 = 4$$
$$S_2 = 4^2 - 2 = 14$$
$$S_3 = 14^2 - 2 = 194$$
$$S_4 = 194^2 - 2 = 37634$$

The test is as follow:

For some $p \geq 3$, which is itself a prime number, $2^p - 1$ is prime if and only if S_{p-1} is divisible by $2^p - 1$. Example: $2^5 - 1 = 31$; because $S_4 = 37634$ and is divisible by 31, 31 must be a prime number.

> **Note** At this point, you may be tempted to question the veracity of a claim I made regarding the reliability of the Lucas-Lehmer test. As I stated at the beginning of this chapter, I will not be demonstrating mathematical proofs. You can spend some time with this test, using various values of S to see for yourself that it does, indeed, work. That is certainly not the same as working out a proof, but it could give you some level of comfort that the test really works.

Relatively Prime, or Co-prime, Numbers

The concept of prime numbers and how to generate them is critical to your study of cryptography. You should also be familiar with the concept of numbers that are *relatively prime*, often called *co-prime* numbers. The concept is actually pretty simple: Two numbers x and y are relatively prime (co-prime) if they have no common divisors other than 1. So, for example, the numbers 8 and 15 are co-prime. The factors of 8 are 1, 2, and 4, and the factors of 15 are 1, 3, and 5. Because these two numbers (8 and 15) have no common factors other than 1, they are relatively prime.

Lots of interesting facts are associated with co-prime numbers, many of which were discovered by Euler, who asked a few simple questions such as this: Given an integer n, how many numbers are co-prime to n? That number is called Euler's totient, the Euler phi function, or simply the totient. The symbol for the totient of a number is shown here:

$$\varphi(n)$$

The term used for integers that are smaller than n and that have no common factors with n (other than 1) is *totative*. For example, 8 is a totative of 15. To check this easily yourself, you will see that 1, 2, 4, 7, 8, 11, 13, and 14 are all co-prime (or relatively prime) with 15. However, 3, 5, 6, 9, 10, and 12 all have common factors with 15.

Note Euler introduced this function in 1763. There was no practical use for it until modern asymmetric cryptography. This is a great example of pure mathematics that is later found to have very important practical applications.

The next question Euler asked was this: What if a given integer, n, is a prime number? How many totatives will it have (that is, what is the totient of n)? Let's consider a prime number—for example, 7. Given that 7 is prime, we know that none of the numbers smaller than 7 have any common factors with 7. So 2, 3, 4, 5, and 6 are all totatives of 7. And since 1 is a special case, it is also a totative of 7, so we find that six numbers are totatives of 7. It turns out that for any n that is prime, the Euler's totient of n is n − 1. So if n = 13, then the totient of n is 12.

And then Euler asked yet another question about co-prime numbers: Assuming we have two prime numbers, m and n. We already know that the totient of each is m − 1 and n − 1, respectively. But what happens if we multiply the two numbers together? So m × n = k; what is the totient of k? You could simply test every number less than k and find the answer. That might work for small values of k, but it would be impractical for larger values. Euler discovered a nice shortcut: If you have two prime numbers (m and n) and multiply them to get k, the totient of k is the totient of m × the totient of n. Put another way, the totient of k is (m − 1)(n − 1).

Let's look at an example. Assume we have two prime numbers, n = 3 and m = 5.

1. Multiply n × m: 3 × 5 = 15.
2. The totient of n is n − 1, or 2.
3. The totient of m is m − 1, or 4.
4. 2 × 4 = 8.
5. The totient of k (15) is 8.

The totient, 15, is a small number so we can test it. The factors of 15 (other than 1) are 3 and 5, which means that 15 has common factors with any multiple of 3 or 5 smaller than 15: 3, 6, 9, 12 and 5, 10. So with what numbers does 15 not have common factors? 1, 2, 4, 7, 8, 11, 13, and 14. If you take a moment to count those, you will see that there are eight numbers. Of course, Euler relied on rigorous mathematical proofs, which we are foregoing in this chapter, but hopefully this example provides you with a comfort level regarding calculating totients.

Now all of this may sound rather obscure, or even unimportant. However, these facts are a very big part of the RSA algorithm that we will be examining in some depth in Chapter 10. In fact, when you first see the RSA algorithm, you will notice several elements discussed in this section.

Important Operations

Some mathematical operations are critical even to a basic understanding of modern cryptographic algorithms. Those of you with a solid foundation in mathematics should already be familiar with these operations, but in case you are not, I will briefly introduce you to them in this section.

Divisibility Theorems

You should be aware of some basics about divisibility that define some elementary facts regarding the divisibility of integers. The following are basic divisibility theorems that you will see applied in later chapters in specific cryptographic algorithms. I recommend that you commit them to memory before proceeding.

For integers a, b, and c, the following is true:

- If a | b and a | c, then a | (b + c). Example: 3 | 6 and 3 | 9, so 3 | 15. (Note that | means *divides*, so in this statement, if a divides b and a divides c, then a will divide b + c.)
- If a | b, then a | bc for all integers c. Example: 5 | 10, so 5 | 20, 5 | 30, 5 | 40, ...
- If a | b and b | c, then a | c. Example: 4 | 8 and 8 | 24, so 4 | 24.

Summation

You have probably seen the summation symbol, Σ, frequently. If not, you will see it later in this book. It is basically a way of adding a sequence of numbers to get their *sum*. It is more convenient to use the summation symbol than expressly write out the summation of a long series of values. Any intermediate result at any given point in the sequences is a *partial sum* (sometimes called a running total or prefix sum). The numbers that are to be added up are often called *addends* or sometimes *summands*. They can be any numbers, but in cryptography, we are most often interested in *summing integers*.

A basic example of summation is shown in Figure 4-1.

The figure states that we are dealing with some integer i. We begin with the value of i set to 1. Add up the i values from 1 until you reach 100. The letter to the right of the summation symbol is the *variable* we are dealing with. The number under the summation is the *initial value* of that variable. Finally, the number over the summation symbol (often denoted with an n)

$$\sum_{i=1}^{100} i$$

FIGURE 4-1   A summation

is the *stopping point*. You can manually add these numbers up, $1 + 2 + 3 + 4 \ldots 100$, if you wish; however, you can use a formula to compute this summation:

$$(n(n+1))/2$$

In our example, that is

$$(100(101))/2 = 5050$$

Note | The notation you see used in Figure 4-1 is often called the "capital Sigma notation," because the Σ is the Greek sigma symbol.

You can do a similar operation with multiplication using the pi symbol, $\prod$. This symbol works exactly like the capital Sigma notation, except rather than adding up the series of values to arrive at a sum, you multiply the series of values to arrive at a *product*.

Logarithms

Logarithms play a very important role in asymmetric cryptography. An entire class of asymmetric algorithms are based on what is called the *discrete logarithm problem*. Most readers encountered logarithms during secondary school.

The *logarithm* of a number is the exponent to which some fixed value (called the base) must be raised to produce that number. Let's assume base 10, for example, and ask, what is the logarithm of 10,000? In other words, what number must 10 be raised to in order to produce the number 10,000? The answer is 4, as $10^4 = 10,000$. Most people are quite comfortable with base 10, which is known as the *common logarithm* in mathematics. However, we can use any base. For example, suppose we want to know the logarithm of 16 in base 2, which we would write as $\log_2(16)$. In other words, what power must 2 be raised to in order to get 16? The answer is 4, as $2^4 = 16$.

Natural Logarithm

The *natural logarithm,* denoted as ln, is widely used in math and science. Natural logarithms use the irrational number e (approximately 2.718) as the base. The natural logarithm of some number x is usually written as ln x but can also be written as $\log_e$ x. As with any logarithm, the natural log is what power e must be raised to in order to give some particular number.

The basic concept of the natural logarithm was developed by Grégoire de Saint-Vincent and Alphonse Antonio de Sarasa in the early 17th century. They were working on problems involving hyperbolic sectors.

Tip
If you are new to logarithms and/or natural logs, you may wish to consult two tutorials to learn more about these topics: "The Common and Natural Logarithms" at http://www.purplemath.com/modules/logs3.htm and "Demystifying the Natural Logarithm (ln)" at http://betterexplained.com/articles/demystifying-the-natural-logarithm-ln/.

Discrete Logarithm

Now that you have a basic grasp of logarithms and even natural logs, we can turn our attention to discussing *discrete logarithms*. These play an important role in the algorithms we will explore in Chapters 10 and 11.

To understand discrete logarithms, keep in mind the definition of a logarithm: the number to which some base must be raised to get another number. Discrete logarithms ask this same question, but do so with regard to a *finite group*. Put more formally, a discrete logarithm is some integer k that solves the equation $x^k = y$, where both x and y are elements of a finite group.

Computing a discrete logarithm is a very difficult problem, which is why discrete logarithms form the basis for some modern cryptographic algorithms. We will take up this topic again in Chapter 10 when we discuss specific algorithms and after we have discussed groups in Chapter 5. For now, note that a discrete logarithm is, essentially, a logarithm within some finite group.

Tip
The Kahn Academy web site provides a very nice introduction to discrete logarithms: https://www.khanacademy.org/computing/computer-science/cryptography/modern-crypt/v/discrete-logarithm-problem.

Modulus Operations

Modulus operations are important in cryptography, particularly in RSA. Let's begin with the most simple explanation, and then delve into more details. To use the modulus operator, simply divide A by N and return the remainder. So, for example,

$$5 \bmod 2 = 1$$
$$12 \bmod 5 = 2$$

Note
I am not using the congruence symbol (≡) here because I am not discussing congruence. I am stating that if you divide 5 by 2, the remainder is 1, and if you divide 12 by 5, the remainder is 2. This is standard to computer programmers but might seem a bit odd to mathematicians. In many programming languages, the % symbol is used to perform the modulus operation.

This explains how to use the modulus operator, and in many cases this is as far as many programming textbooks go. But this still leaves the question of why we are doing this. Exactly what is a modulus? One way to think about modulus arithmetic is to imagine doing any integer math you might normally do, but bind your answers by some number. A classic example used in many textbooks is a clock, which includes numbers 1 through 12, so any arithmetic operation you do has to have an answer of 12 or less. If it is currently 4 o'clock and I ask you to meet me in 10 hours, simple math would say I am asking you to meet me at 14 o'clock. But that is not possible, because our clock is bounded by the number 12! Finding the answer is simple, though: use the mod operator with a modulus of 12 and look at the remainder:

$$14 \bmod 12 = 2$$

So I am actually asking you to meet me at 2 o'clock. (Whether that is A.M. or P.M. depends on the original 4 o'clock, but that is really irrelevant to understanding the concepts of modular arithmetic.) This is an example of how you might use modular arithmetic every day.

Note   Although the basic concept of modular arithmetic dates back to Euclid, who wrote about it in his book *Elements*, the modern approach to modular arithmetic was first published by Carl Friedrich Gauss in his book *Disquisitiones Arithmeticae* in 1801.

Congruence

Congruence in modulus operations is a very important topic and you will see it applied frequently in modern cryptographic algorithms. The symbol $\equiv$ is used to denote congruence in mathematics.

Two numbers a and b are said to be "congruent modulo n" if

$$(a \bmod n) = (b \bmod n) \rightarrow a \equiv b (\bmod n)$$

If two numbers are congruent modulo n, then the difference between a and b will be some multiple of n. To make this clearer, let's return to the clock analogy, in which 14 and 2 are congruent modulo 12. It turns out that the difference between 14 and 2 is 12, a multiple of n (1×12). We also know that 14, or 1400 hours on the 24-hour clock, is 2 o'clock. So when we say that 14 and 2 are congruent modulo 12, we are stating that, at least in reference to modulo 12, 14 and 2 are the same. Here's another example: 17 and 5 are congruent modulo 12. The difference between them is 12. Again using the 24-hour clock to test our conclusions, we find that 1700 hours is the same as 5 P.M.

You should be aware of some basic properties of congruence:

- $a \equiv b \pmod{n}$ if $n | (a - b)$
- $a \equiv b \pmod{n}$ implies $b \equiv a \pmod{n}$
- $a \equiv b \pmod{n}$ and $b \equiv c \pmod{n}$ imply $a \equiv c \pmod{n}$

Congruence Classes

A *congruence class*, or residue class, is a group of numbers that are all congruent for some given modulus.

Consider an example where the modulus is 5. What numbers are congruent modulo 5? Let's begin with 7: 7 mod 5 $\equiv$ 2. Next, we ask what other numbers' mod 5 $\equiv$ 2, and we arrive at an infinite series of numbers: 12, 17, 22, 27, 32 . . . . Notice that this works the other way as well (with integers smaller than the modulus, including negatives). We know that 7 mod 5 $\equiv$ 2, but also 2 mod 5 ≡ 2 (that is, the nearest multiple of 5 would be 0; 0 × 5, thus 2 mod 5 ≡ 2). Make sure you fully understand why 2 mod 5 ≡ 2, then we can proceed to examine negative numbers. Our next multiple of 5 after 0, going backward, is −5 (5 × −1). So −3 mod 5 ≡ 2. We can now expand the elements of our congruence class to include −3, 0, 2, 7, 12, 17, 22, 27, 32, and so on.

You should also note that for any modulus n, there are n congruence classes. If you reflect on this for just a moment you should see that the modulus itself creates a boundary on the arithmetic done with that modulus, so it is impossible to have more congruence classes than the integer value of the modulus.

Modulus operations are very important to several asymmetric cryptography algorithms that we will be examining in Chapter 10. So make certain you are comfortable with these concepts before proceeding.

> **Tip** For more on modulus arithmetic, consult the Rutgers University tutorial "Modular Arithmetic" at www.math.rutgers.edu/~erowland/modulararithmetic.html, or TheMathsters YouTube video "Modular Arithmetic 1" at www.youtube.com /watch?v=SR3oLCYoh-I.

Famous Number Theorists and Their Contributions

When learning any new topic, you may often find it helpful to review a bit of its history. In some cases, this is best accomplished by examining some of the most important figures in that history. Number theory is replete with prominent names. In this section I have restricted myself to a brief biography of mathematicians whose contributions to number theory are most relevant to cryptography.

Fibonacci

Leonardo Bonacci (1170–1250), known as Fibonacci, was an Italian mathematician who made significant contributions to mathematics. He is most famous for the Fibonacci numbers, which represent an interesting sequence of numbers:

$$1, 1, 2, 3, 5, 8, 13, 21, \ldots$$

The sequence is derived from adding the two previous numbers. To put it in a more mathematical format,

$$F_n = F_{n-1} + F_{n-2}$$

So in our example, 2 is 1 + 1, 3 is 2 + 1, 5 is 3 + 2, 8 is 5 + 3, and so on.

The sequence continues infinitely. Fibonacci numbers were actually known earlier in India, but they were unknown in Europe until Fibonacci rediscovered them. He published this concept in his book *Liber Abaci*. Although this number series has many interesting applications, for our purposes, the most important is its use in pseudo-random number generators that we will be exploring in Chapter 12.

Fibonacci was the son of a wealthy merchant and was able to travel extensively. He spent time in the Mediterranean area studying under various Arab mathematicians. In his book *Liber Abaci*, he also introduced Arabic numerals, which are still widely used today.

Fermat

Pierre de Fermat (1601–1665) was trained as a lawyer and was an amateur mathematician, although he made significant contributions to mathematics. He worked with analytical geometry and probability but is best known for several theorems in number theory, which we will look at briefly.

Fermat's little theorem states that if p is a prime number, then for any integer a, the number $a^p - a$ is an integer multiple of p. What does this mean? Let's look at an example: Suppose a = 2 and p = 5. Then $2^5 = 32$ and 32 − 2 is 30, which is indeed a multiple of p (5). This actually turns into a primality test. If you think p is a prime number, you can test it. If it is prime, then a^{p-a} should be an integer multiple of p. If it is not, then p is not prime.

Let's test this on some numbers we know are not prime. Use p = 9: $2^8 - 2 = 256 - 2 = 250$, and 250 is not prime. This is an example of how various aspects of number theory, that might not at first appear to have practical applications, can indeed be applied to practical problems.

Note	This theorem is often stated in a format using modulus arithmetic. However, we have not yet discussed modulus arithmetic so I am avoiding that notation at this time.

Fermat first articulated this theorem in 1640, which he worded as follows:

$$p \text{ divides } a^{p-1} - 1 \text{ whenever p is prime and a is co-prime to p}$$

Fermat is perhaps best known for Fermat's Last Theorem, sometimes called Fermat's conjecture (which, incidentally, is no longer a conjecture). This theorem states that no three positive integers (x, y, z) can satisfy the equation $x^n + y^n = c^n$ for any n that is greater than 2. Put another way, if n > 2, then there is no integer to the n power that is the sum of two other integers to the n power. Fermat first proposed this in 1637, actually in handwritten notes in the margin of his copy of *Arithmetica*, an ancient Greek text written in about 250 C.E. by Diophantus of Alexandria. Fermat claimed to have a proof that would not fit in the margin, but it has never been found. However, his theorem was subsequently proven by Stanford University professor Andrew Wiles in 1994.

Euler

Swiss mathematician and physicist Leonhard Euler (1707–1783) is an important figure in the history of mathematics and number theory. Euler (pronounced *oy*-ler) is considered one of the best mathematicians of all time, and he is certainly the pinnacle of 18th-century mathematics.

Euler's father was a pastor of a church. As a child, Euler and his family were friends with the Bernoulli family, including Johann Bernoulli, a prominent mathematician of the time. Euler's contributions to mathematics are very broad. He worked in algebra, number theory, physics, and geometry. The number e you probably encountered in elementary calculus courses (approximately 2.7182), which is the base for the natural logarithm, is named after Euler, as is the Euler-Mascheroni constant.

Euler was responsible for the development of infinitesimal calculus and provided proof for Fermat's little theorem, as well as inventing the totient function discussed earlier in this chapter. He also made significant contributions to graph theory. Graph theory is discussed later in this chapter in reference to discrete mathematics.

Goldbach

Christian Goldbach (1690–1765) was trained as a lawyer, but he is remembered primarily for his contributions to number theory. It is reported that he had discussions and interactions with a number of famous mathematicians, including Euler. Although he made other contributions to number theory, he is best remembered for Goldbach's conjecture, which, at least as of this writing, is an unsolved mathematical problem. The conjecture can be worded quite simply:

Every integer greater than 2 can be expressed as the sum of two prime numbers. For small numbers, this is easy to verify (though the number 3 immediately poses a problem as mathematicians don't generally consider 1 to be prime):

$$4 = 2 + 2, \text{ both primes}$$

$$5 = 3 + 2, \text{ both primes}$$

$$6 = 3 + 3, \text{ both primes}$$

Although this is true for very large numbers and no exception has been found, it has not been mathematically proven.

Discrete Mathematics

As you learned in the discussion of number theory, some numbers are continuous. For example, real numbers are continuous—that is, there is no clear demarcation point. Consider 2.1 and 2.2 for example, which can be further divided into 2.11, 2.12, 2.13...2.2. And even 2.11 and 2.11 can be further divided into 2.111, 2.112, 2.113...2.12. This process can continue infinitely. Calculus deals with continuous mathematics. One of the most basic operations in calculus, the limit, is a good example of this.

Discrete mathematics, however, is concerned with mathematical constructs that have clearly defined (that is, discrete) boundaries. You can probably already surmise that integers are a major part of discrete mathematics, but so are graphs and sets.

Set Theory

Set theory is an important part of discrete mathematics. A *set* is a collection of objects called the *members* or *elements* of that set. If we have a set, we say that some objects belong (or do not belong) to this set, and are (or are not) in the set. We say also that sets consist of their elements.

As with much of mathematics, terminology and notation is critical. So let's begin our study in a similar fashion, building from simple to more complex concepts. The simplest way I can think of is defining an element of a set: We say that x is a member of set A. This can be denoted as

$$x \in A$$

Sets are often listed in brackets. For example the set of all odd integers < 10 would be shown as follows:

$$A = \{1, 3, 5, 7, 9\}$$

A member of that set would be denoted as follows:

$$3 \in A$$

Negation can be symbolized by a line through a symbol:

$$2 \notin A$$

In this example, 2 is not an element of set A.

If a set is not ending, you can denote that with ellipses. For example, the set of all odd numbers (not just those less than 10) can be denoted like this:

$$A = \{1, 3, 5, 7, 9, 11, ...\}$$

You can also denote a set using an equation or formula that defines membership in that set.

Sets can be related to each other, and the most common relationships are briefly described here:

- **Union**   With two sets A and B, elements that are members of A, B, or both represent the union of A and B, symbolized as $A \cup B$.
- **Intersection**   With two sets A and B, elements that are in both A and B are the intersection of sets A and B, symbolized as $A \cap B$. If the intersection of set A and B is empty (that is, the two sets have no elements in common), the two sets are said to be *disjoint*, or mutually exclusive.
- **Difference**   With two sets A and B, elements that are in one set but not both are the difference between A and B, symbolized as $A \setminus B$.
- **Complement**   With two sets A and B, set B is the complement of set A if B has no elements that are also in A, symbolized as $B = A^c$.
- **Double complement**   The complement of a set's complement is that set itself. In other words, the complement of A^c is A. That may seem odd at first read, but reflect on the definition of the complement of a set for just a moment. The complement of a set has no elements in that set. So it stands to reason that to be the complement of the complement of a set, you would have to have all elements within the set.

These are basic set relationships. Now a few facts about sets:

- **Order is irrelevant** $\{1, 2, 3\}$ is the same as $\{3, 2, 1\}$ or $\{3, 1, 2\}$ or $\{2, 1, 3\}$.
- **Subsets**   Set A could be a subset of set B. For example, if set A is the set of all odd numbers < 10 and set B is the set of all odd numbers < 100, then set A is a subset of set B. This is symbolized as $A \subseteq B$.
- **Power set**   Sets may have subsets. For example, set A is all integers < 10, and set B is a subset of A with all prime numbers < 10. Set C is a subset of A with all odd numbers < 10. Set D is a subset of A with all even numbers < 10. We could continue this exercise making arbitrary subsets such as $E = \{4, 7\}$, $F \{1, 2, 3\}$, and so on. The set of all subsets of a given set is called the *power set* for that set.

Sets also have properties that govern the interaction between sets. The most important of these properties are listed here:

- **Commutative Law**   The intersection of set A with set B is equal to the intersection of set B with set A. The same is true for unions. Put another way, when considering intersections and unions of sets, the order in which the sets are presented is irrelevant. This is symbolized as shown here:

  $(a)\ A \cap B = B \cap A$

  $(b)\ A \cup B = B \cup A$

- **Associative Law**   If you have three sets and the relationships among the three are all unions or all intersections, then the order does not matter. This is symbolized as shown here:

  $(a)\ (A \cap B) \cap C = A \cap (B \cap C)$

  $(b)\ (A \cup B) \cup C = A \cup (B \cup C)$

- **Distributive Law**   This law is a bit different from the Associative Law, and order does not matter. The union of set A with the intersection of B and C is the same as the union of A and B intersected with the union of A and C. This is symbolized as shown here:

  $(a)\ A \cup (B \cap C) = (A \cup B) \cap (A \cup C)$

  $(b)\ A \cap (B \cup C) = (A \cap B) \cup (A \cap C)$

- **De Morgan's Laws**   These laws govern issues with unions and intersections and the complements thereof. These are more complex than the previously discussed laws. Essentially the complement of the intersection of set A and set B is the union of the complement of A and the complement of B. The symbolism of De Morgan's Laws are shown here:

  $(a)\ (A \cap B)^c = A^c \cup B^c$

  $(b)\ (A \cup B)^c = A^c \cap B^c$

These are the basic elements of set theory. You should be familiar with them before proceeding.

Logic

Logic is an important topic in mathematics as well as in science and philosophy. In discrete mathematics, *logic* is a clearly defined set of rules for establishing (or refuting) the truth of a given statement. Although I won't be delving into mathematical proofs in this book, should you choose to continue your study of cryptography, at some point you will need to examine proofs. The formal rules of logic are the first steps in understanding mathematical proofs.

Logic is a formal language for deducing knowledge from a small number of explicitly stated premises (or hypotheses, axioms, or facts). Some of the rules of logic we will examine in this section might seem odd or counterintuitive. Remember that logic is about the structure of the argument, not so much the content.

Before we begin, I will define a few basic terms:

- **Axiom**   An axiom (or *premise* or *postulate*) is something assumed to be true. Essentially, you have to start from somewhere. Now you could, like the philosopher Descartes, begin with, "I think therefore I am" (*Cogito ergo sum*), but that would not be practical for most mathematical purposes. So we begin with some axiom that is true by definition. For example, any integer that is evenly divisible only by itself and 1 is considered to be prime.
- **Statement**   This is a simple declaration that states something is true. For example, "3 is a prime number" is a statement, and so is "16 is 3 cubed"—it is an incorrect statement, but it is a statement nonetheless.
- **Argument**   An argument is a sequence of statements. Some of these statements, the premises, are assumed to be true and serve as a basis for accepting another statement of the argument, called the *conclusion*.
- **Proposition**   This is the most basic of statements. A proposition is a statement that is either true or not. For example, if I tell you that I am either male or female, that is a proposition. If I then tell you I am not female, that is yet another proposition. If you follow these two propositions, you arrive at the conclusion that I am male. Some statements have no truth value and therefore cannot be propositions. For example, "Stop doing that!" does not have a truth value and therefore is not a proposition.

The exciting thing about formal logic is that if you begin with a premise that is true and faithfully adheres to the rules of logic, then you will arrive at a conclusion that is true. Preceding from an axiom to a conclusion is *deductive reasoning*, the sort of reasoning often used in mathematical proofs. *Inductive reasoning* is generalizing from a premise. Inductive reasoning can suffer from overgeneralizing. We will be focusing on deductive logic in this book.

Propositional Logic

You read the definition for a proposition, and you may recall that mathematical logic is concerned with the structure of an argument, regardless of the content. This leads to a common method of presenting logic in textbooks—that is, to ignore actual statements and put characters in their place. Often, p and q are used, and they might represent any propositions you want to make. For example, p could denote "The author of this book has a gray beard" and q could denote "The author of this book has no facial hair." Considering these two propositions it is likely that

> Either p or q is true.
> It is impossible that p and q are both true.
> It is possible that not p is true.
> It is possible that not q is true.

Symbols can be used for each of these statements (as well as other statements you could make). It is important that you become familiar with basic logic symbolism. Table 4-1 gives you an explanation of the most common symbols used in deductive logic.

Table 4-1 is not an exhaustive list of all symbols in logic, but these are the most commonly used symbols. Make certain you are familiar with these symbols before proceeding with the rest of this section.

Several of these symbols are called *connectives*. That just means they are used to connect two propositions. Some basic rules for connectives are shown in Table 4-2.

TABLE 4-1   Symbols Used in Deductive Logic

Symbol	Meaning
∧	The *and* symbol. Sometimes represented with a period (.) or &. Example: p ∧ q means that *both p and q are true.* This is often called the "conjunction of p and q."
∨	The *or* symbol. Sometimes represented as + or ‖. Example: p ∨ q means *either p is true, or q is true, or both are true.* This is often called the "disjunction of p and q."
⊻	The *exclusive or* symbol. Example: p ⊻ q means *either p is true, or q is true, but both are not true.*
∃	This means "there exists." Example: ∃ some p such that p ∧ q means *there exists some p such that p and q are both true.* Example: ∃ x means *there is an x* or *there exists an x.*
∃!	This means "there exists exactly one."
∀	This means "for every." Example: ∀ x means *for every x or for all x.*
⊥	This symbol denotes a contradiction.
→	This means "implies." Example: p → q means *if p is true, that implies that q is true.*
¬	This denotes negation or "not"; sometimes symbolized as !.

TABLE 4-2   Connectives

Connective	Interpretation
$\neg$	A negation: $\neg$p is true if and only if p is false.
$\wedge$	A conjunction: p $\wedge$ q is true if and only if both p *and* q are true.
$\vee$	A disjunction: p $\vee$ q is true if and only if p is true *or* q is true.
$\Rightarrow$	An implication: p $\Rightarrow$ q is false if and only if p is true *and* q is false.

Here are a few basic facts about connectives:

- Expressions on either side of a conjunction are called *conjuncts* (p $\wedge$ q).
- Expressions on either side of a disjunction are called *disjuncts* (p $\vee$ q).
- In the implication p $\Rightarrow$ q, p is called the *antecedent* and q is the *consequence*.
- The order of precedence with connectives is brackets, negation, conjunction, disjunction, implication.

Building Logical Constructs

Now that you are familiar with the basic concepts of deductive logic, and you know the essential symbols, let's practice converting some textual statements into logical structures. That is the first step in applying logic to determine the veracity of the statements. Consider this sample sentence:

> Although both John and Paul are amateurs, Paul has a better chance of winning the golf game, despite John's significant experience.

Now let's restate that using the language of deductive logic. First we have to break down this long statement into individual propositions and assign each to some variable:

p: John is an amateur
q: Paul is an amateur
r: Paul has a better chance of winning the golf game
s: John has significant golf experience

We can now phrase this in symbols:

$$(p \wedge q) \wedge r \wedge s$$

This sort of sentence does not lend itself easily to deducing truth, but it does give us an example of how to take a sentence and rephrase it with logical symbols.

Truth Tables

Once you have grasped the essential concepts of propositions and connectives, your next step is to become familiar with truth tables. Truth tables provide a method for visualizing the truth of propositions.

Here is a simple one. Keep in mind that the actual statement is irrelevant, just the structure. But if it helps you to grasp the concept, P is the proposition "you are currently reading this book."

P	¬P
T	F
F	T

What this table tells us is that if P is true, then not P cannot be true. It also tells us that if P is false, then not P is true. This example is simple, in fact, trivial. All this truth table is doing is formally and visually telling you that either you are reading this book or you are not, and both cannot be true at the same time.

With such a trivial example, you might even wonder why anyone would bother using a truth table to illustrate such an obvious fact. In practice, you'd probably not use a truth table for this example. However, due to the ease most of you will have with comprehending the simple fact that something is either true or not, this makes a good starting point to learn about truth tables. Some of the tables you will see in just a few moments will not be so trivial.

Now let's examine a somewhat more complex truth table that introduces the concept of a conjunction. Again the specific propositions are not important. This truth table illustrates the fact that only if p is true and q is true, will $p \wedge q$ will be true.

p	q	p∧q
T	T	T
T	F	F
F	T	F
F	F	F

What about a truth table for disjunction (the *or* operator)?

p	q	p∨q
T	T	T
T	F	T
F	T	T
F	F	F

You can see that truth table shows, quite clearly, what was stated earlier about the *or* (disjunction) connective.

The *exclusive or* operation is also interesting to see in a truth table. Recall that we stated either p is true or q is true, but not both.

p	q	p ⊻ q
T	T	F
T	F	T
F	T	T
F	F	F

Next we shall examine implication statements. Consider p → q. This is read as p implies q.

Tip	The term *implies*, in logic, is much stronger than in vernacular speech. Here it means that *if you have p, you will have q.*

p	q	p → q
T	T	T
T	F	F
F	T	T
F	F	T

The previous truth tables were so obvious as to not require any extensive explanation. However, this one may require a bit of discussion:

- The first row should make sense to you. If we are stating that p implies q, and we find that p is true and q is true, then, yes, our statement p implies q is true.
- The second row is also obvious. If p is true but q is not, then p implies q cannot be true.

But what about the last two rows?

- We are stating that p implies q; however, in row three we see q is true but p is not. Therefore not p implied q, so our statement that p implies q is not true.
- In the fourth row, if have not p and not q, then p implies q is still true. Nothing in p being false and q being false invalidates our statement that p implies q.

Tip	Several sources can help you learn more about mathematical logic. A good one is the book *Math Proofs Demystified* by Stan Gibilisco (McGraw-Hill Education, 2005).

Combinatorics

Combinatorics is exactly what the name suggests: it is the mathematics behind how you can combine various sets. Combinatorics answers questions such as, how many different ways can you choose from four colors to paint six rooms? How many different ways can you arrange four flower pots?

As you can probably surmise, combinatorics, at least in crude form, is very old. Greek historian Plutarch mentions combinatorial problems, though he did not use the language of mathematics we use today. The Indian mathematician Mahavira, in the ninth century, actually provided specific formulas for working with combinations and permutations. It is not clear if he invented them or simply documented what he had learned from other mathematicians.

Combinatorics are used to address general problems, including the *existence problem* that asks if a specific arrangement of objects exists. The *counting problem* is concerned with finding the various possible arrangements of objects according to some requirements. The *optimization problem* is concerned with finding the most efficient arrangements.

Let's begin our discussion with a simple combinatorics problem. Assume that you are reading this textbook as part of a university course in cryptography. Let's also assume that your class has 30 students, and of those students, 15 are computer science majors and 15 are majoring in something else—we will call these "other."

It should be obvious that there are 15 ways you can choose a computer science major from the class and 15 ways you can choose an other major. This gives you 15×15 ways of choosing a student from the class. But what if you need to choose one student who is either a computer science major *or* an other? This gives you $15 + 15$ ways of choosing one student. You may be wondering why one method used multiplication and the other used addition. The first two rules you will learn about in combinatorics are the *multiplication rule* and the *addition rule*:

- **The multiplication rule**   Assume a sequence of r events that you will call the events E1, E2, and so on. There are n ways in which a specific event can occur. The number of ways an event occurs does not depend on the previous event. This means you must multiply the possible events. In our example, the event was selecting one of the students, regardless of major. So you might select one from computer science or you might select one from other. The multiplication rule is sometimes called the *rule of sequential counting*.
- **The addition rule**   Now suppose there are r events E1, E2, and so on, such that there are n possible outcomes for a given event, but further assume that no two events can occur simultaneously. This means you will use the addition rule, also sometimes called the *rule of disjunctive counting*. The reason for this name is that the addition rule states that if set A and set B are disjoint sets, then addition is used.

I find that when a topic is new to a person, it is often helpful to view multiple examples to fully come to terms with the subject matter. Let's look at a few more examples of selecting from groups, illustrating both the addition rule (sometimes called the *sum rule*) and the multiplication rule (sometimes called the *product rule*).

What happens when you need to pick from various groups? Assume you are about to take a trip and you want to bring some along reading material. You have 5 history books, 3 novels, and 3 biographies. You need to select 1 book from each category. There are 5 different ways to pick a history book, 3 different ways to select a novel, and 3 different ways to choose a biography. The total possible combinations is $5 + 3 + 3$. Why was addition used here? Because each choice can only be made once. You have 5 historical books to choose from, but once you have chosen 1, you cannot select any more. Now you have 3 novels to choose from, but once you have chosen 1, you cannot select any more.

Now let's look at an example where we use the multiplication or product rule. Assume you have 3 rooms to paint and 4 colors of paint. For each room, you can use any of the 4 colors regardless of whether it has been used before. So you have $4 \times 4 \times 4$ possible choices. Why use multiplication rather than addition? Because each choice can be repeated. Assume your 4 colors are green, blue, yellow, and red. You can use green for all 3 rooms if you want, or green for 1 room only, or not use green at all.

The multiplication rule gets modified if selection removes a choice. Supposed that once you have selected a color, you cannot use it again. In the first room you have 4 colors to select from, but in the next room only 3, and in the third room only 2 colors. So the number of possible combinations is $4 \times 3 \times 2$. Selection removes a choice each time.

Selection with removal is actually pretty common. Here's another example: Assume you want to line up 5 people for a picture. It should be obvious that you cannot reuse a person. Once you have lined up the 5 people, no more people are available for selection. So your possible combinations are $5 \times 4 \times 3 \times 2 \times 1$.

Permutations

Permutations are ordered arrangements of things. Because order is taken into consideration, permutations that contain the same elements but in different orders are considered to be distinct. When a permutation contains only some of the elements in a given set, it is called an *r-permutation*. What this means for combinatorics is that the order of the elements in the set matters. Consider the set {a, b, c}. There are six ways to combine this set, if order matters:

- a b c
- a c b
- b a c
- b c a
- c a b
- c b a

Add one more letter to the set, {a, b, c, d}, and there are 24 possible combinations:

abcd	acbd	bcad	bacd	cabd	cbad
abdc	acdb	bcda	badc	cadb	cbda
adbc	adcb	bdca	bdac	cdab	cdba
dabc	dacb	dbca	dbac	dcab	dcba

Fortunately, you don't have to write out the possibilities each time to determine how many combinations of a given permutation there are. The answer is "n!". For those not familiar with the n! symbol, it is the factorial symbol. The n! means $n \times n - 1 \times n - 2 \times n - 3$, and so on. For example 4! is $4 \times 3 \times 2 \times 1$.

Consider ordering a subset of a collection of objects. If there is a collection of n objects to choose from, and you are selecting r of the objects, where $0 < r < n$, then you call each possible selection an *r-permutation* from the collection. What if you have a set of three letters {a, b, c} and you want to select two letters. In other words, you want to select an r-permutation from the collection of letters. How many r-permutations are possible? Six:

| ab | ba | ac | ca | bc | cb |

What if our original collection was four letters {a, b, c, d} and you wanted to select a two-letter r-permutation? You would have 12 possibilities:

| ab | ac | ad | ba | bc | bd |
| ca | cb | cd | da | db | dc |

These examples should illustrate that the number of r-permutations of a set of n objects is $n!/(n - r)!$

To verify this, let's go back to our first example of an r-permutation. We had a set of 3 elements and we wanted to select 2. And $3!$ is $3 \times 2 \times 1 = 6$. The divisor $(n - r)!$ is $(3 - 2)!$, or 1. So we have 6 r-permutations. In the second example, $n = 4$. And $4! = 4 \times 3 \times 2 \times 1 = 24$. The divisor $(n - r)!$ is $(4 - 2)!$, or 2. So we have 12 r-permutations.

Clearly, we could continue exploring combinatorics and delving further into various ways to combine subsets and sets. But at this point, you should grasp the basic concepts of combinatorics. This field is relevant to cryptography in a variety of ways, particularly in optimizing algorithms. (On a personal note, I have found combinatorics to be a fascinating branch of discrete mathematics with numerous practical applications.)

Tip   Combinatorics is a very fascinating topic. The book *Introductory Discrete Mathematics* by V. K. Balakrishnan (Dover Publications, 2010) provides a good chapter on the topic as well as discussions of many other topics covered in this chapter.

Graph Theory

Graph theory is a very important part of discrete mathematics. It is a way to examine objects and the relationships between those objects mathematically. Put formally, a finite graph G(V, E) is a pair (V, E), where V is a finite set and E is a binary relation on V.

Now let's examine that definition in more reader-friendly terms. A graph starts with vertices or nodes, what I previously referred to as *objects*. These objects can be anything. The edges are simply lines that show the connection between the vertices. There are two types of graphs: directed and undirected. In a directed graph, the edges have a direction, in an undirected graph, the edges do not have a direction. The edges are ordered pairs and not necessarily symmetrical. This simply means that the connection between two vertices may or may not be one-way.

Here's an example. Consider two friends, John and Mike. Their relationship, shown in Figure 4-2, is symmetrical. They are each a friend to the other:

John   Mike

FIGURE 4-2   Symmetrical graph

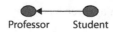
Professor   Student

FIGURE 4-3   Asymmetrical graph

If we use a graph to illustrate the relationship of a student to a professor, the relationship is not symmetrical, as shown in Figure 4-3.

The graph shown in Figure 4-3 is a *directed graph*—that is, there exists a direction to the relationship between the two vertices. Depending on what you are studying, the direction could be either way. For example, if you want to graph the dissemination of knowledge from the professor, then the arrow would point toward the student, and several students would likely be included.

You have already seen the terms *vertex* and *edge* defined. Here are a few other terms I need to define before proceeding:

- **Incidence**   An edge (directed or undirected) is incident to a vertex that is one of its end points.
- **Degree of a vertex**   Number of edges incident to the vertex. Nodes of a directed graph can also be said to have an *in degree* and an *out degree*. The in degree is the total number of edges pointing toward the vertex. The out degree is an edge pointing away, as shown in Figure 4-3.
- **Adjacency**   Two vertices connected by an edge are adjacent.
- **Directed graph**   A directed graph, often simply called a *digraph*, is one in which the edges have a direction.
- **Weighted digraph**   This is a directed graph that has a "cost" or "weight" associated with each edge. In other words, some edges (that is, some relationships) are stronger than others.
- **A complete graph**   This graph has an edge between each pair of vertices. N nodes will mean N × (N − 1) edges.

Once you understand the basic concept of graphs and the relationship between vertices and edges, the next obvious question is, how can you traverse a given graph? This question can be answered in one of several ways. Let's consider the graph shown in Figure 4-4, which has five vertices and seven edges.

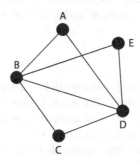

FIGURE 4-4   Traversing a graph

You can traverse a graph in three basic ways:

- **Path**   With a path, no vertex can be repeated—for example, a-b-c-d-e. You can repeat an edge if you want, but not a vertex.
- **Trail**   A trail is the opposite of a path: no edge can be repeated—for example, a-b-c-d-e-b-d.
- **Walk**   There are no restrictions. For example, a-b-e-d-b-c.

Whatever traversal method you use, if you end at the starting point, that is considered *closed*. For example, if you start at vertex b and end at b, then this is closed, whether you use a path, trail, or walk. The length of traversal is simply the count of how many edges you have to cross.

There are two special types of traversal:

- **Circuit**   A closed trail (for example, a-b-c-d-b-e-d-a)
- **Cycle**   A closed path (for example, a-b-c-d-a)

This leads to a few other terms:

- **Acyclic**   A graph wherein there are no cycles
- **Tree**   A connected, acyclic graph
- **Rooted tree**   A tree with a "root" or "distinguished" vertex; the leaves are the terminal nodes in a rooted tree
- **Directed acyclic graph (DAG)**   A digraph with no cycles

Now you should have a basic idea of what a graph is and the different types of graphs. Rather than go deeper into the abstract concepts of graphs, I would like to answer a question that is probably on your mind at this point: What are graphs used for?

Graph theory has many applications. For example, they can help you determine what is the shortest (or longest) path between two vertices/nodes? Or what path has the least weight (as opposed to least length) between two vertices/nodes? If you reflect on those two questions for just a moment, you will see that there are clear applications to computer networks. Graph theory is also used to study the structure of a web site and connected clients. Problems in travel are obviously addressed with graph theory. There are applications in particle physics, biology, and even political science.

  An excellent resource for a novice learning discrete mathematics is the book *Discrete Mathematics Demystified* by Steven Krantz (McGraw-Hill Education, 2008).

Conclusions

This chapter covered the basic mathematical tools you will need in order to understand cryptographic algorithms later in the book. In this chapter, you were introduced to number systems. Most importantly, you were given a thorough introduction to prime numbers, including how to generate prime numbers. The concept of relatively prime or co-prime was also covered. These are important topics that you should thoroughly understand and that are applied in the RSA algorithm.

You also saw some basic math operations, such as summation and logarithms, and were introduced to discrete logarithms. The discussion of modulus operations is critical for your understanding of asymmetric algorithms. The chapter concluded with an introduction to discrete mathematics, including set theory, logic, combinatorics, and graph theory. Each topic was briefly covered in this chapter; if you thoroughly and completely understand what was discussed in this chapter, it will be sufficient for you to continue your study of cryptography. The key is to ensure that you do thoroughly and completely understand this chapter before proceeding further. If needed, reread the chapter and consult the various study aids that were referenced.

Test Your Knowledge

1. Two vertices connected by an edge are _____.
2. The statement "Any number $n \geq 2$ is expressible as a unique product of 1 or more prime numbers" describes what?
3. $\log_3 27 =$ _____
4. A circuit is a closed _____.
5. Are the numbers 15 and 28 relatively prime?
6. A _____ is a group of numbers that are all congruent for some given modulus.
7. _____ is a deterministic test of primality that works on Mersenne numbers.
8. _____ are logarithms in respect to a finite group.
9. Set B is the _____ of set A if B has no elements that are also in A. This is symbolized as B = Ac.
10. _____ are ordered arrangements of things.

Answers

1. adjacent
2. The fundamental theorem of arithmetic
3. 3
4. trail
5. Yes
6. congruence class
7. The Lucas-Lehmer test
8. Discrete logarithms
9. complement
10. Permutations

Endnote

1. Edna E. Kramer, *The Nature and Growth of Modern Mathematics*, (Princeton University Press, 1983).

5 Essential Algebra

In this chapter we will cover the following:

- Groups, rings, and fields
- Diophantine equations
- Basic matrix algebra
- Algorithms
- The history of algebra

Certain aspects of algebra are very important to the cryptographic algorithms you will be exploring later in this book. Those of you with a solid background in mathematics might be wondering how I could cover such a broad topic in a single chapter. Those of you without a solid background in mathematics might be wondering if you can learn enough and grasp enough of the concepts to apply them to cryptography later on.

Let me address these questions before you continue reading. As I did with Chapter 4, in this chapter I'm going to focus only on the basic information you need to help you understand the cryptographic algorithms covered later. Certainly, each of these topics could be given much more coverage. Entire books have been written on abstract algebra, matrix mathematics, and algorithms—in fact, some rather large tomes have been written just on algorithms! But you don't necessarily need all those details to understand what you will encounter in this book. I would, however, certainly recommend that you explore these topics in more depth at some point. In this chapter, as with the last, I won't delve into mathematical proofs. This means that you must accept a few things simply on faith—or you can refer to numerous mathematical texts that do indeed provide proofs for these concepts.

Those of you with a less rigorous mathematical background should keep in mind that, although you'll need to have a firm grasp of the concepts presented in this chapter, you don't need to become a mathematician (though I would be absolutely delighted if this book motivated you to study mathematics more deeply). It might take a mathematician to create cryptographic algorithms, but anyone can understand the algorithms I'll present here. The ultimate goal of this book is to help you understand existing cryptography. I will provide links to resources where you can get additional information and explanations if you need it.

Abstract Algebraic Structures

If you think of algebra only as solving linear and quadratic equations, as you probably did in secondary school, these first algebraic concepts might not seem like algebra at all. But solving such equations is only one application of algebra. A far more interesting topic, and one more pertinent to cryptography, is the study of *sets* and operations you can perform on those sets. This is the basis for *abstract algebra*. Mathematics students frequently struggle with these concepts, but I will endeavor to make them as simple as I can without leaving out any important details.

Special sets of numbers and the operations that can be accomplished on those numbers are important to abstract algebra, and *groups*, *rings*, and *fields* are simply sets of numbers with associated operations.

Let's begin with some examples. Think about the set of real numbers, which is an infinite set, as you know. What operations can you do with numbers that are members of this set in which the result will still be within the set? You can add two real numbers, and the answer will always be a real number. You can multiply two real numbers, and the answer will always be a real number. What about the inverse of those two operations? You can subtract two real numbers and the answer will always be a real number. You can divide two real numbers and the answer will always be a real number (of course division by zero is undefined). At this point, you may think all of this is absurdly obvious, and you might even think it odd that I would spend a paragraph discussing it. However, let's turn our attention to sets of numbers in which all of these facts are *not* true.

The set of all integers is an infinite set, just like the set of real numbers. You can add any two integers and the sum will be another integer. You can multiply any two integers and the product will be an integer. So far, this sounds just like the set of real numbers. So let's turn our attention to the inverse operations. You can subtract any integer from another integer and the answer is an integer. But what about division? There are an infinite number of scenarios in which you cannot divide one integer by another to arrive at another integer. For example, dividing 6 by 2, 10 by 5, 21 by 3, or infinitely more examples, gives you an integer. But divide 5 by 2, or 20 by 3, and the answer is *not* an integer; instead, it's a *rational number*. And there are infinitely more examples like this. Therefore, if I want to limit myself only to integers, I cannot use division as an operation.

Let's continue with examples for a moment to help demonstrate these concepts. Imagine that you want to limit your mathematics to an artificial world in which only integers exist. (Set aside, for now, any considerations of why you might do this, and just focus on this thought experiment for a moment.) In this artificial world that you have created, the addition operation exists and functions as it always has, and so does the inverse of addition, subtraction. The multiplication operation behaves as you would expect. In this imaginary world, however, the division operation simply does not exist, because it has the very real possibility of producing non-integer answers, and such answers do not exist in our imaginary world of "only integers."

And one last hypothetical situation should help clarify these basic points. What if you limit yourself to natural numbers, or counting numbers, only. You can add any two counting numbers and the answer will always be a natural number. You can also multiply any two natural numbers and rest assured that the product will be another natural number. You can also subtract some natural numbers and the answer will be a natural number—but there are infinitely many cases for which this is not true. For example, if you attempt to subtract 7 from 5, the answer is a negative number, which is *not* a natural number. In fact, any time you attempt to subtract a larger natural number from a smaller natural number, the result will not be a natural number. Furthermore, division is just as tricky with natural numbers as it is with integers. In an infinite number of cases, the answer will not be a natural number. In this imaginary world of only natural numbers, addition and multiplication work exactly as you would expect. But their inverse operations, subtraction and division, simply do not exist.

Abstract algebra concerns itself with structures just like this. These structures (groups, rings, fields, and so on) comprise a set of numbers and certain operations that can be performed on those numbers. The only operations allowed in a given structure are those whose result would fit within the prescribed set of numbers. You were introduced to similar concepts in Chapter 4, with modulo arithmetic, where the numbers used were integers bound by the modulo.

Don't be overly concerned with the term *abstract algebra*. Some sources call it *modern algebra*—but since it dates back a few centuries, that may be a misnomer. Later in this book, when we discuss asymmetric cryptography—particularly in Chapter 11—you'll see several practical applications. Even the symmetric algorithm, Advanced Encryption Standard (AES), which you will study in Chapter 7, applies some of these structures.

Groups

A *group* is an algebraic system consisting of a set, which includes an identity element, one operation, and its inverse operation. An *identity element* is a number within a set that, when combined with another number in some operation, leaves that number unchanged. Mathematically, the identity element I can be expressed as follows:

$$a * I = a$$

where * is any operation that you might specify—not necessarily multiplication.

With respect to the addition operation, 0 (zero) is the identity element. You can add 0 to any member of any given group, and you will still have 0. With respect to multiplication, 1 is the identity element. Any number multiplied by 1 is still the same number.

Every group must satisfy four properties: closure, associativity, identity, and invertibility:

- *Closure* is the simplest of these properties. This was discussed a bit earlier in this chapter. Closure means that any operation performed on a member of the set will result in an answer that is also a member of the set.
- *Associativity* means that you can rearrange the elements of a set of values in an operation without changing the outcome. For example $(2 + 2) + 3 = 7$. But if I change the order and instead write $2 + (2 + 3)$, the answer is still 7.
- *Identity* was already discussed.
- *Invertibility* simply means that a given operation on an element in a set can be inverted. Subtraction is the inversion of addition; division is the inversion of multiplication.

Think back to the example set of integers. Integers constitute a group. First there is an identity element, zero. There is also one operation (addition) and its inverse (subtraction). Furthermore you have closure. Any element of the group (that is, any integer) added to any other element of the group (any other integer) still produces a member of the group (in other words, the answer is still an integer).

Abelian Group

An abelian group, or commutative group, has an additional property called the *commutative* property: $a + b = b + a$ if the operation is addition, and $ab = ba$ if the operation is multiplication. The commutative requirement simply means that applying the group operation (whatever that operation might be) does not depend on the order of the group elements. In other words, whatever the group operation is, you can apply it to members of the group in any order you want.

To use a trivial example, consider the group of integers with the addition operation. Order does not matter:

$$4 + 2 = 2 + 4$$

Therefore, the set of integers with the operation of addition is an abelian group.

> **Tip**   Obviously, division and subtraction operations could never be used for an abelian group, because the order of elements changes the outcome of the operation.

Cyclic Group

A cyclic group has elements that are all powers of one of its elements. So, for example, if you start with element x, then the members of a cyclic group would be

$$x^{-2}, x^{-1}, x^0, x^1, x^2, x^3, \dots$$

Of course, the other requirements for a group, as discussed previously, would still apply to a cyclic group. The basic element x is considered to be the *generator* of the group, since all other members of the group are derived from it. It is also referred to as a *primitive element* of the group. Integers could be considered a cyclic group, with 1 being the primitive element (the generator). All integers can be expressed as a power of 1 in this group. This may seem like a rather trivial example, but it is easy to understand.

Rings

A *ring* is an algebraic system consisting of a set, an identity element, two operations, and the inverse operation of the first operation. That is the formal definition of a ring, but it may seem a bit awkward at first read, so let's examine this concept a bit further. If you think back to our previous examples, it should occur to you that when we are limited to two operations, they are usually addition and multiplication. And addition is the easiest to implement, with subtraction being the inverse.

A ring is essentially just an abelian group that has a second operation. We have seen that the set of integers with the addition operation form a group, and furthermore they form an abelian group. If you add the multiplication operation, the set of integers with both the addition and the multiplication operations form a ring.

Fields

A *field* is an algebraic system consisting of a set, an identity element for each operation, two operations, and their respective inverse operations. A field is like a group that has two operations rather than one, and it includes an inverse for both of those operations. It is also the case that every field is a ring, but not every ring will necessarily be a field. For example, the set of integers is a ring, but not a field (because the inverse of multiplication can produce answers that are not in the set of integers). Fields also allow for division (the inverse operation of multiplication), whereas groups do not.

A classic example is the field of rational numbers. Each number can be written as a ratio (a fraction) such as x/y (x and y could be any integers), and the additive inverse is simply −x/y. The multiplicative inverse is y/x.

Galois Fields

Galois fields are also known as *finite fields*. You will learn more about Évariste Galois himself in the "History Highlights" section of this chapter. These fields are very important in cryptography, and you will see them used in later chapters. They are called finite fields because they have a finite number of elements. If you think about some of the groups, rings, and fields we have discussed, you'll realize they were infinite. The set of integers, rational numbers, and real numbers are all infinite. But Galois fields are finite.

In a Galois field, there are some integers such that n repeated terms equals zero. Put another way, there is some boundary on the field that makes it finite. The smallest n that satisfies this is a prime number referred to as the *characteristic* of the field. You will often see a Galois field defined as follows:

$$GF(p^n)$$

In this case, the GF does not denote a function. Instead, this statement is saying that there is a Galois field with p as the prime number (the characteristic mentioned previously), and the field has p^n elements. So a Galois field is some finite set of numbers (from 0 to p^n-1) and some mathematical operations (usually addition and multiplication) along with the inverses of those operations.

Now you may immediately be wondering, how can a finite field even exist? If the field is indeed finite, would it not be the case that addition and multiplication operations could lead to answers that don't exist within the field? To understand how this works, think back to the modulus operation discussed in Chapter 4. Essentially, operations "wrap around" the modulus. If we consider the classic example of a clock, then any operation whose answer would be more than 12 simply wraps around. The same thing occurs in a Galois field: Any answer greater than p^n simply wraps around.

Let's look at an example—another trivial example but it makes the point. Consider the Galois field $GF(3^1)$. First, I hope you realize that 3^1 is the same as 3—most texts would simply write this as GF(3). So we have a Galois field defined by 3. In any case, addition or multiplication of the elements would exceed the number 3, so we simply wrap around. This example is easy to work with because it has only three elements: 1, 2, 3. Considering operations with those elements, several addition operations pose no problem at all:

$$1 + 1 = 2$$

$$1 + 2 = 3$$

However, others would be a problem,

$$2 + 2 = 4$$

except that we are working within a Galois field, which is similar to modulus operations, so $2 + 2 = 1$ (we wrapped around at 3). Similarly, $2 + 3 = 2$.

The same is true with multiplication (in both cases, we wrap around at 3):

$$2 \times 2 = 1$$

$$2 \times 3 = 0$$

In cryptography, we deal with Galois fields that are more complicated than this trivial example, but the principles are exactly the same.

Diophantine Equations

In a Diophantine equation, you are interested only in the integer solutions to the equation. Thus, a linear Diophantine equation is a linear equation $ax + by = c$ with integer coefficients for which you are interested only in finding integer solutions.

There are two types of Diophantine equations: *Linear Diophantine* equations have elements that are of degree 1 or 0. *Exponential Diophantine* equations have at least one term that has an exponent greater than 1.

The word *Diophantine* comes from Diophantus of Alexandria, a third-century C.E. mathematician who studied such equations. You have actually seen Diophantine equations before, though you might not have realized it. The traditional Pythagorean theorem can be a Diophantine equation if you are interested in only integer solutions, which can be the case in many practical applications.

The simplest Diophantine equations are linear and are of this form,

$$ax + by = c$$

where a, b, and c are all integers. There is an integer solution to this problem, if and only if c is a multiple of the greatest common divisor of and b. For example, the Diophantine equation $3x + 6y = 18$ does have solutions (in integers), since $\gcd(3,6) = 3$, which does indeed evenly divide 18.

Matrix Math

A *matrix* is a rectangular arrangement, or array, of numbers in rows and columns. Rows run horizontally and columns run vertically. The dimensions of a matrix are stated m × n, where m is the number of rows and n is the number of columns. Here is an example:

$$\begin{pmatrix} 5 & 0 & 2 & -2 \\ 3 & 1 & 3 & 4 \\ -5 & 2 & 2 & 1 \end{pmatrix}$$

I will focus on 2 × 2 matrices for the examples in this section, but a matrix can be of any number of rows and columns, and it need not be a square. A vector can be considered a 1 × m matrix. In the preceding matrix example, you could have a vertical vector such as 5, 3, –5 or a horizontal vector such as 5, 0, 2, –2. A vector that is vertical is called a column vector, and one that is horizontal is called a row vector.

There are different types of matrices:

- **Column matrix**   A matrix with only one column
- **Row matrix**   A matrix with only one row
- **Square matrix**   A matrix that has the same number of rows and columns
- **Equal matrices**   Two matrices that have the same number of rows and columns (the same dimensions) and all their corresponding elements are exactly the same
- **Zero matrix**   A matrix that contains all zeros

Matrix Addition and Multiplication

If two matrices are of the same size, they can be added together by adding each element together. Consider the following example:

$$\begin{matrix} 1 & 2 \\ 6 & 3 \end{matrix} + \begin{matrix} 3 & 2 \\ 1 & 1 \end{matrix} = \begin{matrix} 4 & 4 \\ 7 & 4 \end{matrix}$$

Start with the first row and first column in the first matrix (which is 1) and add that to the first row and the first column of the second matrix (which is 3); thus in the sum matrix, the first row and first column is 3 + 1 or 4. You repeat this for each cell.

Subtraction works similarly:

$$\begin{matrix} 1 & 2 \\ 6 & 3 \end{matrix} - \begin{matrix} 3 & 2 \\ 1 & 1 \end{matrix} = \begin{matrix} -2 & 0 \\ 5 & 2 \end{matrix}$$

Multiplication, however, is a bit more complicated. Let's take a look at an example multiplying a matrix by a *scalar* (a single number):

$$5 * \begin{matrix} 1 & 2 \\ 6 & 3 \end{matrix}$$

You simply multiply the scalar value by each element in the matrix:

$$5 * \begin{matrix} 1 & 2 \\ 6 & 3 \end{matrix} = \begin{matrix} 5 & 10 \\ 30 & 15 \end{matrix}$$

Multiplication of two matrices is a bit more complex. You can multiply two matrices only if the number of columns in the first matrix is equal to the number of rows in the second matrix. You multiply each element in the first row of the first matrix by each element in the first column of the second matrix. Then you multiply each element of the second row of the first matrix by each element of the second column of the second matrix.

Let's look at a conceptual example:

$$\begin{matrix} a & b \\ c & d \end{matrix} * \begin{matrix} e & f \\ g & h \end{matrix}$$

$$a * e + b * g$$

$$a * f + b * h$$

$$c * e + d * g$$

$$c * f + d * h$$

The product will be

$$(a*e+b*g)(a*f+b*h)$$
$$(c*e+d*g)(c*f+d*h)$$

Now if that is still not clear, we can examine a concrete example:

$$\begin{matrix} 1 & 2 \\ 6 & 3 \end{matrix} * \begin{matrix} 3 & 2 \\ 1 & 1 \end{matrix}$$

We begin with

$$1 * 3 + 2 * 1 = 5$$

$$1 * 2 + 2 * 1 = 4$$

$$6 * 3 + 3 * 1 = 21$$

$$6 * 2 + 3 * 1 = 15$$

The final answer is

$$\begin{matrix} 5 & 4 \\ 21 & 15 \end{matrix}$$

This is why you can multiply two matrices only if the number of columns in the first matrix is equal to the number of rows in the second matrix.

It is important that you remember that matrix multiplication, unlike traditional multiplication (with scalar values), is not commutative. Recall that the commutative property states a * b = b * a. If a and be are scalar values, then this is true; however, if they are matrices, this is not the case. For example, consider the matrix multiplication shown here.

$$\begin{Bmatrix} 2 & 4 \\ 3 & 1 \end{Bmatrix} \times \begin{Bmatrix} 1 & 2 \\ 3 & 4 \end{Bmatrix} = \begin{Bmatrix} 12 & 20 \\ 6 & 10 \end{Bmatrix}$$

Now if we simply reverse the order, you can see that an entirely different answer is produced, as shown here.

$$\begin{Bmatrix} 1 & 2 \\ 3 & 4 \end{Bmatrix} \times \begin{Bmatrix} 2 & 4 \\ 3 & 1 \end{Bmatrix} = \begin{Bmatrix} 8 & 6 \\ 18 & 16 \end{Bmatrix}$$

Matrices are not commutative.

This example illustrates the rather important fact that matrix multiplication is not commutative.

Tip   If you need a bit more practice with matrix multiplication, try FreeMathHelp.com at www.freemathhelp.com/matrix-multiplication.html.

Matrix Transposition

Matrix *transposition* simply reverses the order of rows and columns. Although we have focused on 2×2 matrices, the transposition operation is most easily seen with a matrix that has a different number of rows and columns. Consider the matrix shown next.

$$\begin{Bmatrix} 2 & 2 & 1 \\ 3 & 1 & 4 \end{Bmatrix}$$

A 3×2 matrix

To transpose the matrix, the rows and columns are switched, creating a 2×3 matrix. The first row is now the first column. You can see this in the next illustration.

The transposition of a matrix

Submatrix

A *submatrix* is any portion of a matrix that remains after deleting any number of rows or columns. Consider the matrix shown here:

$$\begin{Bmatrix} 3 & 6 & 5 \\ 3 & 2 & 1 \\ 2 & 0 & 3 \\ 1 & 2 & 1 \end{Bmatrix}$$

A 3×4 matrix

If you remove the second column and second row,

$$\begin{bmatrix} 3 & 5 \\ 2 & 3 \\ 1 & 1 \end{bmatrix}$$

you are left with the matrix shown here:

$$\begin{Bmatrix} 3 & 5 \\ 2 & 3 \\ 1 & 1 \end{Bmatrix}$$

A 2×3 matrix

This matrix is a submatrix of the original matrix.

Identity Matrix

An *identity matrix* is actually rather simple. Think back to the identity property of groups. An identity matrix accomplishes the same goal, so that multiplying a matrix by its identity matrix leaves it unchanged. To create an identity matrix, you'll need to have all the elements along the main diagonal set to 1 and the rest set to 0. Consider the matrix shown in Figure 5-1.

$$\begin{Bmatrix} 1 & 2 \\ 3 & 4 \end{Bmatrix}$$

FIGURE 5-1 A 2×2 matrix

$$\begin{Bmatrix} 1 & 0 \\ 0 & 1 \end{Bmatrix}$$

FIGURE 5-2   The identity matrix

Now consider the identity matrix. It must have the same number of columns and rows, with its main diagonal set to all 1's and the rest of the elements all 0's. You can see the identity matrix in Figure 5-2.

If you multiple the original matrix in Figure 5-3 by the identity matrix, the product will be the same as the original matrix. You can see this in Figure 5-3.

> **Note**
> In these examples, I have focused not only on square, 2×2, matrices but also on matrices that consist of only integers. A matrix can consist of rational numbers, real numbers, or even functions. But since the goal was to provide an introduction to the concepts of matrix algebra, I have not delved into those nuances.

One application of matrix algebra is with linear transformations. A *linear transformation*, sometimes called a *linear mapping* or a *linear function*, is some mapping between two vector spaces that has the operations of addition and scalar multiplication.

> **Note**
> Wolfram MathWorld (http://mathworld.wolfram.com/VectorSpace.html) defines a vector space as follows: "A vector space V is a set that is closed under finite vector addition and scalar multiplication." In other words, a vector space is a collection of objects (in our case, integers) called vectors, which may be added together and multiplied ("scaled") by numbers called scalars.

Consider matrix multiplication (either with a scalar or with another matrix). That process maps each element in the first matrix to some element in the second matrix. This is a good example of a linear transformation. This process has many practical applications in physics, engineering, and cryptography.

> **Tip**
> For general tutorials on matrix algebra, the web site S.O.S. Mathematics offers a helpful set of tutorials at www.sosmath.com/matrix/matrix.html.

$$\begin{Bmatrix} 1 & 2 \\ 3 & 4 \end{Bmatrix} \times \begin{Bmatrix} 1 & 0 \\ 0 & 1 \end{Bmatrix} = \begin{Bmatrix} 1 & 2 \\ 3 & 4 \end{Bmatrix}$$

FIGURE 5-3   The product of a matrix and its identity matrix

Algorithms

All the cryptography you will study from this point on consists of various algorithms. Those of you who have studied computer science have probably taken a course in data structures and algorithms. This section will introduce you to some concepts of algorithms and will then discuss general algorithm analysis in the context of sorting algorithms. At the conclusion of this section, we'll study a very important algorithm.

Basic Algorithms

An *algorithm* is simply a systematic way of solving a problem. If you follow the procedure you get the desired results. Algorithms are a routine part of computer programming. Often the study of computer algorithms centers on sorting algorithms. The sorting of lists is a very common task and therefore a common topic in any study of algorithms.

It is also important that we have a clear method for analyzing the efficacy of a given algorithm. When considering any algorithm, if the desired outcome is achieved, then clearly the algorithm works. But the real question is, how well did it work? If you are sorting a list of 10 items, the time it takes to sort the list is not of particular concern. However, if your list has 1 million items, the time it takes to sort the list, and hence the algorithm you choose to perform the task, is of critical importance. Similar issues exist in evaluating modern cryptographic algorithms. It is obviously imperative that they work (that is, that they are secure), but they also have to work efficiently. For example, e-commerce would not be so widespread if the cryptographic algorithms used provided for an unacceptable lag.

Fortunately, there are well-defined methods for analyzing any algorithm. When analyzing algorithms we often consider the *asymptotic* upper and lower bounds. Asymptotic analysis is a process used to measure the performance of computer algorithms. This type of performance is based on a factor called *computational complexity*, which is usually a measure of either the time it takes or the resources (memory) needed for an algorithm to work. An algorithm can usually be optimized for time or for resources, but not both. The asymptotic upper bound is the worst-case scenario for the given algorithm, whereas the asymptotic lower bound is a best case.

Some analysts prefer to use an average case; however, knowing the best and worst cases can be useful in some situations. In simple terms, both the asymptotic upper and lower bounds must be within the parameters of the problem you are attempting to solve. You must assume that the worst-case scenario will occur in some situations.

The reason for this disparity between the asymptotic upper and lower bounds has to do with the initial state of a set. If you are applying a sorting algorithm to a set that is at its maximum information entropy (state of disorder), then the time it takes for the sorting algorithm to function will be the asymptotic upper bound. If, on the other hand, the set is very nearly sorted, then your algorithm may approach or achieve the asymptotic lower bound.

Perhaps the most common way to evaluate the efficacy of a given algorithm is the *Big O notation*. This method measures the execution of an algorithm, usually the number of iterations required, given the problem size n. In sorting algorithms, n is the number of items to be sorted. Stating some algorithm f(n) = O(g(n)) means it is less than some constant multiple of g(n). (The notation is read, "f of n is Big O of g of n.") Saying an algorithm is 2n means that it will have to execute two times the number of items on the list. Big O notation essentially measures the asymptotic upper bound of a function, and it is also the most often used analysis.

Big O notation was first introduced by German mathematician Paul Bachmann in 1894 in his book *Analytische Zahlentheorie*, a work on analytic number theory. The notation was later popularized in the work of another German mathematician, Edmund Landau, and the notation is sometimes referred to as a "Landau symbol."

Omega notation is the opposite of Big O notation. It is the asymptotic lower bound of an algorithm and gives the best-case scenario for that algorithm. It provides the minimum running time for an algorithm.

$$\Theta$$

Theta notation combines Big O and Omega to provide the average case (average being arithmetic mean in this situation) for the algorithm. In our analysis, we will focus heavily on the Theta, also often referred to as the *Big O running time*. This average time gives a more realistic picture of how an algorithm executes.

> **Note**   It can be confusing when a source refers to a "Big O running time" other than a Theta. I found several online sources that used "O notation," when clearly what they were providing was actually Θ. It is also possible that both could give the same answer.

Now that you have an idea of how the complexity and efficacy of an algorithm can be analyzed, let's take a look at a few commonly studied sorting algorithms and apply these analytical tools.

Sorting Algorithms

Sorting algorithms are often used to introduce someone to the study of algorithms, because they are relatively easy to understand and they are so common. Because we have not yet explored modern cryptography algorithms, I will use sorting algorithms to illustrate concepts of algorithm analysis.

Elementary implementations of the merge sort sometimes use three arrays—one array for each half of the data set and one to store the final sorted list in. There are nonrecursive versions of the merge sort, but they don't yield any significant performance enhancement over the recursive algorithm used on most machines. In fact, almost every implementation you will find of merge sort will be recursive, meaning that it simply calls itself repeatedly until the list is sorted.

The name derives from the fact that the lists are divided, sorted, and then merged, and this procedure is applied recursively. If you had an exceedingly large list and could separate the two sublists onto different processors, then the efficacy of the merge sort would be significantly improved.

Quick Sort

The *quick sort* is a very commonly used algorithm. Like the merge sort, it is recursive. Some books refer to the quick sort as a more effective version of the merge sort. In fact, the quick sort is the same as a merge sort (n ln n), but the difference is that the average case is also its best-case scenario (lower asymptotic bound). However, it has an $O(n^2)$, which indicates that its worst-case scenario is quite inefficient. For very large lists, the worst-case scenario may not be acceptable.

This recursive algorithm consists of three steps (which resemble those of the merge sort):

1. Choose an element in the array to serve as a pivot point.
2. Split the array into two parts. The split will occur at the pivot point. One array will include elements larger than the pivot and the other will include elements smaller than the pivot. One or the other should also include the pivot point.
3. Recursively repeat the algorithm for both halves of the original array.

One very interesting point is that the efficiency of the algorithm is significantly impacted by which element is chosen as the pivot point. The worst-case scenario of the quick sort occurs when the list is sorted and the leftmost element is chosen—this gives a complexity of $O(n^2)$. Randomly choosing a pivot point rather than using the leftmost element is recommended if the data to be sorted isn't random. As long as the pivot point is chosen randomly, the quick sort has an algorithmic complexity of $O(n \log n)$.

Bubble Sort

The *bubble sort* is the oldest and simplest sort in use. By simple, I mean that from a programmatic point of view it is very easy to implement. Unfortunately, it's also one of the slowest. It has a complexity of $O(n^2)$. This means that for very large lists, it is probably going to be too slow. As with most sort algorithms, its best case, or lower asymptotic bound, is $O(n)$.

The bubble sort works by comparing each item in the list with the item next to it, and then swapping them if required. The algorithm repeats this process until it makes a pass all the way through the list without swapping any items (in other words, all items are in the correct order). This causes larger values to "bubble" to the end of the list while smaller values "sink" toward the beginning of the list, thus the name of the algorithm.

The bubble sort is generally considered to be the most inefficient sorting algorithm in common usage. Under best-case conditions (the list is already sorted), the bubble sort can approach a constant n level of complexity. General-case is an $O(n^2)$.

Even though it is one of the slower algorithms available, the bubble sort is used often simply because it is so easy to implement. Many programmers who lack a thorough enough understanding of algorithm efficiency and analysis depend on the bubble sort.

Now that we have looked at three common sorting algorithms, you should have a basic understanding of both algorithms and algorithm analysis. Next we will turn our attention to an important algorithm that is used in cryptography: the Euclidean algorithm.

Euclidean Algorithm

The *Euclidean algorithm* is a method for finding the greatest common divisor of two integers. That may sound like a rather trivial task, but with larger numbers that is not the case. It also happens that this algorithm plays a role in several cryptographic algorithms you will see later in this book. The Euclidean algorithm proceeds in a series of steps such that the output of each step is used as an input for the next one.

Here's an example: Let k be an integer that counts the steps of the algorithm, starting with 0. Thus, the initial step corresponds to k = 0, the next step corresponds to k = 1, and then k = 2, k = 3, and so on. Each step after the first begins with two remainders, r_{k-1} and r_{k-2}, from the preceding step. You will notice that at each step, the remainder is smaller than the remainder from the preceding step. So that r_{k-1} is less than its predecessor r_{k-2}. This is intentional, and it is central to the functioning of the algorithm. The goal of the kth step is to find a quotient qk and remainder r_k such that the equation is satisfied:

$$r_{k-2} = qk\ r_{k-1} + r_k$$

where $r_k < r_{k-1}$. In other words, multiples of the smaller number r_{k-1} are subtracted from the larger number r_{k-2} until the remainder is smaller than r_{k-1}.

Let's look at an example.

$$\text{Let } a = 2322, b = 654$$

$$2322 = 654\cdot3 + 360 \text{ (360 is the remainder)}$$

This tells us that the greatest common denominator of the two initial numbers, gcd(2322, 654), is equal to gcd(654, 360). These are still a bit unwieldy, so let's proceed with the algorithm.

$$654 = 360\cdot1 + 294 \text{ (the remainder is 294)}$$

This tells us that gcd(654, 360) is equal to gcd(360, 294).

In the following steps, we continue this process until there is nowhere to go:

$$360 = 294\cdot1 + 66 \quad \text{gcd}(360, 294) = \text{gcd}(294, 66)$$

$$294 = 66\cdot4 + 30 \quad \text{gcd}(294, 66) = \text{gcd}(66, 30)$$

$$66 = 30\cdot2 + 6 \quad \text{gcd}(66, 30) = \text{gcd}(30, 6)$$

$$30 = 6\cdot5 \quad \text{gcd}(30, 6) = 6$$

Therefore, gcd(2322,654) = 6.

This process is quite handy and can be used to find the greatest common divisor of any two numbers. And, as I previously stated, this will play a role in the cryptography you will study later in this book.

> **Tip**
> If you need a bit more on the Euclidean algorithm, there are some very helpful resources on the Internet. Rutgers University has a nice simple page on this issue, www.math.rutgers.edu/~greenfie/gs2004/euclid.html, as does the University of Colorado at Denver, www-math.ucdenver.edu/~wcherowi/courses/m5410/exeucalg.html.

Designing Algorithms

Designing an algorithm is a formal process that provides a systematic way of solving a problem. Therefore, it should be no surprise that there are systematic ways of designing algorithms. In this section we will examine a few of these methods.

The "divide-and-conquer" approach to algorithm design is a commonly used approach. In fact, it could be argued that it is the most commonly used approach. It works by recursively breaking down a problem into sub-problems of the same type until these sub-problems become simple enough to be solved directly. Once the sub-problems are solved, the solutions are combined to provide a solution to the original problem. In short, you keep subdividing the problem until you find manageable portions that you can solve, and after solving those smaller, more manageable portions, you combine those solutions to solve the original problem.

When you're approaching difficult problems, such as the classic Tower of Hanoi puzzle, the divide-and-conquer method often offers the only workable way to find a solution. The divide-and-conquer method often leads to algorithms that are not only effective, but also efficient.

The efficiency of the divide-and-conquer method can be examined by considering the number of sub-problems being generated. If the work of splitting the problem and combining the partial solutions is proportional to the problem's size n, then there are a finite number p of sub-problems of size ~ n/p at each stage. Furthermore, if the base cases require O (that is, constant-bounded) time, then the divide-and-conquer algorithm will have O(n log n) complexity. This is often used in sorting problems to reduce the complexity from O(n2). An O of n log n is fairly good for most sorting algorithms.

In addition to allowing you to devise efficient algorithms for solving complex problems, the divide-and-conquer approach is well suited for execution in multi-processor machines. The sub-problems can be assigned to different processors to allow each processor to work on a different sub-problem. This leads to sub-problems being solved simultaneously, thus increasing the overall efficacy of the process.

The second method is the *greedy approach*. The textbook *An Introduction to Algorithms*, by Thomas Cormen, Charles Leiserson, Ronald Rivest, and Clifford Stein (MIT Press, 2009), defines *greedy algorithm*s as algorithms that select what appears to be the most optimal solution in a given situation. In other words, a solution is selected that is ideal for a specific situation, but it might not be the most effective solution for the broader class of problems. The greedy approach is used with optimization problems. To provide a precise description of the greedy paradigm, we must first consider a more detailed description of the environment in which most optimization problems occur. Most optimization problems include the following:

- A collection of candidates—a set, a list, an array, or another data structure. How the collection is stored in memory is irrelevant.

- A set of candidates that have previously been used.
- A predicate solution that is used to test whether or not a given set of candidates provides an efficient solution. This does not check to determine whether those candidates provide an optimal solution, just whether or not they provide a working solution.
- Another predicate solution (feasible) to test whether a set of candidates can be extended to a solution.
- A selection function, which chooses some candidate that has not yet been used.
- A function that assigns a value to a solution.

Essentially, an optimization problem involves finding a subset S from a collection of candidates C, where that subset satisfies some specified criteria. For example, the criteria may be "a solution such that the function is optimized by S." Optimization may denote any number of factors, such as minimized or maximized. Greedy methods are distinguished by the fact that the selection function assigns a numerical value to each candidate C and chooses that candidate for which

$$\text{SELECT}(C) \text{ is largest}$$

or

$$\text{SELECT}(C) \text{ is smallest}$$

All greedy algorithms have this same general form. A greedy algorithm for a particular problem is specified by describing the predicates and the selection function. Consequently, greedy algorithms are often very easy to design for optimization problems.

The general form of a greedy algorithm is as follows:

functionselect (C : candidate_set) returncandidate;

functionsolution (S : candidate_set) returnboolean;

functionfeasible (S : candidate_set) returnboolean;

> **Tip**   *An Introduction to Algorithms* is an excellent source for learning about algorithms. It is often used as a textbook in university courses. If you are looking for a thorough discussion of algorithms, I recommend this book.

P vs. NP

You have probably heard this issue bandied about quite a bit, even if you don't have a rigorous mathematical background. It was even featured in an episode of the television drama *Elementary*. It involves a question that has significant implications for cryptography.

Many problems in mathematics are solvable via some *polynomial* equation, though not all problems are solvable in this fashion. Those that are not solvable are referred to as *NP*, or *not polynomial* (also known as *nondeterministic polynomial time* or *not solvable in polynomial time*). In complexity theory, *NP-complete* (NP-C) problems are the most difficult problems to solve because there are no polynomial equations for their solutions. That concept should be simple enough. *P* is *polynomial*, or more exactly, *problems solvable in polynomial time*. So what is the question that "P versus NP" addresses?

The question has to do with the fact that, to date, no one has proven that there is no polynomial solution for any NP-complete problem. If someone could provide a polynomial solution for *any* NP-complete problem, this would prove that *all* NP-complete problems *do* have a polynomial solution (in short, it would prove that there is no such thing as an NP-complete problem). In other words, as far as we know, there might be some polynomial time solution to these NP problems, but no one has proven that they cannot be solved in polynomial time.

Tip   When I say "proven" I mean provided with a mathematical proof.

There are essentially three classes of problems: *P* problems can be solved in polynomial time. *NP* problems cannot be solved in polynomial time, but they can be verified that a given solution is correct. *NP-C* problems simply cannot be addressed in any fashion in polynomial time.

One example of an NP-C problem is the subset sum problem, which can be summarized as follows: Given a finite set of integers, determine whether any non-empty subset of them sums to zero. A proposed answer is easy to verify for correctness; however, to date, no one has produced a faster way to solve the problem than simply to try each and every single possible subset. This is very inefficient.

At present, all known algorithms for NP-C problems require time that is super-polynomial in the input size. In other words, there is no polynomial solution for any NP-C problem. Therefore, to solve an NP-C problem, one of the following approaches is used:

- **Approximation** An algorithm is used that quickly finds a suboptimal solution that is within a certain known range of the optimal one. In other words, an approximate solution is found.
- **Probabilistic** An algorithm is used that provably yields good average runtime behavior for a given distribution of the problem instances.
- **Special cases** An algorithm is used that is provably fast if the problem instances belong to a certain special case. In other words, an optimal solution is found only for certain cases of the problem.
- **Heuristic** An algorithm that works well on many cases, but for which there is no proof that it is always fast. Heuristic methods are also considered *rule-of-thumb*.

We have examined NP-C problems in a general way, but now let's look at a formal definition. A problem *C* is NP-C if

it is in NP

and

every other problem in NP is reducible to it.

In this instance, *reducible* means that for every problem L, there is a polynomial-time many-one reduction, a deterministic algorithm that transforms instances $l \in L$ into instances $c \in C$, such that the answer to c is yes if and only if the answer to l is yes.

As a consequence of this definition, if you have a polynomial time algorithm for C, you could solve all problems in NP in polynomial time. This means that if someone ever finds a polynomial solution for any NP-C problem, then all problems have a solution, as I mentioned earlier.

In *An Introduction to Algorithms*, NP-C problems are illustrated by showing a problem that can be solved with a polynomial time algorithm, along with a related NP-C problem—for example, finding the shortest path is a polynomial time algorithm, whereas finding the longest path is an NP-C problem.

This formal definition was proposed by computer scientist Stephen Cook in 1971, who also showed that the Boolean satisfiability problem is NP-C.

> **Note** The details of the Boolean satisfiability problem are not really pertinent to our current discussion. If you are interested in more details, see the Association of Computing Machinery (ACM) paper on the topic: http://cacm.acm.org /magazines/2014/3/172516-boolean-satisfiability/fulltext.

Since Cook's original results, thousands of other problems have been shown to be NP-C by reductions from other problems previously shown to be NP-C; many of these problems are collected in Michael Garey and David Johnson's book *Computers and Intractability: A Guide to the Theory of NP-Completeness* (W.H. Freeman, 1979).

What does all of this have to do with cryptography? Actually quite a lot. As you will see in Chapters 10 and 11, modern public-key cryptography is based on mathematical problems that are very difficult to solve; these are NP problems (they cannot be solved in polynomial time). If someone were to prove that these NP problems actually had a polynomial time solution, that would seriously degrade the security of all modern public-key cryptography. As you will also see, public-key cryptography is critical to many modern technologies, including e-commerce.

> **Note** The P versus NP issue is a wonderful example of how mathematics that may seem abstract can have very real and practical implications.

History Highlights

In this section, I'll provide a basic overview of some of the more important highlights in the history of algebra. The development of algebra progressed through three stages:

- **Rhetorical** No use of symbols, verbal only
- **Syncopated** Abbreviated words
- **Symbolic** Use of symbols, used today

The *rhetorical stage* is so named because rather than use modern symbols, algebraic problems were described in words. As you might imagine, this was a serious impediment to the development of algebra. Consider for a moment your secondary school algebra courses, and imagine how difficult they would have been if you had to work without any symbols! The early Babylonian and Egyptian mathematicians used rhetorical algebra. The Greeks and Chinese did as well.

It was Diophantus, who you read about earlier in this chapter, who first used *syncopated* algebra in his book *Arithmetica*. Syncopated algebra used abbreviations rather than words.

Around 1500 C.E., symbols began to replace both syncopated and rhetorical algebra. By the 17th century, symbols were the primary way of performing mathematics. However, even then, the symbols used were not exactly the same as those you are most likely familiar with today.

Algebra is divided into two types:

- **Classical algebra** Equation solving—the type of algebra you probably studied in secondary school. It is concerned with trying to find solutions to particular problems, such as quadratic equations.
- **Abstract/modern algebra** Study of groups, or specialized sets of numbers and the operations on them—such as the groups, rings, and fields you read about earlier in this chapter.

The word *algebra* has an interesting origin. It was derived from the word *jabr*, an Arabic word used by mathematician Mohammed ibn-Mūsā al-Khwārizmī. In his book, *The Compendious Book on Calculation by Completion and Balancing*, written around the year 820 C.E., he used the word *jabr* to transpose subtracted terms to the other side of the equation— this is the cancelling you first encountered in secondary school. Eventually, the term *al-jabr* became *algebra*.

Our modern concepts of algebra evolved over many years—in fact, centuries—and has been influenced by many cultures.

Ancient Mediterranean Algebra

Ancient Egyptian mathematicians were primarily concerned with linear equations. One important document, the Rhind Papyrus (also known as the Ahmes Papyrus), written around 1650 B.C.E., appears to be a transcription of an even earlier work that documents ancient Egyptian mathematics. The Rhind Papyrus contains linear equations.

The Babylonians used rhetorical algebra and were already thinking about quadratic and cubic equations. This indicates that their mathematics were more advanced than that of the ancient Egyptians.

Ancient Greeks were most interested in geometric problems, and their approach to algebra reflects this. The "application of areas" was a method of solving equations using geometric algebra. It was described in Euclid's *Elements*. Eventually the Greeks expanded even beyond that. In the book *Introductio Arithmetica*, by Nicomachus (60–120 C.E.), a method called the "bloom of Thymaridas" described a rule used for dealing with simultaneous linear equations. Greeks also studied number theory, beginning with Pythagoras and continuing with Euclid and Nicomachus.

As pivotal as the ancient Greek work in geometry was, their algebra had severe limitations. They did not recognize negative solutions, and such solutions were rejected. They did realize that irrational numbers existed, but they simply avoided them, considering them not to be numbers.

Ancient Chinese Algebra

At least as early as 300 B.C.E., the Chinese were also developing algebra. The book *The Nine Chapters on the Mathematical Art* comprised 246 problems. The book also dealt with solutions to linear equations, including solutions with negative numbers.

Ancient Arabic Algebra

Arab contributions to mathematics are numerous. Of particular note is Al-Karaji (c. 953–1029 C.E.), who has been described by some as the first person to adopt the algebra operations we are familiar with today. Al-Karaji was first to define the monomials x, x^2, x^3, as well as the fractions thereof: $1/x$, $1/x^2$, $1/x^3$, and so on. He also presented rules for multiplying any two of these. Al-Karaji started a school of algebra that flourished for several hundred years.

Omar Khayyám (1048–1131 C.E.), another prominent Arab mathematician, poet, and astronomer, created a complete classification of cubic equations with geometric solutions found by means of intersecting conic sections. He also wrote that he hoped to give a full description of the algebraic solution of cubic equations in his book *The Rubáiyát*:

> If the opportunity arises and I can succeed, I shall give all these fourteen forms with all their branches and cases, and how to distinguish whatever is possible or impossible so that a paper, containing elements which are greatly useful in this art, will be prepared.[1]

Indian and other cultures' mathematicians also significantly contributed to the study of algebra. In the western world, mathematics stagnated until the 12th century, when various translations of Arabic and Latin works became available in Europe, reigniting interest in mathematics.

Important Mathematicians

To give you a thorough understanding of the history of algebra, in this section, I will discuss a few of the more important mathematicians, providing you with a brief biographical sketch. Complete coverage of all relevant mathematicians would take several volumes.

Diophantus

You were briefly introduced to Diophantus, the third-century mathematician, when I discussed Diophantine equations. Diophantus was the first Greek mathematician to recognize fractions as numbers, and he introduced syncopated algebra. Unfortunately, little is known about his life.

Interestingly, the following phrase was an algebra problem written rhetorically in the Greek Anthology (assembled around 500 C.E. by Metrodorus):

> His boyhood lasted 1/6th of his life.
> He married after 1/7th more.
> His beard grew after 1/12th more.
> And his son was born 5 years later.
> The son lived to half his father's age.
> And the father died 4 years after the son.

The solution to this is that he married at the age of 26 and died at 84.

Tartaglia

Niccolo Tartaglia (c. 1499–1557) was an Italian mathematician and engineer. He applied mathematics to study how cannonballs are fired and what path they travel. Some consider him to be the father of ballistics. His first contribution to mathematics was a translation of Euclid's *Elements*, published in 1543. This was the first-known translation of that work into any modern European language. He also published original works, most notably his book *General Trattato di Numeri et Misure* (*General Treatise on Number and Measure*) in 1556, which has been widely considered one of the best works on mathematics of the 16th century.

Tartaglia was known for his solutions to cubic equations. He shared his solutions with fellow mathematician Gerolamo Cardano, on the condition that Cardano keep them secret. However, many years later, Cardano published Tartaglia's solution, giving Tartaglia full credit. (This, however, did not assuage Tartaglia's anger.)

Descartes

René Descartes (1596–1650) may be better known for his work in philosophy, but he was also a mathematician who used symbolic algebra. He used lowercase letters from the end of the alphabet (x, y, z) to denote unknown values and lowercase letters from the beginning of the alphabet (a, b, c) for constants. The Cartesian coordinate system that most students learn in primary or secondary school was named after Descartes, and he is often called the "father of analytical geometry," a combination of algebraic methods applied to geometry. His work also provided a foundation that was later applied by both Leibniz and Newton in the invention of calculus.

Galois

French mathematician Évariste Galois (1811–1832) made a number of important contributions to mathematics. Perhaps two of the most important, at least in reference to our current study of algebra, are his contributions to group theory (namely the Galois field, which we have discussed) and Galois theory. (The details of Galois theory are not necessary for our exploration of cryptography. However, it provided an important advancement in abstract algebra that involves both group theory and field theory.) Interestingly, in 1828, he tried to enter the École Polytechnique, a prestigious French mathematics institute, and failed the oral exam. So he entered the far less esteemed École Normale. A year later, he published his first paper on the topic of continued fractions.

> **Note**
>
> Popular conception views mathematicians as a rather quiet group, timidly working with formulas and proofs. Galois is one (of many) evidences that this perception is simply not true (or at least not always true). He had quite a colorful, and at times violent life. In 1831, Galois quit school to join an artillery unit of the military, which was later disbanded as several of the officers were accused of plotting to overthrow the government (they were later acquitted). Galois was known for rather vocal and extreme political protests, including proposing a toast to King Louis Philippe while holding a dagger above his cup. This was interpreted as a threat on the king's life, and he was arrested but later acquitted. Galois was also arrested on Bastille Day while participating in a protest wearing the uniform of his disbanded artillery unit and carrying several weapons (a rifle, a dagger, and multiple pistols). He spent several months in jail for this incident. On May 30,1832, he was shot in a duel and later died of the wounds he suffered.

Conclusions

We explored several topics in this chapter, including groups, rings, and fields. These algebraic structures, particularly Galois fields, are very important to cryptography. Make certain you are familiar with them before proceeding to Chapter 6. Diophantine equations are so common in algebra that at least a basic familiarity of them is also important.

Next, we studied matrix algebra; matrices are not overly complex, as you read in the fundamentals explained in this chapter. You should be comfortable with matrices and the basic arithmetic operations on matrices, which are used in some cryptographic algorithms.

This chapter also introduced you to algorithms. An understanding of the sorting algorithms is not as critical as having a conceptual understanding of algorithms and algorithm analysis. Finally, you were introduced to some basics of the history of algebra. As with Chapters 3 and 4, the topics in this chapter are foundational and necessary for your understanding of subsequent chapters.

> **Note**
>
> Each of the topics presented in this chapter is the subject of entire books. This chapter provided a basic introduction—just enough information to help you understand the cryptography discussed later in this book. If you want to delve deeper into cryptography, you can study these various topics in the texts mentioned in this chapter as well as in other texts.

Test Your Knowledge

1. A _____ is any equation for which you are interested only in the integer solutions to the equation.

2. A matrix that has all 1's in its main diagonal and the rest of the elements are 0 is called what?
   A. Inverse matrix
   B. Diagonal matrix
   C. Identity matrix
   D. Reverse matrix

3. Omega notation is _____.
   A. the asymptotic upper bound of an algorithm
   B. the asymptotic lower bound of an algorithm
   C. the average performance of an algorithm
   D. notation for the row and column of a matrix

4. A _____ is an algebraic system consisting of a set, an identity element, two operations, and the inverse operation of the first operation.
   A. ring
   B. field
   C. group
   D. Galois field

5. A _____ is an algebraic system consisting of a set, an identity element for each operation, two operations, and their respective inverse operations.
   A. ring
   B. field
   C. group
   D. Galois field

6. Yes or No: Is the set of integers a group with reference to multiplication?

7. Yes or No: Is the set of natural numbers a subgroup of the set of integers with reference to addition?

8. If a | b and a | c, then _____.

9. A group that also has the commutative property is a _____ group.

10. _____ is a process used to measure the performance of computer algorithms.

Answers

1. Diophantine equation
2. C
3. B
4. C
5. B
6. Yes
7. No
8. a | (b + c)
9. abelian
10. Asymptotic analysis

Endnote

1. From Omar Khayyám, *The Rubáiyát of Omar Khayyám.*

PART II

Symmetric Ciphers and Hashes

6 Feistel Networks

In this chapter we will cover the following:

- Cryptographic keys
- Feistel functions
- Pseudo-Hadamard transforms
- MDS matrix
- S-boxes and P-boxes
- Symmetric algorithms
- Methods for improving symmetric algorithms

This chapter is the first of two chapters regarding symmetric ciphers. Before I dive into the topic of this chapter, Feistel networks, you need to understand what a symmetric cipher is and the different types of symmetric ciphers. A *symmetric cipher* is an algorithm that uses the same key to decrypt the message that was used to encrypt the message, as demonstrated in Figure 6-1.

The process is rather straightforward, and a decryption key functions much like a key in a physical door—that is, the same key used to lock the door is used to unlock it. This is probably the modality of cryptography that is easiest for cryptography novices to learn. Symmetric cryptography offers some significant advantages over *asymmetric* cryptography (which we will examine in Chapters 10 and 11). For example, symmetric cryptography is faster than asymmetric and it is just as secure though it uses a smaller key.

Although the classic cryptography discussed in Chapters 1 and 2 could be considered symmetric ciphers, for the purposes of our current discussion we are contemplating only modern ciphers. With that in mind, symmetric algorithms can be classified in two major ways: block ciphers and stream ciphers. A block cipher literally encrypts the data in blocks—64-bit blocks are common, although some algorithms use larger blocks (for example, AES uses a 128-bit block). Stream ciphers encrypt the data as a stream, 1 bit at a time.

Modern block ciphers use a combination of substitution and transposition to achieve both confusion and diffusion (recall those concepts from Chapter 3). Remember that *substitution* is changing some part of the plain text for some matching part of cipher text. The Caesar and Atbash ciphers are simple substitution ciphers. *Transposition* is the swapping of blocks of cipher text. For example, for the text *I like icecream*, you could transpose or swap every three-letter sequence (or block) with the next and get *ikeI l creiceam*. (Of course, modern block

A key has to be exchanged before communications begin.

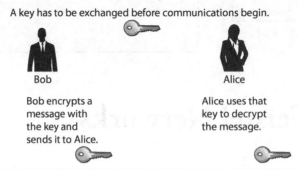

Bob

Alice

Bob encrypts a
message with
the key and
sends it to Alice.

Alice uses that
key to decrypt
the message.

FIGURE 6-1 **Symmetric cryptography**

ciphers accomplish substitution and transposition at the level of bits, or rather blocks of bits, and this example uses characters. However, the example illustrates the concept.)

There are two major types of block ciphers: *Feistel networks* (such as the Data Encryption Standard, DES) and *substitution-permutation networks* (Advanced Encryption Standard, AES). In this chapter we will examine several Feistel ciphers. Some, such as DES, will be discussed in thorough detail; others will be describe in general terms. Chapter 7 discusses substitution-permutation networks as well as stream ciphers.

It is not critical that you memorize every algorithm in this chapter, even those that are described in detail. It is recommended, however, that you pay particular attention to DES and Blowfish. Then study the other algorithms just enough to understand how they differ from DES and Blowfish. The goal of this chapter is to provide you with a solid understanding of Feistel ciphers.

> **Note** As with previous chapters, I will also provide sources of more information, such as books and web sites. I am aware that web sites may not always be up and available, but they are also easy and free to access. If a given URL is no longer available, I suggest you simply use your favorite search engine to search the topic. My web site, www.cryptocorner.com/, will always include links if you want to explore these topics.

Cryptographic Keys

Before we start looking at Feistel ciphers, you need to have a basic understanding of cryptographic keys and how they are used. With all block ciphers, there are two types of keys: cipher keys and round keys.

The cipher key is a random string of bits that is generated and exchanged between parties that want to send encrypted messages to each other. When someone says a particular algorithm has a certain key size, they are referring to this cipher key. For example, DES uses a 56-bit cipher key. How that key is exchanged between the two parties is not relevant at this point. Later in the chapter, when I discuss asymmetric cryptography and Secure Sockets Layer/ Transport Layer Security (SSL/TLS), you'll read about key exchange.

| Note | The cipher key is actually a pseudo-random number, but we will discuss that in more detail in Chapter 12. For now, just understand that the cipher key is a number generated by some algorithm, such that it is at least somewhat random. The more random it is, the better. |

In addition to the cipher key, all block ciphers have a second algorithm called a *key schedule* which derives a unique key, called a *round key*, from the cipher key for each round of the cipher. For example, DES has a 56-bit cipher key, but it derives 48-bit round keys for each of its 16 rounds. The key schedule is usually rather simple, mostly consisting of shifting bits. Using a key schedule, each round uses a key that is slightly different from the previous round. Because both the sender (who encrypts the message) and the receiver (who must decrypt the message) are using the same cipher key as a starting point and are using the same key schedule, they will generate the same round keys.

Why do it this way? If you wanted a different key for each round, why not just generate that many cipher keys? For example, why not create 16 DES keys? There are two answers. The first concerns the time needed. Using pseudo-random-number generators to generate keys is computationally more intensive than most key scheduling algorithms and thus much slower. And there is the issue of key exchange: If you generate multiple cipher keys, you have to exchange all of those keys. It is much easier to generate a single cipher key, exchange that key, and then derive round keys from the cipher key.

Feistel Function

At the heart of most block ciphers is a *Feistel function*, also known as a Feistel network or a Feistel cipher. Because this particular class of block cipher forms the basis for so many symmetric ciphers, it is one of the most influential developments in symmetric block ciphers.

It is named after its inventor, German-born physicist and cryptographer Horst Feistel. Although most known for his contributions to DES, Feistel made other important contributions to cryptography. He invented the Lucifer cipher, the precursor to DES. He also worked for the U.S. Air Force on Identify Friend or Foe (IFF) devices. Feistel held a bachelor's degree from MIT and a master's from Harvard, both in physics.

A simple view of the Feistel function is shown in Figure 6-2. The process is not too difficult to understand if you take it one step at a time. Trying to grasp the entire process at once, however, might prove difficult if this is new to you.

| Note | Often when I am teaching cryptography, I stop at each step and inquire if the class understands so far. You might do this as you read this section. You can apply that same technique to all the algorithms you will read about from this point forward in the book. |

The function starts by splitting the block of plain text data into two parts, traditionally termed L_0 and R_0. The specific size of the plain text block varies from one algorithm to another: 64-bit and 128-bit sizes are commonly used in many block ciphers. If you are using a 64-bit block, you have 32 bits in L_0 and 32 bits in R_0. The 0 subscript simply indicates that this is the initial round. The next round is L_1 and R_1, and then L_2 and R_2, and so on, for as many rounds as that particular cipher uses.

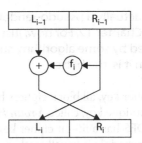

FIGURE 6-2 Feistel—a simple view

After the initial bock of plain text is split into two halves, the round function F is applied to one of the two halves. (The *round function* is a function performed with each iteration, or round, of the Feistel cipher.) The details of the round function F can vary with different implementations. They are usually simple functions that allow for increased speed of the algorithm. (For now, simply treat the round function as a "black box"; I will get to the details of each round function in the specific algorithms I examine—DES, Blowfish, and so on.) In every case, however, at some point in the round function, the round key is XOR'd with the block of text input into the round function—this is, in fact, usually the first step of the round function.

The output of the round function F is then XOR'd with the other half (the half that was not subjected to the round function). What this means is that, for example, L_0 is passed through the round function F, and the result is XOR'd with R_0. Then the halves are transposed. So L_0 gets moved to the right and R_0 gets moved to the left.

This process is repeated a given number of times. The main difference between various Feistel functions is the exact nature of the round function F and the number of iterations. You can see this process in Figure 6-3.

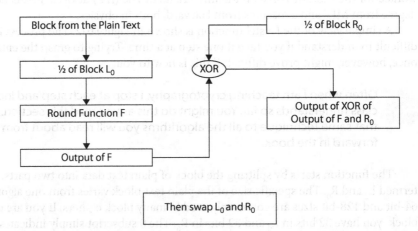

FIGURE 6-3 Feistel function process

This basic structure can provide a very robust basis for cryptographic algorithms. The swapping of the two halves guarantees that some transposition occurs, regardless of what happens in the round function. The Feistel function is the basis for many algorithms, including DES, CAST-128, Blowfish, Twofish, RC5, FEAL (Fast data Encipherment ALgorithm), MARS, TEA (Tiny Encryption Algorithm), and others. But it was first used in IBM's Lucifer algorithm (the precursor to DES).

> **Note** How many rounds do you need to make a Feistel secure? Famed computer scientists Michael Luby and Charles Rackoff analyzed the Feistel cipher construction and showed that if the round function is a cryptographically secure pseudo-random function, three rounds is sufficient to make the block cipher a pseudo-random permutation, while four rounds is sufficient to make it a "strong" pseudo-random permutation.

Unbalanced Feistel

A variation of the Feistel network, the Unbalanced Feistel cipher, uses a modified structure, where L_0 and R_0 are not of equal lengths. So L_0 might be 32 bits and R_0 could be 64 bits (making a 96-bit block of text). This variation is used in the Skipjack algorithm. You can see this process in Figure 6-4.

Pseudo-Hadamard Transform

The pseudo-Hadamard transform (PHT) is a technique applied in several symmetric ciphers. Fortunately, it is simple to understand. A PHT is a transformation of a bit string that is designed to produce diffusion in the bit string. The bit string must be an even length because it is split into two equal halves—so, for example, a 64-bit string is divided into two 32-bit halves. To compute the transform of a, you add $a + b \pmod{2^n}$. To compute the transform of b, you add

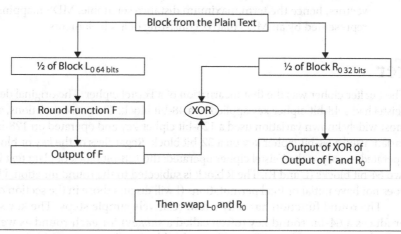

FIGURE 6-4 Unbalanced Feistel function

$a + 2b$ (mod 2^n). The n is the number of bits of each half—in our example, 32. Here's a more formal mathematical notation:

$$a` \equiv a + b \text{ (mod } 2^n)$$

$$b` \equiv a + 2b \text{ (mod } 2^n)$$

The key is that this transform is reversible, as you can see here:

$$a \equiv 2a` - b` \text{(mod } 2^n)$$

$$b \equiv a` - b` \text{(mod } 2^n)$$

PHT is a simple transform, and because of its simplicity it is computationally fast, making it attractive for cryptographic applications.

MDS Matrix

An MDS (Maximum Distance Separable) matrix represents a function and is used in several cryptographic algorithms, including Twofish. Here's a simplified definition of the MDS matrix: "An m × n matrix over a finite field is an MDS matrix if it is the transformation matrix of a linear transformation." This definition is adequate for you to understand how algorithms like Twofish are designed. If you are seeking a more mathematically rigorous definition of MDS matrices, consider this quote:

> MDS code over a field is a linear mapping from a field elements to b field elements, producing a composite vector of a+b elements with the property that the minimum number of non-zero elements in any non-zero vector is at least b+1. Put another way, the "distance" (i.e., the number of elements that differ) between any two distinct vectors produced by the MDS mapping is at least b+1. It can easily be shown that no mapping can have a larger minimum distance between two distinct vectors, hence the term maximum distance separable. MDS mappings can be represented by an MDS matrix consisting of a × b elements.[1]

Lucifer

The Lucifer cipher was the first incarnation of a Feistel cipher. The original description by Horst Feistel had a 48-bit cipher key applied to a 48-bit block. There are variations, and perhaps the most widely known variation used a 128-bit cipher key and operated on 128-bit blocks. Another variant used a 64-bit cipher key on a 32-bit block. Regardless of the key or block size, Lucifer operated exactly as the Feistel cipher operated: the 128-bit block of plain text is separated into two 64-bit blocks (L and R). The R block is subjected to the round function. Unlike DES, Lucifer does not have initial or final permutations (I will discuss those in the section on DES).

The round function has only a few, relatively simple steps. The key schedule algorithm produces a 64-bit round key (often called a *subkey*) for each round as well as 8 bits called *interchange control bits* (ICBs). The 64-bit block to be encrypted is treated as a series of

..atched to each of the bytes of the 64-bit block. If the
..n the left nibble and right nibble of the first byte of the block
. bit of the ICB is a 1, then the two nibbles are left unchanged.
bit of the ICB is a 0, the nibbles of the second byte of the block are
..ontinues through all 8 bits of the ICB and all 8 bytes of the block. Because
.. ..nerated each round with the round key, it changes each round. This gives a
transposition in the round function that is based on the key. After swapping based on the
ICB is completed, the output bits are XOR'd again with the round key. The output of that
is input into the *substitution boxes*, or *S-boxes*—tables that take input and produce output
based on that input. In other words, an S-box is a substitution box that substitutes new
values for the input.

> **Note**   Several block ciphers have key-dependent functionality. In some cases, such
> as Lucifer, the cipher is simply deciding whether or not to execute a basic
> transposition. In other algorithms, the round key can be used to generate the
> S-boxes. Key dependency does make an algorithm more resistant to some types
> of cryptanalysis.

The key-scheduling algorithm is simple. Each round, the 128-bit cipher key is shifted in a
shift register. The left 64 bits form the round key and the right 8 bits form the ICB. After each
round, the 128 bits are shifted 56 bits to the left.

> **Note**   Some sources say that Feistel first suggested the simple name DEMONSTRATION
> cipher, and then shortened it to DEMON. From that, the Lucifer cipher name
> evolved.

As you can see, Lucifer is relatively simple; however, consider how much change is
actually taking place. First, individual bytes of plain text have their nibbles (4-byte halves)
swapped based on the ICB. Then the result is XOR'd with the round key. Then that output
is subjected to an S-box. In these three steps, the text is subjected to transposition as well as
multiple substitutions. Then consider that the most widely known variant of Lucifer (the
128-bit key and 128-bit block variant) uses 16 rounds. So the aforementioned transposition
and substitutions will be executed on a block of plain text 16 times.

To get a good idea of just how much this alters the plain text, consider a simplified
example. In this case, we won't have any S-boxes—just transposition and an XOR operation.
Let's begin with a single word of plain text:

```
Attack
```

If we convert that to ASCII codes, and then convert those to binary, we get this:

```
01000001 01110100 01110100 01100001 01100011 01101011
```

Now let's assume we have a cipher key that is just 8 random bits. We are not even going to
alter this each round, as most real algorithms do. Our key for this example is this:

```
11010011 00110110
```

Furthermore, to make this similar to Lucifer but simpler, we will swap nibbles on every other byte, and we will do the entire text at once, instead of one block at a time. So round one is like this:

Plain text: 01000001 01110100 01110100 01100001 01100011 01101011

Swapped: 00010100 01110100 01000111 01100001 00110110 01101011

(Only every other block is swapped.)
XOR with key produces this:

11000111 01000010 10010100 01010111 11100101 01011101

Converted to ASCII is

199 66 148 87 229 93

You can find ASCII tables on the Internet (such as www.asciitable.com/) to convert this to actual text, which yields the following:

199 = a symbol, not even a letter or number

66 = B

148 = a symbol, not even a letter or number

87 = W

229 = a symbol, not even a letter or number

93 =]

Consider that this is the output after one round—and it was an overly simplified round at that. This should give you some indication of how effective such encryption can be.

DES

The Data Encryption Standard is a classic in the annals of cryptography. It was selected by the National Bureau of Standards as an official Federal Information Processing Standard (FIPS) for the United States in 1976. Although it is now considered outdated and is not recommended for use, it was the premier block cipher for many years and is worthy of study. The primary reason it is no longer considered secure is because of its small key size, though the algorithm is quite sound. Many cryptography textbooks and university courses use DES as the basic template for studying all block ciphers. We will do the same and give this algorithm more attention than most of the others do.

Tip   For a thorough discussion of the technical details of DES, refer to the actual government standard documentation: U.S. Department of Commerce/National Institute of Standards and Technology FIPS Publication 46-3, at http://csrc.nist .gov/publications/fips/fips46-3/fips46-3.pdf. For a less technical but interesting animation of DES, you can try http://kathrynneugent.com/animation.html.

DES uses a 56-bit cipher key applied to a 64-bit block. There is actually a 64-bit key, but 1 bit of every byte is used for error correction, leaving just 56 bits for actual key operations.

DES is a Feistel cipher with 16 rounds and a 48-bit round key for each round. Recall from the earlier discussion on keys that a round function is a subkey that is derived from the cipher key each round, according to a key schedule algorithm. DES's general functionality follows the Feistel method of dividing the 64-bit block into two halves (of 32 bits each, as this is not an unbalanced Feistel cipher), applying the round function to one half, and then XOR'ing that output with the other half.

The first issue to address is the key schedule. How does DES generate a new subkey each round? The idea is to take the original 56-bit key and to permute it slightly each round, so that each round is applying a slightly different key, but one that is based on the original cipher key. To generate the round keys, the 56-bit key is split into two 28-bit halves, and those halves are circularly shifted after each round by 1 or 2 bits. This will provide a different subkey each round. During the round-key generation portion of the algorithm (recall that this is referred to as the *key schedule*) each round, the two halves of the original cipher key (the 56 bits of key the two endpoints of encryption must exchange) are shifted a specific amount. The amount is shown in this table:

Round	Shift to the Left
1	1
2	1
3	2
4	2
5	2
6	2
7	2
8	2
9	1
10	2
11	2
12	2
13	2
14	2
15	2
16	1

Once the round key has been generated for the current round, the next step is to address the half of the original block that will be input into the round function. Recall that the two halves are each 32 bits, and the round key is 48 bits. That means that the size of the round key does not match the size of the half block to which it is going to be applied. (You cannot really XOR a 48-bit round key with a 32-bit half block unless you simply ignore 16 bits of the round key. If you did so, you would basically be making the round key effectively shorter and thus less secure, so this is not a good option.) So the 32-bit half needs to be expanded to 48 bits before it is XOR'd with the round key. This is accomplished by replicating some bits so that the 32-bit half becomes 48 bits: The 32-bit section to be expanded is divided into 4-bit sections (eight 4-bit sections). The bits on each end are duplicated, adding 16 bits to the original 32, for a total of 48 bits. It is important that you keep in mind that the bits on each end were duplicated, because this item will be key later in the round function.

Perhaps this example will help you to understand what is occurring at this point. Let's assume 32 bits, as shown here:

```
11110011010111111111000101011001
```

Divide that into eight sections of 4 bits each, as shown here:

```
1111 0011 0101 1111 1111 0001 0101 1001
```

Now each of these has its end bits duplicated, as shown here:

```
1111  becomes  111111

0011  becomes  000111

0101  becomes  001011

1111  becomes  111111

1111  becomes  111111

0001  becomes  000011

0101  becomes  001011

1001  becomes  110011
```

The resultant 48-bit string is next XOR'd with the 48-bit round key. That is the extent of the round key being used in each round. It is then dispensed with, and on the next round another 48-bit round key will be derived from the two 28-bit halves of the 56-bit cipher key.

Now we have the 48-bit output of the XOR operation, which is split into eight sections of 6 bits each. For the rest of this explanation, I will focus on just one of those 6-bit sections, but keep in mind that the same process is done to all eight sections.

The 6-bit section is used as the input to an S-box. The S-boxes used in DES are then published—the first of which is shown in Figure 6-5.

Notice that Figure 6-5 is simply a lookup table. The 2 bits on either end are shown in the leftmost column and the 4 bits in the middle are shown in the top row. They are cross-matched, and the resulting value is the output of the S-box. For example, with the previous demonstration numbers, our first block would be 111111. So you would find 1xxxx1 on the left and x1111x on the top. The resulting value is 13 in decimal or 1101 in binary.

	x0000x	x0001x	x0010x	x0011x	x0100x	x0101x	x0110x	x0111x	x1000x	x1001x	x1010x	x1011x	x1100x	x1101x	x1110x	x1111x
0yyyy0	14	4	13	1	2	15	11	8	3	10	6	12	5	9	0	7
0yyyy1	0	15	7	4	14	2	13	1	10	6	12	11	9	5	3	8
1yyyy0	4	1	14	8	13	6	2	11	15	12	9	7	3	10	5	0
1yyyy1	15	12	8	2	4	9	1	7	5	11	3	14	10	0	6	13

FIGURE 6-5   **The first DES A-box**

> **Note**   Recall that during the expansion phase we duplicated the outermost bits, so when we come to the S-box phase and drop the outermost bits, no data is lost. As you will see in Chapter 8, this is called a "compression S-box," and they are difficult to design properly.

At the end of this, you will have produced 32 bits that are the output of the round function. Then, in keeping with the Feistel structure, they get XOR'd with the 32 bits that were not input into the round function, and the two halves would be swapped. DES is a 16-round Feistel cipher, meaning this process is repeated 16 times.

This leaves two items to discuss regarding DES: the initial permutation, or IP, and the final permutation, which is an inverse of the IP, as shown in Figure 6-6. (This figure is an excerpt from the Federal Information Processing Standards Publication 46-3.[2])

The initial permutation mentioned earlier is simply a transposition of the bits in the 64-bit plain text block. This occurs before the rounds of DES are executed, and then the reverse transposition occurs after the rounds of DES have completed. Basically, the first 58th bit is moved to the first bit spot, the 50th bit to the second bit spot, the 42nd bit to the third bit spot, and so on. The specifics are shown in Figure 6-7.

> **Note**   Earlier in this chapter we looked at a very simplified version of the Lucifer cipher, and you could see that it was quite effective at altering the plain text. It should be obvious to you that DES is at least as effective as Lucifer. The small key size is the only reason DES is no longer considered secure. Furthermore, DES is probably the most widely studied symmetric cipher, and certainly the most often cited Feistel cipher. It is important that you fully understand this cipher before you move on to the rest of this chapter. You may need to re-read this section a few times to make sure you fully grasp the details of DES.

3DES

Eventually, it became obvious that DES would no longer be secure. The U.S. federal government began a contest seeking a replacement cryptography algorithm. However, in the meantime, 3DES (Triple DES) was created as an interim solution. Essentially, it "does" DES three times, with three different keys. Triple DES uses a "key bundle," which comprises three DES keys—K1, K2, and K3. Each key is a standard 56-bit DES key. There were some variations that would use the same key for K1 and K3, but three separate keys is considered the most secure.

S-Box and P-Box

An S-box, or substitution box, is a table that substitutes some output for a given input; it defines that each of the input bits is substituted with a new bit. A *P-box*, or *permutation box*, is a variation on the S-box. Instead of each input bit being mapped to a bit found in a lookup table as with the S-box, the bits in the P-box that are input are also transposed, or permuted— that is, some may be transposed, while others are left in place. For example, a 6-bit P-box may

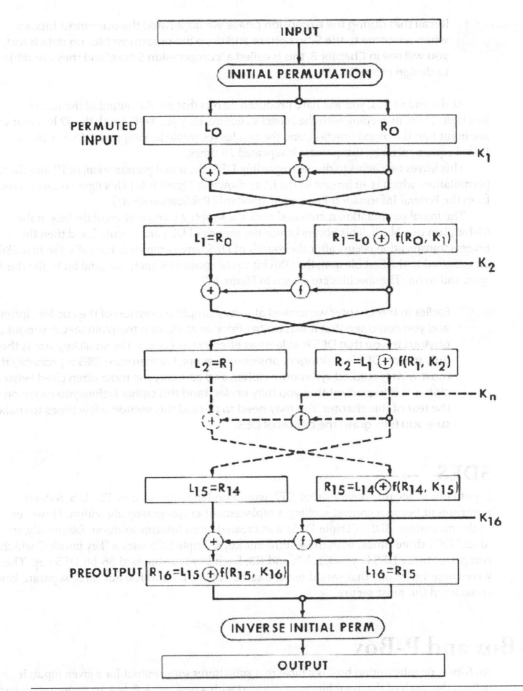

FIGURE 6-6   DES overview from FIPS 46-3

58	50	42	34	26	18	10	2
60	52	44	36	28	20	12	4
62	54	46	38	30	22	14	6
64	56	48	40	32	24	16	8
57	49	41	33	25	17	9	1
59	51	43	35	27	19	11	3
61	53	45	37	29	21	13	5
63	55	47	39	31	23	15	7

FIGURE 6-7 DES initial permutation

swap the first and fourth bits, swap the second and third bit, but leave the fifth bit in place. S-boxes and P-boxes are discussed in detail in Chapter 8.

GOST

GOST is a DES-like algorithm developed by the Soviet and Russian governments in the 1970s. It was first classified but was released to the public in 1994. This 32-round Feistel cipher uses a 64-bit block and a key of 256 bits. (GOST is an acronym for *gosudarstvennyy standart,* which translates into English as "state standard." The official designation is GOST 28147-89.)

GOST was meant as an alternative to the U.S. DES algorithm and has some similarities to DES. It uses a 64-bit block and a 256-bit key with 32 rounds. Like DES, GOST uses S-boxes; unlike DES, the original S-boxes were classified. The round key for GOST is relatively simple: Add a 32-bit subkey to the block, modulo 2^{32}, and then submit the output to the S-boxes. The output of the S-boxes is routed to the left by 11 bits.

The key schedule is as follows: Break the 256-bit cipher key into eight separate 32-bit keys. Each of these keys will be used four times.

Each of eight S-boxes is 4-by-4 and they are implementation dependent—that means that they are generated, for example using a pseudo-random-number generator. Because the S-boxes are not standardized, each party using GOST needs to ensure that the other party is using the same S-box implementation. The S-boxes each take in 4 bits and produce 4 bits. This is different from DES, in which the S-boxes take in 6 bits and produce 4 bits of output.

The round function is very simple, so to compensate for this, the inventors of GOST used 32 rounds (twice that of DES) and the S-boxes are secret and implementation-specific. Although the diversity of S-boxes can make certain types of cryptanalysis more difficult on GOST, it also means the individuals implementing GOST must be very careful in their creation of the S-boxes.

Blowfish

Blowfish is a symmetric block cipher that was published in 1993 by Bruce Schneier, who stated that Blowfish is unpatented and will remain so in all countries. He placed the algorithm in the public domain to be freely used by anyone, which has made Blowfish popular in open source utilities.

> **Note**   Schneier is a very well-known American cryptographer known for his work on the Blowfish and Twofish ciphers as well as his extensive cryptanalysis of various ciphers. He is also the author of the book *Applied Cryptography: Protocols, Algorithms, and Source Code in C* (Wiley, 1996). Schneier maintains a security blog and writes extensively on general network security as well as cryptography-related topics.

The Blowfish cryptography algorithm was intended as a replacement for DES. Like DES, it is a 16-round Feistel cipher working on 64-bit blocks. However, unlike DES, it can have varying key sizes ranging from 32 bits to 448 bits. Early in the cipher, the cipher key is expanded. Key expansion converts a key of at most 448 bits into several subkey arrays totaling 4168 bytes.

The cipher itself is a Feistel cipher, so the first step is to divide the block into two halves. For example, a 64-bit block is divided into L_0 and R_0. Now there will be 16 rounds.

The S-boxes are key dependent (as you will see later in this section). That means rather than be standardized as they are in DES, they are computed based on the key. There are four S-boxes, each 32 bits in size. Each S-box has 256 entries:

s1/0, s1/1, s1/2...s1/255

s2/0, s2/1, s2/2...s2/255

s3/0, s3/1, s3/2...s3/255

s4/0, s4/1, s4/2...s4/255

Blowfish uses multiple subkeys (also called round keys). One of the first steps in the cipher is to compute those subkeys from the original cipher key. This begins with an array called the *P-array*. Each element of the P-array is initialized with the hexadecimal digits of pi, after the 3—in other words, only the values after the decimal point. Each element of the P-array is 32 bits in size. Here are the first few digits of pi in decimal:

```
3.1415926535589979323846264
```

Here is the same number in hexadecimal:

```
2B992DDFA23249D6
```

There are 18 elements in the P-array, each 32 bits in size. They are labeled simply P1, P2, and so on, to P18. The four S-boxes are each 32 bits in size and are also initialized with the digits of pi. Then the first 32 bits of the cipher key are XOR'd with P1, the next 32 bits are XOR'd with P2, and so on. This continues until the entire P-array has been XOR'd with bits from the cipher key. When the process is done, the P-array elements are each hexadecimal digits of pi XOR'd with segments of the cipher key.

The next step might seem confusing, so pay close attention. You take an all-zero string and encrypt it with the Blowfish algorithm using the subkeys you just generated (that is, the P-array). Then replace P1 and P2 with the output of that encryption. Encrypt that output using Blowfish, this time using the new modified keys (the P1 and P2 were modified by the last step). Then replace P3 and P4 with the output of that step. This process continues until all the entries of the P-array and all four S-boxes have been replaced with the output of this continually evolving Blowfish algorithm.[3]

Despite the complex key schedule, the round function itself is rather simple:

1. The 32-bit half is divided into 4 bytes, designated a, b, c, and d.
2. Then this formula is applied.[4]

The F function is: $F(xL) = ((S1,a + S2,b \bmod 2^{32}) \text{ XOR } S3,c) + S4,d \bmod 2^{32}$
You can see this process in Figure 6-8.

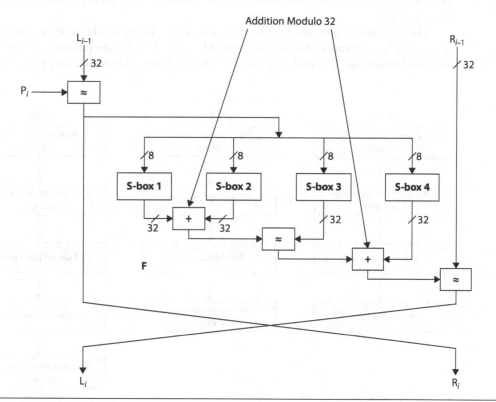

FIGURE 6-8   Blowfish round function

Twofish

Twofish was one of the five finalists of the AES contest (which we will explore in more detail in Chapter 7). It is related to the block cipher Blowfish, and Bruce Schneier was part of the team that worked on this algorithm. Twofish is a Feistel cipher that uses a 128-bit block size and key sizes of 128, 192, and 256 bits. It also has 16 rounds, like DES. Like Blowfish, Twofish is not patented and is in the public domain, so it can be used by anyone without restrictions.

Also like Blowfish, Twofish uses key-dependent S-boxes and has a fairly complex key schedule. There are four S-boxes, each 8 bit–by–8 bit. The cipher key is split in half; one half is used as a key, and the other half is used to modify the key-dependent S-boxes.

Twofish uses key whitening, a process in which a second key is generated and XOR'd with the block. This can be done before or after the round function. In the case of Twofish, it occurs both before and after. You can see this in Figure 6-9.

The plain text is key whitened prior to the application of the Twofish algorithm and again after the application of the Twofish algorithm. In the Twofish documentation, this is referred to as *input whitening* and *output whitening*. With Twofish, 128 bits of key material is used for the input and output whitening.

Twofish has some aspects that are not found in most other Feistel ciphers, the first of which is the concept of the cycle. Every two rounds are considered a cycle. The design of Twofish is such that in one complete cycle (two rounds), every bit of plain text has been modified once.

The plain text is split into four 32-bit words. After the input whitening are 16 rounds of Twofish. In each round, the two 32-bit words on the left side are put into the round function (remember all Feistel ciphers divide the plain text, submitting only part of it to the

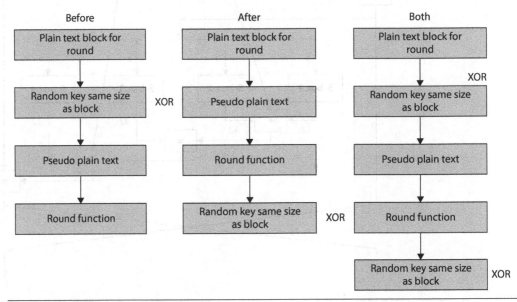

FIGURE 6-9 Key whitening in Twofish

round function). Those two 32-bit words are submitted to the key dependent S-boxes and then mixed using an MDS matrix. Then the results from this process are combined using the pseudo-Hadamard transform. After this is complete, the results are XOR'd with the right two 32-bit words (that were previously left untouched) and swapped for the next round.

There is one nuance to the XOR of the left and right halves. The two 32-bit words on the right are given a slight rotation. One 32-bit word is rotated 1 bit the left, and then after the XOR, the other 32-bit word is rotated 1 bit to the right.

An overview of Twofish is shown in Figure 6-10. Note that this image is the diagram originally presented in Schneier's (et al.) paper on Twofish.[5]

If you want to delve into more detail with Twofish, I recommend the paper that Schneier wrote on Twofish (see the Endnotes for this chapter). You may also want to consult the book *The Twofish Encryption Algorithm: A 128-Bit Block Cipher* by Kelsey, Whiting, Wagner, and Ferguson (Wiley, 1999).

> **Note** Neils Ferguson is a very well-known cryptographer who has worked on Twofish as well as the Helix cipher. He collaborated with Schneier on several projects including the Yarrow and Fortuna pseudo-random-number generators. We will examine both of those in Chapter 12. In 2007, Ferguson and Dan Shumow presented a paper that described a potential cryptographic backdoor in the Dual_EC_DRBG pseudo-random-number generator. Later disclosures by Edward Snowden (the former CIA contractor who leaked classified information) revealed that there was indeed a cryptographic backdoor in Dual_EC_DRBG. We will examine those issues in Chapter 18.

Skipjack

The Skipjack algorithm was developed by the NSA and was designed for the clipper chip. Although the algorithm was originally classified, it was eventually declassified and released to the public. The clipper chip had built-in encryption; however, a copy of the decryption key would be kept in a key escrow in case law enforcement needed to decrypt data without the device owner's cooperation. This feature made the process highly controversial. The Skipjack algorithm was designed for voice encryption, and the clipper chip was meant for secure phones.

Skipjack uses an 80-bit key to encrypt or decrypt 64-bit data blocks. It is an unbalanced Feistel network with 32 rounds. Skipjack's round function operates on 16-bit words. It uses two different types of rounds, called the A and B rounds. In the original specifications, A and B were termed *stepping rules*. First step A is applied for 8 rounds, step B for 8 rounds, and then the process is repeated, totaling 32 rounds.

Skipjack makes use of an S-box that is rather interesting. The documentation refers to it as the "G function" or "G permutation." It takes a 16-bit word as input along with a 4-byte subkey. This G permutation includes a fixed byte S-table that is termed the "F-table" in the Skipjack documentation.

The A round is accomplished by taking the 16-bit word, called *W1*, and submitting it to the G box. The new W1 is produced by XOR'ing the output of the G box with the counter and then with W4. The W2 and W3 words shift one register to the right, becoming W3 and W4. This is shown in Figure 6-11, which is taken directly from the NIST specification for Skipjack.[6]

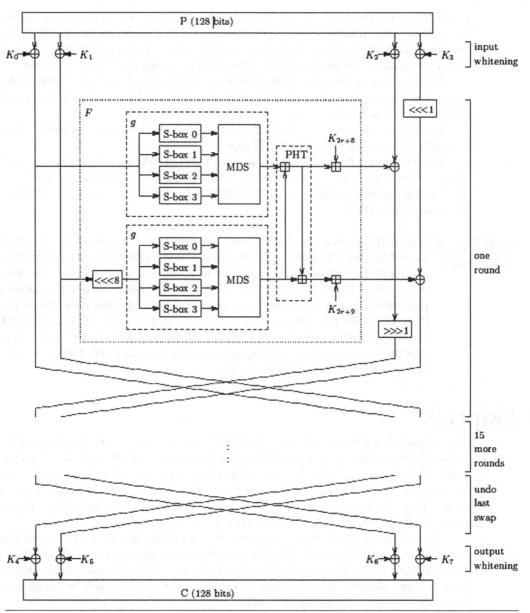

FIGURE 6-10   The original Twofish diagram

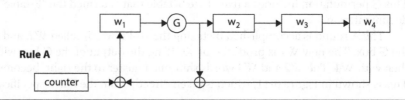

FIGURE 6-11   Skipjack A round

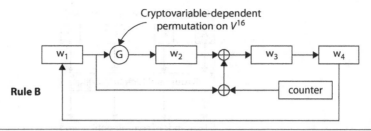

FIGURE 6-12   Skipjack B round

The B round is similar, with slight differences, shown in Figure 6-12 (also taken from the specification documentation).

The Skipjack algorithm is considered to be robust. However, the key escrow issue made it unacceptable to many civilian vendors, who feared that the U.S. government would, at will, be able to eavesdrop on communications encrypted with Skipjack. For this reason, the Skipjack algorithm did not gain wide acceptance and usage.

CAST

There are two well-known versions of CAST: CAST-128 and CAST-256. CAST-256 was a candidate in the AES contest and is based on the earlier CAST-128. CAST-128 is used in some versions of PGP (Pretty Good Privacy). The algorithm was created by Carlisle Adams and Stafford Tavares. CAST-128 can use either 12 or 16 rounds, working on a 64-bit block. The key sizes are in 8-bit increments, ranging from 40 bits to 128 bits, but only in 8-bit increments. The 12-round version of CAST-128 is used with key sizes less than 80 bits, and the 16-round version is used with key sizes of 80 bits or longer. CAST-128 has 8 S-boxes, each 32 bits in size.

FEAL

FEAL (Fast data Encipherment ALgorithm) was designed by Akihrio Shimizu and Shoji Miyaguchi and published in 1987. There are variations of the FEAL cipher, but all use a 64-bit block and essentially the same round function. FEAL-4 uses 4 rounds, FEAL-8 uses 8 rounds, FEAL-N uses N rounds, chosen by the implementer. This algorithm has not done well under cryptanalysis. Because several weaknesses have been found in the algorithm, it is not considered secure.

MARS

MARS was IBM's submission to the AES contest and was one of the final five finalists. It was designed by a team of cryptographers that included Don Coppersmith, a mathematician who was involved in the creation of DES and worked on various other cryptological topics such as cryptanalysis of RSA. The algorithm uses a 128-bit block with a key size that varies between 128 and 448 bits, in 32-bit increments.

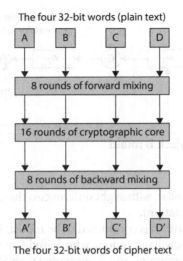

The four 32-bit words (plain text)

FIGURE 6-13   General overview of MARS

MARS divides the input into the round function into four 32-bit words labeled A, B, C, and D. The algorithm has three phases: an 8-round phase that does forward mixing, a 16-round phase that is the core of the algorithm, then an 8-round phase that does backward mixing.

A general overview of MARS is shown in Figure 6-13.

As mentioned, MARS can use a cipher key of 128 to 448 bits, divided into four to fourteen 32-bit words. MARS uses a key schedule that expands the user-supplied cipher key into a key array of forty 32-bit words.

MARS uses a single but very large S-box, a table of 512, 32-bit words to which the operations are applied. The original specification for MARS[7] actually described the algorithm entirely in an image, which is shown in Figure 6-14.

In Figure 6-14, you can see that A, B, C, and D are the 32-bit words that are input, and R and M are intermediate steps in the algorithm. Most of the algorithm consists of bit-shifting (denoted by the >>> and <<< symbols) and XOR'ing. The S represents the S-box (or a portion thereof). Even though it was not chosen in the AES contest, MARS, like the other five finalists, is a secure algorithm that you should feel confident using.

TEA

TEA, or Tiny Encryption Algorithm, was created by David Wheeler and Roger Needham and first publicly presented in 1994. This simple algorithm is easy to implement in code. It is a Feistel cipher that uses 64 rounds (note that this is a suggestion, and it can be implemented with fewer or more rounds). The rounds should be even in number, however, since they are implemented in pairs called *cycles*.

TEA uses a 128-bit key operating on a 64-bit block. It also uses a constant that is defined as 2^{32}/the golden ratio. This constant is referred to as *Delta*, and in each round a multiple of Delta is used.[8] The 128-bit key is split into four 32-bit subkeys labeled K[0], K[1], K[2],

```
// Forward Mixing
(A,B,C,D) = (A,B,C,D) + (K[0],K[1],K[2],K[3])
For i = 0 to 7 do {
        B = (B ⊕ S₀[A]) + S₁[A>>>8]
        C = C + S₀[A>>>16]
        D = D ⊕ S₁[A>>>24]
        A = (A>>>24) + B(if i=1.5) + D(if i=0.4)
        (A,B,C,D) = (B,C,D,A)
}
// Cryptographic Core
For i = 0 to 15 do {
        R = ((A<<<13) × K[2i+5]) <<< 10
        M = (A + K[2i+4]) <<< (low 5 bits of (R>>>5))
        L = (S[M] ⊕ (R>>>5)) ⊕ R) <<< (low 5 bits of R)
        B = B + L(if i<8) ⊕ R(if i≥8)
        C = C + M
        D = D ⊕ R(if i<8) + L(if i≥8)
        (A,B,C,D) = (B,C,D,A<<<13)
}
// Backward Mixing
For i = 0 to 7 do {
        A = A - B(if i=3,7) - D(if i=2,6)
        B = B ⊕ S₁[A]
        C = C - S₀[A<<<8]
        D = (D - S₁[A<<<16]) ⊕ S₀[A<<<24]
        (A,B,C,D) = (B,C,D,A<<<24)
}
(A,B,C,D) = (A,B,C,D) - (K[36],K[37],K[38],K[39])
```

NOTE: $S_0[X]$ and $S_1[X]$ use low 8 bits of X. S[X] uses low 9 bits of X.
S is the concatenation of S_0 and S_1.

FIGURE 6-14   MARS in detail

and K[3]. Rather than use the XOR operation, TEA uses addition and subtraction, but done mod 2^{32}. The block is divided into two halves, R and L, and R is put through the round function.

The round function takes the R half and performs a left shift of 4. The result of that operation is added to K[0] (keep in mind that all addition is being done mod 2^{32}). The result of that operation is added to Delta (recall that Delta is the current multiple of the 2^{32}/the golden ratio). The result of that operation is then shifted right 5 and added to K[1]. That is the round function. As with all Feistel ciphers, the result of the round function is XOR'd with L, and then L and R are swapped for the next round.

Note If you are not familiar with the golden ratio (also called the *golden mean* and *divine proportion*), it is a very interesting number. Two quantities are said to be in the golden ratio if their ratio is the same as the ratio of their sum to the larger of the two quantities. This can be expressed as (a + b)/a = a/b. The ratio is 1.6180339887.... It is an irrational number and appears in many places, including the paintings of Salvador Dali. Mathematicians throughout history including Pythagoras and Euclid have been fascinated by the golden ratio.

TEA is a simple Feistel cipher and is often included in programming courses because writing it in code is relatively simple. You can find numerous examples of TEA in various programming languages, including Java, C, and C++, on the Internet.

LOKI97

LOKI97, another candidate in the AES contest, was developed by Lawrie Brown. There have been other incarnations of the LOKI cipher, namely LOKI89 and LOKI91. The earlier versions used a 64-bit block.

LOKI97 uses 16 rounds (like DES) and a 128-bit block. It operates with key sizes of 128, 192, or 256 bits (as does AES). It has a complex round function, and the key schedule is accomplished via an unbalanced Feistel cipher. The algorithm is freely available.

The key schedule is treated as four 64-bit words: $K4_0$, $K3_0$, $K2_0$, $K1_0$. Depending on the key size used, the four 64-bit words may need to be generated from the key provided. In other words, if there is a cipher key less than 256 bits, then there is not enough material for four 64-bit words, but the missing material for 192- and 128-bit cipher keys is generated. The key schedule itself uses 48 rounds to generate the subkeys.

The round function is probably one of the most complex for a Feistel cipher, certainly more complex than the algorithms we have examined in this chapter. More detail can be found on the Internet in the 1998 paper "Introducing the New LOKI97 Block Cipher," by Lawrie Brown and Josef Pieprzyk.

Camellia

Camellia is a Japanese cipher that uses a block size of 128 bits and key sizes of 128, 192, or 256 bits (like AES). With a 128-bit key, Camellia uses 18 rounds, but with the 192- or 256-bit key it uses 24 rounds—note that both of these rounds are multiples of 6 (18 and 24). Every six rounds, a transformation layer is applied called the "FL function." Camellia uses four S-boxes, and uses key whitening on the input and output.

 Note   Some browsers, such as Chrome, prefer to use Camellia for encryption. They will attempt to negotiate with the server, and if the server can support Camellia, the browser will select it over AES.

ICE

ICE, or Information Concealment Engine, was developed in 1997. It is similar to DES, but it uses a bit permutation during its round function that is key dependent. ICE works with 64-bit blocks using a 64-bit key and 16 rounds. The algorithm is in the public domain and not patented. A faster variant of ICE, called Thin-ICE, uses only 8 rounds.

Simon

Simon is actually a group of block ciphers. What makes it interesting is that it was released by the NSA in 2013. It has many variations—including, for example, a variation that uses 32-bit blocks with a 64-bit key and 32 rounds. However, if you use a 64-bit block, you can choose between 96- and 128-bit keys and either 42 or 44 rounds. The largest block size, 128 bits, can use key sizes of 128, 192, or 256 bits with either 68, 69, or 72 rounds.

Symmetric Methods

Several methods can be used to alter the way a symmetric cipher works. Some of these are meant to increase the security of the cipher.

ECB

The most basic encryption mode is the electronic codebook (ECB) mode, in which the message is divided into blocks, and each block is encrypted separately. The problem, however, is that if you submit the same plain text more than once, you always get the same cipher text. This gives attackers a place to begin analyzing the cipher to attempt to derive the key. Put another way, ECB is simply using the cipher exactly as it is described without any attempts to improve its security.

CBC

When using cipher-block chaining (CBC) mode, each block of plain text is XOR'd with the previous cipher text block before being encrypted. This means there is significantly more randomness in the final cipher text. This is much more secure than ECB mode and is the most common mode. This process is shown in Figure 6-15.

> **Tip**   There really is no good reason to use ECB over CBC, if both ends of communication can support CBC. CBC is a strong deterrent to known plain text attacks and is a cryptanalysis method we will examine in Chapter 17.

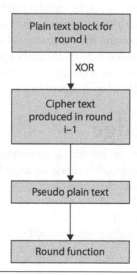

FIGURE 6-15   Cipher-block chaining mode

The only issue with CBC is the first block. There is no preceding block of cipher text with which to XOR the first plain text block. It is common to add an initialization vector to the first block so that it has something to be XOR'd with. The initialization vector (IV) is basically a pseudo-random number, much like the cipher key. Usually an IV is used only once, so it is called a *nonce* (number only used once). The CBC mode is fairly old—it was introduced by IBM in 1976.[9]

PCBC

The propagating cipher-block chaining (PCBC) mode was designed to cause small changes in the cipher text to propagate indefinitely when decrypting and encrypting. This method is sometimes called plain text cipher-block chaining. The PCBC mode is a variation on the CBC mode of operation. It is important to keep in mind that the PCBC mode of encryption has not been formally published as a federal standard.

CFB

In cipher feedback (CFB) mode, the previous cipher text block is encrypted, and then the cipher text produced is XOR'd back with the plain text to produce the current cipher text block. Essentially, it loops back on itself, increasing the randomness of the resultant cipher text. Although CFB is very similar to CBC, its purpose is a bit different. The goal is to take a block cipher and turn it into a stream cipher. Output feedback mode is another method used to transform a block cipher into a synchronous stream cipher. We will examine both of these in more detail in Chapter 7.

Conclusions

In this chapter you have seen the different types of symmetric ciphers and studied Feistel ciphers in detail. It is critical that you fully understand the general Feistel structure and important that you have a strong understanding of DES and Blowfish before proceeding to the next chapter. Other algorithms were presented in this chapter. Although you need not memorize every single algorithm, the more algorithms you are familiar with, the better.

You have also learned some new mathematics in this chapter, such as the pseudo-Hadamard transform. Just as important, you have seen improvements to symmetric ciphers with techniques such as cipher block chaining.

Test Your Knowledge

1. _____ has an 80-bit key and is an unbalanced cipher.
2. _____ is a Feistel cipher using variable length key sizes from 32 bits to 448 bits.
3. The following formulas describe the _____.
   A. $a` \equiv a + b \pmod{2^n}$
   B. $b` \equiv a + 2b \pmod{2^n}$
4. Which of the following is a Russian cipher much like DES?
   A. Blowfish
   B. CAST
   C. FEAL
   D. GOST

5. What is the proper term for the algorithm used to derive subkeys (round keys) from the cipher key?
   A. Key algorithm
   B. Sub key generator
   C. Key schedule
   D. Round key generator
6. Which algorithm described in this chapter was an unbalanced Feistel cipher used with the clipper chip?
7. _____ used input whitening and output whitening as well as a pseudo-Hadamard transform.
8. _____ divides the input into the round function into four 32-bit words labeled A, B, C, and D, and then uses three phases: the 16-round phase that is the core of the algorithm, and pre- and post-phases of forward and backward mixing.
9. With a 128-bit key, Camellia uses _____ rounds, but with the 192- or 256-bit key it uses _____ rounds.
10. With _____, each block of plain text is XOR'd with the previous cipher text block before being encrypted.

Answers

1. Skipjack
2. Blowfish
3. pseudo-Hadamard transform
4. D
5. C
6. Skipjack
7. Twofish
8. MARS
9. 18 and 24
10. cipher-block chaining

Endnotes

1. Lan Luo, Zehui Qu, and Chaoming Song, "Precise Transformation of Feistel to SP Fuse into LFSR," http://image.sciencenet.cn/olddata/kexue.com.cn/upload/blog/file/2010/4/2010421154425312167.pdf.
2. FIPS, Federal Information Processing Standards Publication: Data Encryption Standard (DES), http://csrc.nist.gov/publications/fips/fips46-3/fips46-3.pdf.
3. For more information on Blowfish and the variable-length key, 64-bit block cipher, see "Fast Software Encryption," by Bruce Schneier, at www.schneier.com/paper-blowfish-fse.html.
4. For more information on the equation, see "Blowfish," by Kevin Allison, Keith Feldman, and Ethan Mick at www.cs.rit.edu/~ksf6458/cryptography/Final.pdf.
5. B. Schneier, J. Kelsey, D. Whiting, D. Wagner, C. Hall, and N. Ferguson, "Twofish: A 128-Bit Block Cipher," 1998, www.schneier.com/paper-twofish-paper.pdf.

6. NIST Skipjack and KEA Algorithm Specifications, 1998, http://csrc.nist.gov/groups/ST/toolkit/documents/skipjack/skipjack.pdf.

7. C. Burwick, D. Coppersmith, E. Avignon, R. Gennaro, S. Halevi, C. Jutla, S. Matyas, L. O'Connor, M. Peyravian, D. Safford, and N. Zunic, "The MARS Encryption Algorithm," 1999, http://citeseerx.ist.psu.edu/viewdoc/download?doi=10.1.1.35.5887&rep=rep1&type=pdf.

8. D. Wheeler and R. Needham, "TEA, a Tiny Encryption Algorithm," www.cix.co.uk/~klockstone/tea.pdf.

9. The CBC mode was introduced by IBM in 1976. (US Patent 4074066. W. Ehrsam, C. Meyer, J. Smith, and W. Tuchman, "Message verification and transmission error detection by block chaining," 1976, www.google.com/patents/US4074066.)

7

Substitution-Permutation Networks

In this chapter we will cover the following:

- Advanced Encryption Standard
- Serpent algorithm
- SAFER ciphers
- Stream ciphers

A *substitution-permutation network* (SPM) is a series of operations linked together. The most notable difference between an SPM and a Feistel cipher is that in SPM, the plain text block is not split in half but is operated on as a whole. The block is subjected to alternating rounds or layers of operations, including substitution or permutation boxes (S-boxes or P-boxes), in order to generate the cipher text.

Replacing DES

DES (Data Encryption Standard) is a solid cipher with a robust algorithm, but with a key that was too small. Certainly in the late 1970s and early 1980s it was adequate, but, eventually, as computing power increased, it became clear that a replacement was needed for DES. A contest was undertaken spanning from 1997 to 2000 to find a replacement for DES.

On January 2, 1997, when the National Institute of Standards and Technology (NIST) announced the contest, the search was on to find a replacement for DES. However, it was not until September 12 of that year that NIST announced the general criteria: Contestant algorithms had to be block ciphers that supported a block size of 128 bits as well as key sizes of 128, 192, and 256 bits. For the next several months, 15 different algorithms were submitted from a variety of countries: CAST-256, CRYPTON, DEAL (Data Encryption ALgorithm), DFC (Decorrelated Fast Cipher), E2, FROG (Frequency-Resolved Optical Gating), HPC (Hasty Pudding Cipher), LOKI97, MAGENTA (Multifunctional Algorithm for General-purpose Encryption and Network Telecommunication Applications), MARS (Multivariate Adaptive Regression Splines), RC6, Rijndael, SAFER+, Serpent, and Twofish. Many of these, while not ultimately selected, were solid algorithms. In Chapter 6 we examined MARS and CAST-256.

In this chapter you will learn about a few of the others, though our primary focus will be on AES itself.

The algorithms where subjected to a variety of tests, including common cryptanalysis attacks. The ES1 Candidate Conference was held in August 1998 and the AES2 was in March 1999. In August 1999 the process had narrowed down the candidate list to five algorithms: MARS, RC6, Rijndael, Serpent, and Twofish. These are often referred to in the literature as the AES finalists. All five of these are robust algorithms and are widely used today. Then in October 2000, the NIST announced that the Rijndael cipher had been chosen. In computer security literature, you will see the same algorithm referred to as Rijndael or AES, but cryptography literature usually refers to Rijndael.

Advanced Encryption Standard

The Advanced Encryption Standard (AES), the Rijndael block cipher, was ultimately chosen as a replacement for DES in 2001 after a five-year process. AES is designated as Federal Information Processing Standard (FIPS) 197. The importance of AES cannot be overstated. It is widely used around the world and is perhaps the most widely used symmetric cipher. Of all the algorithms discussed in this chapter, AES is the one you should give the most attention to.

AES can have three different key sizes: 128, 192, or 256 bits. The three different implementations of AES are AES 128, AES 192, and AES 256. The block size can also be 128, 192, or 256 bits. The original Rijndael cipher allowed for variable block and key sizes in 32-bit increments; however, the U.S. government uses these three key sizes with a 128-bit block as the standard for AES.

This algorithm was developed by two Belgian cryptographers, Vincent Rijmen and Joan Daemen. Rijmen helped design the Whirlpool cryptographic hash (which we will study in Chapter 9) and worked on ciphers such as KHAZAD, Square, and SHARK. Daemen has worked extensively on the cryptanalysis of block ciphers, stream ciphers, and cryptographic hash functions.

Rijndael Steps

Rijndael uses a substitution-permutation matrix rather than a Feistel network. The Rijndael cipher works by first putting the 128-bit block of plain text into a 4-by-4–byte matrix. This matrix is termed the *state*, and it will change as the algorithm proceeds through its steps. The first step is to convert the plain text block into binary, and then put it into a matrix, as shown in Figure 7-1.

11011001	01110010	10110000	11101010
01011111	00011001	11011001	10011001
10011100	11011101	00011001	11111101
11011001	10001001	11011001	10001001

FIGURE 7-1 The Rijndael matrix first step

The algorithm consists of a few relatively simple steps that are used during various rounds.

1. **AddRoundKey**   Each byte of the state is combined with the round key using bitwise XOR. This is where Rijndael applies the round key generated from the key schedule.
2. **SubBytes**   In this nonlinear substitution step, each byte is replaced with another according to a lookup table. This is where the contents of the matrix are put through the S-boxes. Each S-box is 8 bits.
3. **ShiftRows**   In this transposition step, each row of the state is shifted cyclically a certain number of steps. The first row is left unchanged. Every byte in the second row is shifted 1 byte to the left (with the far left wrapping around). Every byte of the third row is shifted 2 to the left, and every byte of the fourth row is shifted 3 to the left (again wrapping around). This is shown next. Notice that the bytes are simply labeled by their row and then a letter, such as 1a, 1b, 1c, 1d.

Initial State					After Shift Rows			
1a	1b	1c	1d		1a	1b	1c	1d
2a	2b	2c	2d		2b	2c	2d	2a
3a	3b	3c	3d		3c	3d	3a	3b
4a	4b	4c	4d		4d	4a	4b	4c

4. **MixColumns**   A mixing operation operates on the columns of the state, combining the 4 bytes in each column. Each column of the state is multiplied with a fixed polynomial. Each column (remember the matrix we are working with) is treated as a polynomial within the Galois field (2^8). The result is multiplied with a fixed polynomial $c(x) = 3x^3 + x^2 + x + 2$ modulo $x^4 + 1$. This step can also be viewed as a multiplication by the particular matrix in the finite field $GF(2^8)$. This is often shown as matrix multiplication, as shown next. In other words, you take the 4 bytes and multiply them by the matrix, yielding a new set of 4 bytes:

$$\begin{bmatrix} 2 & 3 & 1 & 1 \\ 1 & 2 & 3 & 1 \\ 1 & 1 & 2 & 3 \\ 3 & 1 & 1 & 2 \end{bmatrix} \begin{bmatrix} a_0 \\ a_1 \\ a_2 \\ a_3 \end{bmatrix} = \begin{bmatrix} b_0 \\ b_1 \\ b_2 \\ b_3 \end{bmatrix}$$

Rijndael Outline

With the aforementioned steps in mind, the following information shows how those steps are executed in the Rijndael cipher. For 128-bit keys, there are 10 rounds; for 192-bit keys, there are 12 rounds; and for 256-bit keys, there are 14 rounds.

Key Expansion   The round keys are derived from the cipher key using the Rijndael key schedule, which is described in more detail later in this chapter.

Initial Round   The initial round executes the AddRoundKey step—simply XOR'ing with the round key. This initial round is executed once, and then the subsequent rounds are executed.

In the AddRoundKey step, the subkey is XOR'd with the state. For each round that follows, a subkey is derived from the main key using the Rijndael key schedule; each subkey is the same size as the state.

Rounds   This phase of the algorithm executes several steps in the following order:

1. SubBytes
2. ShiftRows
3. MixColumns
4. AddRoundKey

Final Round   This round includes everything the rounds phase includes, except no MixColumns:

1. SubBytes
2. ShiftRows
3. AddRoundKey

Rijndael S-Box

The S-box of Rijndael is fascinating to study. (We will look more deeply into S-boxes in Chapter 8. However, a brief description is warranted here.) The S-box is generated by determining the multiplicative inverse for a given number in $GF(2^8) = GF(2)[x]/(x^8 + x^4 + x^3 + x + 1)$, Rijndael's finite field (zero, which has no inverse, is set to zero). In other words, the S-boxes are based on a mathematical formula. In fact, there are variations of the standard Rijndael S-box. It will still operate as any other S-box, taking in bits as input and substituting them for some other bits. You can see the standard Rijndael S-box in Figure 7-2.

Rijndael Key Schedule

As with other ciphers we have examined, Rijndael uses a key schedule to generate round keys from the original cipher key. The key schedule uses three operations that are combined to create the key schedule:

- **Rotate**   The first operation is simply to take a 32-bit word (in hexadecimal) and to rotate it 8 bits (1 byte) to the left.
- **Rcon**   This is the term that the Rijndael documentation uses for the exponentiation of 2 to a user-specified value. However, this operation is not performed with regular integers, but in Rijndael's finite field. In polynomial form, 2 is $2 = 00000010 = 0\,x^\wedge7 + 0\,x^\wedge6 + 0\,x^\wedge5 + 0\,x^\wedge4 + 0\,x^\wedge3 + 0\,x^\wedge2 + 1\,x + 0$.
- **Inner loop**   The key schedule has an inner loop that consists of the following steps:

  1. The input is a 32-bit word and at an iteration number i. The output is a 32-bit word.
  2. Copy the input over to the output.
  3. Use the previously described rotate operation to rotate the output 8 bits to the left.
  4. Apply Rijndael's S-box on all 4 individual bytes in the output word.

	0	1	2	3	4	5	6	7	8	9	a	b	c	d	e	f
00	63	7c	77	7b	f2	6b	6f	c5	30	01	67	2b	fe	d7	ab	76
10	ca	82	c9	7d	fa	59	47	f0	ad	d4	a2	af	9c	a4	72	c0
20	b7	fd	93	26	36	3f	f7	cc	34	a5	e5	f1	71	d8	31	15
30	04	c7	23	c3	18	96	05	9a	07	12	80	e2	eb	27	b2	75
40	09	83	2c	1a	1b	6e	5a	a0	52	3b	d6	b3	29	e3	2f	84
50	53	d1	00	ed	20	fc	b1	5b	6a	cb	be	39	4a	4c	58	cf
60	d0	ef	aa	fb	43	4d	33	85	45	f9	02	7f	50	3c	9f	a8
70	51	a3	40	8f	92	9d	38	f5	bc	b6	da	21	10	ff	f3	d2
80	cd	0c	13	ec	5f	97	44	17	c4	a7	7e	3d	64	5d	19	73
90	60	81	4f	dc	22	2a	90	88	46	ee	b8	14	de	5e	0b	db
a0	e0	32	3a	0a	49	06	24	5c	c2	d3	ac	62	91	95	e4	79
b0	e7	c8	37	6d	8d	d5	4e	a9	6c	56	f4	ea	65	7a	ae	08
c0	ba	78	25	2e	1c	a6	b4	c6	e8	dd	74	1f	4b	bd	8b	8a
d0	70	3e	b5	66	48	03	f6	0e	61	35	57	b9	86	c1	1d	9e
e0	e1	f8	98	11	69	d9	8e	94	9b	1e	87	e9	ce	55	28	df
f0	8c	a1	89	0d	bf	e6	42	68	41	99	2d	0f	b0	54	bb	16

FIGURE 7-2   **Rijndael S-box**

5. On only the first (leftmost) byte of the output word, XOR the byte with 2 to the power of (i-1). In other words, perform the rcon operation with i as the input, and exclusive or the rcon output with the first byte of the output word.

The key schedule for Rijndael is one of the more complex key schedules found in symmetric ciphers. Because the key schedules for 128-bit, 192-bit, and 256-bit encryption are very similar, with only some constants changed, the following key size constants are defined here:

- n has a value of 16 for 128-bit keys, 24 for 192-bit keys, and 32 for 256-bit keys.
- b has a value of 176 for 128-bit keys, 208 for 192-bit keys, and 240 for 256-bit keys (with 128-bit blocks as in AES, it is correspondingly larger for variants of Rijndael with larger block sizes).

Once you have the appropriate constants, the steps of the Rijndael key schedule can be executed:

1. The first n bytes of the expanded key are the encryption key.
2. Set the rcon iteration value i to 1.
3. When the desired b bytes of expanded key are reached, do the following to generate n more bytes of expanded key:
4. Do the following to create 4 bytes of expanded key:
   A. Create a 4-byte temporary variable, t.
   B. Assign the value of the previous 4 bytes in the expanded key to t.
   C. Perform the key schedule core (see above) on t, with i as the rcon iteration value.
   D. Increment i by 1.
   E. XOR t with the 4-byte block n bytes before the new expanded key. This becomes the next 4 bytes in the expanded key.

5. Then do the following three times to create the next 12 bytes of expanded key:
    A. Assign the value of the previous 4 bytes in the expanded key to t.
    B. XOR t with the 4-byte block n bytes before the new expanded key. This becomes the next 4 bytes in the expanded key.
6. If you are processing a 256-bit key, do the following to generate the next 4 bytes of expanded key:
    A. Assign the value of the previous 4 bytes in the expanded key to t.
    B. Run each of the 4 bytes in t through Rijndael's S-box.
    C. XOR t with the 4-byte block n bytes before the new expanded key. This becomes the next 4 bytes in the expanded key.
7. If you are processing a 128-bit key, do not perform the following steps. If you are processing a 192-bit key, run the following steps twice. If you are processing a 256-bit key, run the following steps three times:
    A. Assign the value of the previous 4 bytes in the expanded key to t.
    B. XOR t with the 4-byte block n bytes before the new expanded key. This becomes the next 4 bytes in the expanded key.

Serpent Algorithm

The Serpent algorithm, invented by Ross Anderson, Eli Biham, and Lars Knudsen, was submitted to the AES competition but was not selected because its performance is slower than AES. However, in the ensuing years since the AES competition, computational power has increased dramatically, which has led some experts to reconsider the use of Serpent on modern systems.

Anderson worked with Biham on the Tiger cryptographic hash and other algorithms. He also designed the PIKE stream cipher. Biham is an Israeli cryptographer who is well known for his extensive contributions to cryptography, including inventing the topic of differential cryptanalysis with Adi Shamir (we will study differential cryptanalysis in Chapter 17).

 Note Throughout this book, you will read brief biographies of people who have made significant contributions to cryptography. I recommend you take a bit more time, when you can spare it, to delve more deeply into the biographies of the people mentioned. They can provide significant insights into the field of cryptography.

Serpent has a block size of 128 bits and can have a key size of 128, 192, or 256 bits, much like AES. The algorithm is also a substitution-permutation network like AES. It uses 32 rounds working with a block of four 32-bit words. Each round applies one of eight 4-bit-to-4-bit S-boxes 32 times in parallel. Serpent was designed so that all operations can be executed in parallel.[1]

Serpent S-Boxes and Key Schedule

The inventors of DES stated in the original proposal that they had initially considered using the S-boxes from DES, because those S-boxes had been thoroughly studied. However, they abandoned that idea in favor of using S-boxes optimized for more modern processors.

There are 33 subkeys or round keys, each 128 bits in size. The key length could have been variable, but for the purposes of the AES competition, the key sizes were fixed at 128, 192, and 256 bits.

The Serpent Algorithm

The Serpent cipher begins with an initial permutation (IP), much as DES does. It then has 32 rounds, each consisting of a key-mixing operation (simply XOR'ing the round key with the text), S-boxes, and a linear transformation (except for the last round). In the final round, the linear transformation is replaced with a key-mixing step. Then there is a final permutation (FP). The IP and FP do not have any cryptographic significance; instead, they simply optimize the cipher.

The cipher uses one S-box per round, so during R_0, the S_0 S-box is used, and then during R_1, the S_1 S-box is used. Because there are only eight S-boxes, each is used four times, so that R_{16} reuses S_0.

It should be obvious that Serpent and Rijndael have some similarities. The following table shows a comparison of the two algorithms.

	Serpent	Rijndael
Rounds	32	10, 12, 14
Key size	128, 192, 256	128, 192, 256
Round function operations	XOR, S-boxes, and a linear transformation	S-boxes, row shifting, column mixing, and XOR
S-box	eight S-boxes, each 4-by-4	One 8-by-8 S-box
Speed	Slower	Faster

Clearly, Serpent has more rounds than Rijndael, but the round functions of the two algorithms are different enough that simply having more rounds does not automatically mean Serpent is more secure.

Square

The Square cipher was the forerunner to the Rijndael cipher. It was invented by Joan Daemen, Vincent Rijmen, and Lars Knudsen and first published in 1997.[2] It uses a 128 block size with a 128-bit key working in eight rounds. Given the success of AES, the Square cipher has largely become a footnote in the history of cryptography.

You have already become acquainted with Rijmen and Daemen earlier in this book. Lars Knudsen is a well-known Danish cryptographer who has done extensive work with analyzing block ciphers, cryptographic hash functions, and message authentication codes. He received his doctorate from Aarhus University in 1994.

SHARK

SHARK was invented by a team of cryptographers including Rijmen, Daemen, Bart Preneel, Antoon Bosselaers, and Erik De Win.[3] SHARK uses a 64-bit block with a 128-bit key and operates in six rounds (the original SHARK used six rounds). It has some similarities to the

Rijndael cipher, including the use of S-boxes that are based on GF(2^8). (Remember that GF is a Galois field defined by a particular prime number raised to some power.) Like Rijndael (and unlike DES) the S-boxes take a fixed number of bits and put out the same number of bits. (Recall that DES S-boxes took in 6 bits and produced 4 bits.)

The original paper for SHARK described two different ways to create a key schedule algorithm (recall that the key schedule creates round keys from the cipher key). The first method took n bits of the round input that were XOR'd with n bits of the cipher key. The result was the round key. The second method used an affine transformation.

> **Note**   An affine transformation is a function between affine spaces that preserves points, straight lines, and planes. This is often applied to geometry but works well with matrix mathematics. For more details on affine transformations, the textbook chapter "Matrix Algebra and Affine Transformations" from Clemson University is a good resource: http://people.cs.clemson.edu/~dhouse/courses/401/notes/affines-matrices.pdf.

The specific affine transformation used in SHARK is as follows: Let K_i be a key-dependent invertible (n × n) matrix over GF(2^m). The operation on that matrix is shown here:

$$Y = k_i \cdot X \oplus K_i$$

The SHARK affine transformation

The general flow of the SHARK algorithm is shown in Figure 7-3, which is a figure from the original SHARK paper.

SAFER Ciphers

SAFER (Secure And Fast Encryption Routine) is actually a family of ciphers invented by a team that included James Massey (one of the creators of IDEA, a well-known block cipher). The older versions include SAFER K and SAFER SK, and the newer versions are SAFER+ and SAFER++. The first SAFER cipher was published in 1993 and used a key size of 64 bits. It was eponymously named SAFER K-64. There was also a 128-bit version named SAFER K-128.

Cryptanalysis uncovered weaknesses in the original design, specifically in the key schedule. Thus an improved key schedule was designed and the variants were named SAFER SK-64 and SAFER SK-128. (The SK stands for Safer Key schedule.)

SAFER+ was an improvement published in 1998 and submitted to the AES competition. Some Bluetooth implementations used SAFER+ for generating keys and as a message authentication code, but not for encrypting traffic.

The key size used with SAFER obviously depends on the particular variant of SAFER in use. The number of rounds can range from 6 to 10, with more rounds being used with larger key sizes. However, all the various SAFER variations use the same round function. They differ in key size, key schedule, and total number of rounds.

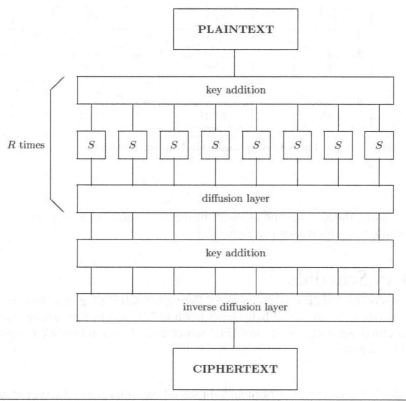

FIGURE 7-3   The SHARK cipher from the original paper

The Round Function

The 64-bit block of plain text is converted into eight blocks, each with 8 bits. Each round consists of an XOR with the round key, the output of which is submitted to the S-boxes, and the output of that is subjected to another XOR with a different round key. This is shown in Figure 7-4.

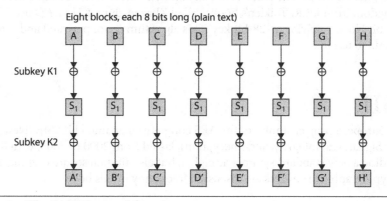

FIGURE 7-4   The SAFER round function

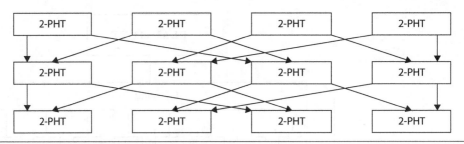

FIGURE 7-5   The SAFER pseudo-Hadamard transforms

After the XOR'ing and S-boxes, the text is subjected to three pseudo-Hadamard transforms. This is shown in Figure 7-5.

Key Schedule

Each of the SAFER variations has a different key scheduling algorithm. For example, SAFER+ expands a 16-, 24-, or 32-byte cipher key into 272, 400, or 528 subkey bytes (these are bytes, not bits). An overview of the SAFER structure is shown in Figure 7-6, from the original SAFER paper.

 Note   You can find the original SAFER K-64 paper by James Massey at http://citeseerx .ist.psu.edu/viewdoc/download?doi=10.1.1.3.4781&rep=rep1&type=pdf.

KHAZAD

The KHAZAD algorithm was designed by Rijmen (one of the creators of the Rijndael cipher) and Paulo Barreto. The name is not an acronym but is derived from a fictional Dwarven kingdom from J.R.R. Tolkien's books called Khazad-dûm. KHAZAD uses eight rounds on a 64-bit block, applying a 128-bit key. This algorithm is not patented and is free to anyone who wants to use it.

NESSIE

In Europe, a project similar to the AES competition, named NESSIE (New European Schemes for Signatures, Integrity, and Encryption), lasted from 2000 to 2003, with the goal of not only finding a new standard symmetric cipher, but also finding secure cryptographic primitives. Cryptographic primitives are discussed frequently in this book.

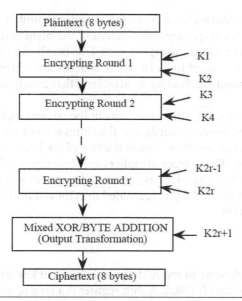

FIGURE 7-6 Overview of the SAFER function from the original paper

---

Note Cryptographic primitives are basic cryptographic algorithms used to build cryptographic protocols. Cryptographic hashes, symmetric algorithms, and asymmetric algorithms all qualify as cryptographic primitives. These primitives are combined to create cryptographic protocols such as Secure Sockets Layer (SSL) and Transport Layer Security (TLS), which you will study in Chapter 13.

Several algorithms of various types were selected in the competition, including the block ciphers MISTY1, Camellia, SHACAL-2, and AES/Rijndael. RSA was also one of the three asymmetric algorithms selected. For cryptographic hashes and message authentication codes, HMAC and SHA were chosen as well as Whirlpool.

Stream Ciphers

A stream cipher is a special type of symmetric cipher. Both Feistel ciphers and SPMs break the plain text into blocks and then encrypt each block. Stream ciphers take each bit of plain text and encrypt it with the key stream to produce the cipher text stream. The combination is usually done via XOR operations.

There are two types of stream ciphers: synchronous and self-synchronizing. In a synchronous stream cipher (sometimes called a binary additive stream cipher), the key is a stream of bits produced by some pseudo-random number generator. The production of this key stream is completely independent of the plain text. The key stream is XOR'd with the plain text to produce the cipher text. This is called a *synchronous cipher* because the sender and receiver need to be in synch. If digits are added or removed from the message during transmission (such as by an attacker), that synchronization is lost and needs to be restored.

Self-synchronizing ciphers use parts of the current cipher text to compute the rest of the key stream. In other words, the algorithm starts with an initial key stream, like an initialization vector, and then creates the rest of the key stream based on the cipher text already produced. These types of ciphers are sometimes called cipher text autokeys. The idea was patented in 1946, long before the advent of modern computer systems. With self-synchronizing ciphers, if digits are added or removed in transit, the receiving end can still continue to decrypt.

LFSR

There are multiple ways to create the pseudo-random key stream. One of these is to use *linear feedback shift registers* (LFSRs). A shift register is a type of register found in digital circuits—basically a chain of flip-flops that shifts the data stored in it by 1 bit, thus the name. LFSRs are chosen because they are easy to implement in hardware. An LFSR uses its previous state to form the input for the current state.

Usually a linear function is used to modify the data in each round, and most often an XOR is used. The LFSR is given an initial value, or seed. Then the register will shift that value and then XOR it with the previous value. Consider this rather simplified example:

Input: `0101110`

First, it is shifted by the LFSR:

`0010111`

Then that value is XOR'd with the previous state:

`0101110 XOR 0010111= 0111001`

This can be repeated with yet another shift and another XOR operation. You will see LSFRs used later in the book when we discuss pseudo-random number generators.

RC4

RC4, designed by Ron Rivest, is a widely known and used stream cipher, perhaps the most widely known. The RC stands for Ron's cipher or Rivest cipher. Ron Rivest is a name that is very familiar in cryptography. He is the *R* in *RSA*, which we will explore in Chapter 10. RC4 is widely used in many security situations, including WEP (Wired Equivalent Privacy) and TLS. However, the algorithm was designed in 1987, and some experts have expressed concerns about its security. Some speculate that it can be broken, and many people recommend no longer using it in TLS. Nevertheless, it is the most widely known of stream ciphers and has a similar place in the history and study of stream ciphers as DES has in block ciphers.

RC4 Key Scheduling

The key scheduling algorithm is rather simple. It begins with an internal state that is denoted by a capital *S*. This state is a 256-*byte* array. (Although most of what you have seen so far involves bits, not bytes, this is not a typo.) There are two indexes, usually named i and j. These indexes are used to point to individual elements in the array. The key scheduling algorithm involves shuffling this array.

The first step in this algorithm involves initializing the state with what is termed the *identity permutation*. This means that the first element is initialized to 0, the second element to 1, the third to 0, and so on. Now, obviously, this is not very random at all, and in fact it is the antithesis of randomness. So the next step consists of shuffling, which involves iterating 256 times, performing the following actions:

1. Compute j = j + S[i] + key[i mod keylength].
2. Swap S[i] and S[j].
3. Increment i.

After 256 iterations of this, the array should be shuffled well. If you happen to have some programming experience, the following pseudo-code may assist you in understanding the shuffling:

```
for i from 0 to 255
    S[i] := i
end for loop
    j := 0
for i from 0 to 255
    j := (j + S[i] + key[i mod keylength]) mod 256
swap values of S[i] and S[j]
end for loop
```

You may argue that this is too predictable, because it would generate the same key each time. And if the algorithm stopped here, you would be correct. This is generating a state that will be used to create the key stream. But we are not done yet.

The rest of the algorithm allows for the generation of a key stream of any size. The goal is to create a key stream of the same size as the message you want to encrypt.

The first step is to initialize the two pointers i and j, and then generate the key stream 1 byte at a time. For each new byte, the algorithm takes the following steps:

1. Compute new value of i and j:

   i := (i + 1) % 256

   j := (j + S[i]) % 256

2. Swap S[i] and S[j].
3. Retrieve the next byte of the key stream from the S array at the index:

   S[i]+S[j]% 256

Again, if you have some background in programming, you may find it easier to understand this using pseudo code:

```
i = 0
j = 0
While generating the output:
    i := (i + 1) mod 256
    j := (j + S[i]) mod 256
Swap values of S[i] and S[j]:
    K := S[(S[i] + S[j]) mod 256]
output K
end while loop
```

Once you have generated the key stream, you XOR it with the plain text to encrypt, or XOR it with the cipher text to decrypt. One of the security issues with RC4 is that it does not use a *nonce* (a number only used once) along with the key. This means that if a key is being used repeatedly, it can be compromised. More modern stream ciphers, such as eSTREAM, specify the use of a nonce.

In 1994, Rivest published RC5 and then later, working with Matt Robshaw, Ray Sidney, and Yiqun Yin, he released RC6. However, both RC5 and RC6 are block ciphers, not stream ciphers. In fact, RC6 was designed for the AES competition.

FISH

The FISH (FIbonacci SHrinking) algorithm was published by the German engineering firm Siemens in 1993. It is a software-based stream cipher using a *Lagged Fibonacci generator* along with a concept borrowed from the shrinking generator ciphers.

A Lagged Fibonacci generator (LFG) is a particular type of pseudo-random-number generator. It is based on the Fibonacci sequence. Recall that the Fibonacci sequence is essentially this:

$$F_n = F_{n-1} + F_{n-2}$$

This can be generalized to

$$X_n = X_{n-l} + X_{n-k} \pmod m \text{ where } 0 < k < l$$

For most cryptographic applications, the m is some power of 2. Lagged Fibonacci generators have a maximum period of $(2^k - 1)*2^{m-1}$. This brings us to the topic of the period of a pseudo-random-number generator (PRNG). With any PRNG, if you start with the same seed you will get the same sequence. The period of a PRNG is the maximum of the length of the repetition-free sequence.

Note   Ross Anderson's paper "On Fibonacci Keystream Generators" (http://www.cl.cam .ac.uk/~rja14/Papers/fibonacci.pdf) provides a very good discussion of Fibonacci-based key generation.

PIKE

The PIKE algorithm was published in a paper by Ross Anderson as an improvement on FISH. In that paper, Anderson showed that FISH was vulnerable to known plain-text attacks. PIKE is both faster and stronger than FISH. The name PIKE is not an acronym, but a humorous play on FISH, a pike being a type of fish.

eSTREAM

The eSTREAM project was a European search for new stream ciphers that ran from 2004 until 2008. It began with a list of forty ciphers and used three phases to narrow that list to seven ciphers. Four were meant for software implementations (HC-128, Rabbit, Salsa20/12, and SOSEMANUK) and three (Grain v1, MICKEY v2, and Trivium) for hardware. Brief descriptions of some of these ciphers are provided here:

SNOW

SNOW 1.0 was submitted to the NESSIE project and has since been supplanted by SNOW 2.0 and SNOW 3G. The SNOW cipher works on 32-bit words and can use either a 128-or 256-bit key. The cipher uses an LFSR along with a Finite State Machine (FSM).

Rabbit

Rabbit was designed by Martin Boesgaard, Mette Vesterager, Thomas Pederson, Jesper Christiansen, and Ove Scavenius. It is a stream cipher that uses a 128-bit key along with a 64-bit initialization vector. The cipher uses an internal state that is 513 bits. That consists of eight variables, each 32 bits in size; eight counters that are also 32 bits in size; and 1 counter bit. The variables are denoted as $x_{j,i}$, meaning the state of the variable of subsystem j at iteration i. The counter variables are denoted by $c_{j,i}$.

> **Note** The entire algorithm is described in the original paper, "The Stream Cipher Rabbit," which can be found online at http://cr.yp.to/streamciphers/rabbit/desc.pdf.[4]

HC-128

HC-128 was invented by Hongjun Wu. It uses a 128-bit key with a 128-bit initialization vector. HC-128 consists of two secret tables, each with 512, 32-bit elements. At each step, one element of a table is updated with a nonlinear feedback function. All the elements of the two tables will get updated every 1024 steps. At each step, one 32-bit output is generated from the nonlinear output filtering function.

> **Note** The algorithm is described in detail in the paper, "The Stream Cipher HC-128," at www.ecrypt.eu.org/stream/p3ciphers/hc/hc128_p3.pdf. In 2004, Wu published HC-256, which uses a 256-bit key and a 256-bit initialization vector.

MICKEY

MICKEY (Mutual Irregular Clocking KEYstream) generator was invented by Steve Babbage and Mathew Dodd. It uses an 80-bit key and a variable-length initialization vector (up to 80 bits in length).

MISTY1

MISTY1 (Mitsubishi Improved Security Technology) was invented by Matsue Mitsuru, Ichikawa Tetsuya, Sorimachi Toru, Tokita Toshio, and Yamagishi Atsurhio (note that the initials of the inventors' first names also spell MISTY). It is a patented algorithm but can be used for free for academic purposes. MISTY1 is a Feistel network that uses 64-bit blocks and a key size of 128 bits. Its round function is a three-round Feistel network, so it is essentially a Feistel within a Feistel.

A5

A5/1 is a stream cipher that was used in GSM (Global System for Mobile Communications, also known as 2g) cell phones. It was originally a secret but eventually was made public. A variation, A5/2, was developed specifically to be weaker for export purposes.

 U.S. law prevents exporting cryptographic tools greater than a certain strength.

The KASUMI algorithm is used in A5/3, and it is also used in UMTS (Universal Mobile Telecommunications System, also known as 3G). In January 2010, Orr Dunkelman, Nathan Keller, and Adi Shamir released a paper showing that they could break KASUMI with a related key attack—the attack, however, was not effective against MISTY1.

 You can read their paper, "A Practical-Time Attack on the A5/3 Cryptosystem Used in Third Generation GSM Telephony," at https://eprint.iacr.org/2010/013.pdf.

One-Time Pad

If used properly, the one-time pad is the only truly uncrackable encryption technique. It should be clear that this is true only if used properly. This idea was first described in 1882, but it was later rediscovered and patented in the early 20th century. In this technique, a random key is used that is as long as the actual message. If the key is sufficiently random, there will be no periods in the key, and periods in keys are used as part of cryptanalysis. The second aspect of this technique is actually in the name: the key is used for a single message and then discarded and never used again. Should the encryption somehow be broken and the key discovered (and this has never been done), it would cause minimal damage because that key will never be used again.

The patented version of this was invented in 1917 by Gilbert Vernam working at AT&T. It was patented in 1919 (U.S. Patent 1,310,719) and was called a Vernam cipher. It worked with teleprinter technology (the state of the art at that time). It combined each character of the message with a character on a paper tape key.

One-time pads are often described as being "information-theoretically secure." This is because the cipher text provides no information about the original plain text. Claude Shannon, the father of information theory, said that the one-time pad provided "perfect secrecy."

It should be obvious, however, that there are logistical issues with the one-time pad, since each message needs a new key. As you will see in Chapter 12, generating random numbers can be computationally intensive, with the issue of key exchange. Imagine for a moment that secure web site traffic was conducted with a one-time pad. That would require that a key be generated and exchanged for each and every packet sent between the web browser and the server. The overhead would make communication impractical. For this reason, one-time pads are used only in highly sensitive communications wherein the need for security makes the cumbersome nature of key generation and exchange worth the effort.

Conclusions

In this chapter you have learned about substitution-permutation networks as well as stream ciphers. The most important algorithm to know well is AES/Rijndael. The other algorithms are interesting, but the focus was on AES because it is widely used around the world, and within the United States it is a national standard.

Pseudo-random-number generators were also discussed, in relation to creating stream ciphers. PRNGs will be covered in much more detail in Chapter 12.

Test Your Knowledge

1. AES using a 192-bit key uses _____ rounds.
2. What happens in the rotate phase of the Rijndael key schedule?
3. _____ is a 32-round substitution-permutation matrix algorithm using key sizes of 128, 192, or 256 bits.
4. The _____ algorithm is a stream cipher developed by Siemens that uses the Lagged Fibonacci generator for random numbers.
5. What are the two types of stream ciphers?
6. _____ uses a 64-bit block with a 128-bit key and operates in six rounds.
7. In _____, there are 33 subkeys or round keys, each 128 bits in size.
8. The _____ key scheduling algorithm begins with a 256-byte array called the *state*.
9. Briefly describe the Rijndael shift rows step.
10. Which of the following steps does not occur in the final round of Rijndael?
    A. SubBytes
    B. ShiftRows
    C. MixColumns
    D. AddRoundKey

Answers

1. 12
2. The rotate operation rotates a 32-bit word (in hexadecimal) 8 bits to the left.
3. Serpent
4. FISH
5. synchronous and self-synchronizing
6. SHARK
7. Serpent
8. RC4
9. Each row of the state is shifted cyclically a certain number of steps. The first row is unchanged, the second row shifted 1 byte to the left, the third row 2 bytes to the left, and the fourth row 3 bytes to the left.
10. C

Endnotes

1. For more information, see "Serpent: A Proposal for the Advanced Encryption Standard," by Anderson, Biham, and Knudsen, at www.cl.cam.ac.uk/~rja14/Papers/serpent.pdf.
2. For more information, see the article "The Block Cipher SQUARE," at http://citeseerx .ist.psu.edu/viewdoc/summary?doi=10.1.1.55.6109.
3. See "The Cipher Shark," at www.cosic.esat.kuleuven.be/publications/article-55.pdf.
4. M. Boesgaard, M. Vesterager, T. Christensen, and Erik Zenner, "The Stream Cipher Rabbit," http://cr.yp.to/streamciphers/rabbit/desc.pdf.

8 S-Box Design

In this chapter we will cover the following:

- The purpose of studying S-boxes
- Types of S-boxes
- Design criteria for S-boxes
- The DES S-box
- The AES S-box
- AES S-box variations

You'll recall that a substitution box (S-box) is an integral part of many ciphers. In fact, it is often the key to the overall security of a given cipher. From the Data Encryption Standard (DES) to more modern ciphers, S-boxes have provided a means of altering the cipher text, and even transposing text, that goes far beyond simple XOR operations. An S-box is a lookup table in which m number of input bits are replaced with n number of output bits.

In his paper "A New Method for Generating High Non-linearity S-Boxes," Petr Tesař states, "All modern block and stream ciphers have one or more non-linear elements. S-box is one of the most used non-linear cornerstones of modern ciphers."[1]

Nonlinearity is an important concept in cryptography. The goal of any cipher is to have the output look as much like a random number as possible, and still be something we can decrypt later to get back the original plain text. Unfortunately, operations such as XOR are linear. S-boxes provide a very good source of nonlinearity in any block cipher.

Why Study S-Box Design?

Many cryptography textbooks provide scant, if any, coverage of S-box design. Usually the S-boxes used in DES or AES are explained in varying levels of detail, but that is the extent of the coverage. And many texts don't go into any real depth on AES S-box design. So why devote an entire chapter to the study of S-boxes? Why not follow the de facto standard in cryptography texts and simply gloss over this topic? Put another way, why should you devote time to studying this topic? There are actually three primary reasons you should study S-box design. Each is explained in detail in the following sections.

Critical to Block Ciphers

You are already aware that S-boxes form a major part of most block ciphers and that they are the primary source for nonlinearity in modern block ciphers. It would be impossible to study symmetric cryptography thoroughly without knowing a bit about S-boxes. If you do not understand S-boxes, you will be forced to treat a portion of most block ciphers as simply a "black box," having no real understanding of what happens inside or why. This fact should be readily apparent from the algorithms you studied in Chapters 6 and 7.

Consider the Feistel ciphers you studied in Chapter 6. The XOR operation forms a part of every Feistel cipher. In most round functions, there is an XOR with the round key, and of course there is a transposition of the two halves of the block each round. But the real substance of encrypting comes from the S-box. Without it, Feistel ciphers would be extremely weak and would not be acceptable for modern use. In fact, without the S-boxes, many block ciphers would not be much better than combining a substitution cipher such as Caesar with a transposition cipher such as rail-fence, and executing it several times.

Designing Ciphers

Should you ever be involved in the design of a symmetric cipher, you will need to design S-boxes. These are often key to the security of a symmetric cipher. It will be important that you understand the principles of S-box design.

Note	Usually designing your own cipher is a bad idea. It is most likely that in attempting such a task, you will create a cipher that is, at best, weak. However, someone must create the new ciphers that appear from time to time, so clearly some people do create new ciphers that are secure. My recommendation is that you carefully study cryptography for several years, looking at existing ciphers in detail. Before considering developing your own cipher, you must thoroughly understand a wide range of existing ciphers. Consider the inventors of the algorithms you have read about in Chapters 6 and 7. All had extensive related education, such as in mathematics, and all have worked in the field of cryptography for many years. This is not a field in which a novice is likely to make a substantive contribution. Becoming a cryptographer is a lengthy process. This book may be the first step on that journey. Then, if after careful and in-depth study, you are compelled to create a new cipher, submit it to the peer review process so that experts in the field can evaluate your idea.

It is difficult to overemphasize the importance of the S-box in designing a block cipher. Anna Grocholewska-Czurylo, in her paper "Cryptographic Properties of Modified AES-Like S-Boxes," describes the importance of S-boxes as follows:

> S-box design is usually the most important task while designing a new cipher. This is because an S-box is the only nonlinear element of the cipher upon which the whole cryptographic strength of the cipher depends. New methods of attacks are constantly being developed by researchers, so S-box design should always be one step ahead of those pursuits to ensure cipher's security.[2]

Altering S-Boxes

Finally, there are some organizations, primarily governments, who want the security of well-known algorithms such as Advanced Encryption Standard (AES), but also want an implementation that is private to their organization. One reason this may be desirable in some situations is that it provides an extra layer of security. Should an outside party obtain the symmetric key being used, but apply it to intercepted cipher text using the standard Rijndael cipher, the message will not be decrypted. The interest in this topic has increased as awareness of cryptographic backdoors has increased, particularly when such backdoors are used in random-number generators that generate keys for algorithms such as AES. We will study cryptographic backdoors in detail in Chapter 18.

In 2013, then CIA employee Edward Snowden released classified documents that indicated that the U.S. National Security Agency (NSA) had placed backdoors in some random-number generators. This prompted some concern as to the dependability of widely used random-number generators. Some governments considered simply redesigning the S-boxes of AES so that their specific AES implementation was not standard, so that even if the key were generated from a backdoor, an attacker would still have to know the specifics of the organization's AES implementation to compromise their security.

General Facts about S-Boxes

The core of most block ciphers (including Blowfish, AES, DES, Serpent, GOST, and so on) is the S-box. An S-box provides the source of nonlinearity for a given cryptographic algorithm. Other facets of the algorithm are typically just various swapping mechanisms and exclusive or (XOR) operations. The XOR, in particular, provides no diffusion or confusion in the resulting cipher text. (Recall that these concepts were discussed in Chapter 3.) In fact, the basis of differential cryptanalysis is the fact that the XOR operation maintains the characteristics found in the plain text to cipher text. We will closely examine differential cryptanalysis in Chapter 17.

According to Grocholewska-Czurylo,[3] "S-box design is usually the most important task while designing a new cipher. This is because an S-box is the only nonlinear element of the cipher upon which the whole cryptographic strength of the cipher depends." Although other aspects of a given S-box clearly have an impact on the security and efficiency of a given block cipher, the S-box is the core of the security. For this reason, proper S-box design is imperative.

Types of S-Boxes

S-boxes can be grouped into two types: substitution boxes and permutation boxes. A *substitution* box substitutes input bits for output bits. A *permutation* box (sometimes called a P-box) transposes the bits. It is often the case that cryptologists use "S-box" to refer to either type.

Let's first consider a simple 3-bit S-box that performs substitution. Each 3 bits of input are mapped to the 3 bits of output. This S-box is shown in Figure 8-1. The first bit of input is on the left, the second 2 bits are on the top. By matching those you will identify the output bits.

	00	11	10	01
1	101	011	100	111
0	010	000	001	110

FIGURE 8-1   A 3-bit S-box

For example, with this S-box, an input of 110 would produce an output of 100. An input of 100 would produce an output of 101. This S-box is very simple and does not perform any transposition. (Note that the values of output were chosen at random.)

A P-box is an S-box that transposes, or permutes, the input bits. It may, or may not, also perform substitution. Figure 8-2 shows a P-box.

Of course, in the process of permutation, the bit is also substituted. For example, if the least significant bit in the input is transposed with some other bit, then the least significant bit in the output is likely to have been changed. In the literature, you will often see the term *S-box* used to denote either a substitution box or a permutation box. This makes complete sense when you consider that, regardless of which type it is, one inputs some bits and the output is different bits. So for the remainder of this chapter, I will use the term *S-box* to denote either a substitution or permutation box.

Whether an S-box or a P-box, there are three subclassifications: straight, compressed, and expansion. A straight S-box takes in a given number of bits and puts out the same number of bits. This is the design approach used with the Rijndael cipher and is frankly the easiest and most common form of S-box.

A *compression S-box* puts out fewer bits than it takes in. A good example of this is the S-box used in DES, in which each S-box takes in 6 bits but outputs only 4 bits. Keep in mind, however, that in the DES algorithm, there is a bit expansion phase earlier in the round function. In that case, the 32 input bits are expanded by 16 bits to create 48 bits. So when eight inputs of 6 bits each are put into each DES S-box, and only four are produced, the difference is 16 (8 × 2). So the bits being dropped off are those that were previously added. You can see a compression S-box in Figure 8-3.

The third type of S-box, similar to a compression S-box, is the *expansion S-box*. This S-box puts out more bits than it takes in. This can be accomplished by simply duplicating some of the input bits. This is shown in Figure 8-4.

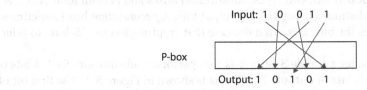

FIGURE 8-2   A P-box

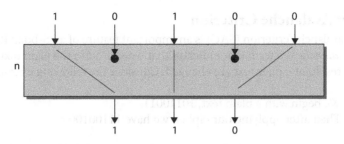

FIGURE 8-3   A compression S-box

Significant issues are associated with both compression and expansion S-boxes. The first issue is reversibility, or decryption. Since either type of S-box alters the total number of bits, reversing the process is difficult. You have to be very careful in the design of such an algorithm, or it is likely that decryption will not be possible. The second issue is a loss of information, particularly with compression S-boxes. In the case of DES, prior to the S-box, certain bits are replicated. Thus what is lost in the compression step are duplicate bits and no information is lost. In general, working with either compression or expansion S-boxes will introduce significant complexities in your S-box design. Therefore, straight S-boxes are far more common.

Design Considerations

Regardless of the type or category of S-box that is being created, any S-box must exhibit certain features in order to be effective. You cannot simply put together any substitution scheme you want and create a good S-box. It is not enough that it simply substitutes values; an S-box must also provide confusion and diffusion. The efficacy of an S-box is usually measured by examining three separate criteria that contribute to its security: strict avalanche criterion, balance, and bit independence criterion.

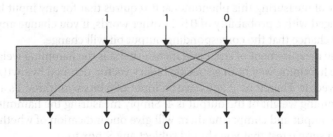

FIGURE 8-4   An expansion S-box

Strict Avalanche Criterion

Strict avalanche criterion (SAC) is an important feature of an S-box.[4] Remember from Chapter 3 that *avalanche* is a term that indicates that when 1 bit in the plain text is changed, multiple bits in the resultant cipher text are changed. Consider the following example:

1. We begin with a plain text, 10110011.
2. Then after applying our cipher, we have 11100100.

But what if, prior to encrypting the plain text, we change just 1 bit of the plain text—for example, the third bit from the left, so we have 10010011? In an cipher with no avalanche, the resulting cipher text would change by only 1 bit, perhaps 11100101. Notice that the only difference between this cipher text and the first cipher text is the last, or least significant, bit. This shows that a change of 1 bit in the plain text changed only 1 bit in the cipher text. That is no avalanche. However, if our algorithm has some avalanche, then changing the plain text from

```
10110011
```

to

```
10010011
```

will change more than 1 bit in the cipher text. In this case, before the change in plain text, remember our cipher text was

```
11100100
```

Now, if our cipher has some avalanche, we expect more than 1 bit in the cipher text to change, perhaps 2 bits:

```
10100101
```

Notice that the second and last bits are different. So a change in 1 bit of the plain text produced a change in 2 bits in the cipher text. Ideally, we would like to get more avalanche than this, as much as having a change in a single bit of plain text change half the cipher text bits. Without some level of avalanche, a cryptanalyst can examine changes in input and the corresponding changes in output and make predictions about the key. It is therefore critical that any cipher exhibit at least some avalanche.

In most block ciphers, the primary way to achieve avalanche is to use an S-box. SAC is one way of measuring this phenomena; it requires that for any input bit, the output bit should be changed with a probability of 0.5. In other words, if you change any given input bit, there is a 50/50 chance that the corresponding output bit will change.

One measurement of strict avalanche criteria is the hamming weight. Recall from Chapter 3 that the hamming weight of a specific binary vector, denoted by hwt(x), is the number of 1's in that vector. Therefore, if you have an input of 8 bits with three 1's and an output of four 1's, the hamming weight of the output is 4. Simply measuring the hamming weight of the input and the output and comparing them will give one indication of whether or not SAC is satisfied. This is a simple test that you should subject any S-box to.

Balance

Balance is also important in effective S-box design. Various papers provide slightly different definitions of balance.[5] However, in the current context, perhaps the best definition is that each output symbol should appear an equal number of times when the input is varied over all possible values. Some sources address S-boxes with unequal input and output, though it's safe to say that an S-box with n input bits and m output bits, m < n, is balanced if every output occurs 2^{n-m} times. So an S-box with a 6-bit input and 4-bit output would need each output bit to occur four times (2^{6-4}).

Bit Independence Criterion

The bit independence criterion (BIC) is the third criteria for good S-box design.[6] Bit independence criterion states that output bits j and k should change independently when any single input bit i is inverted, for all i, j, and k. The output bits change independently of each other. They are, of course, dependent on the input bits.

Approaches to S-Box Design

A number of approaches to S-box design are currently in use:

- One method simply uses a pseudo-random number generator for each entry in the S-box. The problem with this approach, however, is that you will not be able to predict whether or not your S-box actually fulfills the three criteria for an effective S-box. Instead, you will have to test extensively.
- A second approach is the human-made approach, in which some person (or persons) manually selects the values for the S-box—hopefully based on sound criteria. This was the method used in DES, and, in fact, the details of how the S-box for DES was designed are not public information. The actual S-boxes for DES are public, but the methodology for designing them is not. These S-boxes were designed in cooperation with the NSA.
- Another approach uses some mathematical-based method to generate the values for the S-box. This is the method used in AES.

The DES S-Box

As discussed in Chapter 6, the NSA was involved in the creation of DES—specifically in the S-box design. In fact, Alan Konheim, one of the IBM designers who worked on DES, is quoted as saying, "We sent the S-boxes off to Washington. They came back and were all different."[7] This led many people to believe that there might be a cryptographic backdoor embedded in the DES S-boxes, which would allow the NSA to break DES-encrypted communications easily. However, many years of study and analysis have not revealed any such backdoor.

The DES S-boxes convey a resistance to differential cryptanalysis, which we will study in Chapter 17. In fact, it has been discovered that even a small change to the DES S-box can significantly weaken its resistance to differential cryptanalysis. Differential cryptanalysis was unknown to the public at the time DES was invented (differential cryptanalysis was introduced—at least publically—by Eli Biham and Adi Shamir in the late 1980s). It is interesting to note that both Biham and Shamir noticed that DES is very resistant to differential cryptanalysis.[8] It therefore seems most likely that the NSA was aware of differential cryptanalysis long before it was publically known, and DES was created to be resistant to that attack.

The Actual S-Boxes for DES

Although the DES S-box design choices themselves have not been made public, we can derive some knowledge from studying them. As far as is publically known, the S-boxes are not derived from a mathematical formula, as the S-boxes in AES are. It seems that each substitution was specifically and manually chosen. Figure 8-5 shows DES S-boxes 1 through 8.

	x0000x	x0001x	x0010x	x0011x	x0100x	x0101x	x0110x	x0111x	x1000x	x1001x	x1010x	x1011x	x1100x	x1101x	x1110x	x1111x
0yyyy0	14	4	13	1	2	15	11	8	3	10	6	12	5	9	0	7
0yyyy1	0	15	7	4	14	2	13	1	10	6	12	11	9	5	3	8
1yyyy0	4	1	14	8	13	6	2	11	15	12	9	7	3	10	5	0
1yyyy1	15	12	8	2	4	9	1	7	5	11	3	14	10	0	6	13

S-box 1

	x0000x	x0001x	x0010x	x0011x	x0100x	x0101x	x0110x	x0111x	x1000x	x1001x	x1010x	x1011x	x1100x	x1101x	x1110x	x1111x
0yyyy0	15	1	8	14	6	11	3	4	9	7	2	13	12	0	5	10
0yyyy1	3	13	4	7	15	2	8	14	12	0	1	10	6	9	11	5
1yyyy0	0	14	7	11	10	4	13	1	5	8	12	6	9	3	2	15
1yyyy1	13	8	10	1	3	15	4	2	11	6	7	12	0	5	14	9

S-box 2

	x0000x	x0001x	x0010x	x0011x	x0100x	x0101x	x0110x	x0111x	x1000x	x1001x	x1010x	x1011x	x1100x	x1101x	x1110x	x1111x
0yyyy0	10	0	9	14	6	3	15	5	1	13	12	7	11	4	2	8
0yyyy1	13	7	0	9	3	4	6	10	2	8	5	14	12	11	15	1
1yyyy0	13	6	4	9	8	15	3	0	11	1	2	12	5	10	14	7
1yyyy1	1	10	13	0	6	9	8	7	4	15	14	3	11	5	2	12

S-box 3

	x0000x	x0001x	x0010x	x0011x	x0100x	x0101x	x0110x	x0111x	x1000x	x1001x	x1010x	x1011x	x1100x	x1101x	x1110x	x1111x
0yyyy0	7	13	14	3	0	6	9	10	1	2	8	5	11	12	4	15
0yyyy1	13	8	11	5	6	15	0	3	4	7	2	12	1	10	14	9
1yyyy0	10	6	9	0	12	11	7	13	15	1	3	14	5	2	8	4
1yyyy1	3	15	0	6	10	1	13	8	9	4	5	11	12	7	2	14

S-box 4

	x0000x	x0001x	x0010x	x0011x	x0100x	x0101x	x0110x	x0111x	x1000x	x1001x	x1010x	x1011x	x1100x	x1101x	x1110x	x1111x
0yyyy0	2	12	4	1	7	10	11	6	8	5	3	15	13	0	14	9
0yyyy1	14	11	2	12	4	7	13	1	5	0	15	10	3	9	8	6
1yyyy0	4	2	1	11	10	13	7	8	15	9	12	5	6	3	0	14
1yyyy1	11	8	12	7	1	14	2	13	6	15	0	9	10	4	5	3

S-box 5

FIGURE 8-5 S-boxes 1 through 8

	x0000x	x0001x	x0010x	x0011x	x0100x	x0101x	x0110x	x0111x	x1000x	x1001x	x1010x	x1011x	x1100x	x1101x	x1110x	x1111x
0yyyy0	12	1	10	15	9	2	6	8	0	13	3	4	14	7	5	11
0yyyy1	10	15	4	2	7	12	9	5	6	1	13	14	0	11	3	8
1yyyy0	9	14	15	5	2	8	12	3	7	0	4	10	1	13	11	6
1yyyy1	4	3	2	12	9	5	15	10	11	14	1	7	6	0	8	13

S-box 6

	x0000x	x0001x	x0010x	x0011x	x0100x	x0101x	x0110x	x0111x	x1000x	x1001x	x1010x	x1011x	x1100x	x1101x	x1110x	x1111x
0yyyy0	4	11	2	14	15	0	8	13	3	12	9	7	5	10	6	1
0yyyy1	13	0	11	7	4	9	1	10	14	3	5	12	2	15	8	6
1yyyy0	1	4	11	13	12	3	7	14	10	15	6	8	0	5	9	2
1yyyy1	6	11	13	8	1	4	10	7	9	5	0	15	14	2	3	12

S-box 7

	x0000x	x0001x	x0010x	x0011x	x0100x	x0101x	x0110x	x0111x	x1000x	x1001x	x1010x	x1011x	x1100x	x1101x	x1110x	x1111x
0yyyy0	13	2	8	4	6	15	11	1	10	9	3	14	5	0	12	7
0yyyy1	1	15	13	8	10	3	7	4	12	5	6	11	0	14	9	2
1yyyy0	7	11	4	1	9	12	14	2	0	6	10	13	15	3	5	8
1yyyy1	2	1	14	7	4	10	8	13	15	12	9	0	3	5	6	11

S-box 8

FIGURE 8-5 (*Continued*)

As you know, DES S-boxes are compression S-boxes. They take in 6 input bits and produce 4 output bits. Examine S-box 1, and you can see how this is done. All possible combinations of the middle 4 bits of the input are listed on the top row of the S-box. All possible combinations of the outer 2 bits are listed on the far left column. By matching the outer bits on the left with the inner bits on the top, you can find the output bits. Some substitutions change several bits. For example, in S-box 1, an input of all 0's, 000000 produces 1110. However, others produce far less change—for example, again focusing on S-box 1, an input of 001000 produces 0010. A simple shift of the 1 to the right.

Although most of the S-boxes provide a different substitution for any input, there is some overlap. For example, inputting 000110 in either S-box 2 or S-box 3 will produce 1110. In several cases, different inputs to an S-box produce the same output. For example, in S-box 5, notice that an input of 000001 produces 1110. However, an input of 111110 also produces 1110.

There has been no public disclosure as to why the specific design choices for DES S-boxes were made. As mentioned, resistance to differential cryptanalysis appears to have played a significant role. However, another factor is the nature of these S-boxes as compression boxes. It is difficult to design an S-box that uses compression without losing data. In the case of DES, it is possible only because an earlier step in the algorithm expanded bits. At least some of the design choices in DES are related to providing the compression without losing data.

The Rijndael S-Box

Given the prominence of AES, the Rijndael S-box is a good candidate for analysis. In fact, this is probably the most important portion of this chapter. Before we delve deeply into the S-boxes for Rijndael, let's look at some of the mathematics behind the S-box design. The actual Rijndael S-box is shown in Figure 8-6.

The Irreducible Polynomial

The Rijndael S-box is based on a specific irreducible polynomial in a specific Galois field:

$$GF(2^8) = GF(2)[x]/(x^8 + x^4 + x^3 + x + 1)$$

In hexadecimal, this is 11B; in binary, it is 100011011.

> **Note**   An irreducible polynomial cannot be factored into the product of two other polynomials; in other words, it cannot be reduced. This is in reference to a specific field—with the irreducible polynomial we are considering, it is in reference to the Galois field GF(2^8). Put more formally, a polynomial is irreducible in GF(p) if it does not factor over GF(p). Otherwise, it is reducible.

Why was this specific irreducible polynomial chosen? Does it have some special property that makes it more suitable for cryptography? To answer that question, let's consider the actual words of the inventors of Rijndael: "The polynomial m(x) ('11B') for the multiplication in GF(2^8) is the first one of the list of irreducible polynomials of degree 8."[9] In other words, they looked at a list of irreducible polynomials in a specific text and chose the first one. This is important to keep in mind. Any irreducible polynomial of the appropriate size can be used.

```
    | 0   1   2   3   4   5   6   7   8   9   a   b   c   d   e   f
- --| --|--|--|--|--|--|--|--|--|--|--|--|--|--|--|--|
00 | 63  7c  77  7b  f2  6b  6f  c5  30  01  67  2b  fe  d7  ab  76
10 | ca  82  c9  7d  fa  59  47  f0  ad  d4  a2  af  9c  a4  72  c0
20 | b7  fd  93  26  36  3f  f7  cc  34  a5  e5  f1  71  d8  31  15
30 | 04  c7  23  c3  18  96  05  9a  07  12  80  e2  eb  27  b2  75
40 | 09  83  2c  1a  1b  6e  5a  a0  52  3b  d6  b3  29  e3  2f  84
50 | 53  d1  00  ed  20  fc  b1  5b  6a  cb  be  39  4a  4c  58  cf
60 | d0  ef  aa  fb  43  4d  33  85  45  f9  02  7f  50  3c  9f  a8
70 | 51  a3  40  8f  92  9d  38  f5  bc  b6  da  21  10  ff  f3  d2
80 | cd  0c  13  ec  5f  97  44  17  c4  a7  7e  3d  64  5d  19  73
90 | 60  81  4f  dc  22  2a  90  88  46  ee  b8  14  de  5e  0b  db
a0 | e0  32  3a  0a  49  06  24  5c  c2  d3  ac  62  91  95  e4  79
b0 | e7  c8  37  6d  8d  d5  4e  a9  6c  56  f4  ea  65  7a  ae  08
c0 | ba  78  25  2e  1c  a6  b4  c6  e8  dd  74  1f  4b  bd  8b  8a
d0 | 70  3e  b5  66  48  03  f6  0e  61  35  57  b9  86  c1  1d  9e
e0 | e1  f8  98  11  69  d9  8e  94  9b  1e  87  e9  ce  55  28  df
f0 | 8c  a1  89  0d  bf  e6  42  68  41  99  2d  0f  b0  54  bb  16
```

FIGURE 8-6   Rijndael S-box

The text that Daemen and Rijmen consulted for their list of irreducible polynomials was *Introduction to Finite Fields and Their Applications*, by Rudolf Lidl and Harald Niederreiter (Cambridge University Press, 1986, revised in 1994). You can check the same source that was cited by the inventors of Rijndael. Here are a few irreducible polynomials from that list (in binary form, but you can place them in polynomial or hex form if you want):

```
100101011
```

```
100111001
```

```
100111111
```

```
101001101
```

```
101011111
```

```
101110111
```

```
110001011
```

You may have noticed that all of these, and the one chosen for Rijndael, have nine digits. Why use degree 8 (nine digits)—isn't that one too many? According to the algorithm specification, "Clearly, the result will be a binary polynomial of degree below 8. Unlike for addition, there is no simple operation at byte level."

The reason an irreducible polynomial must be used, instead of just any polynomial (or a primitive polynomial), is that Rijndael is trying to make a nonlinear permutation function that has diffusion, spreading input bits to output bits in a nonlinear way.

Multiplicative Inverse

In mathematics, the reciprocal, or multiplicative inverse, of a number x is the number that, when multiplied by x, yields 1. The multiplicative inverse for the real numbers, for example, is $1/x$. To avoid confusion by writing the inverse using set-specific notation, it is generally written as x^{-1}.

Multiplication in a Galois field, however, requires more tedious work. Suppose f(p) and g(p) are polynomials in GF(pn), and let m(p) be an irreducible polynomial (or a polynomial that cannot be factored) of degree at least n in GF(pn). We want m(p) to be a polynomial of degree at least n so that the product of two f(p) and g(p) does not exceed 11111111 = 255, because the product needs to be stored as a byte. If h(p) denotes the resulting product, then

$$h(p) \equiv (f(p) * g(p))(\bmod m(p))$$

On the other hand, the multiplicative inverse of f(p) is given by a(p) such that

$$(f(p) * a(p))(\bmod m(p)) \equiv 1$$

Note that calculating the product of two polynomials and the multiplicative inverse of a polynomial requires both reducing coefficients modulo p and reducing polynomials modulo m(p). The reduced polynomial can be calculated easily with long division, while the best way to compute the multiplicative inverse is by using the extended Euclidean algorithm. The details on the calculations in GF(2^8) is best explained in the example that follows.

Finite field multiplication is more difficult than addition and is achieved by multiplying the polynomials for the two elements concerned and collecting like powers of x in the result. Since each polynomial can have powers of x up to 7, the result can have powers of x up to 14 and will no longer fit within a single byte.

This situation is handled by replacing the result with the remainder polynomial after division by a special eighth order irreducible polynomial, which, as you may recall for Rijndael, is

$$m(x) = x^8 + x^4 + x^3 + x + 1$$

The finite field element {00000010} is the polynomial x, which means that multiplying another element by this value increases all its powers of x by 1. This is equivalent to shifting its byte representation up by 1 bit so that the bit at position i moves to position $i+1$. If the top bit is set prior to this move, it will overflow to create an x^8 term, in which case the modular polynomial is added to cancel this additional bit, leaving a result that fits within a single byte.

For example, multiplying {11001000} by x, that is {00000010}, the initial result is 1{10010000}. The "overflow" bit is then removed by adding 1{00011011}, the modular polynomial, using an XOR operation to give a final result of {10001011}. However, you need not calculate the multiplicative inverse manually. The table in Figure 8-7 provides multiplicative inverses.

Affine Transformation

This concept originates in graphics and is also used in transforming graphics. Moving pixels in one direction or another is very similar to moving a value in a matrix, so the concept gets applied to matrices (as in AES). In geometry, an affine transformation—or affine map or

	0	1	2	3	4	5	6	7	8	9	a	b	c	d	e	f
00	--	01	8d	f6	cb	52	7b	d1	e8	4f	29	c0	b0	e1	e5	c7
10	74	b4	aa	4b	99	2b	60	5f	58	3f	fd	cc	ff	40	ee	b2
20	3a	6e	5a	f1	55	4d	a8	c9	c1	0a	98	15	30	44	a2	c2
30	2c	45	92	6c	f3	39	66	42	f2	35	20	6f	77	bb	59	19
40	1d	fe	37	67	2d	31	f5	69	a7	64	ab	13	54	25	e9	09
50	ed	5c	05	ca	4c	24	87	bf	18	3e	22	f0	51	ec	61	17
60	16	5e	af	d3	49	a6	36	43	f4	47	91	df	33	93	21	3b
70	79	b7	97	85	10	b5	ba	3c	b6	70	d0	06	a1	fa	81	82
80	83	7e	7f	80	96	73	be	56	9b	9e	95	d9	f7	02	b9	a4
90	de	6a	32	6d	d8	8a	84	72	2a	14	9f	88	f9	dc	89	9a
a0	fb	7c	2e	c3	8f	b8	65	48	26	c8	12	4a	ce	e7	d2	62
b0	0c	e0	1f	ef	11	75	78	71	a5	8e	76	3d	bd	bc	86	57
c0	0b	28	2f	a3	da	d4	e4	0f	a9	27	53	04	1b	fc	ac	e6
d0	7a	07	ae	63	c5	db	e2	ea	94	8b	c4	d5	9d	f8	90	6b
e0	b1	0d	d6	eb	c6	0e	cf	ad	08	4e	d7	e3	5d	50	1e	b3
f0	5b	23	38	34	68	46	03	8c	dd	9c	7d	a0	cd	1a	41	1c

FIGURE 8-7 Multiplicative inverses

an affinity—(from the Latin, *affinis*, "connected with") between two vector spaces (strictly speaking, two affine spaces) consists of a linear transformation followed by a translation. In general, an affine transform is composed of linear transformations (rotation, scaling, or shear) and a translation (or shift). For our purposes, it is just a word for a linear transformation.

Generating the S-Box

The Rijndael S-box can be generated with a series of shift operations; in fact, this is exactly how it is usually implemented in programming. These shifts essentially accomplish the same process as matrix multiplication.

The matrix multiplication can be calculated by the following algorithm:

1. Store the multiplicative inverse of the input number in two 8-bit unsigned temporary variables: s and x.
2. Rotate the value s 1 bit to the left; if the value of s had a high bit (eighth bit from the right) of 1, make the low bit of s 1; otherwise the low bit of s is 0.
3. XOR the value of x with the value of s, storing the value in x.
4. For three more iterations, repeat steps 2 and 3 a total of four times.
5. The value of x will now have the result of the multiplication.

After the matrix multiplication is complete, XOR the resultant value by the decimal number 99 (the hexadecimal number 0x63, the binary number 1100011, and the bit string 11000110 representing the number in least significant bit first notation). This value is termed the *translation vector*. This last operation, the final XOR, is meant to prevent any situation wherein the output is the same as the input—in other words to prevent S-box(a)=a.

An Example Generating the S-Box

It may be helpful for you to see an actual example generating the S-box.

1. Take a number for GF(2^8)—let's pick 7. Looking at the multiplicative inverse table gives us d1 in hex or 11010001 in binary.
2. Now we need to do four iterations of the process of affine transformation. We start by putting the multiplicative inverse into two variables s and x:
   s = 11010001
   x = 11010001
3. Now we simply rotate s(10001101) to the left = 00011010
   • If the high bit is 1 make the low bit 1
   • Else low bit is 0
4. Now in this case, the high bit was 1, so we change the low bit, thus
   s = 00011011
5. XOR that number with x so 00011011 XOR 10001101= 10010110
   s = 00011011; x = 10010110
6. Next rotate s (00011011) to the left = 00110110.
   A. If this still gives us 00110110, XOR with x, so
      00110110 XOR 10010110 = 10100000
      s = 00110110; x = 10100000

7. Next rotate s(00110110) to the left = 01101100.
   A. If this still gives us 01101100, XOR with x, so
      01101100 XOR 10100000= 11001100
      s = 01101100; x = 11001100
8. Next rotate s(01101100) to the left = 11011000.
   A. If this still gives us 11011000, XOR with x, so
      01101100 XOR 11001100= 00010100
      s = 11011000; x = 00010100
9. Now x (00010100) gets XOR'd with decimal 99 (hex x63 binary 1100011) = 1110111
   or 77.

Remember the output of the matrix multiplication (which we have accomplished via shift operations) is finally XOR'd with the translation vector (decimal 99). This process allows you to create the Rijndael S-box, and it is in fact how that S-box is often created in code.

Changing the Rijndael S-Box

After studying the previous section, you should realize that there are three factors in generating the AES S-box. The first is the selection of the irreducible polynomial—in this case it was $P = x^8 + x^4 + x^3 + x + 1$, which is 11B in hexadecimal notation, or 100011011 in binary numbers. As I mentioned previously, the creators of the Rijndael cipher stated clearly that this number was chosen simply because it was the first on the list of irreducible polynomials of degree 8 in the reference book they chose. That means that you could choose other irreducible polynomials.

In fact, you can choose from a total of 30 irreducible polynomials of degree 8, and this gives you 29 alternatives to the traditional S-box for AES, each with well-tested security. For more details on this alternative, you can look into Rabin's test for irreducibility (see http://math.stackexchange.com/questions/528552/rabins-test-for-polynomial-irreducibility-over-mathbbf-2). In their paper "Random S-Box Generation in AES by Changing Irreducible Polynomial," Das, Sanjoy, Subhrapratim, and Subhash[10] demonstrated an equally secure variation of the Rijndael, by changing the chosen irreducible polynomial. You can use any of the 30 possible irreducible polynomials; each of these is equally secure to the original Rijndael cipher S-box.

> **Note**   Altering the Rijndael S-box is practical only if you have the ability to ensure that all parties to encrypted communication will be using your modified S-box. If you simply modify the S-box on your end, you would render communication with other parties impossible. Even though those other parties will have the same key and the same algorithm (AES), they will be using standard S-boxes. This is why altering AES S-boxes is primarily an issue for government entities that want to have secure communication with a limited number of involved parties.

A second option, one that may be the simplest to implement, is to change the translation vector (the final number you XOR with). Obviously, there are 255 possible variations. Rather than use 0x63, you can use any of the other possible variations for that final byte. Although simple to implement, it may be more difficult to test. Some variations might adversely affect one of the three criteria that you are attempting to maintain. In fact, selecting the wrong translation vector may lead to no change at all when it is applied to the product of the preceding matrix multiplication.

The third method is to change the affine transform, and this can be more difficult to implement but safe if you simply alter parameters within the existing transform. Section 5.2 of Sinha and Arya's paper "Algebraic Construction and Cryptographic Properties of Rijndael Substitution Box"[11] discusses this in detail. According to Cui, et al.,[12] the choice of affine transformation matrix or irreducible polynomial has no significant impact on the security of the resultant cipher text.

Conclusions

The S-box (or in some cases, S-boxes) is a critical part of most block ciphers. To understand any block cipher fully, you need to have some understanding of S-box design. S-boxes fall into two main categories: substitution and permutation. Either of these can be divided into three subcategories: straight, compression, and expansion.

In addition to S-boxes in general, the Rijndael S-box warrants particular attention. In addition to the standard Rijndael S-box commonly used, three relatively simple methods can be used to alter the S-box used in the Rijndael cipher. This will lead to permutations of Rijndael that are equal, or very nearly equal, in security to the original cipher. Using such permutations can lead to private versions of the AES algorithm, which can be useful for certain governmental and military applications.

If you want to delve into S-box design beyond the scope of this chapter, unfortunately there are no books on S-box design. As mentioned, many cryptography texts avoid this topic altogether or provide cursory coverage. You may, however, find a few sources useful (beyond those cited in the chapter endnotes), which can be found online using a Google search:

- Dawson and Tavares, "An Expanded Set of S-box Design Criteria Based on Information Theory and Its Relation to Differential-Like Attacks."
- Adams and Tavares, "The Use of Bent Sequences to Achieve Higher-Order Strict Avalanche Criterion in S-Box Design."

Test Your Knowledge

1. In mathematics, the _____ of a number x is the number that, when multiplied by x, yields 1.
2. What is the irreducible polynomial used in standard AES?
3. What is the strict avalanche criterion in S-box design?
4. What is the bit independence criterion in S-box design?
5. What is the value of the Rijndael translation vector?
6. How many irreducible polynomials are there for the generation of the Rijndael S-box?
7. What is the primary advantage that DES S-boxes convey on the DES cipher?
8. A _____ provides the source of nonlinearity for a given cryptographic algorithm.
9. An S-box that transposes bits is called a _____.
10. What are the two concerns with using a compression S-box?

Answers

1. multiplicative inverse
2. $x^8 + x^4 + x^3 + x + 1$
3. The S-box must produce at least 50 percent avalanche.
4. The resulting bits must be independent of each other.
5. Decimal 99, hex x63, or binary 1100011
6. 30
7. Resistance to differential cryptanalysis
8. substitution box
9. permutation box
10. Loss of data and an inability to decrypt enciphered messages

Endnotes

1. Petr Tesař, "A New Method for Generating High Non-linearity S-Boxes," (p. 1), 2010, www.radioeng.cz/fulltexts/2010/10_01_023_026.pdf.
2. A. Grocholewska-Czurylo, "Cryptographic Properties of Modified AES-Like S-Boxes," *Annales UMCS Informatica, AI XI*(2), (2011): 37–48.
3. Ibid.
4. For more about the avalanche effect, see "Differential Cryptanalysis of DES-like Cryptosystems" by E. Biham and A. Shamir, at http://zoo.cs.yale.edu/classes/cs426/2012/bib/biham91differential.pdf.
5. One article that provides information about balancing S-box cryptographic functions is "Improving the Strict Avalanche Characteristics of Cryptographic Functions," by J. Seberry, X. Zhang, and Y. Zheng, at www.uow.edu.au/~jennie/WEBPDF/1994_09.pdf.
6. For more information about BIC, see "Good S-Boxes Are Easy to Find," by Carlisle Adams and Stafford Taveres, published in the *Journal of Cryptology*, vol. 3, no. 1 (1990), pp. 27–41.
7. Bruce Schneier, *Applied Cryptography* (Wiley, 1996), p. 280.
8. Biham and Shamir, http://zoo.cs.yale.edu/classes/cs426/2012/bib/biham91differential.pdf.
9. J. Daemen and V. Rijmen, "AES Proposal: Rijndael," 1999, http://csrc.nist.gov/archive/aes/rijndael/Rijndael-ammended.pdf.
10. I. Das, R. Sanjoy, N. Subhrapratim, and M. Subhash, "Random S-Box Generation in AES by Changing Irreducible Polynomial," 2012. You can purchase and download the document from the IEEE Xplore Digital Library (http://ieeexplore.ieee.org/Xplore/home.jsp).
11. S. Sinha and C. Arya, "Algebraic Construction and Cryptographic Properties of Rijndael Substitution Box," 2012, http://publications.drdo.gov.in/ojs/index.php/dsj/article/viewFile/1439/605.
12. J. Cui, L. Huang, H. Zhong, C. Chang, and W. Yang, "An Improved AES S-Box and Its Performance Analysis," 2011, www.ijicic.org/ijicic-10-01041.pdf.

9

Cryptographic Hashes

In this chapter we will cover the following:

- What is a cryptographic hash?
- Specific algorithms
- Message authentication codes (MACs)
- Applications of cryptographic hashes

In the preceding eight chapters, we examined cryptography as a means of keeping information confidential. Cryptographic hashes are not concerned with protecting confidentiality, however; instead, they are concerned with ensuring integrity. Computer security has a handful of bedrock concepts upon which it is built. The CIA triangle, consisting of *confidentiality*, *integrity*, and *availability*, is one such concept. Different technologies support different aspects of the CIA triangle. For example, backups, disaster recovery plans, and redundant equipment support availability. Certainly encrypting a message so others cannot read it supports confidentiality. Cryptographic hashes are about supporting integrity.

As with previous chapters, some algorithms in this chapter will be discussed in depth, while others will be briefly described. The goal is not necessarily for you to memorize every major cryptographic hashing function, but to gain a general familiarity with cryptographic hashes. It is also important that you understand how cryptographic hashing algorithms are used to support security.

What Is a Cryptographic Hash?

A cryptographic hash is a special type of algorithm. William Stallings, in his book *Network Security Essentials*, describes a hash as follows:

1. H can be applied to a block of data of variable size.
2. H produces a fixed-length output.
3. H(x) is relatively easy to compute for any given x, making both hardware and software implementations practical. X is whatever you input into the hash.
4. For any given value h, it is computationally infeasible to find x such that H(x) = h. This is sometimes referred to in the literature as the *one-way property*.

5. For any given block x, it is computationally infeasible to find y !=x such that H(y) = H(x). This is sometimes referred to as *weak collision resistance*.

6. It is computationally infeasible to find any pair x, y such that H(x) = H(y). This is sometimes referred to as *strong collision resistance*.[1]

Note William Stallings received his Ph.D. in computer science from the Massachusetts Institute of Technology. He has authored several computer science and security textbooks as well as a number of scientific articles.

Stallings's definition is accurate, but it may be a bit technical for the novice. Allow me to explain the properties of a cryptographic hash in a manner that is a bit less technical, but no less true. In order to be a cryptographic hash function, an algorithm needs to have three properties.

First, *the function must be one way*. That means it cannot be "unhashed." This may seem a bit odd at first—an algorithm that is not reversible? In fact, it is not simply difficult to reverse, but it is literally impossible to reverse—like trying to unscramble a scrambled egg and put it back in the shell. When we examine specific hashing algorithms later in this chapter, you'll understand why a cryptographic hash is irreversible.

Second, *a variable-length input must produce a fixed-length output*. That means that no matter what size of input you have, you will get the same sized output. Each particular cryptographic hash algorithm has a specific sized output. For example, the Secure Hash Algorithm (SHA-1) produces a 160-bit hash. It does not matter whether you input 1 byte or 1 terabyte; you'll still get out 160 bits. How do you get fixed-length output regardless of the size of the input? Different algorithms will each use its own specific approach, but in general, it involves compressing all the data into a block of a specific size. If the input is smaller than the block, you can pad it.

Consider the following example, which is trivial and for demonstrative purposes. It would not suffice as a secure cryptographic hash. We will call this the *trivial hashing algorithm* (THA):

1. If the input is less than 64 bits, pad it with 0's until you achieve 64 bits. If it is greater than 64 bits, divide it into 64-bit segments. Make sure the last segment is exactly 64 bits, even if you need to pad it with 0's.

2. Divide each 64-bit block into two halves.

3. XOR the left half of each block with the right half.

4. If there is more than one block, start at the first block, XOR'ing it with the next block. Continue this until you reach the last block. The output from the final XOR operation is your hash. If you had only one block, the result of XOR'ing the left half with the right half is your hash.

Note I cannot emphasize enough that this would not be secure. It is very easy to envision collisions occurring in this scenario—quite easily, in fact. However, this does illustrate a rather primitive way in which the input text can be condensed (or padded) to reach a specific size.

Third, *there should be few or no collisions*. That means if you hash two different inputs, you should not get the same output. Why "few or no" rather than no collisions, when the preference is for no collisions? If you use SHA-1, then you have a 160-bit output, and that means about 1.461×10^{48} possible outputs. Clearly, you could have trillions of different inputs and never see a collision. For most people, this qualifies as "no collisions." In the interest of being accurate, however, I cannot help but note that it is at least theoretically possible that two inputs could produce the same output, even though that has never yet occurred and the possibility is incredibly remote. Thus the caveat "few or no collisions."

How Are Cryptographic Hashes Used?

Cryptographic hashes can be used in many ways, and this section discusses some of the most common uses. Each will depend on one or more of the three key properties of a cryptographic hash, as discussed in the previous section. Reading this section should help you understand the importance of cryptographic hashes in computer security.

Message Integrity

One common use of hashing algorithms is to ensure message integrity. Obviously, messages can be altered in transit, either intentionally or accidentally. You can use hashing algorithms to detect any alterations that have occurred. Consider, for example, an e-mail message. If you put the body of the message into a hashing algorithm—say, SHA-1—the output is a 160-bit hash. That hash can be appended at the end of the message.

> **Note** Another term for *hash* is *message digest*, or just *digest*.

When the mail is received, the recipient can recalculate the cryptographic hash of the message and compare that result to the hash that was attached to the message. If the two do not match exactly, this indicates that some alteration in the message has occurred and that the message contents are no longer reliable.

Cryptographic hashes are also used in file integrity systems. For example, the popular Tripwire product (both the open source Linux version and the Windows version) creates a cryptographic hash of key files (as designated by the Tripwire administrator). At any time, a hash of the current file can be compared to the previously computed cryptographic hash to determine whether there has been any change in the file. This can detect anything from a simple edit of a file such as a spreadsheet to an executable that has been infected with a Trojan horse.

> **Note** A Trojan horse is a program or file that has malware attached to it. Often, attackers use wrapper programs to tie a virus or spyware to a legitimate program. A user who executes the legitimate program may inadvertently launch the malware.

Password Storage

Cryptographic hashes also provide a level of security against insider threats. Consider the possibility, for example, that someone with access to a system, such as a network administrator, has malicious intentions. This person may simply read a user's password from the database, and then use that user's login credentials to accomplish some attack on the system. Then, should the attack become known, it is the end user who will be a suspect, not the administrator who actually perpetrated the breach. One way to avoid this is to store passwords in a cryptographic hash. When the user logs into the system, whatever password is typed in is hashed and then compared to the hash in the database. If they match exactly, the user is logged into the system.

Given that the database stores only a hash of the password, and hashes are not reversible, even a network administrator or database administrator cannot retrieve the password from the database. If someone attempts to type in the hash as a password, the system will hash whatever input is placed into the password field, thus yielding a hash different from the one stored in the database. The storing of passwords as a hash is widely used and strongly recommended.

Hashing is, in fact, how Windows stores passwords. For example, if your password is *password*, then Windows will first hash it producing something like this:

```
0BD181063899C9239016320B50D3E896693A96DF
```

That hash will be stored in the Security Accounts Manager (SAM) file in the Windows System directory. When you log on, Windows cannot "un-hash" your password. Instead, it hashes whatever password you type in and compares that result with what is stored in the SAM file. If they match (exactly), then you can log in.

Forensic Integrity

When you conduct a forensic examination of a hard drive, one of your first steps is to create an image of the drive and perform the analysis on the image. After creating an image, you must verify that the imaging process was accurate. To do this, you create a hash of the original and a hash of the image and compare the two. This is where the "variable-length input produces fixed-length output" and "few or no collisions" comes in. If you have a terabyte drive, for example, and you image it, you must ensure that your image is an exact copy. The fact that the hash is only a fixed size, such as 160 bits for SHA-1, is very useful. It would be quite unwieldy if the hash itself was the size of the input. Comparing terabyte-sized hashes would be problematic at best.

If you make a hash of the original and the image, and then compare them, you can verify that everything is copied exactly into the image. If the variable-length input produced a fixed-length output, then you would have hashes that were humongous and that took forever to compute. Also, if two different inputs could produce the same output, you could not verify that the image was an exact copy.

Merkle-Damgård

Before we delve into specific hashing algorithms, it is worthwhile to examine a function that is key to many commonly used cryptographic hashes. A *Merkle-Damgård function* (also called a *Merkle-Damgård construction*) is a method used to build hash functions. Merkle-Damgård functions form the basis for MD5, SHA1, SHA2, and other hashing algorithms.

> **Note**   To read more about Merkle-Damgård functions, see the article "Merkle-Damgård Revisited: How to Construct a Hash Function," at http://www.cs.nyu.edu/~puniya/papers/merkle.pdf.

Computer scientist Ralph Merkle co-invented cryptographic hashing and published his findings in his 1979 doctoral dissertation. The function starts by applying some padding function to create an output that is of some particular size (256, 512, or 1024 bits, and so on). The specific size will vary from one algorithm to another, but 512 bits is a common size used by many algorithms. The function then processes blocks one at a time, combining the new block of input with the block from the previous round (recall our earlier THA example that took output from one block and combined it with the next). Put another way, if you break up a 1024-bit message into four 256-bit blocks, block 1 will be processed, and then its output will be combined with block 2 before block 2 is processed. Then that output will be combined with block 3 before it is processed. And, finally, that output is combined with block 4 before that block is processed. Merkle-Damgård is often referred to as a "compression function," because it compresses the entire message into a single output block.

The algorithm starts with some initial value or initialization vector that is specific to the implementation. The final message block is always padded to the appropriate size (256, 512 bits, and so on) and includes a 64-bit integer that indicates the size of the original message.

Specific Algorithms

You can use a variety of specific algorithms to create cryptographic hashes. Remember that to be a viable cryptographic hash, an algorithm needs three properties:

1. Variable-length input produces fixed-length output
2. Few or no collisions
3. Not reversible

A variety of cryptographic hashing functions meet these three criteria. In the United States as well as much of the world, the MD5 and SHA algorithms are the most widely used, and thus will be prominently covered in this chapter.

Checksums

A checksum is a much simpler algorithm than a cryptographic hash and can serve similar purposes—for example, a checksum can check for message integrity. The word *checksum* is often used as a generic term for the actual output of a specific algorithm. The algorithms are often called a *checksum function* or *checksum algorithm*.

Longitudinal Parity Check

One of the simplest checksum algorithms is the longitudinal parity check. It breaks data into segments (called words) with a fixed number of bits. Then the algorithm computes the XOR of all of these words, with the final result being a single word or checksum. Here's an example: Assume a text that says this:

```
Euler was a genius
```

Then convert that to binary (first converting to ASCII codes, and then converting that to binary):

```
01000101 01110101 01101100 01100101 01110010 00100000 01110111 01100001
01110011
00100000 01100001 00100000 01100111 01100101 01101110 01101001 01110101
01110011
```

The segments can be any size, but let's assume a 2-byte (16-bit) word. So this text is now divided into nine words (shown here separated with brackets):

```
[01000101 01110101] [01101100 01100101] [01110010 00100000] [01110111 01100001]
[01110011 00100000] [01100001 00100000] [01100111 01100101] [01101110 01101001]
[01110101 01110011]
```

The next step is to XOR the first word with the second:

```
01000101 01110101 XOR 01101100 01100101 = 0010100100010000
```

Then that result is XOR'd with the next word:

```
0010100100010000 XOR 00100000 01110111 = 0000100101100111
```

This process is continued with the result of the previous XOR, which is then XOR'd with the next word until a result is achieved. That result is called the *longitudinal parity check*.

This type of checksum (as well as others) works well for error detection. The checksum of a message can be appended to a message. The recipient then recalculates the checksum and compares it. Checksums are usually much faster than cryptographic hashes. However, collisions are possible (different inputs producing identical outputs).

Fletcher Checksum

The Fletcher checksum is an algorithm for computing a position-dependent checksum. Devised by John G. Fletcher at Lawrence Livermore Labs in the late 1970s, this checksum's objective was to provide error-detection properties that were those of a cyclic redundancy check but with the lower computational effort associated with summation techniques. The Fletcher checksum works by dividing the input into words and computing the modular sum of those words. Any modulus can be used for computing the modular sum. The checksum is appended to the original message, and the recipient recalculates the checksum and compares it to the original.

MD5

This 128-bit hash is specified by RFC 1321. Designed by Ron Rivest in 1991 to replace and improve on the MD4 hash function, MD5 produces a 128-bit hash, or digest. As early as 1996, a flaw was found in MD5 and by 2004 it was shown that MD5 was not collision resistant.

The first step in the algorithm is to break the message to be encrypted into 512-bit segments, each consisting of sixteen 32-bit words. If the last segment is less than 512 bits, it is padded to reach 512 bits. The final 64 bits represents the length of the original message.

Because MD5 ultimately seeks to create a 128-bit output, it works on a 128-bit state that consists of four 32-bit words labeled A, B, C, and D. These 32-bit words are initialized to some fixed constant. The algorithm has four rounds consisting of a number of rotations and binary operations, with a different round function for each round. Since MD5 is a Merkle-Damgård function, the following steps are taken for each 512-bit block. If the message is more than 512 bits, final output of a given block is then combined with the next block until the last block is reached.

1. Round 1: B is XOR'd with C. The output of that operation is OR'd with the output of the negation of B XOR'd with D.
2. Round 2: B is XOR'd with D. The output of that operation is OR'd with the output of C XOR'd with the negation of D.
3. Round 3: B is XOR'd with C. The output is XOR'd with D.
4. Round 4: C is XOR'd with the output of B, which is OR'd with the negation of D.

These round functions are often denoted as F, G, H, and I, with F being round 1, G being round 2, H being round 3, and I being round 4.

The algorithm is illustrated in Figure 9-1. The blocks A–D have already been explained. The F in Figure 9-1 represents the round function for that given round (F, G, H, or I depending on the round in question). The message word is M_i and K_i is a constant. The <<< denotes a binary left shift by s bits. After all rounds are done, the A, B, C, and D words contain the digest, or hash, of the original message.

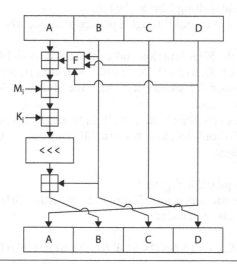

FIGURE 9-1   The MD5 algorithm

SHA

The Secure Hash Algorithm is perhaps the most widely used hash algorithm today, with several versions, all of which are considered secure and collision free:

- **SHA-1** This 160-bit hash function resembles the earlier MD5 algorithm. It was designed by the National Security Agency (NSA) to be part of the Digital Signature Algorithm (DSA).
- **SHA-2** These are two similar hash functions with different block sizes and are known as SHA-256 and SHA-512. They differ in the word size; SHA-256 uses 32-byte (256-bit) words, and SHA-512 uses 64-byte (512-bit) words. Truncated versions of each standard are known as SHA-224 and SHA-384; these were also designed by the NSA.
- **SHA-3** The latest version of SHA was adopted in October 2012.

SHA-1

Much like MD5, SHA-1 uses some padding and 512-bit blocks. The final block must be 448 bits, followed by a 64-bit unsigned integer that represents the size of the original message. Because SHA-1 is also a Merkle-Damgård function, each 512-bit block undergoes a step-by-step process (shown a bit later). If the message is more than 512 bits, final output of a given block is combined with the next block until the last block is reached.

Unlike MD5, SHA1 uses five blocks, often denoted as h1, h2, h3, h4, and h5. These are initialized to some constant value. The message to be hashed is changed into characters and converted to binary format. The message is padded so it evenly breaks into 512-bit segments with the 64-bit original message length at the end.

Each 512-bit segment is divided into sixteen 32-bit words. The first step after preparing the message is a process that will create 80 words from the 16 in the block. This is a loop that will be executed until a given condition is true. First, the 16 words in the 512-bit block are put into the first 16 words of the 80-word array. The other words are generated by XOR'ing previous words and shifting 1 bit to the left.

Then you loop 80 times through a process that does the following:

1. Calculates the SHA function and a constant K, both based on the current round.
2. Sets word E = D, word D = C, word C = B after rotating B left 30 bits; word B = 1, word A = word A rotated left 5 bits + the SHA function + E + K + word [i], where i is the current round.
3. Concatenates the final hash as A, B, C, D, and E; this has five final words (each 32-bit), whereas MD5 only had four, because MD5 produces a 128-bit digest and SHA-1 produces a 160-bit digest.

This process is depicted in Figure 9-2.

Notice the round function in Figure 9-2. Like MD5, SHA-1 has a varying round function that changes slightly each round:

Variation 1: f(t;B,C,D) = (B AND C) OR ((NOT B) AND D) (0 <= t <= 19)

Variation 2: f(t;B,C,D) = B XOR C XOR D   (20 <= t <= 39)

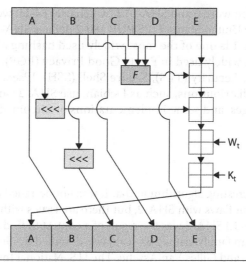

FIGURE 9-2 The SHA-1 algorithm

Variation 3: f(t;B,C,D) = (B AND C) OR (B AND D) OR (C AND D) (40 <= t <=59)

Variation 4: f(t;B,C,D) = B XOR C XOR D   (60 <= t <= 79)

> **Note** At this point, you may find both MD5 and SHA-1 to be a bit convoluted, and that's OK. Remember the goal is to have a nonreversible algorithm. So the convoluted steps are designed simply to scramble the message so that it cannot be unscrambled.

If you have a programming background or are simply familiar with algorithm analysis, you may find the following pseudo-code helpful in understanding SHA-1:

```
For loop on k = 1 to L
     (W(0),W(1),...,W(15)) = M[k] /* Divide M[k] into 16 words */
     For t = 16 to 79 do:
          W(t) = (W(t-3) XOR W(t-8) XOR W(t-14) XOR W(t-16)) <<< 1
          A = H0, B = H1, C = H2, D = H3, E = H4
          For t = 0 to 79 do:
               TEMP = A<<<5 + f(t;B,C,D) + E + W(t) + K(t) E = D, D = C,
                    C = B<<<30, B = A, A = TEMP
          End of for loop
          H0 = H0 + A, H1 = H1 + B, H2 = H2 + C, H3 = H3 + D, H4 = H4 + E
End of for loop
```

SHA-2

SHA-2 is similar in structure and function to SHA-1, and it is also a Merkle-Damgård construction. However, it has a variety of sizes, the most common of which are SHA-256 (which uses 32-bit words) and SHA-512 (which uses 64-bit words); there is also SHA-224 and SHA-384. In the United States, FIPS PUB 180-2 defines SHA-2 as a standard.

While SHA-1 is one of the most widely used hashing algorithms in existence today, SHA-2 is widely used in Pretty Good Privacy (PGP), Secure Sockets Layer (SSL), Transport Layer Security (TLS), Secure Shell (SSH), IPsec, and other security protocols. Certain Linux distributions, such as Debian, use SHA-2 variations to authenticate software packages, and some implementations of Bitcoin also use SHA-2 to verify transactions.

SHA-3

SHA-3 is an interesting algorithm in that it was not designed to replace SHA-2. (There are no known significant flaws with SHA-2, but there are issues with MD-5 and at least theoretical issues with SHA-1.) SHA-3 was the result of a contest to find a new hashing algorithm. The original algorithm family, named Keccak, was designed by Guido Bertoni, Joan Daemen, Michaël Peeters, and Gilles Van Assche. The U.S. National Institute of Standards and Technology (NIST) published FIPS 202,[2] which standardized the use of SHA-3.

Unlike SHA-1 and SHA-2 that use a Merkle-Damgård construction, SHA-3 uses a *sponge construction* (also known as a sponge function), which is a type of algorithm that uses an internal state and takes input of any size to produce a specific-sized output. This makes it a good fit for cryptographic hashes that need to take variable-length input to produce fixed-length output.

Any sponge construction uses three components: a state, usually called S, that is of some fixed size; some function, f, that transforms the state; and a padding function to ensure the output is of the proper size.

The state is usually divided into two sections, denoted R and C. The R represents the size bitrate and the C is the size of the capacity. The bitrate is simply the base size for the algorithm. Just as Merkle-Damgård constructions might use 512-bit blocks, sponge constructions have a certain base size, and the entire input must be a multiple of that size. The padding function ensures that the input is a multiple of R.

The sponge function consists of iterations of the following steps:

1. The state (S) is initialized to 0.
2. The input string is padded using the padding function.
3. R is XOR'd with the first *r*-bit block of padded input. (Remember R is the bit size being used as a base for this implementation.)
4. S is replaced by F(S). The function F is specific to a particular sponge function.
5. R is then XOR'd with the next *r*-bit block of padded input.
6. Steps 4 and 5 continue until the end of the input, at which time, the output is produced as follows:
   A. The R portion of the state memory is the first *r*-bits of output.
   B. If more output bits are desired, S is replaced by F(S).
   C. The R portion of the state memory is the next *r*-bits of output.

Note
This is a generic overview of the essentials of a sponge construction; there can be variations on this process. The details of the function F will vary with specific implementations. In SHA-3, the state consists of a 5 × 5 array of 64-bit words, 1600 bits total. The authors claim 12.5 cycles per byte on an Intel Core 2 CPU. In hardware implementations, it was notably faster than all other finalists. The permutations of SHA-3 that were approved by the NIST include 224-, 256-, 384-, and 512-bit outputs.

RIPEMD

RACE Integrity Primitives Evaluation Message Digest is a 160-bit hash algorithm developed in Belgium by Hans Dobbertin, Antoon Bosselaers, and Bart Preneel. This algorithm has 128-, 256-, and 320-bit versions, called RIPEMD-128, RIPEMD-256, and RIPEMD-320, respectively.

RIPEMD-160 replaces the original RIPEMD, which was found to have collision issues. The larger bit sizes make this far more secure that MD5 or RIPEMD. RIPEMD-160 was developed in Europe as part of the RIPE project and is recommended by the German Security Agency. The authors of the algorithm describe RIPEMD as follows:

> RIPEMD-160 is a fast cryptographic hash function that is tuned towards software implementations on 32-bit architectures. It has evolved from the 256-bit extension of MD4, which was introduced in 1990 by Ron Rivest. Its main design feature[s] are two different and independent parallel chains, the result of which are combined at the end of every application of the compression function.[3]

The RIPEMD-160 algorithm is slower than SHA-1 but perhaps more secure (at least according to some experts). The general algorithm uses two parallel lines of processing, each consisting of five rounds and 16 steps.

Note
Because the five rounds are in parallel, some sources describe RIPEMD as using ten rounds. Either description is accurate, depending on your perspective.

As with many other hashing algorithms, RIPEMD works with 512-bit segments of input text. It must first pad, so that the final message block is 448 bits plus a 64-bit value that is the length of the original message. (You may have noticed by now that padding is a very common approach to creating hashing algorithms.)

The initial five-word buffer (each word being 32 bits, for a total of 160 bits) is initialized to a set value. The buffers are labeled A, B, C, D, and E (as you have seen with previous algorithms). The message being hashed is processed in 512-bit segments, and the final output is the last 160 bits left in the buffer when the algorithm has completed all rounds.

Tiger

Tiger is designed using the Merkle-Damgård construction. Tiger produces a 192-bit digest. This cryptographic hash was invented by Ross Anderson and Eli Biham and published in 1995.

> **Note**
> You were introduced to Ross Anderson and Eli Biham in Chapter 7. These very prominent cryptographers are individually quite accomplished, and they have frequently collaborated in their work. Anderson is currently Cambridge University's head of cryptography and professor in security engineering. Biham is a prominent Israeli cryptographer who has done extensive work in symmetric ciphers, hashing algorithms, and cryptanalysis.

The one-way compression function operates on 64-bit words, maintaining three words of state and processing eight words of data.[4] There are 24 rounds, using a combination of operation mixing with XOR and addition/subtraction, rotates, and S-box lookups, and a fairly intricate key scheduling algorithm for deriving 24 round keys from the eight input words.

HAVAL

HAVAL is a cryptographic hash function. Unlike MD5, but like most other modern cryptographic hash functions, HAVAL can produce hashes of different lengths—128, 160, 192, 224, and 256 bits. HAVAL enables users to specify the number of rounds (three, four, or five) to be used to generate the hash. HAVAL was invented by Yuliang Zheng, Josef Pieprzyk, and Jennifer Seberry in 1992.

> **Note**
> Yuilang Zheng is, as of this writing, a professor at the University of North Carolina who has also worked in ciphers such as SPEED and the STRANDOM pseudo-random-number generator. Josef Pieprzyk is a professor at Queensland University of Technology in Australia and is known for his work on the LOKI family of block ciphers. Jennifer Seberry is currently a professor at the University of Wollongong in Australia and is notable not only for her work in cryptography, but for being the first female professor of computer science in Australia. She also has worked on the LOKI family of ciphers as well as the Py stream cipher.

Whirlpool

Whirlpool, invented by Paulo Barreto and Vincent Rijmen, was chosen as part of the NESSIE project (mentioned in Chapter 7) and has been adopted by the International Organization for Standardization (ISO) as a standard. Whirlpool is interesting because it is a modified block cipher. It is a common practice to create a hashing algorithm from a block cipher. In this case, the square cipher (precursor to Rijndael) was used as the basis. Whirlpool produces a 512-bit digest and can take in inputs up to 2^{256} bits in size.[5] The algorithm is not patented and can be used free of charge.

> **Note**
> Vincent Rijmen was one of the creators of the Rijndael cipher, which was chosen to become AES. Paulo Barreto is a Brazilian cryptographer who also worked on the Anubis and KHAZAD ciphers. He has worked on various projects with Rijmen and published papers on elliptic curve cryptography, discussed in Chapter 11.

Skein

The Skein cryptographic hash function was one of the five finalists in the NIST competition. Entered as a candidate to become the SHA-3 standard, it lost to Keccak. Skein was created by Bruce Schneier, Stefan Lucks, Niels Ferguson, Doug Whiting, Mihir Bellare, Tadayoshi Kohno,

Jon Callas, and Jesse Walker. It is based on the Threefish block cipher, which is compressed using the Unique Block Iteration (UBI) chaining mode while leveraging an optional low overhead argument system for flexibility.

> **Note** Both Bruce Schneier and Niels Ferguson are well-known cryptographic researchers. Stefan Lucks is primarily known for his work on cryptanalysis. Mihir Bellare is a professor at University of California San Diego and has published several papers on cryptography as well as earning the 2003 RSA's Sixth Annual Conference Award for outstanding contributions in the field of mathematics. Jon Callas is known primarily for his work with the Internet Engineering Task Force in establishing standards such as OpenPGP. Whiting also worked on the Twofish algorithm. Tadayoshi Kohno is an adjunct professor at the University of Washington and has published various computer security–related papers. Jesse Walker has published a number of cryptography-related papers and been a guest speaker on cryptography.

FSB

The Fast Syndrome-Based (FSB) hash functions are a family of cryptographic hash functions introduced in 2003 by Daniel Augot, Matthieu Finiasz, and Nicolas Sendrier.[6]

> **Note** Daniel Augot is a French researcher known for work in cryptography as well as algebraic coding theory. Matthieu Finiasz has numerous publications covering a wide variety of cryptographic topics. Nicolas Sendrier is a French researcher with extensive publications in both cryptography and computer security.

FSB is distinctive in that it can, at least to a certain extent, be proven to be secure. Breaking FSB is at least as difficult as solving a certain NP-complete problem known as *Regular Syndrome Decoding*. What this means, in practical terms, is that FSB is provably secure. (You read about NP-complete problems in Chapter 5.)

Security and efficiency are often conflicting goals, and provably secure algorithms are often a bit slower. Therefore, as you might expect, FSB is slower than many traditional hash functions and uses a lot of memory. There have been various versions of FSB, one of which was submitted to the SHA-3 competition, which was rejected.

GOST

This hash algorithm was initially defined in the Russian government standard GOST R 34.11-94 Information Technology – Cryptographic Information Security – Hash Function. The GOST algorithm produces a fixed-length output of 256 bits. The input message is broken up into chunks of 256-bit blocks. If a block is less than 256 bits, the message is padded to bring the length of the message up to 256 bits. The remaining bits are filled up with a 256-bit integer arithmetic sum of all previously hashed blocks, and then a 256-bit integer representing the length of the original message, in bits, is produced. It is based on the GOST block cipher period.

Attacks on Hashes

How does someone go about attacking a hash? Of particular interest are hashes used for password storage. The most common attack on hashed passwords is a *preimage attack*. In the security community, this is often done using a rainbow table, which reverses cryptographic hash functions.

In 1980, Martin Hellman described a cryptanalytic technique that reduces the time of cryptanalysis by using precalculated data stored in memory. This technique was improved by Rivest before 1982. Basically, these types of password crackers are working with precalculated hashes of all passwords available within a certain character space, be that a-z, a-zA-z, or a-zA-Z0-9, and so on. If you search a rainbow table for a given hash, whatever plain text you find must be the text that was input into the hashing algorithm to produce that specific hash.

A rainbow table can get very large very fast. Assume that the passwords must be limited to keyboard characters, and that leaves 52 letters (26 uppercase and 26 lowercase), 10 digits, and roughly 10 symbols, or about 72 characters. As you can imagine, even a six-character password has a large number of possible combinations. (Recall the discussion of combinatorics in Chapter 4.) There is a limit to how large a rainbow table can be, and this is why longer passwords are more secure that shorter passwords.

> **Note**
>
> As a practical matter, some utilities were designed to crack Windows passwords that include rainbow tables on a Linux live CD. The utility will boot to Linux and then attempt to grab the Windows SAM file, where hashes of passwords are stored, and run those through rainbow tables to get the passwords. This is another reason why longer passwords are a good security measure.

Salt

In hashing, the term *salt* refers to random bits that are used as one of the inputs to the hash. Essentially, the salt is intermixed with the message that is to be hashed. Consider this example password:

```
pass001
```

In binary, that is

```
01110000 01100001 01110011 01110011 00110000 00110000 00110001
```

A salt algorithm inserts bits periodically. Suppose we insert bits every fourth bit, giving us the following:

```
0111100001 0110100011 0111100111 0111100111 0011100001 0011100001 0011100011
```

If you convert that to text you would get

```
xZ7◇ ◇#
```

Someone using a rainbow table to try and derive salted passwords would get the incorrect password back and would not be able to log in to the system. Salt data makes rainbow tables harder to implement. The rainbow table must account for the salting algorithm as well as the hashing algorithm.

MAC and HMAC

As you know, hashing algorithms are often used to ensure message integrity. If a message is altered in transit, the recipient can compare the hash received against the hash computed and detect the error in transmission. But what about intentional alteration of messages? What happens if someone alters a message intentionally, deletes the original hash, and recomputes a new one? Unfortunately, a simple hashing algorithm cannot account for this scenario. A message authentication code (MAC), however—specifically a keyed-hash message authentication code (HMAC)—can detect intentional alterations in a message. A MAC is also often called a keyed cryptographic hash function,[7] and its name should tell you how it works.

Let's assume you are using MD5 to verify message integrity. To detect an intercepting party intentionally altering a message, both the sender and recipient must previously exchange a key of the appropriate size (in this case, 128 bits). The sender will hash the message and then XOR that hash with this key. The recipient will hash what she receives and XOR that computed hash with the key. Then the two hashes are exchanged. Should an intercepting party simply recompute the hash, he will not have the key to XOR that with (and may not even be aware that it should be XOR'd) and thus the hash the interceptor creates won't match the hash the recipient computes and the interference will be detected.

Another common way of accomplishing a MAC is called a *cipher block chaining MAC* (CBC-MAC). In this case, a block cipher is used (any cipher will do) rather than a hash. The algorithm is used in CBC mode. Only the final block is used for the MAC. You can use any block cipher you choose.

> **Note** Recall that CBC mode XOR's the cipher text from each block with that of the next block before encrypting it.

Conclusions

This chapter offered a broad overview of cryptographic hashes. The first important things you should absolutely commit to memory are the three criteria for an algorithm to be a cryptographic hash. You should also be familiar with the practical applications of cryptographic hashes.

You have also been exposed to several cryptographic hashing algorithms, some in more detail than others. The SHA family of hashing algorithms is the most widely used, and thus is the most important for you to be familiar with. The other algorithms presented in this chapter are widely used and warrant some study—perhaps in depth. You can find a great deal of information, including research papers, on the Internet.

Test Your Knowledge

1. _____ is a message authentication code that depends on a block cipher wherein only the final block is used.
2. The _____ works by first dividing the input into words and computing the modular sum of those words.

3. What hashing algorithm that uses a modified block cipher was chosen as part of the NESSIE project?
4. What algorithm was ultimately chosen as SHA-3?
5. What are the three properties all cryptographic hash functions must exhibit?
6. What is the compression function used as a basis for MD5, SHA1, and SHA2?
7. _____ was developed in Europe and is recommended by the German Security Agency.
8. Which algorithm discussed in this chapter was published in 1995 and produces a 192-bit digest?
9. _____ was one of the five finalists in the SHA-3 competition (but did not win) and is based on the Threefish block cipher.
10. Which hash functions introduced in this chapter have provable security?

Answers

1. CBC-MAC
2. Fletcher checksum
3. Whirlpool
4. Keccak
5. a) Variable-length input produces fixed-length output; b) no collisions; c) not reversible
6. Merkle-Damgård
7. RIPEMD-160
8. Tiger
9. Skein
10. Fast Syndrome-Based (FSB) hash functions

Endnotes

1. William Stallings, *Network Security Essentials: Applications and Standards*, 5th ed. (Prentice Hall, 2013).
2. National Institute of Standards and Technology, *SHA-3 Standard: Permutation-Based Hash and Extendable-Output Functions*, 2014, http://csrc.nist.gov/publications/drafts/fips-202/fips_202_draft.pdf.
3. B. Preneel, H. Dobbertin, and A. Bosselaers, "The Cryptographic Hash Function RIPEMD-160," 1997, www.cosic.esat.kuleuven.be/publications/article-317.pdf.
4. For more information, see "Tiger: A Fast New Hash Function," at www.cl.cam.ac.uk/~rja14/Papers/tiger.pdf.
5. For more information, see "The Whirlpool Secure Hash Function" by William Stallings, at www.seas.gwu.edu/~poorvi/Classes/CS381_2007/Whirlpool.pdf.
6. For more information, see "A Family of Fast Syndrome Based Cryptographic Hash Functions," at http://lasec.epfl.ch/pub/lasec/doc/AFS05.pdf.
7. RFC 2104, "HMAC: Keyed-Hashing for Message Authentication," describes HMAC in detail. See https://tools.ietf.org/html/rfc2104.

10 Common Algorithms

In this chapter we will cover the following:

- What is asymmetric cryptography?
- RSA
- Diffie-Hellman
- ElGamal
- MQV
- Homomorphic encryption
- Applications

I n this chapter we will discuss asymmetric cryptography, including its general concepts and usage, as well as an in-depth discussion of the more common asymmetric algorithms. You will apply the mathematics you learned about in Chapters 4 and 5.

Note	Where necessary, I will provide a brief reminder of the mathematical principles covered earlier in the book. However, if those chapters were new or difficult for you, you may want to review them before proceeding with this chapter.

What Is Asymmetric Cryptography?

In asymmetric cryptography, as the name suggests, one key is used to encrypt a message and a different (but related) key is used to decrypt it. This concept often baffles those new to cryptography and students in network security courses. How can it be that a key used to encrypt will not also decrypt? This will be clearer to you once we examine a few algorithms and you see the actual mathematics involved. For now, set that issue to one side and simply accept that one key encrypts but cannot decrypt the message; another key is used to decrypt it.

Asymmetric cryptography is a powerful concept because symmetric cryptography (which you studied in Chapters 6 and 7) has a serious problem. That problem is key exchange and the potential for compromise. Let's look at an example to demonstrate. For some reason, all security and cryptography books like to use the fictitious characters Alice, Bob, and Eve to explain how asymmetric cryptography works, and I will continue that tradition here.

Let's assume, then, that Alice would like to send Bob a message. But Alice is concerned that Eve might eavesdrop (thus her name!) on the communication. Now let's further assume that they don't have asymmetric cryptography—all they have are the symmetric ciphers (which you learned about in Chapters 6 and 7). Further, Bob and Alice do not live in the same location, so how can they exchange a key so that they might encrypt messages? Any method (other than asymmetric cryptography) has the very real chance of being compromised, short of a secure/trusted courier manually taking the keys to the two parties. (If a courier was needed to exchange keys every time secure communication was required, then we would not have online banking, e-commerce, or a host of other useful technologies.)

With public key/asymmetric cryptography, Alice will get Bob's public key and use that to encrypt the message she sends to Bob. If Eve intercepts the message and gains access to Bob's public key, that's OK, because that key won't decrypt the message. Only Bob's private key will do so, and this he safeguards. You can see the process in Figure 10-1.

If Bob wants to respond to Alice, he reverses the process. He gets Alice's public key and encrypts a message to her—a message that only *her* private key will decrypt.

Asymmetric cryptography solves the problem of key exchange. It does not impede security, even if literally every person on the planet has both Bob's and Alice's public keys. Those keys can be used only to encrypt messages to Bob and Alice (respectively) and cannot decrypt the messages. So as long as Bob and Alice keep their private keys secret, secure communication is achieved with no problems in key exchange.

This basic concept of two keys—one key being public and another being private—is why this is often called *public key* cryptography. The term *asymmetric cryptography* is also used because the two keys are not the same—they are not symmetrical. Unfortunately, this is as far as many security courses go in explaining asymmetric cryptography—but, of course, we will be delving into the actual algorithms.

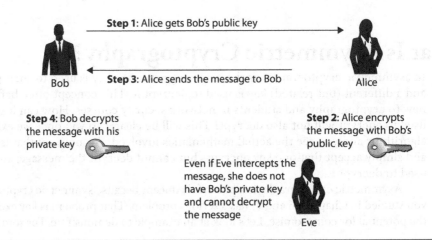

FIGURE 10-1   **Alice sends Bob a message with asymmetric cryptography.**

RSA

RSA may be the most widely used asymmetric algorithm, and it is certainly one of the most well-known. This public key method was developed in 1977 by three mathematicians—Ron Rivest, Adi Shamir, and Leonard Adleman. The name RSA is derived from the first letter of each mathematician's last name. The algorithm is based on prime numbers and the difficulty of factoring a large number into its prime factors.

Note	The three inventors of RSA are very well-known and respected cryptographers. Ron Rivest has been a professor at MIT and invented several algorithms including RC2, RC4, RC5, MD2, MD4, MD5, and MD6. Adi Shamir is an Israeli cryptographer and one of the inventors of differential cryptanalysis. Leonard Adleman has made significant contributions to using DNA as a computational system.

As often happens in the history of cryptography, it turns out that a similar system was developed earlier in England, but it was classified. In 1973, Clifford Cocks developed a system that remained classified until the late 1990s. Cocks worked for the English government, specifically the Government Communications Headquarters (GCHQ). He went on to develop other, nonclassified cryptographic innovations. In 2001 he invented one of the early identity-based encryption methodologies using aspects of number theory.

The RSA Algorithm

To create the public and private key pair, you start by generating two large random primes, p and q, of approximately equal size. You need to select two numbers so that when multiplied together, the product will be the size you want (such as 2048 bits, 4096 bits, and so on).

Next, multiply p and q to get n:

$$\text{Let } n = pq$$

The next step is to multiply *Euler's totient* for each of these primes.

Tip	You'll recall reading about Euler's totient in Chapter 4. Two numbers are considered co-prime if they have no common factors. For example, if the original number is 8, then 8 and 9 would be co-prime—8's factors are 2 and 4, and 9's factors are 3. Euler asked a few questions about co-prime integers. Given a number X, how many numbers smaller than X are co-prime to X? We call that number *Euler's totient*, or just the totient. It just so happens that for prime numbers, this is always *the number minus 1*. So, for example 7 has 6 numbers that are co-prime to it.

When you multiply two primes together, you get a composite number, and there is no easy way to determine the Euler's totient of a composite number. Recall that Euler found that if you multiply any two prime numbers together, the Euler's totient of that product is the Euler's totient of each prime multiplied together. So here's our next step:

$$\text{Let } m = (p - 1)(q - 1)$$

So m is the Euler's totient of n.

Now we are going to select another number—we will call this number e. The number e should be co-prime to m. Frequently, a prime number is chosen for e; that way, if e does not evenly divide m, then we are confident that e and m are co-prime, because e does not have any factors to consider.

> **Note**   Many RSA implementations use $e = 216 + 1 = 65537$. This is considered large enough to be effective but small enough to still be fast.

At this point, we have almost completed generating the key. Now we must find a number d that, when multiplied by e and modulo m, would yield a 1. (Note that *modulo* means to divide two numbers and return the remainder—for example, 8 modulo 3 would be 2.) In other words,

$$\text{Find } d, \text{ such that } de \% m = 1$$

Now you will publish e and n as the public key. Keep d as the secret key. To encrypt, you simply take your message raised to the e power and modulo n.

$$C = M^e \% n$$

To decrypt, you take the cipher text and raise it to the d power modulo n.

$$P = C^d \% n$$

RSA Example 1

Let's look at an example that might help you better understand. Of course, RSA would be done with very large integers, but to make the math easy to follow, small integers are used in this example. (Note that this example is from Wikipedia.)

1. Choose two distinct prime numbers, such as p = 61 and q = 53.
2. Compute n = pq, giving n = 61 × 53 = 3233.
3. Compute the totient of the product as $\varphi(n) = (p - 1)(q - 1)$ giving $\varphi(3233) = (61 - 1) \times (53 - 1) = 3120$.
4. Choose any number 1 < e < 3120 that is co-prime to 3120. Choosing a prime number for e leaves us only to check that e is not a divisor of 3120. Let e = 17.
5. Compute d, the modular multiplicative inverse of e, yielding d = 2753.

The public key is (n = 3233, e = 17). For a padded plaintext message m, the encryption function is $m^{17} \pmod{3233}$.

The private key is (n = 3233, d = 2753). For an encrypted cipher text c, the decryption function is $c^{2753} \pmod{3233}$.

RSA Example 2

For those of you who are new to RSA, or new to cryptography in general, it might be helpful to see one more example, with even smaller numbers.

1. Select primes: p = 17 and q = 11.
2. Compute n = pq = 17 × 11 = 187.

3. Compute ø(n) = (p − 1)(q − 1) = 16 × 10 = 160.
4. Select e: gcd(e,160) = 1; choose e = 7.
5. Determine d: de = 1 mod 160 and d < 160. Value is d = 23 since 23 × 7 = 161 = 10 × 160 + 1.
6. Publish public key (7 and 187).
7. Keep secret private key 23.

If you are struggling with the concepts of RSA key generation, I suggest you first work through these two examples. Because the complete process as well as the answers are provided for you, it will be easy for you to check your work. You may also want to work through a few more examples. Start with any two prime numbers that are small enough to make the calculations feasible.

Factoring RSA Keys

You may be thinking, couldn't someone take the public key and use factoring to derive the private key? Well, hypothetically yes. However, it turns out that factoring really large numbers into their prime factors is extremely difficult—a more technical description would be that it is computationally infeasible, because there is no efficient algorithm for doing it. And when I say large numbers, RSA can use 1024-, 2048-, 4096-, 8192-bit and larger keys—those are extremely large numbers. Here's an example of a 2048-bit number represented in decimal format:

```
51483247893254789632147780069501356699875410025145630214586147855148324789
32547896321477800695015148324789325478963214778006950135669987541002514563
02145861478551483247893254789632147780069501325666312458863144587702335658
8896350232358658900145221478533654
```

In most modern implementations, at least as of this writing, 2048 bits is the smallest RSA key used. Reflect on the rather large number above and contemplate attempting to factor that number.

There are mathematical techniques that will improve the process, but nothing that makes factoring such large numbers a feasible endeavor. Of course, should anyone ever invent an efficient algorithm that will factor a large number into its prime factors, RSA would be dead.

There certainly have been incidents where someone was able to factor a small RSA key. In 2009, Benjamin Moody factored a 512-bit RSA key in 73 days. In 2010, researchers were able to factor a 768-bit RSA key. Due to these advances in factorization, modern implementations of RSA are using larger key sizes.[1] In Chapter 17 we will examine cryptanalysis techniques used on RSA.

Tip   This section provides a basic introduction to RSA. A great resource for delving deeper into RSA is the book *Cryptanalysis of RSA and Its Variants* by M. Jason Hinek (Chapman and Hall/CRC, 2009). You also might find it interesting to read the paper "Fast Variants of RSA" by Dan Boneh and Hovav Shacham, at https://cseweb.ucsd.edu/~hovav/dist/survey.pdf.

The Rabin Cryptosystem

This algorithm was created in 1979 by Israeli cryptographer Michael Rabin, who is a recipient of the Turing Award. You can think of the Rabin cryptosystem as an RSA cryptosystem in which the value of e and d are fixed.

$$e = 2 \text{ and } d = 1/2$$

The encryption is $C \equiv P^2 \pmod{n}$ and the decryption is $P \equiv C^{1/2} \pmod{n}$.

Here is a very trivial example to show the idea:

1. Bob selects $p = 23$ and $q = 7$.
2. Bob calculates $n = p \times q = 161$.
3. Bob announces n publicly; he keeps p and q private.
4. Alice wants to send the plain text message $M = 24$. Note that 161 and 24 are relatively prime; 24 is in the group selected, Z_{161}*.

Encryption: $C \equiv 24^2 \mod 161 = 93$, and sends the cipher text 93 to Bob.

> **Note**   This algorithm is not as widely used as RSA or Diffie-Hellman, but I present it here to give you a general overview of alternative asymmetric algorithms.

The Turing Award

The Turing award is a prize given every year by the Association for Computing Machinery (ACM) to a computer scientist whose contributions are lasting and of major importance. Some people call this award the Nobel Prize for computing. It is named after Alan Turing. Some notable recipients are Edgar F. Codd, who won the award for creating the concept of relational databases; Niklaus Wirth, who developed several programming languages, including Pascal and ALGOL-w; and Alan Kay, for his work in object-oriented programming, including leading the team that developed the Smalltalk programming language.

Diffie-Hellman

Although some security textbooks state that RSA was the "first asymmetric algorithm," this is not accurate. In fact, Diffie-Hellman was the first publically described asymmetric algorithm. This cryptographic protocol allows two parties to establish a shared key over an insecure channel. In other words, Diffie-Hellman is often used to allow parties to exchange a symmetric key through some unsecure medium, such as the Internet. It was developed by Whitfield Diffie and Martin Hellman in 1976.

Note As you already saw with RSA, one problem with working in cryptology is that much of the work is classified. You could labor away and create something wonderful…that you cannot tell anyone about. Then, to make matters worse, years later someone else might develop something similar and release it, getting all the credit. This is exactly the situation with Diffie-Hellman. It turns out that a similar method had been developed a few years earlier by Malcolm J. Williamson of the British Intelligence Service, but it was classified.

The system has two parameters called p and g. Parameter p is a prime number and parameter g (usually called a *generator*) is an integer less than p, with the following property: for every number n between 1 and $p - 1$ inclusive, there is a power k of g such that $n = g^k \bmod p$.

Let's revisit our old friends Alice and Bob to illustrate this:

1. Alice generates a random private value a and Bob generates a random private value b. Both a and b are drawn from the set of integers.
2. They derive their public values using parameters p and g and their private values. Alice's public value is $g^a \bmod p$ and Bob's public value is $g^b \bmod p$.
3. They exchange their public values.
4. Alice computes $g^{ab} = (g^b)^a \bmod p$, and Bob computes $g^{ba} = (g^a)^b \bmod p$.
5. Since $g^{ab} = g^{ba} = k$, Alice and Bob now have a shared secret key k.

This process is shown in Figure 10-2.

ElGamal

First described by Egyptian cryptographer Taher ElGamal in 1984, ElGamal is based on the Diffie-Hellman key exchange algorithm and is used in some versions of Pretty Good Privacy (PGP). The ElGamal algorithm has three components: the key generator, the encryption algorithm, and the decryption algorithm.

Both parties know p and g

Alice

1. Alice generates a
2. Alice's public value is $g^a \bmod p$
3. Alice computes $g^{ab} = (g^b)^a \bmod p$

Since $g^{ab} = g^{ba}$ they now have a shared secret key usually called k ($K = g^{ab} = g^{ba}$)

Bob

1. Bob generates b
2. Bob's public value is $g^b \bmod p$
3. Bob computes $g^{ba} = (g^a)^b \bmod p$

FIGURE 10-2   Diffie-Hellman process

Here's an example, with Alice and Bob:

1. Alice generates an efficient description of a multiplicative cyclic group G of order q with generator g.

> **Note**   You should remember groups from Chapter 5. A cyclic group is generated by a single element—in this case, that is the generator g. With a multiplicative cyclic group, each element can be written as some power of g.

2. Next Alice chooses a random number x from a set of numbers $\{0, \ldots, q - 1\}$.
3. Then Alice computes $h = g^x$. Remember g is the generator for the group and x is a random number from within the group.
4. h, G, q, and g are the public key, and x is the private key.
5. If Bob wants to encrypt a message m with the public key Alice generated, the following process occurs:
   A. Bob generates a random number y chosen from $\{0, \ldots, q - 1\}$. Y is often called an *ephemeral key.*
   B. Next Bob will calculate c1: $c1 = g^y$.
   C. Next a shared secret, $s = h^y$, is computed.
   D. The message m is converted to m′ of G.
   E. Next Bob must calculate c2: $c2 = m′ * s$.
   F. Bob can now send c1 and c2 = as the encrypted text.
6. To decrypt a message m with the public key the first person generated, the following process occurs:
   A. The recipient calculates $s = c1^x$.
   B. The recipient calculates $m′ = c2 * s^{-1}$.
   C. Finally, m′ is converted back to the plain text m.

> **Note**   This structure should look similar to Diffie-Hellman.

MQV

Like ElGamal, MQV (Menezes–Qu–Vanstone) is a protocol for key agreement that is based on Diffie-Hellman. It was first proposed by Alfred Menezes, Minghua Qu, and Scott Vanstone in 1995 and then modified in 1998. MQV is incorporated in the public-key standard IEEE P1363. HQMV is an improved version. The specific algorithm is related to elliptic curves, and we will address those specifics in Chapter 11.

> **Note**   Alfred Menezes is a professor of mathematics at the University of Waterloo in Canada and the author of several books on cryptography.

Optimal Asymmetric Encryption Padding

OAEP (Optimal Asymmetric Encryption Padding) was introduced in 1994 by M. Bellare and P. Rogaway and is standardized in RFC 2437. OAEP processes the plain text prior to encryption with an asymmetric algorithm. When used with an algorithm such as RSA, it gives a cryptography scheme that is proven to be secure against a chosen plain text attack.

OAEP satisfies the following two goals:

- Adds an element of randomness that can be used to convert a deterministic encryption scheme such as RSA into a probabilistic scheme.
- Prevents partial decryption of cipher texts (or other information leakage) by ensuring that an adversary cannot recover any portion of the plain text without being able to invert the trapdoor one-way permutation f.

Cramer-Shoup

The Cramer-Shoup system is an asymmetric key encryption algorithm that was developed by Ronald Cramer and Victor Shoup in 1998. It is an extension of the ElGamal cryptosystem and was the first efficient algorithm proven to be secure against an adaptive chosen cipher text attack.

Applications

By this point, you should have a general understanding of several asymmetric algorithms and a very good understanding of at least RSA and Diffie-Hellman. Now for a thorough discussion of how asymmetric algorithms are used. In this section we will look at common applications for asymmetric algorithms.

Key Exchange

As you know, symmetric algorithms are much faster than asymmetric, and they achieve the same security with much smaller keys. However, asymmetric algorithms overcome the issue of key exchange. Therefore, it is common for asymmetric algorithms to be used for exactly that purpose. For example, in Secure Sockets Layer (SSL) and Transport Layer Security (TLS), an asymmetric algorithm (such as RSA) is used to exchange a symmetric key (such as AES, Advanced Encryption Standard). This is a common way to use asymmetric algorithms.

Digital Signatures

I am sure you are familiar with the term "digital signatures," but do you know what they are and how they work? Remember that cryptographic algorithms are about protecting confidentiality, ensuring that only the intended recipient can read the message. Essentially, digital signatures reverse asymmetric cryptography, so that they can protect integrity. A digital signature uses the sender's private key and encrypts either the entire message or a portion of it (such as the signature block) so anyone with the sender's public key can decrypt that. A digital signature verifies that the sender really is who he or she claims to be and is an important aspect of message security.

Put another way, assume your boss sends you an e-mail telling you that you have done such a great job, he thinks you should take next week off with pay. It would probably be a good thing to verify that this is legitimate, that he really sent it, and that it's not a prank. What a digital signature does is to take the sender's private key and encrypt either the entire message or a portion (like the signature block). Now anyone with the sender's public key can decrypt that. So let's return to Alice and Bob to see how this works.

Bob wants to send Alice a message and make certain she knows it's from him, so he signs it with his private key. When Alice uses Bob's public key, the message decrypts and she can read it. Now suppose that Bob didn't really send this message. Instead, Eve sent it, pretending to be Bob. Because Eve does not have Bob's private key, she had to use some other key to sign the message. So when Alice tries to decrypt it (that is, verify the signature) with Bob's public key, she will get back gibberish and nonsense, such as that shown in Figure 10-3.

In essence, to have total security for a message, you would execute the following steps:

1. Use a hash, message authentication code (MAC), or hash MAC (HMAC) on the message and put the digest at the end of the message.
2. Digitally sign the message—usually just a portion such as the hash or signature block— with your own private key.
3. Encrypt the message with the recipient's public key.

This process is depicted in Figure 10-4.

The recipient then reverses the process:

1. Decrypts the message with the recipient's private key.
2. Verifies the signature with the sender's public key.
3. Recalculates the hash, MAC, or HMAC and compares it to the one received to ensure that there were no errors in transmission.

More than one type of digital signature exists. The type I just described is the most common and is referred to as a *direct digital signature*. A second type is the *arbitrated digital signature*. It is similar to the process just described, but instead of the sender digitally signing each message, a trusted third party digitally signs the message, attesting to the sender's identity.

```
-------BEGIN SIGNATURE------
uMfgNYjAQFAKgL/ZkBfbeNEsbthba4BlrcnjaqbcKgRCd+R
Hm7LIQUBMVSiA5QYCwNhhb
a5kr4B1Aw7LlOnAelws4S87UX80cLBtBcN6AACf1mC2h+R
b2j5S1qyU+rmXWru+5yYh5x7cxA1ojEHg45Saodi4fRR
=Nv+537y8
------END SIGNATURE------
```

FIGURE 10-3   Without having the appropriate key, all you get is gibberish.

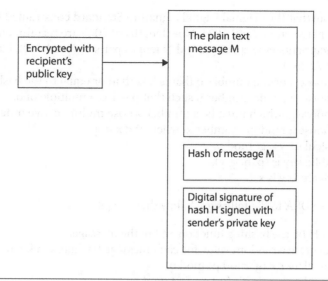

FIGURE 10-4   Message security with digital signatures

A third type of digital signature also exists—the *blind signature*. Basically, a sender makes a signer to sign a message m without knowing m; therefore, this is considered a blind signature. Blind signing can be achieved by a two-party protocol between the sender and the signer that has the following properties.

- In order to sign (by a signer) a message *m*, the sender computes, using a blinding procedure, from m and m* from which m cannot be obtained without knowing a secret, and sends m* to the signer.
- The signer signs m* to get a signature s_{m*} (of m*) and sends s_{m*} to the sender. Signing is done in such a way that the sender can afterward compute, using an unblinding procedure, from signer's signature s_{m*} of m*—the signer signature s_m of m.

This allows the arbiter to sign the message, confirming that it was created on a given date by a specific sender, without knowing the contents of the message.

Digital Signature Algorithm

A digital signature can be done with any asymmetric algorithm; however, some algorithms have been created specifically for digitally signing messages. The Digital Signature Algorithm (DSA) described in U.S. Patent 5,231,668 was filed July 26, 1991, and attributed to David W. Kravitz. It was adopted by the U.S. government in 1993 with FIPS 186. The actual algorithm functions as follows:

1. Choose a hash function (traditionally this has been SHA1, but the stronger the hash the better).
2. Select a key length L and N.

Note that the original Digital Signature Standard constrained L to be a multiple of 64 between 512 and 1024. Now lengths of 2048 are recommended. U.S. government documents now specify L and N length pairs of (1024,160), (2048,224), (2048,256), and (3072,256).

3. Choose a prime number q that is less than or equal to the hash output length.
4. Choose a prime number p such that p − 1 is a multiple of q.
5. Choose g, which must be a number whose multiplicative order modulo p is q.
6. Choose a random number x, where 0 < x < q.
7. Calculate $y = g^x$ mod p.
   Public key is (p, q, g, y).
   Private key is x.

To use DSA to digitally sign, follow these steps:

1. Let H be the hashing function and m the message.
2. Generate a random value for each message k where 0 < k < q.
3. Calculate $r = (g^k$ mod p$)$ mod q.
4. Calculate $s = (k^{-1}(H(m) + x*r))$ mod q.
5. If r or s = 0, then recalculate for a non-zero result (that is, pick a different k).
6. The signature is (r, s).

DSA is a commonly used digital signature algorithm. In Chapter 11 you will see an elliptic curve variation of DSA.

Digital Certificates

A digital certificate is a digital document that contains information about the certificate holder and (if it is an X.509 certificate) the method to verify this information with a trusted third party. Digital certificates are how web sites distribute their public keys to end users, and they are how web sites can be authenticated.

The most common type of certificates is X.509. Before we go further into this topic, you should first get acquainted with the contents of an X.509 certificate:

- **Version**   What version of the X.509 standard is this certificate using.
- **Certificate holder's public key**   One of the reasons we use digital certificates is so that the recipient can get the certificate holder's public key. If you visit a web site that uses SSL/TLS (discussed later in this chapter), your browser gets the web site's public key from the site's digital certificate.
- **Serial number**   This identifies the specific certificate.
- **Certificate holder's distinguished name**   Something to identify the certificate holder uniquely, often an e-mail address or domain name.
- **Certificate's validity period**   How long this certificate is good for.
- **Unique name of certificate issuer**   The preceding items identify the certificate, the certificate holder, and provide the certificate holder's public key. But how do you know this certificate really belongs to who claims it? How do you know it is not a fake? You verify the certificate with a trusted certificate issuer, such as Verisign.

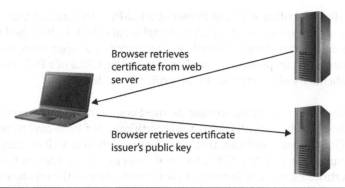

Browser retrieves certificate from web server

Browser retrieves certificate issuer's public key

FIGURE 10-5 Retrieving a digital signature

- **Digital signature of issuer** To prove this certificate was issued by a trusted certificate issuer, that issuer signs the certificate.
- **Signature algorithm identifier** Indicates what digital signing algorithm the certificate issuer used in this process.

For example, when you visit a web site that uses SSL/TLS, your browser will first retrieve the web site's certificate. Then it notes the unique name of the certificate issuer. The browser then retrieves that issuer's public key from the issuer to verify the digital signature. If it is verified, secure communications can proceed. You can see this process in Figure 10-5.

Following are some general terms associated with digital certificates that you should be familiar with:

- **PKI (public key infrastructure)** Uses asymmetric key pairs and combines software, encryption, and services to provide a means of protecting the security of business communication and transactions.
- **PKCS (Public Key Cryptography Standards)** Put in place by RSA to ensure uniform certificate management throughout the Internet.
- **CA (certification authority)** An entity trusted by one or more users to issue and manage certificates.
- **RA (registration authority)** Takes the burden off a CA by handling verification prior to certificates being issued. The RA acts as a proxy between the user and the CA—receiving a request, authenticating it, and forwarding it to the CA.
- **X.509** The international standard for the format and information contained in a digital certificate. X.509 is the most common type of digital certificate in the world. It is a digital document that contains a public key signed by a trusted third party known as a certificate authority.
- **CRL (certificate revocation list)** A list of certificates issued by a CA that are no longer valid. CRLs are distributed in two main ways: via a PUSH model, in which the CA automatically sends out the CRL at regular intervals, and via a pull model, in which the CRL is downloaded from the CA by those who want to see it to verify a certificate.

- **Online Certificate Status Protocol (OCSP)**   An Internet protocol used for obtaining the revocation status of an X.509 digital certificate. It is described in RFC 2560 and is on the Internet standards track. It was created as an alternative to CRLs, specifically to address certain problems associated with using CRLs in a PKI. The OCSP allows the authenticity of a certificate to be verified immediately.

Although X.509 certificates are the most common certificate type, they are not the only type. Usually web sites will use an X.509 certificate, but for e-mail some people use PGP, or Pretty Good Privacy, software that provides encryption as well as integrity. PGP was created by Phil Zimmerman in 1991. PGP software defines its own certificate. It does not have CAs that issue certificates, so there is no third-party verification of the certificate holder's identity. But PGP certificates can be used to exchange public keys. Here are some basic fields found in most PGP certificates:

- PGP version number
- Certificate holder's public key
- Certificate holder's information
- Digital signature of certificate owner
- Certificate's validity period
- Preferred symmetric encryption algorithm for the key

The critical issue to keep in mind with PGP certificates is that they do not include any trusted third-party verification. Therefore, they are not used in applications where such verification is important, such as e-commerce. However, PGP is often used to encrypt e-mail.

SSL/TLS

Chapter 13 covers SSL and TLS fully. This section is meant as a basic introduction to the topic. If you ever use a secure web site—for example, to check your bank account, shop on Amazon .com, or for any sort of e-commerce—you have used SSL/TLS. The Secure Sockets Layer is a technology employed to allow for transport-layer security via public-key encryption. Most web sites now use TLS (the successor to SSL) but the term SSL stuck, so many people simply refer to SSL to mean either SSL or TLS. The SSL/TLS protocol was developed by Netscape for transmitting private documents via the Internet. URLs that require an SSL connection start with *https:* instead of *http:*. SSL/TLS works by using X.509 certificates so the browser can get the web server's public key, and then that public key is used to exchange a symmetric key. There have been several versions as of this writing:

- Unreleased v1 (Netscape)
- Version 2, released in 1995 with many flaws
- Version 3, released in 1996, RFC 6101
- Standard TLS1.0, RFC 2246, released in 1999
- TLS 1.1 defined in RFC 4346 in April 2006
- TLS 1.2 defined in RFC 5246 in August 2008, based on the earlier TLS 1.1 spec
- TLS 1.3 as of July 2014, TLS 1.3

The process of establishing an SSL/TLS connection is actually somewhat straightforward:

1. When the client browser first encounters a web site that indicates the use of SSL/TLS, the client sends the server the client's SSL version number, cipher settings (that is, what algorithms the client is capable of), and some session-specific data.

2. The server responds to the client with similar information from the server: the server's SSL version number, cipher settings, and some session-specific data. The server also sends its X.509 certificate. If mutual authentication is being used, or if the client is requesting a server resource that requires client authentication, the server requests the client's certificate.

3. The client browser first uses the X.509 certificate from the server to authenticate the server. If the server cannot be authenticated, the user is warned of the problem and informed that an encrypted and authenticated connection cannot be established. If the server can be successfully authenticated, the client proceeds to the next step, using the server's public key that the client retrieved from the X.509 certificate.

4. Using all data generated in the handshake thus far, the client creates the premaster secret for the session. Then the client encrypts this premaster secret with the server's public key and sends the encrypted premaster secret to the server.

5. In this optional step, if the server has requested client authentication, the client will also send its own X.509 certificate so that the server can authenticate the client. The server attempts to authenticate the client. If the client cannot be authenticated, the session ends. If the client can be successfully authenticated, the server uses its private key to decrypt the premaster secret, and then performs a series of steps to generate the master secret. These are the exact steps the client will use on the premaster secret to generate the same master secret on the client side.

6. Both the client and the server use the master secret to generate the session keys, which are symmetric keys (using whatever algorithm the client and server agreed upon). All communication between the client and the server after this point will be encrypted with that session key.

7. The client sends a message to the server informing it that future messages from the client will be encrypted with the session key. It then sends a message indicating that the client portion of the handshake is finished. The server responds with a similar message, telling the client that all future messages from the server will be encrypted, and the server portion of the handshake is complete.

This handshake process may seem a bit complex, but it serves several purposes. First, it allows the client to authenticate the server and get the server's public key. It then allows the client and server both to generate the same symmetric key, and then use that key to encrypt all communication between the two parties. This provides a very robust means of secure communication.

Homomorphic Encryption

Homomorphic encryption is about allowing mathematical operations to be performed on data that is still encrypted. In other words, analysis can be conducted on the cipher text itself, without the need to decipher the text first. Before I delve into how this is accomplished, you may find it useful to understand why this is done. In some situations, you may want a third party to calculate some value regarding data, without exposing the party to the actual plain text data. In such situations, homomorphic encryption is the solution.

Homomorphic encryption plays an important part in cloud computing by allowing companies to store encrypted data in a public cloud and still use the cloud provider's analytic tools. The cloud provider can analyze aspects of the data without decrypting the data.

The Pallier cryptosystem is an example of a homomorphic cryptography system. This asymmetric algorithm was invented by Pascal Paillier in 1999 and is one of the modern homomorphic cryptographic algorithms.

Conclusions

This chapter provided an overview of asymmetric cryptography. RSA is the most important algorithm for you to understand from this chapter, which is why you were shown two different examples of RSA. It is imperative that you fully understand RSA before proceeding to the next chapter. The next most important algorithm discussed is Diffie-Hellman. The other algorithms are interesting, and if you proceed further in cryptography you will, undoubtedly, delve deeper into those algorithms.

This chapter also introduced you to applications of cryptography. Digital certificates and SSL/TLS are commonly used, and you need to have a strong understanding of these applications before proceeding. Homomorphic encryption is a relatively new topic, and at this point you need only have a general understanding of what it is.

Test Your Knowledge

1. Which algorithm based on Diffie-Hellman was first described in 1984 and is named after its inventor?
2. U.S. Patent 5,231,668 was filed July 26, 1991, and attributed to David W. Kravitz. The _____ was adopted by the U.S. government in 1993 with FIPS 186.
3. The _____ can be thought of as an RSA cryptosystem in which the value of e and d are fixed: e = 2 and d = 1/2.
4. Explain the basic setup of Diffie-Hellman (the basic math including key generation).
5. Explain RSA key generation.
6. What is the formula for encrypting with RSA?
7. _____ was introduced by Bellare and Rogaway and is standardized in RFC 2437.
8. What does PKCS stand for?
9. What is the most widely used digital certificate standard?
10. X.509 certificates contain the digital signature of who?

Answers

1. ElGamal
2. Digital Signature Algorithm (DSA)
3. Rabin cryptosystem

4. The system has two parameters called p and g. Parameter p is a prime number and parameter g (usually called a generator) is an integer less than p, with the following property: for every number n between 1 and p − 1 inclusive, there is a power k of g such that $n = g^k \bmod p$. One public key is g^a and the other is g^b.

5. Let n = pq. Let m = (p − 1)(q − 1). Choose a small number e, co-prime to m. (Note: Two numbers are co-prime if they have no common factors.) Find d, such that de % m = 1. Publish e and n as the public key. Keep d and n as the secret key.

6. $C = M^e \% n$

7. OAEP (Optimal Asymmetric Encryption Padding)

8. Public Key Cryptography Standards

9. X.509

10. The issuer of the certificate

Endnote

1. For more information, see "Factorization of a 768-bit RSA Modulus," by Kleinjung, Aoki, Franke, et al., at https://eprint.iacr.org/2010/006.pdf.

11 Elliptic Curve Cryptography

In this chapter we will cover the following:

- The basic math of elliptic curves
- Elliptic curve groups as a basis for cryptography
- ECC variations

The elliptic curve may be the most mathematically challenging algorithm that you will encounter in this book, or in any other introductory cryptography book. If you feel uncertain of your mathematical acumen, it might help to review Chapters 4 and particularly 5. Throughout this chapter, brief reminders cover key mathematical concepts to help you follow along. If your goal is a career related to cryptography, then you will at some point need to master this material. However, if you simply want to get a general overview of cryptography, with a primary focus on computer/network security, you will finish this chapter with a broad overview of elliptic curve cryptography.

> **Note** Because this topic is often difficult for many readers, this chapter (albeit a short one) has been devoted to just this topic. Furthermore, in some cases, key concepts are explained more than once with slightly different wording to try and aid your understanding.

Elliptic curve cryptography (ECC) is difficult for many people to learn because few people have prior exposure to the underlying mathematics. If you compare ECC to RSA, for example, the difficulty of ECC is quite clear. Most people were exposed to prime numbers, factoring numbers, raising a number to a certain power, and basic arithmetic in primary and secondary school. But far fewer people were exposed to elliptic curves and discrete logarithms in school.

General Overview

Elliptic curves have been studied, apart from cryptographic applications, for well over a century. As with other asymmetric algorithms, the mathematics have been a part of number theory and algebra long before being applied to cryptography. As you saw in Chapter 10, many asymmetric algorithms depend on algebraic groups. There are multiple ways to form finite groups, including elliptic curves, making them appropriate for cryptographic purposes.

There are two types of elliptic curve groups. The two most common (and the ones used in cryptography) are elliptic curve groups based on Fp, where p is prime, and those based on F2^m. F, as you will see in this chapter, is the field being used. F is used because we are describing a field. ECC is an approach to public-key cryptography based on elliptic curves over finite fields.

> **Tip**
>
> Remember that a *field* is an algebraic system consisting of a set, an identity element for each operation, two operations, and their respective inverse operations. A *finite field*, also called a *Galois field*, is a field with a finite number of elements. That number is called the *order* of the field.

Using elliptic curves for cryptographic purposes was first described in 1985 by Victor Miller (IBM) and Neal Koblitz (University of Washington). The security of ECC is based on the fact that finding the discrete logarithm of a random or arbitrary elliptic curve element with respect to a publicly known base point is difficult to the point of being impractical to do.[1]

> **Note**
>
> Neal Koblitz is a mathematics professor at the University of Washington and a very well-known cryptographic researcher. In addition to his work on ECC, he has published extensively in mathematics and cryptography. Victor Miller is a mathematician with the Institute for Defense Analysis in Princeton. He has worked on compression algorithms, combinatorics, and various subtopics in the field of cryptography.

What Is an Elliptic Curve?

An elliptic curve is the set of points that satisfy a specific mathematical equation. Keep in mind that an elliptic curve is not the same thing as an ellipse and should not be confused with one. The equation for an elliptic curve looks something like this:

$$y^2 = x^3 + Ax + B$$

You can see this equation graphed in Figure 11-1. There are other ways to represent an elliptic curve, but Figure 11-1 is the most common and perhaps the easiest to understand.

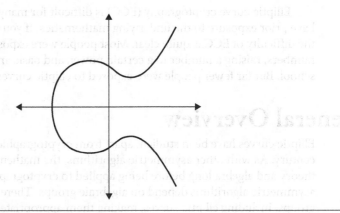

FIGURE 11-1   The graph of an elliptic curve

> **Note** An elliptic curve is not the same as an ellipse.

Another way to describe an elliptic curve is that it is simply the set of points that satisfy an equation that has two variables in the second degree and one variable in the third degree. Notice the horizontal symmetry in the graph in Figure 11-1. Any point on the curve can be reflected about the x-axis without changing the shape of the curve.

In his book *Elliptic Curves: Number Theory and Cryptography*, Professor Lawrence Washington of the University of Maryland describes an elliptic curve a bit more formally:

> ...an elliptic curve E is the graph of an equation of the form $y^2 = x^3 + Ax + B$, where A and B are constants. This will be referred to as the Weierstrass equation for an elliptic curve. We will need to specify what set A, B, x, and y belong to. Usually, they will be taken to be elements of a field, for example, the real numbers R, the complex numbers C, the rational numbers Q, one of the finite fields F_p $(=Z_p)$ for a prime p, or one of the finite fields F_q, where $q = p^k$ with $k \geq 1$.[2]

> **Note** This chapter provides only an overview of elliptic curve cryptography. Washington's book is an excellent source for more detail. There have been two editions of his book; I have both books and I highly recommend them. However, the book assumes a level of mathematical sophistication that this book does not.

The operation used with the elliptic curve is addition (remember that, by definition, a group requires a set along with an operation). Thus elliptic curves form additive groups.

Review of the Definition of Groups in Algebra

A *group* is an algebraic system consisting of a set, an identity element, one operation, and its inverse operation. An *abelian group*, or commutative group, has an additional axiom $a + b = b + a$ if the operation is addition, and $ab = ba$ if the operation is multiplication. A *cyclic group* has elements that are all powers of one of its elements.

Basic Operations on Elliptic Curves

The members of the elliptic curve field are integer points on the elliptic curve. You can perform addition with points on an elliptic curve. Throughout this chapter, as well as in most of the literature on elliptic curves, two points are considered: P and Q. The negative of a point $P = (xP, yP)$ is its reflection in the x-axis: the point $-P$ is $(xP, -yP)$. Notice that for each point P on an elliptic curve, the point $-P$ is also on the curve. Suppose that P and Q are two distinct points on an elliptic curve, and assume that P is not merely the inverse of Q. To add the points P and Q, a line is drawn through the two points. This line will intersect the elliptic curve in

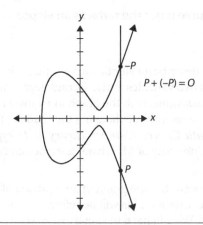

FIGURE 11-2 $P + (-P)$

exactly one more point, called $-R$. The point $-R$ is reflected in the x-axis to the point R. The law for addition in an elliptic curve group is $P + Q = R$.

The line through P and $-P$ is a vertical line that does not intersect the elliptic curve at a third point; thus the points P and $-P$ cannot be added as previously. It is for this reason that the elliptic curve group includes the point at infinity O. By definition, $P + (-P) = O$. As a result of this equation, $P + O = P$ in the elliptic curve group. O is called the additive identity of the elliptic curve group; all elliptic curves have an additive identity. Figure 11-2 shows a graph of an elliptic curve.

To add a point P to itself, a tangent line to the curve is drawn at the point P. If yP is not 0, then the tangent line intersects the elliptic curve at exactly one other point, $-R$. $-R$ is reflected in the x-axis to R. This operation is called "doubling the point P" and is shown in Figure 11-3.

The tangent at P is always vertical if yP = 0.

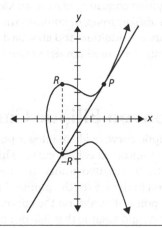

FIGURE 11-3   Doubling the P

If a point P is such that yP = 0, then the tangent line to the elliptic curve at P is vertical and does not intersect the elliptic curve at any other point. By definition, 2P = O for such a point P.

Recall that the field Fp uses the numbers from 0 to p − 1, and computations end by taking the remainder on division by p (i.e. the modulus operations). For example, in F_{23} the field is composed of integers from 0 to 22, and any operation within this field will result in an integer also between 0 and 22.

An elliptic curve with the underlying field of Fp can be formed by choosing the variables a and b within the field of Fp. The elliptic curve includes all points (x,y) that satisfy the elliptic curve equation modulo p (where x and y are numbers in Fp). For example: y^2 mod p = x^3 + ax + b mod p has an underlying field of Fp if a and b are in Fp.

Note   In some cases in this chapter, I use uppercase A and B, and in others, lowercase. In this situation, the case of the letters is irrelevant and you will see both used in the literature. So both are used here to acclimate you to this fact.

If x^3 + ax + b contains no repeating factors, then the elliptic curve can be used to form a group. An elliptic curve group over Fp consists of the points on the corresponding elliptic curve, together with a special point O called the *point at infinity*. There are finitely many points on such an elliptic curve.

At the foundation of every cryptosystem is a hard mathematical problem that is computationally infeasible to solve. The discrete logarithm problem is the basis for the security of many cryptosystems including the ECC. More specifically, the ECC relies upon the difficulty of the *elliptic curve discrete logarithm problem* (ECDLP).

Recall that we examined two geometrically defined operations over certain elliptic curve groups: point addition and point doubling. By selecting a point in a elliptic curve group, you can double it to obtain the point 2P. After that, you can add the point P to the point 2P to obtain the point 3P. The determination of a point nP in this manner is referred to as *scalar multiplication* of a point. The ECDLP is based upon the intractability of scalar multiplication products.

In the multiplicative group Zp*, the discrete logarithm problem is this: given elements r and q of the group, and a prime p, find a number k such that r = qk mod p. If the elliptic curve group is described using multiplicative notation, then the elliptic curve discrete logarithm problem is this: given points P and Q in the group, find the number k such that kP = Q; in this case, k is called the *discrete logarithm* of Q to the base P. When the elliptic curve group is described using additive notation, the elliptic curve discrete logarithm problem is this: given points P and Q in the group, find a number k such that Pk = Q.

The following is a common example used in many textbooks, papers, and web pages. It uses rather small numbers that you can easily work with but makes the general point of how elliptic curve cryptography works. This is not adequate for cryptographic purposes; it is provided only to help you get a feel for how ECC works.

In the elliptic curve group defined by

$$y2 = x3 + 9x + 17 \text{ over F23}$$

What is the discrete logarithm k of Q = (4,5) to the base P = (16,5)?

One way to find k is to compute multiples of P until Q is found. The first few multiples of P are

$$P = (16,5) \quad 2P = (20,20) \quad 3P = (14,14) \quad 4P = (19,20) \quad 5P = (13,10)$$
$$6P = (7,3) \quad 7P = (8,7) \quad 8P = (12,17) \quad 9P = (4,5)$$

Since 9P = (4,5) = Q, the discrete logarithm of Q to the base P is k = 9.

In a real application, k would be large enough such that it would be infeasible to determine k in this manner. This is the essence of ECC. When implementing ECC in the real world, obviously we use larger fields—much larger.

> **Tip**   If you are still struggling with the concepts of elliptic curves, the excellent online tutorial, "A (Relatively Easy to Understand) Primer on Elliptic Curve Cryptography," does a good job of explaining these concepts. You might find that reviewing that tutorial and then rereading this section aids in your understanding. See http://arstechnica.com/security/2013/10/a-relatively-easy-to-understand-primer-on-elliptic-curve-cryptography/.

The Algorithm

In the preceding section we discussed elliptic curves in general; in this section we will discuss specific applications to cryptography. In cryptographic applications, the elliptic curve along with some distinguished point at infinity is used along with the group operation of the elliptic group theory to form an abelian group, with the point at infinity as the identity element. The structure of the group is inherited from the divisor group of the underlying algebraic variety.

For cryptographic purposes, we will restrict ourselves to numbers in a fixed range—only integers are allowed. You must also select a maximum value. If you select the maximum to be a prime number, the elliptic curve is called a "prime curve" and can be used for cryptographic applications.

To use ECC, all parties must agree on all the elements defining the elliptic curve—that is, the domain parameters of the scheme. The field is defined by p in the prime case and the pair of m and f in the binary case. To focus on the prime case (the simpler), the field is defined by some prime number p. The elliptic curve is defined by the constants A and B used in the equation

$$y^2 = x^3 + Ax + B$$

Finally, the cyclic subgroup is defined by its generator (that is, base point) G.

The elliptic curve is the points defined by the preceding equation, with an extra point O, which is called the "point at infinity"—keep in mind that point O is the identity element for this group.[3]

Given a point P = (x,y) and a positive integer n, you define [n]P = P + P + ... + P (n times). The *order* of a point P = (x,y) is the smallest positive integer n such that [n]P = O.

You denote by < P > the *group generated by P*. In other words, < P > = {O, P, P+P, P+P+P, ...}.

Now that you have a group defined by an elliptic curve, the security of elliptic curve cryptography is provided by the ECDLP: given an elliptic curve C defined over F_θ and two points P, Q that are elements of the curve C, find an integer x such that Q = xP.

Discrete Logarithm Review

To understand discrete logarithms, keep in mind the definition of a *logarithm*: the number to which some base must be raised to get another number. Discrete logarithms ask this same question but do so in regard to a finite group. Put more formally, a *discrete logarithm* is some integer k that solves the equation $x^k = y$, where both x and y are elements of a finite group. A discrete logarithm is, essentially, a logarithm within some finite group.

In the preceding section you saw basic math, specifically addition, within an elliptic curve. You can choose any two points on an elliptic curve and produce another point. The process is not particularly complicated. You first begin with two points P1 and P2. These are defined as

$$P1 = (x1, y1)$$

$$P2 = (x2, y2)$$

The curve itself is symbolized as E, given by the equation you already have seen: $y2 = x3 + AX + B$.

Now to define a new point, you call P3, draw a line (let's call it L) through points P1 and P2. You can see that no matter where P1 and P2 are, this line L will intersect E (the elliptic curve) at a third point P3, as shown in Figure 11-4.

You can reflect that across the x-axis (simply change the sign of the y coordinate) and you have P3.

As you already know, an elliptic curve is the set of points that satisfy a specific mathematical equation. The equation for an elliptic curve looks something like this:

$$y^2 = x^3 + ax + b$$

and some point at infinity. This means that choosing different values for a and b changes the elliptic curve.

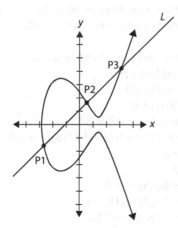

FIGURE 11-4   Line intersecting curve E

The size of the elliptic curve determines the difficulty of finding the discrete logarithm, and thus the security of the implementation. The level of security afforded by an RSA-based system with a large modulus can be achieved with a much smaller elliptic curve group. This is one strong reason why ECC has generated so much interest.

The U.S. National Security Agency has endorsed ECC algorithms and allows their use for protecting information classified up to top secret with 384-bit keys, which is important because 384-bit keys are much smaller than RSA keys. ECC achieves a level of security at least equal to RSA, but with key sizes almost as small as symmetric algorithms such as AES.

ECC Variations

As you can see from the previous sections, elliptic curves form groups, and those groups can be used just as any other algebraic group. The practical implication of this is that you can adapt various algorithms to elliptic curve groups. There are many permutations of elliptic curve cryptography including the following:

- Elliptic Curve Diffie-Hellman (used for key exchange) (ECDH)
- Elliptic Curve Digital Signature Algorithm (ECDSA)
- Elliptic Curve MQV key agreement protocol
- Elliptic Curve Integrated Encryption Scheme (ECIES)

In this section we will take a closer look at two of these.

ECC Diffie-Hellman

Diffie-Hellman, which you studied in Chapter 10, is the oldest key exchange protocol. It is natural to modify for elliptic curves. Elliptic Curve Diffie-Hellman (ECDH) is a key exchange or key agreement protocol used to establish a shared secret over an insecure medium. That shared secret is then either used directly or as the basis to derive another key. In the case of ECDH, the public private key pairs are based on elliptic curves.

- **Public:** Elliptic curve and point (x,y) on curve
- **Secret:** Alice's A and Bob's B
  - Alice computes A(B(x,y))
  - Bob computes B(A(x,y))
  - These are the same since AB = BA.
- **Public:** Curve $y^2 = x^3 + 7x + b$ (mod 37) and point (2,5) $\Rightarrow$ b = 3
- **Alice's secret:** A = 4
- **Bob's secret:** B = 7
  - Alice sends Bob: 4(2,5) = (7,32)
  - Bob sends Alice: 7(2,5) = (18,35)
  - Alice computes: 4(18,35) = (22,1)
  - Bob computes: 7(7,32) = (22,1)

> **Note**   For more details consult NIST document 800-56A Revision 2, at http://nvlpubs .nist.gov/nistpubs/SpecialPublications/NIST.SP.800-56Ar2.pdf.

Elliptic Curve Digital Signature Algorithm

The Digital Signature Algorithm (DSA) was invented specifically for digitally signing messages. Of course, you can use any asymmetric algorithm to sign a message, but the DSA was designed for that purpose. As I mentioned, there is an elliptic curve variation on this algorithm.

To illustrate how this works, let's again consider the fictitious Bob and Alice. First the two parties must agree on some parameters: the curve, denoted as E; the base point/generator of the elliptic curve, denoted as G; and the order of G (an integer), denoted by n. Now to sign a message, Alice takes the following steps:

1. Select a random integer k that is less than n (that is, $k > 1$; $k < n$).
2. Compute $kG = (x_1, y_1)$ and $r = x_1 \bmod n$. If $r = 0$ then go to step 1.
3. Compute $k^{-1} \bmod n$.
4. Compute $e = SHA\text{-}1(m)$. Most digital signature algorithms use a hash; in this case the hash is usually SHA-1. So this is stating that you compute the SHA-1 hash of the message.
5. Compute $s = k^{-1}\{e + d_A \cdot r\} \bmod n$.
6. If $s = 0$, then go to step 1. In other words, keep repeating until s! = 0. This is not usually time-consuming and could happen on the first attempt.
7. Alice's signature for the message m is (r, s).

In order for Bob to verify Alice's signature (r,s), he will execute the following steps:

1. Verify that r and s are integers in $[1, n-1]$.
2. Compute $e = SHA\text{-}1(m)$.
3. Compute $w = s^{-1} \bmod n$.
4. Compute $u_1 = ew \bmod n$ and $u_2 = rw \bmod n$.
5. Compute $(x_1, y_1) = u_1 G + u_2 Q_A$.
6. Compute $v = x_1 \bmod n$.
7. Accept the signature if and only if $v = r$.

This is very much like the traditional DSA, except that it is using elliptic curve groups. ECDSA is quite secure.

> **Note**   There have been a few reported breaches of ECDSA, but those were based on faulty implementations, not on the algorithm itself being insecure. For example, in March 2011, researchers published a paper with the IACR (International Association of Cryptological Research) demonstrating that it is possible to retrieve a TLS private key of a server using OpenSSL in a timing attack. OpenSSL authenticates with ECDSA over a binary field. However, the vulnerability was fixed in a subsequent release of OpenSSL and was an implementation issue, not a flaw in the algorithm.

Conclusions

In this chapter we have examined the use of elliptic curve groups for cryptography. This may be the most mathematically challenging chapter in this entire book. For most security applications, you need only be aware of the general description of the various elliptic curve algorithms. For those of you interested in pursuing cryptography in more depth, this chapter provides an introduction to this topic. Various resources have been suggested in this chapter that will give you more detail and depth on ECC.

Test Your Knowledge

1. Which of the following equations is most related to elliptic curve cryptography?
   A. M^e % n
   B. $P = C^d$ % n
   C. C^e % n
   D. $y^2 = x^3 + Ax + B$
2. Which ECC variation requires the use of SHA?
3. What is an algebraic group?
4. What is a discrete logarithm?
5. What kind of key does ECC DH product?

Answers

1. D
2. ECDSA
3. A group is an algebraic system consisting of a set, an identity element, one operation, and its inverse operation.
4. A discrete logarithm is some integer k that solves the equation $x^k = y$, where both x and y are elements of a finite group.
5. Ephemeral key

Endnotes

1. For more information on ECC, read "Elliptic Curve Cryptography," a paper by Vivek Kapoor, Vivek Sonny Abraham, and Ramesh Singh, at http://csis.bits-pilani.ac.in/faculty/murali/netsec-10/seminar/refs/abhishek3.pdf.
2. Lawrence C. Washington, *Elliptic Curves: Number Theory and Cryptography, Second Edition* (Chapman and Hall/CRC, 2008).
3. For more information on ECC, see the *Guide to Elliptic Curve Cryptography* by Darrel Hankerson, Alfred Menezes, and Scott Vanstone (Springer Professional Computing, 2004).

12 Random Number Generators

In this chapter we will cover the following:

- Properties of pseudo-random numbers
- Tests of randomness
- Algorithmic random number generators
- The Marsaglia CD-ROM

Random numbers are a key part of cryptography. When you generate a key for a symmetric algorithm such as Advanced Encryption Standard (AES), Blowfish, or GOST, you need that key to be very random. Random numbers are also required for initialization vectors used with a variety of algorithms. A truly random number is impossible to generate from a computer algorithm. It is possible to generate a truly random number using other means, including hardware, but not strictly in a software algorithm. Certain naturally occurring phenomena such as radioactive decay can form the basis for true random-number generation. However, this is not a practical source of random numbers for use in cryptographic applications.

Algorithms called *pseudo-random-number generators* (PRNGs) are normally used in cryptography. These algorithms can be used to create long runs of numbers with good random properties, but eventually the sequence repeats.

The need to generate random numbers is nothing new; in fact, many methods of generating random numbers have been around for centuries, though they are usually not sufficient for cryptographic purposes. We will explore some of these in this chapter.

There are three types of PRNGs:

- **Table look-up generators**   Literally a table of precomputed pseudo-random numbers is compiled and numbers are extracted from it as needed.
- **Hardware generators**   Some hardware process, perhaps packet loss on the network card, or fluctuations from a chip, are used to produce pseudo-random numbers.
- **Algorithmic (software) generators**   This type is most commonly used in cryptography, and it's what we will focus our attention on in this chapter.

What Makes a Good PRNG?

You know that a true random-number generator is impractical, but what makes a particular PRNG good enough? Is the output of a given algorithm random enough?

There are some specific properties and standards you can look for in a PRNG, and you can use some tests to measure for randomness. In this section we will look at all three of these items. This information should inform your evaluation of specific algorithms we will explore later in this chapter.

(Desirable) Properties of Pseudo-random Numbers

Before you consider actual algorithms and attempt to evaluate the efficacy of each for cryptographic purposes, it is important that you understand what you are looking for in a cryptographic algorithm. Any good PRNG will generate a sequence of numbers that have the following properties:

- **Uncorrelated sequences**   The sequences are not correlated—there, quite literally, is no correlation between one section of output bits and another. So you cannot take a given stretch of numbers (say 16 bits) and use that to predict subsequent bits.
- **Long period**   Ideally the series of digits (usually bits) should never have any repeating pattern. However, the reality is that some repetition will eventually occur. The distance (in digits or bits) between repetitions is the period of that sequence of numbers. The longer the period, the better. Put another way: we can accept that there will be repeated sequences, but those should be as far apart as possible.
- **Uniformity**   Pseudo-random numbers are usually represented in binary format, with an equal number of 1's and 0's that are not distributed in any discernable pattern. The sequence of random numbers should be uniform and unbiased. If you have significantly more (or significantly less) 1's than 0's, then the output is biased. This category is the one most often used in cryptography. It does not produce a truly random number, but rather a pseudo-random number.
- **Computational indistinguishability**   Any subsection of numbers taken from the output of a given PRNG should not be distinguishable from any other subset of numbers in polynomial time by any efficient procedure. The two sequences are indistinguishable. That does not, however, mean they are identical—it means there is no efficient way to determine specific differences.

Tests of Randomness

How do you know if a PRNG is "random enough"? You can apply a variety of tests to the output of any algorithm to determine the degree of randomness—to determine whether that algorithm is suitable for cryptographic purposes. Let's start with relatively simple tests that you can easily execute. Then I'll provide an overview of more sophisticated statistical tests.

1-D Test

The 1-D frequency test is a simple test that is used as a first pass. In other words, simply passing the 1-D test does not mean an algorithm is suitable for cryptographic purposes. However, if a PRNG fails the 1-D test, there is no need for further testing.

Imagine a number line stretching from 0 to 1, with decimal points in between. Use the random-number generator to plot random points on this line. First, divide the line into a number of "bins" of any size. In the following graph, there are four bins, each with a size of 0.25:

```
| --------- | --------- | --------- | --------- |

    0.25         .50         .75         1.0
```

As random numbers (between 0 and 1.0) are generated, count how many fit into each bin. If the bins fill evenly, that is a good sign that you have random dispersal. If there is a significant preference for one bin over another, then the PRNG is not sufficiently random and has a bias; further testing is not required to determine that it is not useful for cryptographic purposes.

Equidistribution

The equidistribution test, sometimes called the *Monobit frequency test*, is used to determine whether there is an equal distribution of 1's and 0's throughout the output of the PRNG. It seeks to verify that the arithmetic mean of the sequence approaches 0.5. This can be applied to the entire output of a PRNG or to a given segment, though the larger the segment, the more meaningful the test. The further the arithmetic mean is from 0.5, the more of a bias the algorithm is displaying and therefore the less suitable this PRNG is for cryptographic purposes.

This test is described by the National Institute of Standards (NIST) as follows:

> The focus of the test is the proportion of zeroes and ones for the entire sequence. The purpose of this test is to determine whether the number of ones and zeros in a sequence are approximately the same as would be expected for a truly random sequence. The test assesses the closeness of the fraction of ones to zeroes, that is, the number of ones and zeroes in a sequence should be about the same. All subsequent tests depend on the passing of this test; there is no evidence to indicate that the tested sequence is non-random.[1]

This test (also sometimes just called the frequency test) has similarities to the 1-D test in that the purpose is to determine whether there is bias in the output of a given PRNG. The focus of the test is the proportion of 0's and 1's for the entire sequence.

Note | Throughout this chapter, I will use a tool named CrypTool to demonstrate PRNGs as well as randomness tests. This is a free and open source tool you can download from https://www.cryptool.org/en/.

Runs Test

A *run* is an uninterrupted sequence of identical bits. The focus of the runs test is the total number of runs in the sequence. A run of length k consists of exactly k identical bits and is bounded before and after with a bit of the opposite value. The purpose of the runs test is to determine whether the number of runs of 1's and 0's of various lengths is as expected for a random sequence. This test determines whether the oscillation between such 0's and 1's is too fast or too slow. In other words, are the 1's and 0's alternating quickly or slowly?

Fast oscillation occurs when there are a lot of changes, e.g., 010101010 oscillates with every bit.

```
(input) E = 1100100100001111110110101010001000100001011010001100001000110
10011000100110001100110000101000101111000

(input) n = 100

(output) p-value = 0.500798

(conclusion) Since p-value >= 0.01, accept the sequence as random.
```

You can use CrypTool to apply the runs test to a sequence of numbers. You can find the various randomness tests by choosing Analysis | Analyze Randomness, as shown in Figure 12-1.

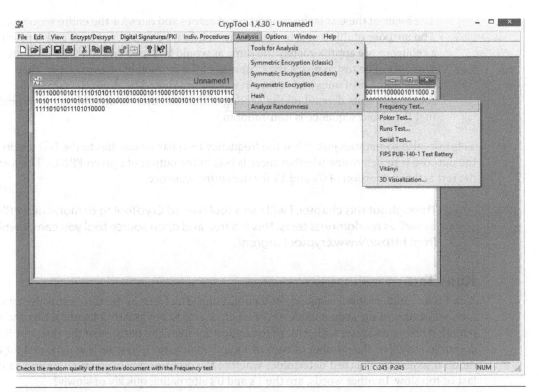

FIGURE 12-1   CrypTool randomness analysis

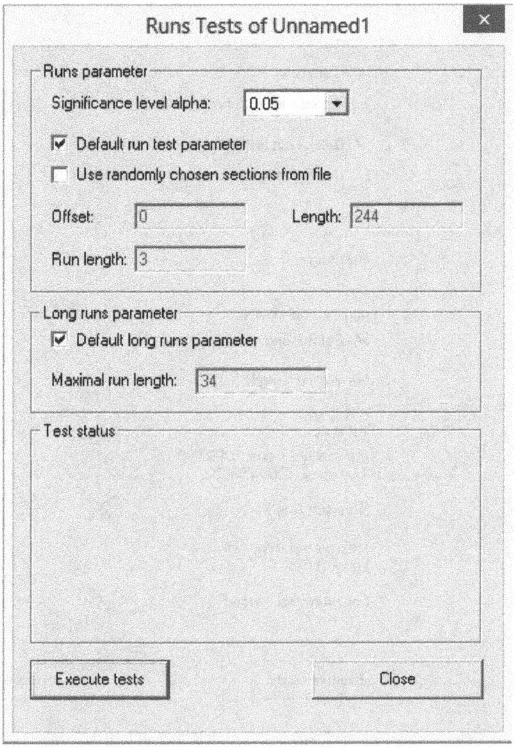

FIGURE 12-2   Runs test parameters

In the output shown previously (1100100100001111110110101010001000100001011010000110000100011010011000100110001100110001010001011000), there is a seemingly random series of 1's and 0's. To apply the runs test to this, you will first be prompted to select some test parameters, as shown in Figure 12-2. For this example, simply use the default parameters. To test this you, select Analysis | Analyze Randomness | Runs Test.

The test results, shown in Figure 12-3, are relatively simple to interpret—and, in this case, the sequence of numbers did not pass a key part of the runs test. If subsequent tests also cast doubt on the particular algorithm used, it should definitely be rejected.

Test for Longest Run of 1's

This test is very similar to the runs test. It tests for the longest uninterrupted series of 1's within a given output for a given PRNG. The purpose of this test is to determine whether the length of the longest run of 1's within the tested sequence is consistent with the length of the longest run of 1's that would be expected in a random sequence.

Poker Test

The poker test for PRNGs is based on the frequency in which certain digits are repeated in a series of numbers. Let's consider a trivial example—a three-digit number. In a three-digit number, there are only three possibilities.

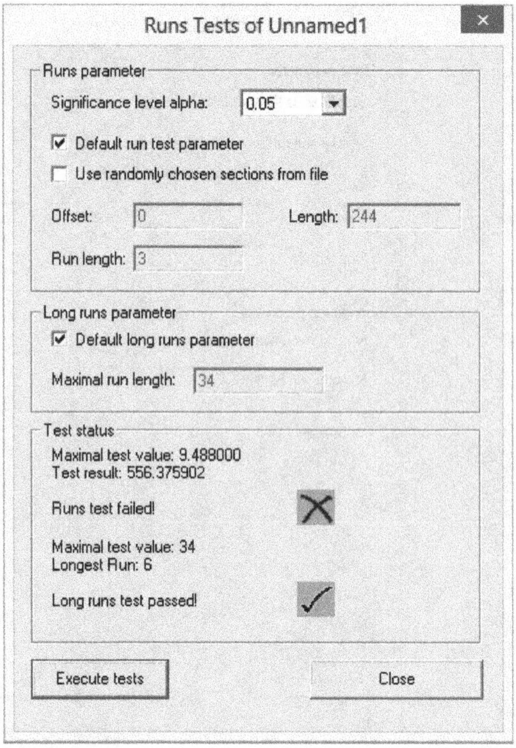

FIGURE 12-3   Runs test results

- All three digits are the same.
- The three digits are all different.
- One digit is different from the other two.

The poker test actually assumes sequences of five numbers (there are five cards in a hand of poker). The five numbers are analyzed to determine whether any sequence appears more frequently than the other possible sequences. This is a rather primitive test. When using CrypTool to execute this test, you will need to select a few simple parameters. For our purposes use the default settings. You can see the results in Figure 12-4.

Chi-Squared Statistical Test

Many statistical tests can be applied to a sequence of numbers to determine how random that sequence is.

Chi Squared   The chi-squared test is a common statistical test used to test a sampling distribution. It is often used to compare observed data with data you would expect to obtain according to a specific hypothesis.

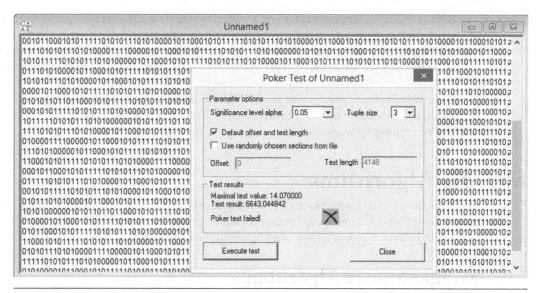

FIGURE 12-4   The poker test

> **Note**
> My purpose is not to evaluate all of the possible tests, but to give you some insight into how you might apply a common statistical test to determining how random a PRNG's output is. If you are not familiar with statistical testing, consult any elementary statistics textbook.

Chi-squared test results are usually reported as a chi^2 measure. A chi^2 measure of ±2 is probably random noise, ±3 probably means the generator is biased, and ±4 almost certainly means the generator is biased. The lower the value, the more random the number sequence; the higher the value, the less random the sequence.

> **Note**
> NIST recommends a number of statistical tests for testing a PRNG. These tests are documented in "Statistical Testing of Random Number Generators" at http://csrc.nist.gov/groups/ST/toolkit/rng/documents/nissc-paper.pdf.

Standards for PRNG

The German Federal Office for Information Security (BSI) has established four criteria for quality of random number generators:

- **K1**   A sequence of random numbers with a low probability of containing identical consecutive elements.
- **K2**   A sequence of numbers that is indistinguishable from "true random" numbers according to specified statistical tests.

- **K3**   It should be impossible for any attacker to calculate, or otherwise guess, from any given subsequence, any previous or future values in the sequence.
- **K4**   It should be impossible for an attacker to calculate, or guess from an inner state of the generator, any previous numbers in the sequence or any previous inner generator states.

To be suitable for cryptography, any PRNG should meet K3 and K4 standards. Obviously, K4 is inclusive of K3 and would be the ideal level to achieve; however, K3 should be suitable for cryptographic purposes.

Specific Algorithms

In this section, I'll start with older algorithms that produce a pseudo-random number, but perhaps one that is not sufficient for cryptographic purposes. Just as I did in Chapters 1 and 2 with historical ciphers, I will start here with historical PRNGs.

Middle-Square Algorithm

The middle-square, or mid-square, is a very old algorithm that was first described by a Franciscan friar in the 13th century. It was reintroduced by John Von Neumann in the 1940s. It is a rather simple method and easy to follow.

Here's a step by step description of the middle-square method:

1. Start with an initial seed (for example, a four-digit integer).
2. Square the number.
3. The middle four digits become the new seed.
4. Divide this value by 10,000 to produce the random number, and go back to step 2.

The following is a concrete example:

1. $x_0 = 1234$
2. x_1: $1234^2 = 01\underline{5227}56 \rightarrow x_1 = 5227$, $R_1 = 0.5227$
3. x_2: $5227^2 = 27\underline{3215}29 \rightarrow x_2 = 3215$, $R_2 = 0.3215$
4. x_3: $3215^2 = 10\underline{3362}25 \rightarrow x_3 = 3362$, $R_3 = 0.3362$

The process is repeated indefinitely, generating a new random number each time. The middle 4 bits of each output is the seed for the next iteration of the algorithm.

This algorithm has some definite limitations. The initial starting value is very important. If you start with all 0's, for example, then you will continue with all 0's. However, if you start with leading 0's followed by some number, the subsequent values produced by the algorithm will be reducing to 0. Certain seed numbers are known to generate short periods of repeating cycles. In fact, the best that you can get from any mid-square implementation of n-digit numbers is a period of 8^n. And some have far shorter periods.

This algorithm makes an excellent introduction to PRNGs, and it is easy to understand and easy to code should you be interested in implementing this in a program. However, it is not adequate for modern cryptographic purposes.

Linear Congruential Generator

A linear congruential generator (LCG) is an algorithm that depends on a linear equation to generate a pseudo-random sequence. More specifically, it depends on a *piecewise* linear congruence equation.

Note A *piecewise* linear function is a linear function that produces different results depending on input. In other words, it functions in pieces. Here is a simple example:

$$f(x) = \begin{pmatrix} X+3 & \text{if} & X > 0 \\ X \wedge 2 & \text{if} & X < 0 \\ X & \text{if} & X = 0 \end{pmatrix}$$

This function performs one of three operations on X, depending on the value of X.

There are a variety of LCGs, but the most common form is

$$X_{n+1} = (aX_n + C) \bmod m$$

- a is the multiplier.
- C is the increment.
- m is the modulus.
- X_0 is the initial value of X.

The period of a general LCG is at most m, so the choice of m is quite critical. Some linear congruential generators have a smaller period than m.

Note Not all LCGs are created equal; some are quite good, others depend heavily on initial conditions, and others are very bad. The RANDU LCG was used in the 1970s. It has a rather poor design and has widely been considered so bad at generating pseudo-random numbers that it caused some to question the efficacy of LCGs in general.

A number of LCGs are built into the random-number generators of various libraries. Each has a value of m sufficient for most random-number purposes. The following table provides details on some of these implementations.

	m (modulus)	a (multiplier)	C (increment)
Borland C/C++	2^{32}	22695477	1
Microsoft Visual/Quick C/C++	2^{32}	214013	2531011
Java's java.util.Random	2^{48}	25214903917	11

LCGs Implemented in Code

LCGs are fast and easy to code. And as you can see, many programming tools, libraries, and languages have LCGs built in, so you need not even code the algorithm itself. Keep in mind, however, that LCGs are not considered random enough for many cryptographic applications. They are a great place to start learning about PRNGs, and for less rigorous applications they might be used in some limited cryptographic scenarios, but in general they are not sufficient for secure cryptography.

> **Note** One of the major issues with cryptography is the implementation. Many common hard drive and file encryption products use sound algorithms such as AES and Blowfish, but they use substandard PRNGs to generate the cipher key for the chosen algorithm. Many programmers are not even aware that the library they are using may not have an adequate PRNG.

CrypTool

CrypTool can also be used to generate random numbers. You can find a few common random number generators in CrypTool by choosing Individual Procedures | Tools | Generate Random Numbers, as shown in Figure 12-5.

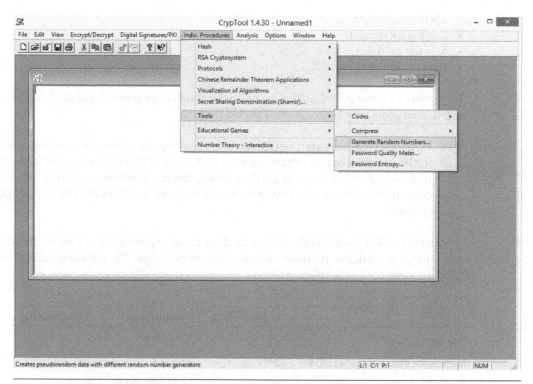

FIGURE 12-5 CrypTool random number generation

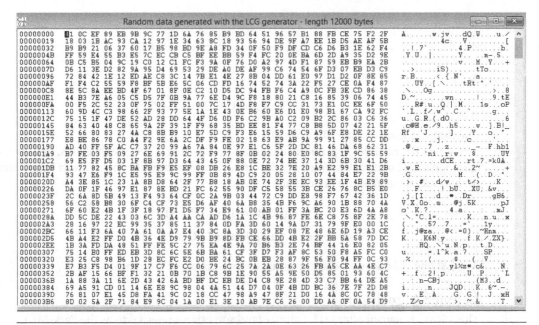

FIGURE 12-6   **CrypTool random numbers from LCG**

As you can see in Figure 12-6, LCG is one of the PRNGs available. It starts with a preset seed of 314149, but you can change that if you want. Using default settings, it produces 1200 bytes of pseudo-random numbers, as shown in the figure.

Note Feel free to test this random number with the randomness tests mentioned earlier in this chapter, which are also available in CrypTool.

Lagged Fibonacci Generators

The Lagged Fibonacci Generator (LFG) is a particular type of LCG that uses the Fibonacci sequence as a base.

Note Recall that the Fibonacci sequence is $Sn = Sn - 1 + Sn - 2$, so that the sequence is 1, 1, 2, 3, 5, 8, 13, 21, 35, and so on.

LFGs come in a variety of forms. If addition is used, it is referred to as an Additive Lagged Fibonacci Generator (ALFG). If multiplication is used, it is referred to as a Multiplicative Lagged Fibonacci Generator or (MLFG). If the XOR operation is used, it is called a Two-tap generalized feedback shift register (GFS).

The basic formula is

$$y = x^k + x^j + 1$$

or

$$y = x^k * x^j + 1 \text{ (multiplicative LCG)}$$

or

$$y = x^k XOR x^j + 1 \text{ (GFS)}$$

The indices j, k are the lags of the generator.

When the modulus is prime, a maximum period of $m^k - 1$ is possible. It is, however, more common to use a modulus which is a power of two, $m = 2^p$, with p being some prime number.[2] In this case, the maximum periods are

For an additive LFG: $(2^k - 1)2^{p-1}$

For a multiplicative LFG: $(2^k - 1)2^{p-3}$

Any LFG must be seeded with the initial k elements of the sequence.

Lehmer Algorithm

This PRNG is named after D.H. Lehmer (and sometimes referred to as the Park-Miller random number generator, after S.K. Park and K.W. Miller). It is the classic example of a linear congruential generator. This algorithm produces a sequence of numbers $\{X_n\}$ using a standard LCG format:

$$X_{n+1} = (a \times X_n + c) \bmod m$$

Here is a relatively simple example:

Given a = 7, c = 0, m = 32, $X_0 = 1$

$X_1 = (7 \times 1 + 0) \bmod 32 = 7$

$X_2 = (7 \times 7 + 0) \bmod 32 = 49/32; Q = 1, R = 17$

$X_3 = (7 \times 17 + 0) \bmod 32 = 119/32; Q = 3, R = 23$

$X_4 = (7 \times 23 + 0) \bmod 32 = 161/32, Q = 5, R = 1$

However, with the small m you would expect a repetition at some point, and indeed you find one:

$X_5 = (7 \times 1 + 0) \bmod 32 = 7/32; Q = 0, R = 7$

Oops!

$X_6 =$ obviously, we are at the same point as X_2 again.

The sequence repeats with a period of 4, and that is clearly unacceptable. Let's consider a few things that can be done to make this acceptable. For a range of m numbers $0 < m < 2^m$, the function should generate all the numbers up to 2^m before repeating. So clearly a large value of m is important. Even a good algorithm with poorly chosen inputs will produce bad results.

Mersenne Twister

The original Mersenne Twister is not suitable for cryptographic purposes, but permutations of it are. This PRNG was invented by Makoto Matsumoto and Takuji Nishimura. It has a very large period, $2^{19937}-1$, which is greater than the many other generators. Its name derives from the fact that its period length is chosen to be a Mersenne prime.

The most commonly used version of the Mersenne Twister algorithm is based on the Mersenne prime $2^{19937}-1$ and uses a 32-bit word. It is often called MT 19937. There is a 64-bit word version called MT 199937-64. The Mersenne Twister is widely used and is implemented in PHP, MATLAB,[3] Microsoft Visual C++,[4] and Ruby.[5]

The algorithm itself can be a bit complex to describe, but the following pseudo-code may help you understand this algorithm if you have even a rudimentary programming background:

```
// Create an array that is 624 bytes in size to store the state of the
// generator
int[0..623] MERSENNE //initial array named MERSENNE
int index = 0          // index


 // Initialize the generator from a seed
functioninit_generator(int seed)
{
index := 0
    MERSENNE [0] := seed
forifrom 1 to 623 { // loop over each element
        MERSENNE [i] := lowest 32 bits of(1812433253 * (MERSENNE[i-1] xor
(right shift by 30 bits(MERSENNE [i-1]))) + i)
    }
}


 // Extract a pseudorandom number based on the index-th value,
 // calling generate_numbers() every 624 numbers
functionextract_number() {
if index == 0
    {
generate_numbers()
    }

int y := MERSENNE [index]
y := y xor (right shift by 11 bits(y))
```

```
y := y xor (left shift by 7 bits(y) and (2636928640))
y := y xor (left shift by 15 bits(y) and (4022730752))
y := y xor (right shift by 18 bits(y))

index := (index + 1) mod 624
return y
 }

// Generate an array of 624 numbers
functiongenerate_numbers()
{
forifrom 0 to 623
   {
int y:=(MERSENNE [i] and 0x80000000) // 32nd bit of MERSENNE [i]
         + (MERSENNE [(i+1) mod 624] and0x7fffffff // bits 0-30

    MERSENNE [i]:= MERSENNE[(i + 397) mod 624] xor (right shift by 1 bit(y))
if (y mod 2) != 0 { // y is odd
         MERSENNE[i] := MERSENNE[i] xor (2567483615)
      }
    }
 }
```

Blum Blum Shub

This algorithm was proposed in 1986 by Lenore Blum, Manuel Blum, and Michael Shub.

> **Note** Lenore Blum is a professor of computer science at Carnegie Mellon University. Manuel Blum is the recipient of the 1995 Turing Award for his work in complexity theory. Michael Shub is a mathematician known for his work in dynamical systems and in the complexity of real number algorithms.

The format of Blum Blum Shub is as follows:

$$X_{n+1} = X_n^2 \bmod M$$

M = pq is the product of two large primes, p and q (this should remind you of the RSA algorithm). At each step of the algorithm, some output is derived from Xn+1. The main difficulty of predicting the output of Blum Blum Shub lies in the difficulty of the "quadratic residuosity problem": given a composite number n, find whether x is a perfect square modulo n. It has been proven that this is as difficult as breaking the RSA public-key cryptosystem, which involves the factoring of a large composite. This makes Blum Blum Shub a quite effective PRNG.

Yarrow

This algorithm was invented by Bruce Schneier, John Kelsey, and Niels Ferguson. Like all of Schneier's inventions, this algorithm is unpatented and open source. Yarrow is no longer recommended by its inventors and has been supplanted by Fortuna.[6] However, it is still an excellent algorithm to study, because it is generally easy to implement, and it does a good job of generating sufficiently random numbers. The general structure of Yarrow is relatively simple to understand. Yarrow has four parts:

- **An entropy accumulator**   Collects semi-random samples from various sources and accumulates them in two pools
- **A generation mechanism**   Generates the PRNG outputs
- **Reseed mechanism**   Periodically reseeds the key with new entries from the entropy pools
- **Reseed control**   Determines when reseeding should occur

The two pools are called the *fast pool* and *slow pool*. The fast pool, as the name suggests, is used frequently to reseed the key, while the slow pool provides very conservative reseeds of the key. Both pools contain a hash of all inputs to that point in time, and both use Secure Hash Algorithm (SHA-1), so they produce a 160-bit hash output. Put more simply, each pool is fed some semi-random source, and that source is then put into a hash. As new data is fed to the pool, the hash is updated. This way, there is a constantly changing hash value that could be used as a key.

The SHA-1 outputs are used to create keys for 3-DES. The outputs from 3-DES are the pseudo-random numbers. Periodically the reseed mechanism goes back to the entropy accumulator to get a new SHA-1 hash so that a new key is used with the 3-DES algorithm. Essentially, the algorithm consists of accumulating semi-random input, hashing that output, and using the hash as a seed/key for a block cipher (in this case, 3-DES).

One reason this algorithm is worthy of study is that the same concepts could be easily modified. Allow me to illustrate with a simple but effective variation:

1. Begin with a poor PRNG such as mid-square. Use that to generate a pool of semi-random numbers. You can seed the PRNG with any value, even a current date/time stamp.
2. Subject each number in the pool to a hashing algorithm of your choice (SHA-1, RIPEMD, and so on).
3. From that pool, select two hashes: one will be the seed, the other will be the input or plain text value subjected to a cipher.
4. Use a block cipher of your choice (Blowfish, AES, Serpent, and so on) in cipher-block chaining mode. The output of that cipher is your random number.

This is provided as an example of how you can take existing cryptographic functions and combine them to produce numbers that should be sufficiently random for cryptographic purposes.

Fortuna

Fortuna is actually a group of PRNGs and has many options for whoever implements the algorithm. It has three main components (note that this is similar to Yarrow):

- A *generator*, which is seeded and will produced pseudo-random data
- The *entropy accumulator*, which collects random data from various sources and uses that to reseed the generator
- The *seed file*, which has initial seed values

The algorithm uses a generator that is based on any good block cipher—DES, AES, Twofish, and so on. The algorithm is run in counter mode. The generator is just a block cipher in counter mode. The counter mode generates a random stream of data, which will be the output of Fortuna. Because it is possible that a sequence would eventually repeat, it is recommended that the key used for the block cipher be periodically replaced.

> **Note**   Counter mode is usually used to turn a block cipher into a stream cipher. It generates the next key-stream block by encrypting successive values of the counter.

After each number is generated, the algorithm generates a fresh new key that is used for the next PRNG. This is done so that if an attacker were to compromise the PRNG and learn the state of the algorithm when generating a given PRNG, this will not compromise previous or subsequent numbers generated by this algorithm.

Reseeding the algorithm is done with some arbitrary string. A hashing algorithm is often used for this purpose, because it produces a somewhat random number itself, making it an excellent seed for Fortuna.

Dual_EC_DRBG

The Dual Elliptic Curve Deterministic Random Bit Generator became well known outside of cryptographic circles when Edward Snowden revealed that the algorithm contained a backdoor inserted by the National Security Agency. The algorithm itself is based on elliptic curve mathematics and was standardized in NIST SP 800-90A.

According to John Kelsey, the possibility of the backdoor by carefully chosen P and Q values was brought up at a meeting of the ANSI X9.82 committee. As a result, a way was specified for implementers to choose their own P and Q values.

In 2007, Bruce Schneier's article, "Did NSA Put a Secret Backdoor in New Encryption Standard?" appeared in *Wired Magazine*. It is based on an earlier presentation by Dan Shumow and Niels Ferguson.

Given that Dual_EC_DRBG is clearly not secure, the details of the algorithm are not important; however, the story of this algorithm illustrates an important point about the relationship between cryptography and network security. Most network security professionals learn only the most elementary facts about cryptography. Major industry security certifications such as the Certified Information Systems Security Professional (CISSP from ISC2), Certified Advanced Security Practitioner (CASP from the Computer

Technology Industry Association), and even many university security textbooks contribute only a surface view of cryptography. This is dramatically illustrated by the story of Dual_EC_DRBG. When Snowden revealed, in 2013, that there was a backdoor in this algorithm, the network security community was stunned. However, the cryptography community had been discussing this possibility for many years. This is, in fact, one of the major purposes of this book you are reading now—to present the world of cryptography in a manner that even general security practitioners can understand.

The Marsaglia CD-ROM

As mentioned earlier in this chapter, you can use tables of pseudo-random numbers as sources for random numbers. George Marsaglia produced a CD-ROM containing 600 MB of random numbers. These were produced using various dependable pseudo-random-number generators, but they were then combined with bytes from a variety of random sources or *semi-random* sources to produce quality random numbers.

The theory behind combining random numbers to create new random numbers can be described as follows: Suppose X and Y are independent random bytes, and at least one of them is uniformly distributed over the values 0 to 255 (the range found in a single byte when expressed in decimal format). Then both the bitwise exclusive-or of X and Y, and X+Y mod 256, are uniformly distributed over 0 to 255. If both X and Y are approximately uniformly distributed, then the combination will be more closely uniformly distributed.

In the Marsaglia CD-ROM, the idea is to get the excellent properties of the pseudo-random-number generator but to further "randomize" the numbers by disrupting any remaining patterns with the combination operation.

Improving PRNGs

There are a number of ways to improve any given PRNG algorithm. You might think that simply creating new PRNG algorithms would be the ideal way to improve randomness; however, that approach can be difficult. You'd then need to subject the new algorithm to lengthy peer review to ensure that a new problem had not been introduced. Furthermore, the more complex an algorithm, the more computationally intensive it will be. So in some cases it is desirable to take an existing algorithm and simply improve it. A few simple methods can be applied to any PRNG to improve randomness.

Shuffling

One of the simplest methods for improving a PRNG is to shuffle the output. Consider the following example:

1. Start with an array of 100 bytes (you can actually use any size, but we will use 100 for this example).
2. Fill that array with the output of the PRNG algorithm you are trying to improve.
3. When a random number is required, combine any two random numbers from the array.

This combination, as described earlier in reference to specific PRNGs, will increase the randomness. You can make it even more random by combining nonsequential elements of the array.

Cryptographic Hash

This method is sometimes used to generate a reasonably secure random number from a PRNG that is not cryptographically secure—such as a simple mid-square method. The methodology is quite simple. You use the PRNG output as the input to a well-known cryptographic hash such as SHA-1. The output should be reasonably random.

Conclusions

In this chapter you were introduced to pseudo-random-number generators. We have looked at specific algorithms, the desirable properties of a PRNG, and specific tests for randomness. It cannot be overstated how important PRNGs are in the creation of cryptographic keys for symmetric algorithms and in the creation of initialization vectors. Even if you use a secure algorithm, if the PRNG used to create the key is not sufficiently random, it will weaken the cryptographic implementation.

Test Your Knowledge

1. What does K3 of the German standard for PRNG state?
2. What is the basic formula for a linear congruential generator?
3. Briefly describe the 1-D test?
4. What is shuffling?
5. Provide a general overview of Yarrow (the major steps).

Answers

1. Given any stream of bits in the output, you cannot predict previous or subsequent bits.
2. $x_n{+}_1 = P_1x_n + P_2 \pmod N$
3. In the 1-D test, you take 0 to 1.0 and divide it into "bins" and fill the bins with output from the PRNG and see if they fill evenly.
4. In shuffling, you mix the output of a PRNG in some fashion to increase entropy.
5. 1) Generate a seed from semi-random sources; 2) hash the output (SHA-1); and 3) feed that output into 3DES.

Endnotes

1. NIST Special Publication 800-22, http://csrc.nist.gov/groups/ST/toolkit/rng/documents/SP800-22b.pdf.
2. S. Aluru, "Lagged Fibonacci Random Number Generators for Distributed Memory Parallel Computers," *Journal of Parallel and Distributed Computing* 45 (1997), 1–12.

3. MathWorks Random Number Generator, www.mathworks.com/help/matlab/ref/randstream.list.html.
4. Microsoft Developer Network, https://msdn.microsoft.com/en-us/library/bb982398.aspx.
5. PHP Manual, http://php.net/manual/en/function.mt-srand.php.
6. B. Schneier, J. Kelsey, and N. Ferguson, "Yarrow-160: Notes on the Design and Analysis of the Yarrow Cryptographic Pseudorandom Number Generator," www.schneier.com/paper-yarrow.pdf.

13 Secure Sockets Layer/Transport Layer Security Protocol

In this chapter we will cover the following:

- Digital signatures
- Digital certificates
- The Public Key Infrastructure (PKI)
- SSL/TLS basics

The preceding 12 chapters have covered the algorithms used in cryptography, including symmetric key cryptography, asymmetric key cryptography, cryptographic hashes, and generating random numbers. In this chapter, as well as the next two chapters, we will be focusing on practical applications of cryptography. Chapter 14 will discuss virtual private networks, and Chapter 15 will cover military applications of cryptography. In this chapter, the primary focus is on Secure Sockets Layer and Transport Layer Security (SSL/TLS) Protocols. However, in order to cover this topic adequately, I will first cover digital signatures, digital certificates, and the Public Key Infrastructure (PKI), all of which are needed for SSL/TLS.

The importance of applied cryptography cannot be overstated. Without modern protocols such as SSL/TLS, modern e-commerce, online banking, and similar technologies would not exist. Although it is certainly important that you understand the mathematics behind cryptography and the actual algorithms being implemented, it is also important that you understand how all of this is used for secure communications.

Digital Signatures

I briefly touched on digital signatures when I discussed asymmetric cryptography in Chapter 10. The concept involves simply reversing some asymmetric algorithm process. A piece of data is encrypted with the sender's public key. Anyone can access the sender's public key and decrypt/verify that message.

There are primarily two types of digital signatures: direct and arbitrated. Each has its own strengths and weaknesses and is thus used in different situations. The question is not which type of signature is best, but rather which is better for a specific situation.

Direct Signature

A direct signature involves only two parties (the sender/signer and the receiver). The signature is usually done in one of two ways: either the entire message is encrypted with the sender's private key, or a cryptographic hash, message authentication code, or HMAC is created that is then encrypted with the sender's private key. In either case, the recipient will obtain the sender's public key to decrypt/verify the message.

With a direct signature, there is no third-party verification of the sender's identity. This type of signature is often used in e-mail communications. Verification is assumed based on the sender's e-mail address and the fact that the recipient used the alleged sender's public key to verify the message and it worked. If the e-mail was spoofed (that is, it was not really the purported sender, but rather someone else faking the sender's e-mail address), then the message signature was actually done with some key other than the purported sender's key, and thus verification would fail. The basic process is shown in Figure 13-1.

A typical direct signature process involves the following steps:

1. Write the message.
2. Create a hash of the message.
3. Sign the hash with the sender's private key.
4. Encrypt the message with the recipient's public key.
5. Send the message.

This multi-step process ensures message integrity with the hash, verifies the identity of the sender with the digital signature, and provides message confidentiality with the encryption. This is diagrammed in Figure 13-2. Note that, in the diagram, H(M) means the cryptographic

Alice

- Alice composes a message
- Alice creates a hash of the message
- Alice encrypts that hash with her private key
- Alice sends message to Bob

Bob

- Bob receives message
- Bob retrieves Alice's public key and decrypts the signature
- Bob then recomputes the hash of the message and compares it to the hash he received

FIGURE 13-1   Direct digital signature process

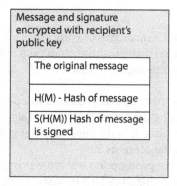

FIGURE 13-2   Typical signature process

hash function of the message M: H is the hashing function and M is the input, or message. The S(H(M)) has similar meaning, with S denoting the digital signature of the hash of the message M.

Arbitrated Digital Signature

An arbitrated digital signature works similarly to a direct signature, but the entity signing the message is not the sender and is instead a third party that is trusted by both sender and receiver. The rest of the process is the same. This sort of digital signature is often used to provide even more assurance that the sender is indeed who they claim to be. A common implementation of this process is shown in Figure 13-3.

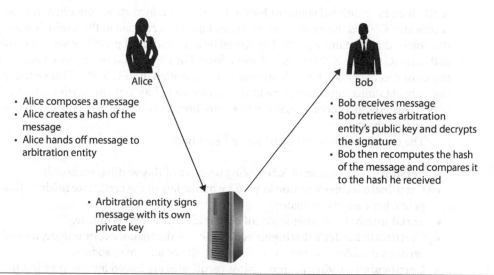

FIGURE 13-3   Arbitrated digital signature

Blind Signatures

The blind signature adds a nuance to the process of arbitrated digital signatures. The signer simply signs a message verifying that the sender did indeed send it, but the signer has no idea what the content of the message is. This allows the signer to verify the origin of the message but not the content.

Think about it like this: Assume you observe a person writing a note, putting it in an envelope, and then sealing the envelope. You then sign the envelope, verifying that the person did indeed write it and place it in the envelope. You can attest to the identity of the sender, but you have no idea what the contents are.

A blind signature is a great option when the privacy of the data being sent is of paramount importance, such as in voting situations or when using private digital currency. Blind signatures provide the enhanced validation of the sender via arbitrated digital signatures, but they protect the privacy of the data.

Digital Certificates

In Chapters 10 and 11 I discussed asymmetric key cryptography, also known as public-key cryptography. The strength of asymmetric cryptography is that there is no issue with key exchange. It is perfectly acceptable for anyone, and indeed everyone, to have access to the public keys of both the sender and receiver. However, this does not answer the question of how such public keys are disseminated. The first step in that process is a *digital certificate*, a digital document that contains some information about the certificate holder and the certificate holder's public key. There are two major types of digital certificates: X.509 and PGP.

X.509

X.509 is an international standard for the format and information contained in a digital certificate. X.509 is the most common type of digital certificate in the world. It is a digital document that contains a public key signed by a trusted third party known as a certificate authority (CA). The X.509 standard was released in 1988. It has been revised since then, with the most recent version being X.509 version 3, specified in RFC 5280.[1] This system supports not only obtaining information about the certificate holder, but also verifying that information with a trusted third party. This is key to secure protocols such as SSL and TLS, as you will see later in this chapter.

The content of an X.509 certificate is listed here:

- **Version**   The version of X.509 being used (as of this writing, version 3).
- **Certificate holder's public key**   The public key of the certificate holder—this is how public keys are disseminated.
- **Serial number**   A unique identifier that identifies this certificate.
- **Certificate holder's distinguished name**   A distinguished, or unique, name for the certificate holder; usually a URL for a web site or an e-mail address.
- **Certificate's validity period**   Most certificates are issued for one year, but the exact validity period is reflected in this field.

- **Unique name of certificate issuer**   Identifies the trusted third party that issued the certificate. Public CAs include Thawte, VeriSign, GoDaddy, and others.
- **Digital signature of issuer**   Confirms that this certificate was really issued by the certificate authority it claims to have been issued by.
- **Signature algorithm identifier**   The signer's public key and the algorithm used, to verify the signer's digital signature.

There are other optional fields, but these are the required fields. Notice that the last three items are about verification. One of the benefits of the X.509 digital certificate is the mechanism for verifying the certificate holder. This is a key to secure communications, not just encrypting the transmissions, but verifying the identity of the parties involved. An overview of the process is provided in Figure 13-4.

This leads to a significant question: Why would you trust the certificate issuer to verify the identity of the certificate holder? Certificates are issued by CAs, entities that are trusted by many different third parties. The major CAs include Symantec, GoDaddy, DigiCert, Global Sign, and Comodo, which are all considered trusted vendors.

> **Note**   Companies and other organizations sometimes publish their own digital certificates, but those are useful only within the organizational network. Because the company's CA is not trusted by other networks, the certificates issued by that CA won't be trusted by other networks.

There are varying levels of digital certificates. Each involves a different level of verification of the certificate holder's identity. The more verification used, the more expensive the certificate:

- **Class 1**   For individuals, intended for e-mail
- **Class 2**   For organizations, for which proof of identity is required; most web sites use a class 2 certificate

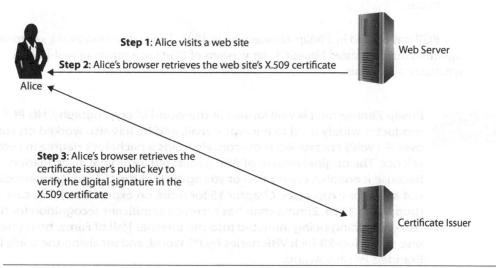

Step 1: Alice visits a web site

Step 2: Alice's browser retrieves the web site's X.509 certificate

Alice

Web Server

Step 3: Alice's browser retrieves the certificate issuer's public key to verify the digital signature in the X.509 certificate

Certificate Issuer

FIGURE 13-4   Verifying X.509 certificates

- **Class 3** For servers and software signing, for which independent verification and checking of identity and authority is done by the issuing CA
- **Class 4** For online business transactions between companies
- **Class 5** For private organizations or governmental security

PGP

The other type of certificate is the Pretty Good Privacy (PGP) certificate. The PGP methodology combines cryptographic hashes, asymmetric cryptography, and symmetric cryptography to create secure communications. Each public key is tied to a username and/or e-mail address, so PGP is often used for e-mail encryption. PGP operates by using certificates, but it uses self-signed digital certificates. That means there is no CA and thus no third-party verification of a sender's identity. This is why PGP certificates are not used for web pages/e-commerce. A PGP certificate includes the following information:

- **PGP version number** The version of PGP is being used.
- **Certificate holder's public key** The public key of the certificate holder. One of the purposes of using digital certificates is to disseminate public keys.
- **Certificate holder's information** Identifies who this certificate belongs to; can be a bit more extensive that the X.509 certificate.
- **Digital signature of certificate owner** Because there is no CA, the certificate owner signs the certificate.
- **Certificate's validity period** How long the certificate is valid for.
- **Preferred symmetric encryption algorithm for the key** Once asymmetric cryptography is in use, what type of symmetric algorithm does the certificate holder prefer to use.

PGP was created by Phillip Zimmerman in 1991. The first version used a symmetric algorithm that he created himself. Later versions of PGP use a variety of well-known symmetric algorithms.

Note Phillip Zimmerman is well known in the world of cryptography. His PGP product is widely used to encrypt e-mail, and he has also worked on voice over IP (VoIP) encryption protocols. He holds a bachelor's degree in computer science. The original release of PGP generated a criminal investigation because it enabled encryption of strengths that the U.S. government did not allow for export (see Chapter 15 for more on export laws). The case was dropped in 1996. Zimmerman has received significant recognition for his work, including being inducted into the Internet Hall of Fame, being named one of the Top 50 Tech Visionaries by *PC World*, and receiving the Louis D. Brandeis Privacy Award.

Public-Key Infrastructure X.509

PKI is the infrastructure required to create and distribute digital certificates. Because digital certificates are the means by which public keys for asymmetric algorithms are disseminated, the PKI is an important part of any implementation of asymmetric cryptography.

One role of the PKI is to bind public keys with some user's identity via a CA. In other words, it is not adequate simply to have public keys widely available; there needs to be some mechanism to validate that a specific public key is associated with a specific user. With PKI, this is done via a CA that validates the identity of the user.

There are several parts to the PKI. Each certificate issuer must be trusted by the other certificate issuers for the certificates to be interchangeable. Consider the process of visiting an online banking site, for example. The site has a digital certificate issued by some CA, which needs to be one that you and the bank both trust. Then later, perhaps you visit an e-commerce web site, which might use an entirely different CA—but it must also be one that you trust.

The CA is responsible for issuing and managing certificates.[2] This includes revoking certificates, which is accomplished in one of two ways:

- **CRL (Certificate Revocation List)**   A list of certificates that have been revoked. These lists are distributed in two ways: via a push model, in which the CA automatically sends the CRL out at regular intervals, and via a pull model, in which the CRL is downloaded from the CA by those who want to see it to verify a certificate. Neither model provides instant, real-time updates.
- **Status checking**   Given that CRLs are not real-time, the Online Certificate Status Protocol (OCSP) was invented to verify whether a certificate is valid or not. OCSP is described in RFC 6960. It uses HTTP to communicate messages and is supported in Internet Explorer 7, Mozilla Firefox 3, and Safari.

The CA is often assisted by a registration authority (RA), which is responsible for verifying the person or entity requesting a digital certificate. Once that identity has been verified, the RA informs the CA that a certificate can be issued.

The *Public-Key Infrastructure X.509 (PKIX)* is the working group formed by the IETF to develop standards and models for the public key infrastructure. Among other things, this working group is responsible for updates to the X.509 standard. The working group involves experts from around the world, each contributing input to the standards.

The *Public-Key Cryptography Standards (PKCS)* is a set of voluntary standards created by RSA and along with several other companies including Microsoft and Apple. As of this writing, there are 15 published PKCS standards:

- PKCS #1: RSA Cryptography Standard
- PKCS #2: Incorporated in PKCS #1
- PKCS #3: Diffie-Hellman Key Agreement Standard
- PKCS #4: Incorporated in PKCS #1
- PKCS #5: Password-Based Cryptography Standard

- PKCS #6: Extended-Certificate Syntax Standard
- PKCS #7: Cryptographic Message Syntax Standard
- PKCS #8: Private-Key Information Syntax Standard
- PKCS #9: Selected Attribute Types
- PKCS #10: Certification Request Syntax Standard
- PKCS #11: Cryptographic Token Interface Standard
- PKCS #12: Personal Information Exchange Syntax Standard
- PKCS #13: Elliptic Curve Cryptography Standard
- PKCS #14: Pseudorandom Number Generators
- PKCS #15: Cryptographic Token Information Format Standard

SSL and TLS Protocol Basics

The Secure Sockets Layer (SSL) protocol has been supplanted by Transport Layer Security (TLS). Both protocols use X.509 certificates for the exchange of public keys and to authenticate them. Many references (books, magazines, courses, and so on) refer to SSL when in fact it is most likely that TLS is being used today. I will use the convention of referring to SSL/TLS when the specific version is not important.

History

When the World Wide Web first began, no one considered security. The Hypertext Transfer Protocol (HTTP), the foundation of communication on the Web, is inherently quite insecure, however, so it didn't take long for computer scientists to realize that security was needed if the Web was to be used for sensitive communications such as financial data. When Netscape invented the SSL protocol, version 1.0 was never released because of significant security flaws. However, version 2.0 was released in 1995 and began to be widely used. But security flaws were found with it as well, and it was subsequently supplanted with version 3.0 in 1996, which was not just a minor improvement over past versions—it was a complete overhaul. It was published as RFC 6101.

TLS 1.0 was released in 1999 and was essentially an upgrade to SSL 3.0. However, it was not compatible with SSL 3.0.[3] TLS 1.0 also added support for the GOST hashing algorithm as an option for message authentication and integrity. Previous versions had supported only MD5 and SHA-1 as hashing message authentication codes.

TLS 1.0 was eventually supplanted by TLS 1.1 in April 2006. It included a number of specific cryptographic improvements, including improved initialization vectors as well as support for cipher block chaining for the Advanced Encryption Standard (AES).

In August 2008, TLS 1.2 was released as RFC 5246.[4] It had many improvements over previous versions, including the following:

- Replaced MD5 and ShAQ with SHA-256
- Supported advanced modes of AES encryption

Note   As of this writing, TLS 1.3 is still in draft and has not been released.

The Handshake Step-by-Step

The process of establishing an SSL/TLS connection is rather complex. The specific steps are described here:[5, 6]

1. Communication begins with the client sending a hello message (see the "Handshake Initiation" sidebar), which contains the client's SSL version number, cipher settings (the algorithms the client supports), session-specific data, and other information that the server needs to communicate with the client using SSL.
2. The server responds with a server hello message, which contains the server's SSL version number, cipher settings, session-specific data, and other information that the client needs to communicate with the server over SSL. The server also sends the client the server's X.509 certificate. The client can use this to authenticate the server and then use the server's public key. In some optional configurations, client authentication is required. In that case, part of the server hello message is a request for the client's certificate.
3. The client uses the server's X.509 certificate to authenticate the server by retrieving the public key of the CA that issued this X.509 certificate and using that to verify the CA's digital signature on the certificate. Assuming authentication works, the client can proceed with confidence with the server.
4. Using all data generated in the handshake thus far, the client creates the premaster secret for the session, encrypts it with the server's public key (obtained from the server's certificate in step 2), and then sends the premaster secret to the server.
5. If the server is configured to require client authentication, it requires that the client send to the server the client's X.509 certificate. The server will use this to attempt to authenticate the client.
6. If client authentication is required and the client cannot be authenticated, the session ends. If the client can be successfully authenticated, the server uses its private key to decrypt the premaster secret sent by the client.
7. Both the client and the server use the premaster secret that was sent from the client to the server to generate the session keys. The session keys are symmetric keys and use whatever algorithm the client and server have agreed upon in steps 1 and 2 of the handshake process.
8. Once the client has completed generating the symmetric key from the premaster secret, the client sends a message to the server stating that future messages from the client will be encrypted with that session key. It then sends an encrypted message indicating that the client portion of the handshake is finished.
9. The server sends a message to the client informing it that future messages from the server will be encrypted with the session key. The server then sends an encrypted message indicating that the server portion of the handshake is finished.

You can see this entire process in Figure 13-5, which shows the basic handshake process, without client authentication.

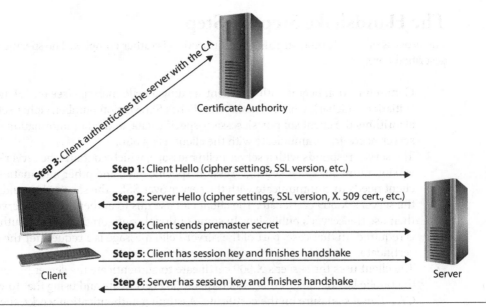

FIGURE 13-5 SSL/TLS handshake process

> **Note**
> Client authentication is not generally used in e-commerce, because it would require each and every client to have an X.509 certificate from a well-known and trusted CA. I suspect that most of you do not have such a certificate. If e-commerce sites did request such a certificate, it might reduce online fraud, but it would also add an extra burden and cost to consumers, who would have to purchase a certificate at an average cost of $19.95 per year.

The SSL/TLS process is very important. If you have ever purchased a product online, checked your bank statement online, or used any secure web site, you have already participated in this process. It is the basis for secure web traffic. Once the handshake is completed, you will notice that your browser URL changes from *http* to *https*, indicating that HTTP is secured by SSL/TLS. Many browsers also display a small visual indicator that the site communications are now secure, as shown here.

Microsoft Internet Explorer displays the indicator at the end of the URL text field, and Mozilla Firefox and Google Chrome display the indicator just before the URL, but both use a padlock indicator.

Handshake Initiation

The hello messages sent from client to server were discussed in "Handshake Step-by-Step." The client hello consists of the following elements:

- **Protocol version**   Indicates if this is SSL version 3, TLS version 1.1, and so on.

- **Random number**   A 32-byte random number; the first 4 bytes are the time of the day in seconds, and the next 28 bits are a random number; used to prevent replay attacks.

- **Session ID**   A 32-byte number used to identify the SSL/TLS session.

- **Compression algorithm**   If compression is used in transmission, the specific algorithm is provided here.

- **Cipher suite**   A list of the cryptographic algorithms the client can use; often common symmetric ciphers such as Blowfish, AES, and so on. May also include hashing or message authentication code algorithms the client is capable of to allow for message integrity.

The server hello is similar, consisting of the following elements:

- **Protocol version**   Indicates if this is SSL version 3, TLS version 1.1, and so on.

- **Random number**   A 32-byte random number. The first 4 bytes are the time of the day in seconds, and the next 28 bits are a random number; used to prevent replay attacks.

- **Session ID**   A 32-byte number used to identify the SSL/TLS session.

- **Compression algorithm**   The server selects one of the algorithms the client has indicated that it can support.

- **Cipher suite**   The server selects one of the algorithms the client has indicated that it can support.

During the handshake, and throughout the SSL/TLS communication process, both client and server send a number of specific error messages to each other. The most critical of these messages is shown in Table 13-1.

SSL/TLS Applications

As mentioned, secure web communications depend on SSL/TLS. If you use the web for e-commerce, online banking, secure social media, or other secure communications, you are using SSL/TLS. Clearly this is a critical technology.

OpenSSL

OpenSSL is a popular open source implementation of SSL/TLS. It is written in C and is widely used for SSL/TLS. The OpenSSL project was founded in 1998 and is widely used today, with literally thousands of web servers running OpenSSL.[7, 8]

TABLE 13-1 SSL/TLS Messages

Message	Description
unexpected_message	The message sent by the other party (client or server) is inappropriate and cannot be processed.
bad_record_mac	Incorrect Message Authentication Code. This indicates that message integrity may be compromised.
decryption_failed	For some reason the party sending this message was unable to decrypt TLS cipher text correctly.
handshake_failure	Unacceptable security parameters; the handshake cannot be completed.
bad_certificate	There is a problem with the X.509 certificate that was sent.
unsupported_certificate	The certificate is unsupported. Either the type or format of the certificate cannot be supported.
certificate_revoked	Certificate has been revoked.
certificate_expired	Certificate has expired.
certificate_unknown	Certificate is unknown. This often happens with self-signed certificates.
unknown_ca	CA unknown. This also happens with self-signed as well as domain certificates.
access_denied	The other party refuses to perform the SSL/TLS handshake.
protocol_version	Protocol version not supported by both parties.
insufficient_security	Security requirements are not met. The minimum security level of one party exceeds the maximum level of the other party. This is not a common error message.

OpenSSL can support a wide range of cryptographic algorithms. For symmetric ciphers it can support DES, AES, Blowfish, 3DES, GOST, CAST 128, IDEA, RC2, RC4, RC5, Camellia, and SEED. For cryptographic hashes, OpenSSL can support MD2, MD4, MD5, SHA-1, SHA-2, RIPEMD-160, GOST, and MDC-2. For asymmetric algorithms, OpenSSL can support Diffie-Hellman, RSA, DSA, and elliptic curve cryptography.

OpenSSL and the Heartbleed Bug

No discussion of OpenSSL would be complete without including the infamous Heartbleed Bug. Heartbleed came down to a very simple flaw—a buffer over-read. The bug involved improper bounds checking that would allow an attacker to read more data than OpenSSL should be able to. The flaw was implemented in the OpenSSL source code repository on December 31, 2011, and was released with OpenSSL version 1.0.1 on March 14, 2012.

Here's how the process worked: A computer at one end of the connection would send a heartbeat request message, simply a request to ensure the other end was still active. This included a 16-bit integer, and the receiving computer would send back the same payload (16 bits). The bug allowed the attacker to set any return length size desired, up to 64KB of data. With this flaw, the attacker would request whatever was in active memory up to 64KB. In the case of servers, this 64KB of data could include other users' keys, credit card information, or other sensitive data. This bug has been patched, and OpenSSL continues to be widely used.

VoIP

Voice over IP (VoIP) is in wide use today. The ability to place phone calls using IP networks is quickly replacing traditional phone calls—at least for many people. VoIP depends primarily on two protocols: Session Initiation Protocol (SIP) establishes a session/phone call; then Real-time Transport Protocol (RTP) transmits the data. In many cases, Secure Real-Time Transport Protocol (sRTP) is used to secure the data. sRTP uses AES encryption. However, that still leaves the initial SIP communication insecure.

Some implementations of VoIP use an SSL/TLS connection established first, and then both SIP and RTP communication are conducted over the SSL/TLS connection. This allows for complete security of the entire communication session.

E-mail

E-mail is usually sent using the Simple Mail Transfer Protocol (SMTP) and received using either Post Office Protocol version 3 (POP3) or Internet Message Access Protocol (IMAP). All of these protocols are quite effective at transferring e-mail, but they are simply not secure. To secure these protocols, SSL/TLS is added. SMTPS (SMTP using SSL/TLS) uses port 465 and can send e-mail over an encrypted channel. IMAPS (IMAP using SSL/TLS) uses port 993 and can retrieve e-mail from the e-mail server over an encrypted channel.

Web Servers

Obviously, SSL/TLS is used to encrypt web traffic. In fact, that may be one of the most common applications of SSL/TLS. The two most common web servers are Apache web server and Microsoft Internet Information Services (IIS). Let's look at configuring SSL/TLS for each of these commonly used web servers.

Apache Web Server

The Apache web server ships by default with many Linux distributions. You can also download Apache for either Linux or Windows at www.apache.org. It is an open source product and a free download. This, combined with its ease of use, has made it a very popular web server.

Depending on the version of Apache being used, the configuration file (httpd.conf) will be found in one of the following two locations:

- /etc/apache2
- /etc/httpd

```
httpd.conf
# allow all ciphers for the initial handshake,
# so export browsers can upgrade via SGC facility
SSLCipherSuite ALL:!ADH:RC4+RSA:+HIGH:+MEDIUM:+LOW:+SSLv2:+EXP:+eNULL

<Directory /usr/local/apache2/htdocs>
# but finally deny all browsers which haven't upgraded
SSLRequire %{SSL_CIPHER_USEKEYSIZE} >= 128
</Directory>
```

FIGURE 13-6   Configure SSL/TLS in Apache

You can configure your web server to accept secure connections and, in some cases, to accept only secure connections simply by changing the httpd.conf file. For example, if you want the server to accept only SSL version 3:

```
SSLProtocol -all +SSLv3
SSLCipherSuite SSLv3:+HIGH:+MEDIUM:+LOW:+EXP
```

Figure 13-6 shows an excerpt from an example httpd.conf file. This excerpt comes from the Apache.org web site.[9]

 Note   Go to the Apache.org web site to find other possible configurations. As you can see, it is a rather trivial matter to enable SSL/TLS for Apache.

Internet Information Services

Microsoft IIS is configured entirely from GUI methods, although it is a lengthy process. Unlike Apache, there is no configuration file to edit. However, the steps are relatively simple, and this section offers a step-by-step guide.

First, navigate to the Control Panel, and then Administrative Tools. This process will be the same in every version of Windows (Windows Vista, 7, 8, 8.1; Server 2003, 2008, 2012; and so on). Under Administrative Tools, you should see Internet Information Services, as shown here.

▸ Control Panel ▸ System and Security ▸ Administrative Tools			
Name	Date modified	Type	Size
Component Services	7/25/2012 3:22 PM	Shortcut	2 KB
Computer Management	7/25/2012 3:19 PM	Shortcut	2 KB
Defragment and Optimize Drives	7/25/2012 3:18 PM	Shortcut	2 KB
desktop.ini	5/1/2014 6:54 AM	Configuration setti...	4 KB
Disk Cleanup	7/25/2012 3:22 PM	Shortcut	2 KB
Event Viewer	7/25/2012 3:20 PM	Shortcut	2 KB
Hyper-V Manager	7/25/2012 3:19 PM	Shortcut	2 KB
Internet Information Services (IIS) Manag...	7/25/2012 3:15 PM	Shortcut	2 KB
iSCSI I...			2 KB
Local S...			2 KB
ODBC			2 KB

Internet Information Services (IIS) Manager
Internet Information Services (IIS) Manager enables you to configure, control, and troubleshoot IIS and ASP.NET.

If you do not see this option, you need to add it. In Windows Client operating systems (Windows 7, 8, and so on), you do this by going to Control Panel and then Programs; turn on Windows Features, as shown next.

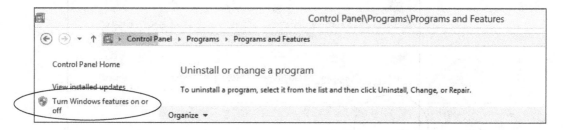

IIS is a part of all versions of Windows and can be turned on or added to any Windows server or client. For servers, you simply use the Add Role function rather than "turn on" features.

Once you have IIS turned on, you can use the IIS manager in the Administrative Tools to configure IIS. There are really two segments to the IIS management: the first is for IIS server-wide, and the second is for specific sites. As you go through these steps, if you do not see an option mentioned, you are probably looking at the wrong aspect of the IIS manager. You can see the server settings circled in Figure 13-7.

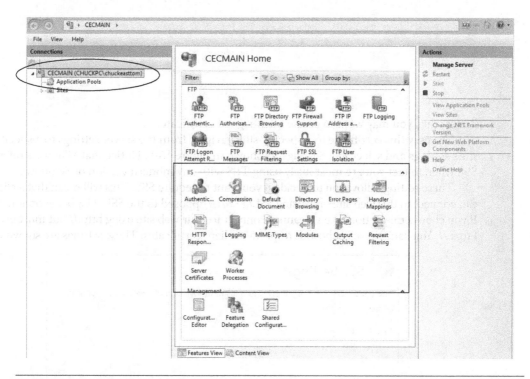

FIGURE 13-7   IIS server settings

Within those server settings you need to select Server Certificates, as shown next.

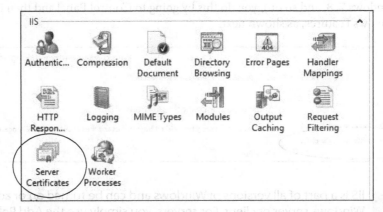

On the right side of the Server Certificates screen is an Actions menu, where, as shown next, you can create a self-signed certificate, create a certificate request, create a domain certificate, or import an existing certificate.

To test this, you may want to create a self-signed certificate.

To apply this certificate to a specific site, navigate from the server settings to a specific site's settings and select SSL Settings, as shown in Figure 13-8. Notice that Windows refers to SSL when in fact you are most likely using TLS with any modern version of Windows.

These settings allow you to decide if you want to require SSL. This will mean that a client can connect to this web site only using SSL/TLS, as opposed to the SSL/TLS being optional. If you choose this option, clients cannot connect to your web site using http:// but must use https://. You can also select how to respond to client certificates. These settings are shown here.

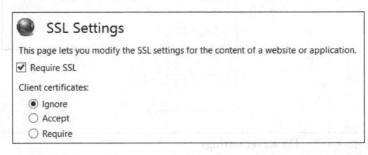

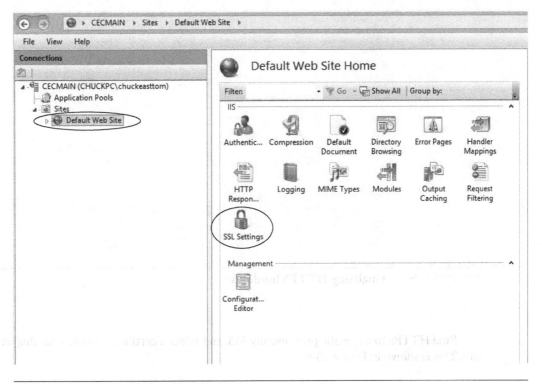

FIGURE 13-8 Site SSL Settings

Finally, set the bindings for this site. When you have navigated to a specific site, the binding's option is on the right side of the screen, as shown next.

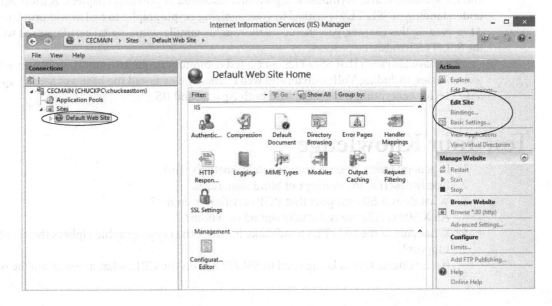

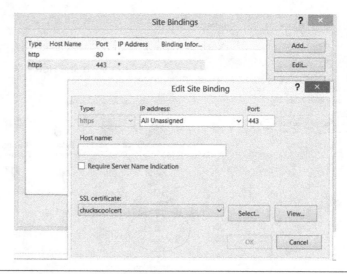

FIGURE 13-9   Finalizing HTTPS bindings

Bind HTTPS to a specific port, usually 443, and select a certificate to use with this web site. This is shown in Figure 13-9.

Conclusions

The SSL and TLS protocols are a cornerstone of modern secure communications. These protocols in turn depend on other technologies such as X.509 certificates, digital signatures, and the symmetric and asymmetric algorithms discussed in previous chapters. A thorough understanding of SSL/TLS is critical to your applying cryptography to real-world problems. After reading this chapter, you should be thoroughly familiar with digital certificates as well as the SSL/TLS handshake process.

You have also seen that SSL/TLS encrypted communications are important in a variety of technologies, including VoIP, e-mail, and web traffic. You explored the basics of setting up SSL/TLS for encrypting web traffic with both Apache and IIS.

Test Your Knowledge

1. In general terms, describe how digital signatures work.
2. Briefly describe the concept of blind signatures.
3. What does X.509 support that PGP certificates do not?
4. An X.509 certificate is digitally signed by whom?
5. What part of the SSL/TLS handshake includes the cryptographic ciphers the client can support?
6. If a certificate that is being used in SSL/TLS is on the CRL, what message will be sent?

7. On what port does secure IMAP operate by default?
8. What is an arbitrated signature?
9. Is voicemail secure?
10. Where is PGP most often used?

Answers

1. The private key is used to encrypt a message, usually the hash of the message, and the receiver uses the public key to verify.
2. Person A needs to send a message to Person B, but a trusted third party C must sign to verify that the data was in fact sent by A. However, A does not want C to see the contents of the message being signed.
3. Third-party authentication
4. The certificate issuer
5. The client hello
6. certificate_revoked
7. 993
8. The signature is from a trusted third party, not the message sender.
9. No, SIP and RTP are not inherently secure. Protocols such as sRTP need to be used to provide security.
10. E-mail encryption

Endnotes

1. IETF, RFC 5280, "Internet X.509 Public Key Infrastructure Certificate and Certificate Revocation List (CRL) Profile," May 2008, www.rfc-editor.org/info/rfc5280.
2. Microsoft Developer Network, "Public Key Infrastructure," https://msdn.microsoft .com/en-us/library/windows/desktop/bb427432(v=vs.85).aspx.
3. Microsoft TechNet, "What Is TLS/SSL?" https://technet.microsoft.com/en-us/library/ cc784450(v=ws.10).aspx.
4. IETF RFC 5246, "The Transport Layer Security (TLS) Protocol Version 1.2," https:// tools.ietf.org/html/rfc5246.
5. IBM Knowledge Center, "An Overview of the SSL or TLS Handshake," www-01 .ibm.com/support/knowledgecenter/SSFKSJ_7.1.0/com.ibm.mq.doc/sy10660_ .htm?lang=en.
6. Microsoft TechNet, "SSL/TLS in Detail," https://technet.microsoft.com/en-us/library/ cc785811(v=ws.10).aspx.
7. Netcraft, "April 2014 Web Server Survey," http://news.netcraft.com/archives/ 2014/04/02/april-2014-web-server-survey.html.
8. BuiltWith, "OpenSSL Usage Statistics: Websites Using OpenSSL," http://trends .builtwith.com/Server/OpenSSL.
9. Apache HTTP Server Version 2.0, "SSL/TLS Strong Encryption: How To," http://httpd .apache.org/docs/2.0/ssl/ssl_howto.html.

14 Virtual Private Networks

In this chapter we will cover the following:

- Authentication
- PPTP
- L2TP
- IPSec
- SSL/TLS VPN
- Secure communications

Virtual private networks (VPNs) are yet another very common application of cryptography. VPNs are designed to provide a secure connection between two sites or between a remote worker and a site. They give you the same connection you would have if you were physically connected to the network—thus the name: it is a virtual connection to a private network. In this chapter we will examine some general concepts as well as specific technologies related to VPNs. We will also look at related technologies that, while not strictly VPNs, are secure remote connections.

The *Dictionary of Computer and Internet Terms* defines a VPN as "a network where data is transferred over the Internet using security features preventing unauthorized access."[1] This is a fairly typical definition, similar to what you would find in any computer dictionary, but not quite detailed enough.

The idea of a VPN is to emulate an actual physical network connection, which means a VPN must provide the same level of access and security as well. To emulate a dedicated point-to-point (PTP) link, data is encapsulated, or wrapped, with a header that provides routing information that allows it to transmit across the Internet to reach its destination. This creates a virtual network connection between the two points. Next, the data is encrypted, thus making that virtual network private.

The question becomes, how does one implement the authentication and encryption required to create a VPN? Several technologies can facilitate establishing a VPN, and each works in a slightly different manner. We will examine each of these in this chapter. Despite the differences in the protocols, the end goals are the same. First authenticate the user to ensure that this user is who they claim to be. Then exchange cryptographic information such as what algorithms to use, and finally establish a symmetric key the two parties can use to secure data between them.

Authentication

Authentication is merely the process of verifying that some entity (be it a user or another system or program) is, indeed, who they claim to be. The most obvious example of authentication occurs when an end user provides a username and password. The password presumably verifies the user's identity. However, as security breaches become more widespread, a simple username and password are no longer adequate. So other types of authentication have been developed:

- **Type I, something you know**   Passwords, PINs, and passphrases are classic examples of Type I authentication. They all have the same weakness, however: they can be easily guessed or stolen.
- **Type II, something you have**   These are physical items, such as a debit card used with ATMs, smart cards, and smart keys. This type of authentication cannot be guessed, but it can certainly be stolen.
- **Type III, something you are**   Biometrics, including fingerprints, retinal scans, facial recognition, even handwriting, all constitute Type III authentication. This is the most secure type of authentication, because it cannot be guessed and cannot be stolen (at least not easily!).

> **Note**   These are the three primary means of authentication, but other methods exist. For example, out-of-band (OOB) authentication involves prompting the user for information from various data sources that is likely to be known only to the authentic user. When you run a credit report online, many systems will prompt you for identifying information such as a Social Security Number (Type I authentication) and ask you questions such as the amount of your monthly credit card payment and current balance. These last two pieces of information are OOB information.

Type I authentication can be used for VPNs and often is. Type II can also be used. The best solution, often called strong authentication, is to combine Type I and Type II authentication. For example, if you want to use an ATM, you must have a debit card (Type II) and a PIN (Type I). Some VPN solutions operate in a similar fashion, requiring a password and perhaps a digital certificate (see Chapter 13 for a detailed discussion of digital certificates), or even a smart card on the client machine. Type III authentication is not appropriate for VPNs in most situations (except for government-controlled classified systems). The cost, overhead, and complexity make biometrics less attractive for VPNs.

In addition to considerations as to what type of authentication to use, you must address the method of transmitting authentication data as well as cryptographic information. This is handled by VPN protocols. Each protocol establishes its own authentication method as well as how to exchange cryptographic data.

Because all VPN protocols include authentication as well as encryption, you need to have a good understanding of authentication protocols. Throughout this book, we have examined a number of cryptographic and hashing algorithms; compared to those, authentication is a relatively simple process. The purpose of authentication is simply to verify that a given entity is who they claim to be. Modern authentication protocols also prevent sophisticated attacks such as session hijacking.

Session hijacking occurs when an attacker waits until a user has authenticated to a system and then takes over that session. Various methods can be used, all of which are at least moderately sophisticated. The key to session hijacking is that the attacker does not actually need to obtain the user's password; the attacker takes over a session after the user has supplied the password to the system.

CHAP

Challenge Handshake Authentication Protocol was specifically designed to prevent session hijacking. The process of CHAP is relatively straightforward:

1. The client sends her username and password to the server (often called the "authenticator" in CHAP documentation).
2. The server/authenticator then requests that the client calculate a cryptographic hash and send that to the server.
3. Periodically, at random intervals, the server/authenticator will request that the client re-present that cryptographic hash. The purpose of this is to detect if session hijacking has occurred, and, if so, terminate that connection.

This process is depicted in Figure 14-1.

Microsoft created its own variation of CHAP, called MS-CHAP. Although MS-CHAP conforms to the general description, the variations are not pertinent to our discussions of VPNs. For example, MS-CHAP v2 provides for mutual authentication, wherein both sides authenticate each other.

EAP

Extensible Authentication Protocol, as the name implies, is a framework that can be modified, or extended, for a variety of purposes. The EAP standard was originally specified in RFC 2284,

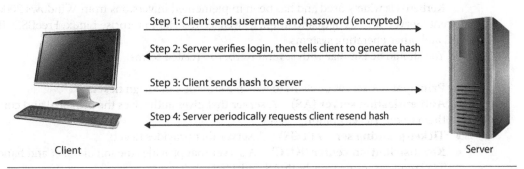

Step 1: Client sends username and password (encrypted)

Step 2: Server verifies login, then tells client to generate hash

Step 3: Client sends hash to server

Step 4: Server periodically requests client resend hash

Client

Server

FIGURE 14-1 The CHAP process

but that was supplanted by RFC 3748, and then later updated by RFC 5247. The various permutations of EAP differ in how authentication material is exchanged. There are many variations of EAP, so let's take a look at just a few.

LEAP

Lightweight Extensible Authentication Protocol was developed by Cisco and has been used extensively in wireless communications. LEAP is supported by many Microsoft operating systems including Windows 7. LEAP uses a modified version of MS-CHAP.

EAP-TLS

Extensible Authentication Protocol–Transport Layer Security uses TLS (see Chapter 13) to secure the authentication process. Most implementations of EAP-TLS use X.509 digital certificates (also discussed in Chapter 13) to authenticate the users.

PEAP

Protected Extensible Authentication Protocol encrypts the authentication process with an authenticated TLS tunnel. PEAP was developed by a consortium including Cisco, Microsoft, and RSA Security. It was first included in Microsoft Windows XP.

EAP-POTP

Protected One-Time Password is a variation of EAP described in RFC 4793. It uses a one-time password token to generate authentication keys and can be used for one-way or bilateral authentication (the client authenticates to the server, and the server authenticates to the client).

An OTP is used only once, and then it is no longer valid. It is often used in conjunction with a device such as a key fob that generates the OTP. The key fob and the server use the same algorithm and tie in the current time stamp to generate the same OTP on both ends. Often this is used in conjunction with a traditional password.

Kerberos

Kerberos is a network authentication protocol designed to provide strong authentication for client/server applications by using symmetric cryptography. It was originally developed at MIT under the name "Project Athena." The protocol was named after the Greek mythological character Kerberos (or Cerberus), the monstrous three-headed guard dog of Hades.

Kerberos is widely used and has been implemented in versions from Windows 2000 to the current (Server 2012 as of this writing), as well as Red Hat Enterprise Linux, FreeBSD, IBM AIX, and other operating systems.

You should be familiar with several Kerberos-related terms:

- **Principal**   A server or client to which Kerberos can assign tickets
- **Authentication server (AS)**   A server that gives authorizes the principal and connects them to the Ticket-granting server
- **Ticket-granting server (TGS)**   A server that provides tickets
- **Key distribution center (KDC)**   A server that provides the initial ticket and handles TGS requests; often runs both AS and TGS services
- **Ticket-granting ticket (TGT)**   The ticket that is granted during the authentication process

- **Ticket**   Used to authenticate to the server; contains client identity, session key, timestamp, and checksum and is encrypted with server's key
- **Session key**   Temporary encryption key

The process itself is purposefully complex to prevent session hijacking attacks and to ensure a more robust and reliable authentication mechanism. There are variations on the process depending on implementation, but the general process is as follows:

1. The client sends a username and password to the authentication server (also known as a server or a service). The username and password are used to generate a session key that the server uses to send messages to the client for this session. The authentication server/service (AS) is usually colocated with the ticket-granting service (TGS) on the key distribution center (KDC) server. Often, the KDC includes the AS and TGS.
2. After the AS has verified the client, it directs the TGS to generate a ticket-granting ticket (TGT). This includes, among other things, the client ID, client network address, client session key, and validity period. All of that information is encrypted with a symmetric key that only the TGS has—in other words, the client cannot decrypt the ticket.
3. When the client wants to access a given service, a message is sent to the KDC consisting of the TGT and the ID of the service requested. A second message is also sent that has the client ID and a timestamp and is encrypted with the session key.
4. If everything checks out, the KDC sends a session ticket back to the client that can be used to access the service in question.
5. The previous information is used to authenticate to the service, so the client accesses that service.

The basic process, without a few nuances, is depicted in Figure 14-2.

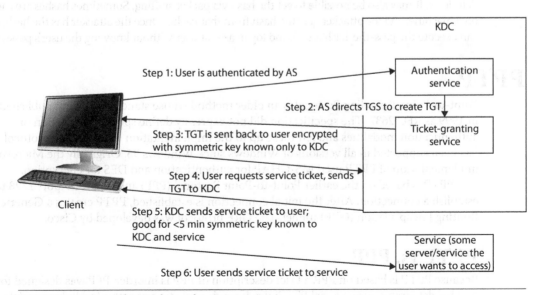

FIGURE 14-2   The Kerberos basic process

The complexity you see in Kerberos is intentional. The constant exchange of encrypted tickets and verification of information makes session hijacking far more difficult. And the combination of the session key with the TGT means an attacker would need to crack two strong encryption keys to subvert the system.

NTLM

NTLM (NT LAN Manager) is not used in modern VPNs but is commonly used in Microsoft products to provide authentication as well as other security services, and you should be familiar with it. Although Microsoft recommends Kerberos as the preferred authentication protocol, many implementations still use NTLM.

NTLM is a three-step process:

1. The client connects to the server, then sends a NEGOTIATE_MESSAGE advertising its capabilities.
2. The server responds with CHALLENGE_MESSAGE. This is used to establish the identity of the client.
3. The process culminates with the client responding to the server's challenge with an AUTHENTICATE_MESSAGE.

Authentication in NTLM is accomplished by sending a hash of the password. NTLM version 1 uses a Data Encryption Standard (DES)–based LanMan hash. NTLM version 2 uses the MD4 cryptographic hash.

NTLM is vulnerable to the pass-the-hash attack, in which the attacker acquires a hash of the user's password and sends that along. The attacker does not know the actual password, but has somehow acquired the hash. This can be done if the user uses the same password for a local password, so the attacker can get that hash from the local Security Account Manager (SAM) file in Windows. It may also be possible to get the hash via packet sniffing. Sometimes hashes are cached on a machine, and the attacker gets the hash from that cache. Once the attacker has the hash, she can execute the pass-the-hash attack and log in as that user without knowing the user's password.

PPTP

Point-to-Point Tunneling Protocol is an older method whose standard was first published in 1999 as RFC 2637. The specification did not expressly define specific encryption or authentication modalities and left these up to the implementation of PPTP. The protocol has been supported in all versions of Windows since Windows 95. Originally the Microsoft implementation of PPTP used MS-CHAP for authentication and DES for encryption.

PPTP is based on the earlier Point-to-Point Protocol (PPP) and uses TCP port 1723 to establish a connection. After the initial connection is established, PPTP creates a Generic Routing Encapsulation (GRE) tunnel. The GRE protocol was developed by Cisco.

PPTP vs. PPP

Because PPTP is based on PPP, a brief description of PPP is in order. PPP was designed for moving datagrams across serial PTP links. It sends packets over a physical link—a serial cable set up between two computers. It is used to establish and configure the communications link and the network layer protocols, and also to encapsulate datagrams. PPP has several components and is actually made up of several protocols, each of which handles a different part of the process. PPP was originally developed as an encapsulation protocol for transporting IP traffic over PTP links. PPP also established a standard for a variety of related tasks, including any transfer of data from one computer to another.

PPP supports these functions by providing an extensible Link Control Protocol (LCP) and a family of Network Control Protocols (NCPs) to negotiate optional configuration parameters and facilities. In addition to IP, PPP supports other protocols. This is no longer such an advantage, however, because now all mainstream networks use TCP/IP. But at the time of the creation of PPTP, Novell used IPX/SPX, Apple used AppleTalk, and UNIX used TCP/IP. Now all of these, as well as Windows, use TCP/IP.

PPTP supports two generic types of tunneling: voluntary and compulsory. In the case of voluntary tunneling, a remote user connects to a standard PPP session that enables the user to log on to the provider's network. The user then launches the VPN software to establish a PPTP session back to the PPTP remote-access server in the central network. This process is called *voluntary tunneling* because the user initiates the process and chooses whether to establish the VPN session. Although not advisable, the user could simply use a standard PPP connection without the benefits of a VPN.

In a compulsory tunneling setup, the only connection available to the host network is via a VPN. A simple PPP connection is not available—only the full PPTP connection, which forces users to use a secure connection. From a security standpoint, this is the preferred option.

PPTP Authentication

When connecting to a remote system, encrypting the data transmissions is not the only facet of security. You must also authenticate the user. PPTP supports two separate technologies for accomplishing this: EAP and CHAP. Both of these were described earlier in this chapter.

PPTP Encryption

The PPP payload is encrypted using Microsoft Point-to-Point Encryption (MPPE) protocol. MPPE was designed specifically for PPTP. It uses RC4 with either a 128-bit, 56-bit, or 40-bit key. Obviously, the 128-bit key is the strongest. One advantage to MPPE is that the encryption keys are frequently changed.[2] During the initial negotiation and key exchange for MPPE, a bit is set to indicate what strength of RC4 to use:

- 128-bit encryption (S bit set)
- 56-bit encryption (M bit set)
- 40-bit encryption (L bit set)

L2TP

The Layer 2 Tunneling Protocol sends its entire packet (both payload and header) via the User Datagram Protocol (UDP). The endpoints of an L2TP tunnel are called the L2TP Access Concentrator (LAC) and the L2TP Network Server (LNS). The LAC initiates a tunnel, connecting to the LNS. After the initial connection, however, communication is bilateral. Like PPTP, L2TP can work in either voluntary or compulsory tunnel mode. However, there is a third option for an L2TP multi-hop connection.

The major differences between L2TP and PPTP are listed here:

- L2TP provides the functionality of PPTP, but it can work over networks other than just IP networks. PPTP can work only with IP networks. L2TP can work with Asynchronous Transfer Mode (ATM), frame relay, and other network types.
- L2TP supports a variety of remote access protocols such as Terminal Access Controller Access Control System Plus (TACACS+) and Remote Authentication Dial-In User Service (RADIUS), while PPTP does not.

Although L2TP has more connection options, it does not define a specific encryption protocol. The L2TP payload is encrypted using Internet Protocol Security (IPSec). RFC 4835 specifies either Triple DES (3DES) or AES encryption. IPSec is considered far more secure that the authentication and encryption used in PPTP.[3]

IPSec

IPSec is probably the most widely used VPN protocol today. Unlike PPTP and L2TP, IPSec provides a complete solution that includes built-in authentication and encryption. IPSec is a security technology used in addition to IP that adds security and privacy to TCP/IP communications. IPSec is incorporated with Microsoft OSs as well as many others. For example, the security settings in the Internet Connection Firewall that ships with Windows XP enables users to turn on IPSec for transmissions. IPSec was developed by the IETF (Internet Engineering Task Force) to support secure exchange of packets. It has been deployed widely to implement VPNs.

IPSec has two encryption modes: transport and tunnel. The transport mode works by encrypting the data in each packet, but it leaves the source and destination address, as well as other header information, unencrypted. The tunnel mode encrypts both the header and the data and is more secure than transport mode but can work more slowly. At the receiving end, an IPSec-compliant device decrypts each packet. For IPSec to work, the sending and receiving devices must share a key, an indication that IPSec is a single-key encryption technology. It also comprises two other protocols beyond the two modes already described: Authentication Header (AH) and Encapsulated Security Payload (ESP).

AH is used to provide for authentication and integrity for packets. It contains several pieces of information, including payload length, an Integrity Check Value (ICV), sequence number, and Security Parameters Index (SPI). The header format is shown in Figure 14-3.

Authentication Header				
Offsets Octet	Octet	0	1	2	3
Octet	Bit	0 1 2 3 4 5 6 7	8 9 10 11 12 13 14 15	16 17 18 19 20 21 22 23	24 25 26 27 28 29 30 31
0	0	Next Header	Payload Length	Reserved	
4	32	Security Parameters Index (SPI)			
8	64	Sequence Number			
c	96	Integrity Check Value (ICV)			

FIGURE 14-3   The Authentication Header

Encapsulated Security Payload Header (ESP)				

Offsets	Octet	0	1	2	3
Octet	Bit	0 1 2 3 4 5 6 7	8 9 10 11 12 13 14 15	16 17 18 19 20 21 22 23	24 25 26 27 28 29 30 31
0	0	Security Parameters Index (SPI)			
4	32	Sequence Number			
8	64	Payload data			
		Padding (0-225 octets)			
				Pad Length	Next Header
		Integrity Check Value (ICV)			

FIGURE 14-4   The ESP header

ESP provides confidentiality as well as authentication and integrity. The ESP header has some items similar to those of the AH. Some of the responsibilities for the two headers overlap. You can see that header in Figure 14-4.

The broad steps of the IPSec process are as follows:

1. Some party decides to initiate an IPSec VPN. That starts the Internet Key Exchange (IKE) process.
2. During IKE phase 1, the peers are authenticated and security associations are negotiated.
3. During IKE phase 2, the security association parameters are negotiated and finalized.
4. Data is transmitted.

One concept you will see regarding IPSec is that of the Security Association (SA), a set of parameters such as algorithms, keys, and other items necessary to encrypt and authenticate. One part of IPSec initiation is to ensure that both peers in an IPSec connection have identical SAs. These are established using the Internet Security Association and Key Management Protocol (ISAKMP). This protocol is most often implemented with IKE, which occurs in two phases.

IKE Phase 1

The primary purpose of the IKE phase 1 is to authenticate the IPSec peers and to set up a secure channel between the peers to enable IKE exchanges. In other words, after the two parties are authenticated, subsequent steps involving the exchange of keys can take place. IKE phase 1 is subdivided into a few phases:

1. Authenticates the identities of the IPSec peers
2. Negotiates a matching IKE SA policy between the peers
3. Uses Diffie-Hellman exchange so that both peers have the same secret key

Using that same secret key, the IKE phase 2 parameters can be securely exchanged.

There are two methods or modes for performing IKE phase 1: the main mode and the aggressive mode.

Main Mode

Main mode is the primary or preferred mode for IKE phase 1. In main mode, there are three two-way exchanges between the initiator and receiver.

In the first exchange, the peers agree on the symmetric algorithms used to secure communication and the cryptographic hashes used to protect integrity. This information is being exchanged via the key established using Diffie-Hellman.

In the second exchange, the two peers generate secret key material used to generate secret keys on both ends. This is similar to the process you saw for SSL/TLS in Chapter 13.

> **Note** The IPSec standard allows for HMAC, SHA1, and SHA2 to be used for authentication and 3DES and AES (both with cipher-block chaining) to be used for encryption.

The third exchange involves each peer verifying the other's identity. At the end of this exchange, the two peers should have identical SAs, and a secure channel exists between the two peers.

Aggressive Mode

Aggressive mode essentially condenses the process of main mode into fewer exchanges. The entire process is condensed into just three packets. All of the information required for the SA is passed by the initiating peer. The responding peer then sends the proposal, key material, and ID, and authenticates the session in the next packet. The initiating peer then replies by authenticating the session. And at that point IKE phase 1 is complete.

IKE Phase 2

You may think that after IKE phase 1 there is nothing left to do. However, IPSec takes additional steps to ensure that communication is secure and authenticated. IKE phase 2 has only one mode, called quick mode, which occurs immediately after IKE phase 1 is complete.

Phase 2 negotiates a shared IPSec policy and then derives secret keying material used for the IPSec security algorithms. Phase 2 also exchanges nonces (Numbers Only used oNCE) that provide protection against a variety of attacks, including replay attacks. The nonces are also used to generate new secret key material and prevent replay attacks. IKE phase 2 can also be used to renegotiate new SAs if the IPSec SA lifetime expires but the peers have not terminated communication.

The basic flow of these phases is shown in Figure 14-5.

> **Note** During establishment of IPSec policies, if a setting called Perfect Forward Secrecy is specified in the IPSec policy, then a new Diffie-Hellman exchange is performed with each iteration of IKE phase 2 quick mode. This means new key material is used each time IKE phase 2 is executed.

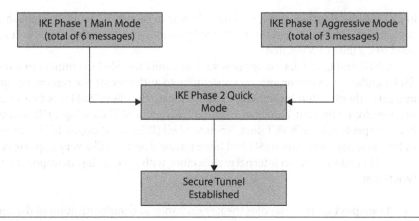

FIGURE 14-5   IKE phases 1 and 2

Although IKE is the most common way to set up SAs, there are other methods, including IPSECKEY DNS records and Kerberized Internet Negotiation of Keys (KINK).

SSL/TLS

A new type of firewall uses Secure Sockets Layer (SSL) or Transport Layer Security (TLS) to provide VPN access through a web portal. Essentially, TLS and SSL are the protocols used to secure web sites. Web site URLs beginning with HTTPS indicate that traffic to and from that site is encrypted using SSL or TLS.

In some VPN solutions, the user simply logs in to a web site that is secured with SSL or TLS, and is then given access to a VPN. It is important that you know that simply visiting a web site that uses SSL or TLS does not mean you are on a VPN. As a general rule, most web sites, such as banking web sites, give you access only to a very limited set of data, such as your account balances. A VPN gives you access to the network—the same or similar access to what you would have if you were physically on that network.

The process to connect, authenticate, and establish the VPN is the same as that described in Chapter 13. The difference is that instead of simply getting secure access to a web site such as a bank or e-commerce site, the end user gets a VPN connection to their network.

Other Secure Communications

A variety of additional secure communications are not considered VPNs, but they do use authentication and encryption to provide secure communication with some endpoint. SSL/TLS communication with a secure web site, described in Chapter 13, would be the most common example of such a communication. In this section, we will look at a few additional communication methods.

SSH

It is common for network administrators to need to use some secure communication channel to access a server. Telnet has long been used for this purpose; however, Telnet sends the data in clear text and is thus insecure. The only way to secure Telnet is to establish a VPN and then connect via Telnet through the VPN. SSH provides an alternative that is secure, without the need to establish a VPN first.

UNIX and UNIX-based systems such as Linux use SSH to connect to a target server. The SSH standard uses asymmetric cryptography to authenticate the remote computer and, when mutual authentication is required, to authenticate the client. SSH was first released in 1995 and was developed by Tatu Ylonen at Helsinki University of Technology. His goal was to replace insecure protocols such as Telnet, Remote Shell (RSH), and rlogin. SSH version 1 was released as freeware. By 1999, OpenSSH had been released and is still a very popular version of SSH.

SSH version 2 has an internal architecture with specific layers responsible for particular functions:

- **Transport layer** Handles the key exchange and authentication of the server. Keys are re-exchanged usually after either 1 hour of time has passed or 1GB of data has been transmitted. This re-negotiation of keys is a significant strength of SSH.
- **User authentication layer** Authenticates the client, usually via password and public key. The password method checks the user's password. The public key method uses either Digital Signature Algorithm (DSA) or RSA key pairs to verify the client's identity, and can also support X.509 certificates.

Generic Security Service Application Program Interface (GSSAPI) authentication is a variation of SSH authentication that allows for the use of either Kerberos or NTLM to authenticate. Although not all versions of SSH support GSSAPI, OpenSSH does.

SSH can be used to provide secure file transfer with technologies such as Secure Copy Protocol (SCP), SSH File Transfer Protocol (SFTP), and Files transferred over Shell Protocol (FISH).

SSH can be configured to use several different symmetric algorithms including AES, Blowfish, 3DES, CAST-128, and RC4. The specific algorithm is configured for each SSH implementation.

Wi-Fi Encryption

One obvious application of cryptography is encrypting wireless communications. Wi-Fi is now ubiquitous. Most homes in North America, Europe, Japan, and much of the world use wireless Internet. Free Wi-Fi can be found at bars, coffee shops, airports, fast food restaurants, and other locations. For a fee, you can even access Wi-Fi in flight on many airlines. The pervasiveness of Wi-Fi means that securing wireless communications is critical.

WEP

Wired Equivalent Privacy was released in 1999. It uses RC4 to encrypt the data and a CRC-32 checksum for error checking. Standard WEP uses a 40-bit key (known as WEP-40) with a 24-bit initialization vector to form 64-bit encryption; 128-bit WEP uses a 104-bit key with a 24-bit initialization vector (IV).

Because RC4 is a stream cipher, the same traffic key must never be used twice. The purpose of an IV, which is transmitted as plain text, is to prevent any repetition, but a 24-bit IV is not long enough to ensure this on a busy network. The IV must never be repeated (recall the concept of a number used only once).

In August 2001, Scott Fluhrer, Itsik Mantin, and Adi Shamir published a cryptanalysis of WEP. They showed that because of the improper implementation of RC4 along with the reuse of initialization vectors, WEP could be cracked with relative ease.

WEP should never be used today unless there is absolutely no other choice. However, the story of WEP illuminates one reason more security professionals need to understand cryptography (and thus the reason I wrote this book). WEP was created by a consortium of computer companies, each contributing engineers to work on the standard. Clearly these were skilled engineers with a solid understanding of network communications—however, they lacked an appropriate knowledge of cryptography and this led to an insecure wireless encryption standard.

WPA

Wi-Fi Protected Access was released in 2003 and was intended as an intermediate step to make up for the issues with WEP while the full implementation of 802.11i (WPA2) was being finalized. One advantage of WPA over WEP is the use of the Temporal Key Integrity Protocol (TKIP), a 128-bit per-packet key that generates a new key for each packet. This regeneration of keys makes WPA much stronger than WEP.

> **Note** 802.11 is the IEEE standard for wireless communications. If you have an "N" router, what you really have is a router that complies with the 802.11n wireless standard. 802.11i is the IEEE standard for wireless security.

WPA operates in one of two modes:

- **WPA-Personal**   Also referred to as *WPA-PSK* (pre-shared key) mode, WPA-Personal is designed for home and small office networks and doesn't require an authentication server. Each wireless network device authenticates with the access point using the same 256-bit key.
- **WPA-Enterprise**   Also referred to as *WPA-802.1x* mode, WPA-Enterprise is designed for enterprise networks and requires a RADIUS authentication server. EAP is used for authentication. EAP has a variety of implementations such as EAP-TLS and EAP-TTLS.

WPA2

WPA2 is the only Wi-Fi encryption protocol that fully implements the IEEE 802.11i standard. It uses a robust set of cryptographic algorithms. Confidentiality is maintained through the use of AES using cipher-block chaining (CBC). Message integrity is protected via message authentication codes (MACs).

WPA2 allows for the optional use of Pairwise Master Key (PMK) caching and opportunistic PMK caching. In PMK caching, wireless clients and wireless access points (WAP) cache the results of 802.1X authentications. This improves access time.

The optional use of pre-authentication allows a WPA2 wireless client to perform an 802.1X authentication with other wireless access points in its range, even though it is still connected to the current WAP. This also speeds connectivity.

In modern Wi-Fi systems, you should always select WPA2 unless you have a compelling reason to use one of the other Wi-Fi protocols. In some cases, you may need to support older systems that cannot perform WPA2.

Conclusions

The point of this and the preceding chapter is to demonstrate common applications of the cryptography you have been studying throughout this book. There are two sides to cryptography: The first is the understanding of the mathematics and algorithms being used to secure communications; the second is to have a working knowledge of the protocols that implement these cryptographic algorithms.

In this chapter we explored some of the most common applications of cryptography, in particular VPNs. You must understand the authentication methods as well as the VPN protocols presented. Most important are CHAP, Kerberos, L2TP, and IPSec. You were also introduced to other applications of cryptography such as Secure Shell (SSH) and Wi-Fi encryption. Both of these are common applications of the cryptographic algorithms you have learned previously in this book.

Test Your Knowledge

1. What is a Kerberos principal?
2. To what attack is NTLM particularly susceptible?
3. The IPSec standard describes three algorithms used for integrity. What are they?
4. What phase of IPSec involves the exchange of nonces?
5. What authentication protocols does PPTP use?
6. Which authentication method is based on periodically re-requesting a hash from the client?
7. How many steps are in IKE phase 1 in aggressive mode?
8. What encryption does PPTP use?
9. What is the major weakness in WEP?
10. Which Wi-Fi encryption protocol completely implements 802.11i?

Answers

1. Any user or computer to whom tickets can be assigned
2. Pass-the-hash
3. HMAC, SHA1, and SHA2
4. IKE phase 2
5. CHAP and EAP
6. CHAP
7. Three
8. MPPE
9. Reusing initialization vectors
10. WPA2

Endnotes

1. D. Downing, M. Covington, and C. Covington, *Dictionary of Computer and Internet Terms*, 10th Ed. (Barron's Educational Series, 2009).
2. G. Pall and G. Zorn, "Microsoft Point-to-Point Encryption (MPPE) Protocol," RFC 3078, www.ietf.org/rfc/rfc3078.txt.
3. IVPN, "PPTP vs. L2TP/IPSec vs. OpenVPN," www.ivpn.net/pptp-vs-l2tp-vs-openvpn.

15 Military Applications

In this chapter we will cover the following:

- NSA and cryptography
- U.S. cryptography laws
- How do other nations use cryptography
- Cryptography and malware
- The Onion Router

It may seem a bit odd to some readers to include a separate chapter specifically for military applications of cryptography. After all, isn't the military the primary user of cryptography? Prior to the Internet and the advent of e-commerce, that was undoubtedly true. However, for the past several decades, banks, e-commerce web sites, and individuals sending e-mail or securing their hard drives all use cryptography. In fact, the civilian applications for cryptography are quite numerous. Most of the cryptography I have discussed thus far in this book is used for civilian purposes, although some of it (such as AES and GOST) is also used for military purposes.

In this chapter, we will specifically examine applications of cryptography that are exclusively (or nearly so) the domain of militaries, governments, and intelligence agencies. Although civilian organizations certainly have a need for secure communications, the need is more pressing in military and intelligence applications for two reasons. First, the stakes are much higher. Rather than money being lost or embarrassing data being leaked, lives might be lost. In the event of armed conflict, a breach of security could provide the opponent with a tactical or even strategic advantage. Second, the nature of the persons attempting to breach government security is far more serious. Militaries are not worried about solo hackers or similar threats so much as concerted efforts by trained intelligence personnel to breach their communication systems.

Note The line between military and law enforcement can sometimes become blurred, especially in regard to dealing with terrorist organizations. Their activities are pursued by law enforcement agencies but also by military and intelligence agencies. International criminal organizations are also the domain of intelligence agencies and law enforcement. In the latter part of this chapter, I will discuss some items that fit in both criminal and terrorist categories.

NSA and Cryptography

It would be impossible to discuss the military applications of cryptography without discussing the U.S. National Security Agency (NSA). In Chapter 2 you read a brief history of the NSA up through the Cold War. In this section I will first discuss the modern cryptographic role of the NSA.

Security Classifications

Throughout this chapter, you will see items designated as "secret" or "top secret." It is important that you understand the meaning of these terms. Each nation has its own security classification system, and even some agencies within the United States have their own systems. In this chapter, the terms used are in reference to U.S. Department of Defense classifications.

The terms "secret" and "top secret" have specific meanings according to a specific hierarchy of classification in the United States. The lowest classification is *confidential*. This is information that might damage national security if disclosed. *Secret* information is data that might cause serious damage to national security if disclosed. *Top secret* information is data that could be expected to cause exceptionally grave damage to national security if disclosed. And there is one more designation: *Top Secret SCI*, or *Sensitive Compartmented Information*. Each of these clearances requires a different level of investigation.

For a *secret* clearance, an applicant undergoes a complete background check, including criminal, work, and credit history, and a check with various national agencies (Department of Homeland Security, Immigration, State Department, and so on) is required. This is referred to as a National Agency Check with Law and Credit (NACLC). The check for employment will cover the last seven years of the person's life and may or may not include a polygraph.

The *top secret* clearance is more rigorous, as you may imagine. Those seeking a top secret clearance require a Single Scope Background Investigation (SSBI)—a complete NACL for the applicant and his or her spouse that goes back at least ten years. It will also involve a subject interview conducted by a trained investigator. Direct verification of employment, education, birth, and citizenship are also required, along with at least four references—at least two of which will be interviewed by investigators. A polygraph is also required. The SSBI is repeated every five years.

SCI clearance is assigned only after a complete SSBI has been completed. An SCI may have its own process for evaluating access; therefore, a standard description of what is involved is not available.

In any clearance investigation, should any issues arise, the scope will be expanded to resolve those issues. For example, if a specific issue arises in regard to the applicant's education, but that education occurred 20 years ago, the investigation would be expanded to address that issue.

NSA Cryptographic Standards

Since the early days of the NSA, the agency has been responsible for U.S. government cryptography. The NSA defines cryptographic algorithms in two ways: via four encryption product types, numbered 1 through 4, and two algorithm suites named Suite A and Suite B.[1]

Note   In this chapter we will be discussing classified equipment and algorithms. However, we will be discussing only those aspects that are accessible in the public domain. So you may find some algorithm descriptions much more vague than the algorithms you have explored earlier in this book. For what should be obvious reasons, it is not possible to provide complete descriptions of classified algorithms in a published book.

Type 1 Products

Type 1 products are endorsed by the NSA for classified purposes in the United States. This often includes equipment and algorithms that are classified, though in some cases classified equipment might use an unclassified algorithm.

HAIPE   A HAIPE (High Assurance Internet Protocol Encryption) device can use both Suite A and Suite B algorithms. A HAIPE device is often used as a secure gateway to connect two sites. HAIPE is essentially a government-enhanced version of IPSec.

HAIPE is based on IPSec with some additional enhancements. One such enhancement is the ability to encrypt multicast data by having all the HAIPE devices that wish to participate in the multicast session share a key in advance. Whereas IPSec uses security associations (SAs) to establish secure tunnels, HAIPE uses an internal Security Policy Database.

HAVE QUICK   HAVE QUICK is a frequency-hopping algorithm originally developed for ultra high frequency (UHF) radios used between ground and air. Military radio traffic hops through a range of frequencies, which makes it very difficult to jam signals. For signals to employ HAVE QUICK, both ends must be initialized with an accurate time of day (often called TOD). They often also use a Word of the Day (WOD) that serves a key for encrypting transmissions. Finally, both ends also use a NET number to select a specific network. HAVE QUICK is not itself an encryption system, but many systems combine HAVE QUICK with encryption to provide confidentiality and prevent jamming.

SINCGARS   The Single Channel Ground and Airborne Radio System is a VHF FM band radio using frequencies from 30 to 87.975 MHz. It is currently used by the U.S. military as well as several other countries. It can provide both single frequency and frequency hopping modes. Early SINCGARS units did not have built-in cryptography and required external cryptographic units. Later versions included built-in cryptographic units.

FIGURE 15-1 SINCGARS system

There have been many models, starting with the RT-1439 produced in 1988. More recent developments include the RT-1523G, RT-1730C and E (for Naval applications), and RT-1702G, made to be carried by an individual solider. One example of these systems is shown in Figure 15-1.

Type 2 Products

Type 2 products are endorsed by the NSA for sensitive but unclassified purposes. The Key Exchange Algorithm (KEA) asymmetrical logarithm and the Skipjack block cipher are examples of Type 2 algorithms, and Type 2 equipment examples include Fortezza, CYPRIS, and others.

Fortezza Plus   The Fortezza Plus card, also known as the KOV-14 card, is a PC card that provides cryptographic functions and keys for secure terminal equipment. The original Fortezza Crypto Card contained a security token. Each user was issued a Fortezza card that included, among other things, private keys used to access sensitive data. The original Fortezza card was developed to use the Skipjack algorithm.

Fortezza Plus is an improvement that uses a classified algorithm. It is used with secure terminal equipment for voice and data encryption. An even more modern improvement on Fortezza Plus is called the KSV-21, which is backward-compatible with the Fortezza Plus card. A Fortezza Crypto Card is shown in Figure 15-2.

Type 3 and 4 Products

Type 3 products are unclassified. Many of the algorithms we have examined in this book so far are in this category, including Data Encryption Standard (DES), Advanced Encryption Standard (AES), and SHA.

FIGURE 15-2 Fortezza Crypto Card

Type 4 products are not endorsed by the NSA for any government use. They are usually products with such weak encryption that they have no practical value.

Suite A

Suite A algorithms are unpublished, classified algorithms used for highly sensitive systems. Suite A algorithms include MEDLEY, SAVILLE, BATON, WALBURN, JOSEKI, and SHILLELAGH.

SAVILLE   The SAVILLE algorithm is often used in voice encryption. Although its details are classified, some indications suggest it may have a 128-bit key.

BATON   The BATON algorithm is classified. However, the publically available standard PKCS#11 has some general information about BATON. Public-Key Cryptography Standard (PKCS) 11 defines an API for cryptographic tokens such as those used in smart cards. BATON is a block cipher that uses a 128-block with a 320-bit key. It can also be used in electronic codebook (ECB) mode with a 96-bit block.

> **Note**   Although this was mentioned earlier in this book, it is worth mentioning again that the NSA using classified documents is not in conflict with Kerckhoffs's principle. To begin with, the NSA is the largest employer of mathematicians and cryptographers in the world. They can subject an algorithm to internal peer review that is quite exhaustive. Furthermore, Kerckhoffs teaches us that the security of a cryptographic mechanism should depend on only the secrecy of the key, not the secrecy of the algorithm. The key word being *depend*. The Suite A algorithms do not depend on the secrecy of the algorithm for security, but they do add a bit of additional security.

Suite B

Suite B algorithms are published, and AES is a perfect example of a Suite B.[2] Suite B includes many algorithms you have already studied in previous chapters, which are all publically available:

- **Advanced Encryption Standard**   If using a 128-bit key, AES is considered secure enough for secret information. If using a 256-bit key, AES is considered secure enough for top-secret information.
- **Elliptic Curve Digital Signature Algorithm** (ECDSA)
- **Elliptic Curve Diffie-Hellman** (ECDH)
- **Secure Hash Algorithm 2** (SHA-2, 256, 384, and 512)
- **Elliptic curve cryptography**   With a 384-bit key, ECC is considered secure enough for top-secret information.

The Modern Role of the NSA

The NSA has been involved in encrypted communications for military purposes since its inception. This involves developing and approving cryptography for U.S. government use, but also attempting to compromise the cryptographic communications of other countries.

In the past several years, NSA involvement in cyber-espionage has increased. The Office of Tailored Access Operations (TAO) is a cyber-warfare and intelligence gathering unit within the NSA. One of its goals is to infiltrate foreign systems. Edward Snowden revealed that the TAO has a suite of software tools used specifically for breaking into these systems.

Despite the NSA expanding into areas of cyber-espionage and cyber-warfare, its primary role is still to provide secure communications. The NSA leads the U.S. government in creating and approving cryptography. For example, for the past few years, the NSA has been recommending moving from RSA to ECC. And many U.S. government agencies are now using a variation of ECC, including ECDSA and ECDH. Data mining and similar roles involve heavy use of both mathematics and computer science, so it is only natural that the NSA be involved in those activities.

U.S. Cryptography Laws and Regulations

Export laws regarding cryptography were quite strict until the turn of the 21st century. In fact, U.S. cryptography export laws have undergone gradual changes since the 1990s.

One of the first changes came in 1992, when 40-bit RC2 and RC4 became available to export and was no longer governed by the State Department, but was instead managed by the Commerce Department. When Netscape developed Secure Sockets Layer (SSL), this required a reexamination of cryptographic export laws. The U.S. version of SSL used RSA with key sizes of 1024 bits and larger, along with Triple DES (3DES) or 128-bit RC3. The international version used 40-bit RC4.

There were various legal challenges to cryptography export rules throughout the early 1990s. The expansion of e-commerce and online banking also required some rethinking of these export laws. Prior to 1996, the U.S. government regulated most cryptography exports under the auspices of the Arms Export Control Act and the International Traffic in Arms Regulations. Cryptography was treated much like weapons and ammunition. In 1996, President Bill Clinton signed an executive order that moved commercial cryptography off of the munitions list, and since then it has been treated as standard commerce. In 1999, regulations were again relaxed to allow export of 56-bit symmetric keys (DES) and 1024-bit RSA.

Currently, the following technologies are exempt from any export controls:[3]

- Software or hardware specifically designed for medical use
- Cryptography specifically used for copyright or intellectual property protections

As of this writing, exporting cryptographic products from the United States to other nations requires a license from the U.S. Department of Commerce. For the most part, prior restrictions have been relaxed—for example, McAfee Data Protection Suite, which includes encryption, has been granted an ENC/Unrestricted license exception by the Department of Commerce.

When exporting any software that includes cryptographic functions, one must check with the appropriate government entity within one's country. In the United States, if you export such software without obtaining proper licensure, you can be fined. For example, in 2014, Wind River Systems (a subsidiary of Intel) was fined $750,000 for exporting encryption to several countries, including China, Russia, and Israel.[4]

In the United States, cryptography (as well as many other items) for use in government systems is regulated by the Federal Information Processing Standard. Civilian use of cryptography is not regulated (except for the export of cryptography).

Cryptography in Other Nations

Although the NSA is an obvious starting point for examining government-sponsored cryptography, it is not the only place to look. Clearly, other nations develop their own cryptographic systems and standards. In some cases the cryptography developed is applied to military and/or classified purposes. In this section we will take a brief look at how other nations deal with cryptography.

This information is very important for a few reasons. First, you may not reside within the United States. Or you may travel abroad and be subject to the cryptography laws of the nations you visit. And should you be involved in the creation, design, or sale of cryptographic products, a knowledge of international laws is important.

International Regulations and Agreements

Governments have an interest in regulating the import and export of cryptographic equipment and software. The export issue may be more obvious, so let's begin with that. If a nation has cryptographic software or hardware that is highly secure, that government may want to limit its export to other countries. It is not in any government's interest to hand other nations its means to secure communications. Import restrictions may not be so obvious, however. One major reason for such restrictions is the fear of cryptographic backdoors (see Chapter 18). Essentially there is a concern that if products are imported from foreign nations, those products could contain backdoors that subvert security.

COCOM and the Wassenaar Arrangement

There have been attempts to regulate and standardize the export of various products considered to be of strategic military value, including both munitions and cryptographic products. One early attempt was the Coordinating Committee for Multilateral Export Controls (COCOM), which consisted of Australia, Belgium, Canada, Denmark, France, Germany, Greece, Italy, Japan, Luxemburg, The Netherlands, Norway, Portugal, Spain, Turkey, United Kingdom, and the United States. Other nations did not join the committee but cooperated with the standards it set: Austria, Finland, Hungary, Ireland, New Zealand, Poland, Singapore, Slovakia, South Korea, Sweden, Switzerland, and Taiwan.

In 1991, COCOM decided to allow the export of mass-market software that implemented cryptography. In 1995, the successor to COCOM, the Wassenaar Arrangement on Export Controls for Conventional Arms and Dual-Use Goods and Technologies (often simply called the Wassenaar Arrangement), was created.[5]

> **Note** The name comes from the town where the original agreement was reached in 1995. The town of Wassenaar is a suburb of The Hague in the Netherlands. As of this writing, 41 countries have signed the Wassenaar Arrangement.

The Wassenaar Arrangement followed most of the COCOM recommendations but provided a specific exception for the use of mass-market and public domain cryptographic software. It also included a personal use exception that allowed the export of products that were for the user's personal use (such as encrypting their laptop hard drive).

In 1998, the Wassenaar Arrangement was revised to allow the following:

- Export for all symmetric cryptography products using keys up to 56 bits
- Export for all asymmetric cryptography products using keys up to 512 bits
- Export for elliptic curve–based asymmetric products using keys up to 112 bits
- Export of mass-market products (software and hardware) using keys up to 64 bits

> **Note** In 2000, the Wassenaar Arrangement lifted the 64-bit limit for mass-market cryptographic products.

Specific Government Regulations

The European Union (EU) regulates cryptography exports under the "Council Regulation (EC) No 1334/2000 setting up a Community regime for the control of exports of dual-use items and technology." The EU essentially follows the Wassenaar Arrangement with a few exceptions:

- Export from one EU member nation to another is relaxed, with the notable exception of cryptanalysis products.
- Exceptions can be applied to exporting to certain nations including Canada, Australia, Japan, and the United States.

Australia regulates the export of cryptographic products via the Defense and Strategic Goods List. This regulation is notable in that it includes a specific exemption for public-domain software. In 2001, Australia passed the Cybercrime Act of 2001, which included a clause requiring the release of encryption keys or decrypting the data if a court order was issued. Australia passed its Defense Trade Control Act of 2012, which describes "dual use goods" (products with both military and civilian use) and includes segments on electronics and telecommunication. However, its requirements on encryption are not very clear, and some are concerned that it could lead to criminalizing the teaching of cryptography.[6]

China first implemented the Commercial Use Password Management Regulations in 1999, which requires a license from the government before cryptographic functions can be imported or exported. In 2000, the Chinese government clarified this order, indicating that the order refers to products that have cryptography as a core function. Products such as mobile phones and web browsers, for which cryptographic functions are ancillary, are exempted.

Several nations require a license to use encrypted communications. In Iran, a license is required to use cryptography for any communications. Israel requires a license from the government to export or import cryptographic products. Pakistan requires government approval for the sale or use of cryptography products.

India, under the Information Technology Act 2000, does not require a license, but any organization or individual must cooperate with any agency of the government to assist in decrypting data if requested.

Although Russia has signed the Wassenaar Arrangement, its laws go a bit further. A license is required to import cryptography products manufactured outside of Russia. Exporting cryptography requires government approval.

Belarus has strict regulations regarding the import and export of cryptography. A license is required for the design, production, sale, repair, and operation of cryptography. Along with other countries, Belarus may not recognize a personal use exception.

| Tip | Many of us use encrypted hard drives on our personal computers. If you plan to travel internationally, be sure to check the laws of the countries you will be traveling through before you go to determine if you must comply with particular laws or regulations. It may be necessary for you to take a separate laptop that does not include encryption. |

Belgium passed the Law on Information-Science Crime in 2000, in which Article 9 allows a court to issue an order to a person who is suspected of having "special knowledge" of encryption services to provide information to law enforcement on how to decrypt data. This means that if a suspect has encrypted data, the court can order the vendor of the cryptography product to provide assistance in decrypting the data. Failure to comply can result in 6 to 12 months of incarceration.

> **Note** There has been a great deal of debate regarding how to handle evidence that has been encrypted by parties suspected of criminal activity. Currently, the United States has no laws compelling anyone to reveal encrypted data or to assist in decrypting the data, although there has been discussion of creating such laws, which now exist in several other countries.

Cryptography and Malware

Malware, even cryptographic malware, may seem to be an unrelated topic for this chapter. How does malware relate to military applications of cryptography? As cyber-warfare becomes increasingly real, malware that uses cryptography in one form or another has become a common weapon used by governments and other entities.

The term "cryptovirology" is sometimes applied to the study of how cryptography is combined with malware. One application of cryptography with malware is the use of encryption to protect a virus from detection; this is an example of an "armored virus."[7] One of the first armored viruses was the Cascade virus, which was discovered in the late 1980s. This clearly demonstrates that using encryption to bolster viruses is not a new technique.

Malware encryption is done not only to prevent detection, but also to make it difficult to analyze the malware. To use encryption the malware needs at least three components:

- The actual malware code (which is encrypted)
- A module to perform encryption/decryption
- A key

Cryptoviral extortion, or ransomware, is another application of cryptovirology. *Ransomware* is malware that, once it has infected the target machine, encrypts sensitive files on that machine. The machine user is then sent a ransom message, demanding money for the attacker to decrypt the files. The One_Half virus, first reported in 2007, would encrypt certain files but did not demand ransom.[8] The PGPCoder, or GPCode (Virus.Win32.Gpcode.ag), used a 660-bit version of RSA to encrypt certain files. It then asked for a ransom. If the ransom was paid, the victim was sent a key to decrypt the files.

The infamous CryptoLocker is one of the most widely known examples of a cryptovirus that was first discovered in 2013. CryptoLocker used asymmetric encryption to lock the user's files. Several varieties of the virus have been detected, including CryptoWall, which was first found in August 2014.[9] It looked and behaved much like CryptoLocker, but in addition to encrypting sensitive files, it would communicate with a command and control server, and even take a screenshot of the infected machine. In March 2015, a variation of CryptoWall was discovered, which is bundled with the spyware TSPY_FAREIT.YOI and actually steals credentials from the infected system in addition to holding files for ransom.[10]

Note	The viruses mentioned here are just a sample of viruses that use encryption. The purpose of this chapter is not to educate you on viruses, but the line between viruses and cryptography is becoming blurred. As you have seen, cryptography can be used with malware to create both new forms of malware (ransomware) and enhanced viruses (armored viruses).

Weaponized Malware

Moving forward, we should expect to see more examples of malware-based attacks and state-sponsored malware espionage, as indicated in the "Worldwide Threat Assessment of the US Intelligence Community" report.[11] Several nations have either already been discovered to have been engaged in such activities or are strongly suspected of being engaged in such activities. Most analysts believe that the Stuxnet and Flame viruses were designed for the express purpose of cyber-espionage and/or sabotage of the Iranian government.[12]

Stuxnet Virus

As the first example of cyber-warfare via malware infections, consider the Stuxnet virus. Stuxnet first spread via infected thumb drives; however, after it infected a machine, it would spread over the entire network and even over the Internet. The Stuxnet virus then searched for a connection to a specific type of programmable logic controller (PLC), specifically the Siemens STEP 7 software. Once Stuxnet discovered that PLC, the virus would load its own copy of a specific dynamic link library (DLL) to monitor the PLC and then alter the PLC's functionality. It was meant to target only centrifuge controllers involved in Iran's uranium enrichment program.[13] Clearly this was meant to be a targeted attack, but it spread beyond the intended targets. Although many reported no significant damage from Stuxnet, outside the Iranian reactors, it was detected on numerous machines. Although the Stuxnet targeting was clearly inadequate, its design was classic virus design. Stuxnet has three modules: a worm that executes routines related to the attack, a link file that executes the propagated copies of the worm, and a rootkit responsible for hiding files and processes, with the goal of making it more difficult to detect the presence of Stuxnet.

Note	It is not the purpose of this chapter to explore the intricacies of Stuxnet. Rather Stuxnet is introduced as both an example of state-sponsored malware attacks and at least an attempt to target such attacks.

Flame Virus

The Flame virus was first discovered in May 2012 in Iran.[14] It was spyware that recorded keyboard activity and network traffic; it took screenshots and was even reported to record Skype conversations. It would also turn the infected computer into a Bluetooth beacon that attempted to download information from nearby Bluetooth-enabled devices.

Kaspersky Labs reported that the Flame file contained an MD5 hash that appeared only on machines in the Middle East. This indicated the possibility that the virus authors intended to target the malware attack to a specific geographical region. The Flame virus also appears to have had a kill function that would allow someone controlling it to send a signal directing it to delete all traces of itself. These two items indicate an attempt to target the malware, though like Stuxnet, the outcome of that targeting was less than optimal.

Cyber-Warfare

Cyber-warfare may seem like a topic far removed from cryptography. Although a complete discussion of cyber-warfare is beyond the scope of this text, it is appropriate to introduce the topic briefly. As you have already seen, weaponized malware is an element of cyber-warfare, and cryptovirology certainly has a role to play.

Let's begin by defining cyber-warfare. According to the Rand Corporation, "Cyber warfare involves the actions by a nation-state or international organization to attack and attempt to damage another nation's computers or information networks through, for example, computer viruses or denial-of-service attacks."[15] Cyber-warfare is not just a topic for science fiction. Here are a few real-world incidents:

- In 2008, Central Command (CENTCOM) was infected with spyware. CENTCOM is the U.S. Army entity that is responsible for command and control throughout the Middle East and Central Asia. This means that during the conflicts in Iraq and Afghanistan, spyware was infecting a critical military system for at least a certain period of time.
- In 2009, drone video feed was compromised. In Afghanistan, an unknown attacker was able to tap into the video feed of a U.S. drone and watch the video feed.
- On December 4, 2010, a group calling itself the Pakistan Cyber Army hacked the web site of India's top investigating agency, the Central Bureau of Investigation (CBI).
- In December 2009, hackers broke into computer systems and stole secret defense plans of the United States and South Korea. Authorities speculated that North Korea was responsible. The information stolen included a summary of plans for military operations by South Korean and U.S. troops in case of war with North Korea, though the attacks were traced back to a Chinese IP address.
- The security firm Mandiant tracked several advanced persistent threats (APTs) over a period of seven years, all originating in China, specifically Shanghai and the Pudong region. These APTs were named APT1, APT2, and so on. The attacks were linked to the UNIT 61398 of the Chinese military. The Chinese government regards this unit's activities as classified, but it appears that offensive cyber-warfare is one of its tasks. Just one of the APTs from this group compromised 141 companies in 20 different industries. APT1 was able to maintain access to victim networks for an average of 365 days, and in one case for 1764 days. APT1 is responsible for stealing 6.5 terabytes of information from a single organization over a 10-month timeframe.

Each of these incidents reveals that cyber-warfare and cyber-espionage are indeed realities. However, they further demonstrate the role cryptography plays in at least some cyber-warfare; for example, in the drone incident of 2008, it is likely that the encrypted communications with the drone were compromised in some fashion. At a minimum, each of these incidents reveals the need for robust, secure communications.

TOR

TOR, or The Onion Router, may not seem like a military application of cryptography, but it is appropriate to cover this topic in this chapter for two reasons:

- The TOR project is based on an earlier Onion Routing protocol developed by the U.S. Navy specifically for military applications. So TOR is an example of military technology being adapted to civilian purposes.
- TOR is used by privacy advocates every day, but it is also used by terrorist groups and organized crime.

TOR consists of thousands of volunteer relays spread around the world. Each relay uses encryption to conceal its origin and the final destination of the traffic passing through it. Each relay is able to decrypt only one layer of the encryption, revealing the next stop in the path. Only the final relay is aware of the destination, and only the first relay is aware of the origin. This makes tracing network traffic practically impossible.

The basic concepts for Onion Routing were developed at the U.S. Naval Research Laboratory in the mid-1990s and later refined by the Defense Advanced Research Projects Agency (DARPA). The goal was to provide secure intelligence communication online.

Onion routers communicated using Transport Layer Security (TLS, see Chapter 13) and ephemeral keys. Ephemeral keys are created for one specific use and then destroyed immediately afterward. In TOR, 128-bit AES is often used as the symmetric key.[16]

Although the TOR network is a very effective tool for maintaining privacy, it has also become a way to hide criminal activity. Some markets on the TOR network are used expressly to sell and distribute illegal products and services, and stolen credit card numbers and other financial data are a common product on TOR markets. A screenshot of one of these markets is shown in Figure 15-3.

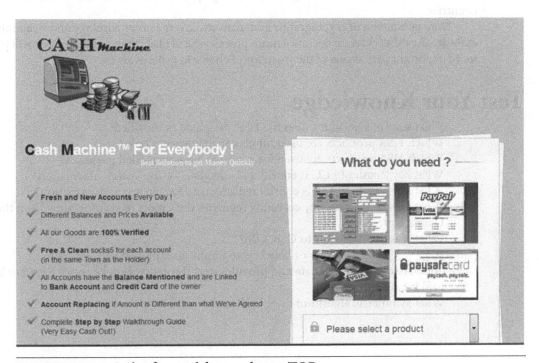

FIGURE 15-3   Stolen financial data market on TOR

Even more serious criminal activity can be found on TOR, including child pornography, weapons, and other distributors like the Hitman Network that even purport to perform murder for hire. More closely related to military and intelligence operations, various terrorists groups are reported to have used TOR for communication and recruitment. TOR's anonymity makes it a perfect venue for terrorist communications. The criminal activity on TOR also provides a means for fundraising for terrorist organizations.

> **Note** In 2015, Ross Ulbricht, the founder of Silk Road—the most well-known of the TOR markets—was sentenced to life in prison. Many people on various news outlets claim that this sentence is draconian. And one can certainly argue the merits of any sentence. But allow me to offer some food for thought. Silk Road was not simply a venue for privacy, or even for marijuana exchanges. It became a hub for massive drug dealing, including heroin, cocaine, meth, and other serious drugs. It was also used to traffic arms, stolen credit cards, child pornography, and even murder for hire. The venue Ulbricht created was a hub for literally thousands of very serious felonies.

Conclusions

In this chapter we examined various military and government applications of cryptography. We looked at the NSA classifications of cryptography as well as specific military applications. We also examined various laws regarding cryptography for the United States and other countries.

The examination of cryptography and malware covered cryptovirology and weaponized malware. As cyber-warfare becomes more prevalent, it is likely that cryptovirology will play a more important part as one of the weapons of choice in cyber-war.

Test Your Knowledge

1. What suite of algorithms does the NSA designate as classified?
2. Which NSA products are used for classified purposes only?
3. Which NSA products are used for sensitive but unclassified purposes?
4. What key length of ECC is considered adequate for top secret information?
5. What key length of AES is considered adequate for top secret information?
6. What government agency currently regulates the export of cryptography from the United States?
7. What was the successor to COCOM?
8. _____ is the study of how cryptography is combined with malware.
9. Software that encrypts data and provides only the decryption key once a fee has been paid is called _____.
10. What symmetric algorithm does TOR use?

Answers

1. Suite A
2. Type 1
3. Type 2
4. 384 bits
5. 256 bits
6. Department of Commerce
7. The Wassenaar Arrangement
8. Cryptovirology
9. ransomware
10. AES

Endnotes

1. Cryptology Museum, "NSA Encryption Products," www.cryptomuseum.com/crypto/usa/nsa.htm.
2. National Security Agency, "Suite B Cryptography," www.nsa.gov/ia/programs/suiteb_cryptography/.
3. Bureau of Industry and Security, U.S. Department of Commerce, "Identifying Encryption Items," www.bis.doc.gov/index.php/policy-guidance/encryption/identifying-encryption-items#One.
4. John Leyden, "US government fines Intel's Wind River over crypto exports," *The Register*, www.theregister.co.uk/2014/10/17/intel_subsidiary_crypto_export_fine/.
5. The Wassenaar Arrangement, www.wassenaar.org.
6. Daniel Mathews, "Paranoid defence controls could criminalise teaching encryption," http://theconversation.com/paranoid-defence-controls-could-criminalise-teaching-encryption-41238.
7. PC Encyclopedia, "Definition of: armored virus," www.pcmag.com/encyclopedia/term/63208/armored-virus.
8. Symantec, "One_Half," www.symantec.com/security_response/writeup.jsp?docid=2000-121513-2517-99.
9. Dell SecureWorks, "CryptoWall Ransomware," www.secureworks.com/cyber-threat-intelligence/threats/cryptowall-ransomware/.
10. Antony Joe Melgarejo, "CryptoWall Ransomware Partners with FAREIT Spyware," http://blog.trendmicro.com/trendlabs-security-intelligence/cryptowall-3-0-ransomware-partners-with-fareit-spyware/.
11. James R. Clapper, February 26, 2015, "Worldwide Threat Assessment of the US Intelligence Community," www.dni.gov/files/documents/Unclassified_2015_ATA_SFR_-_SASC_FINAL.pdf.
12. R. Langner, "Stuxnet: Dissecting a Cyberwarfare Weapon," *IEEE Security & Privacy*, vol. 9, no. 3 (2011).

13. David E. Sanger, "Obama Order Sped Up Wave of Cyberattacks Against Iran," *The New York Times*, June 1, 2012, www.nytimes.com/2012/06/01/world/middleeast/obama-ordered-wave-of-cyberattacks-against-iran.html.

14. Ellen Nakashima, Greg Miller, and Julie Tate, "U.S., Israel developed Flame computer virus to slow Iranian nuclear efforts, officials say," *Washington Post*, June 19, 2012, www.washingtonpost.com/world/national-security/us-israel-developed-computer-virus-to-slow-iranian-nuclear-efforts-officials-say/2012/06/19/gJQA6xBPoV_story.html.

15. Rand Corporation, "Cyber Warfare," www.rand.org/topics/cyber-warfare.html.

16. R. Dingledine, N. Mathewson, and P. Syverson, "Tor: The Second-Generation Onion Router," www.onion-router.net/Publications/tor-design.pdf.

16 Steganography

In this chapter we will cover the following:

- Steganography basics
- The history of steganography
- Modern methods and algorithms
- Tools for steganography
- Steganalysis
- Distributed steganography

Strictly speaking, steganography is not cryptography, but the topics are often covered in the same course or textbook, as they are here, because both technologies seek to prevent unwanted parties from viewing certain information. Cryptography attempts to accomplish this by applying mathematics to make the message undecipherable without a key. Steganography attempts to secure data by hiding it in other innocuous media. In this chapter, we will examine how steganography works, the history of steganography, methods and tools used in steganography, and how to detect the use of steganography.

Steganography Basics

Steganography is the art and science of writing a hidden message in such a way that no one, apart from the sender and intended recipient, suspects that the message exists; it's a form of security through obscurity. Often the message is hidden in some other file, such as a digital picture or audio file, to defy detection.

The advantage of steganography over cryptography alone is that messages do not attract attention to themselves. If no one is aware that the message exists, then no one will try to decipher it. In many cases, messages are encrypted and also hidden via steganography.

The most common implementation of steganography uses the least significant bits (LSBs) in a file to store data. By altering the LSB, you can hide additional data without altering the original file in any noticeable way.

There are a few basic steganography terms you should know:

- **Payload** The data to be covertly communicated—in other words, the message you want to hide

- **Carrier** The signal, stream, or data file into which the payload is hidden
- **Channel** The type of medium used, such as still photos, video, or sound files

The most common way steganography is accomplished today is by manipulating the LSBs in a graphics file. Every graphics file includes a certain number of bits per unit of the file. For example, an image file in Windows has 24 bits per pixel—8 bits for red, 8 bits for green, and 8 bits for blue. If you change the least significant of those bits, then the change is not noticeable with the naked eye. And you can hide information in the LSBs of an image file.

Let's walk through the basic concept of altering the LSB. Consider the cover of this book, shown in Figure 16-1.

Let's select a single pixel—in this case, it's located in the lower-right part of the image, circled in white in Figure 16-2. You can see the RGB (Red, Green, and Blue) settings in the figure: Red 91, Green 16, and Blue 10.

Let's change the color red by just 1 bit—the LSB. Decimal value 91, when converted to binary, is 1011011. So let's change that last bit, resulting in 1011010, which would be 90 in decimal. Figure 16-3 shows the difference that occurs by changing 1 bit of that pixel. As you can see, it is impossible to tell a difference.

Given that the average picture is made of tens of thousands of pixels, you could change the LSB of thousands of these pixels, and in those LSBs, you could store some covert message. That message would be undetectable to the human eye. This is the basic concept behind modern steganography.

FIGURE 16-1   This book's cover

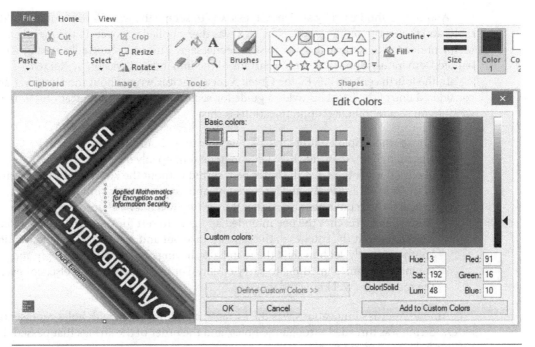

FIGURE 16-2   Selecting a single pixel

Steganography History

In modern times, steganography involves the digital manipulation of files to hide messages. However, the concept of hiding messages is nothing new, and many methods have been used to do this throughout history.

For example, in ancient China, message senders wrapped notes in wax and the messenger swallowed them for transport. If the messenger was intercepted in transit, no matter how thoroughly he was searched, the message could not be found. In ancient Greece, a messenger's head might be shaved, a message written on his head, then his hair was allowed to grow back. Obviously, this method had some significant drawbacks—in particular, it took a long time to prepare a message for transport. This method was reported by the Greek historian Herodotus, who claimed that this method was used to warn Greece of the impending Persian invasion.

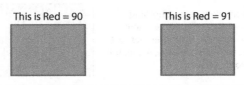

FIGURE 16-3   One bit changed in a picture

Another method used by ancient Greeks was to scrape the wax off of a wooden folding table, and then write on the wood. New wax was then applied to cover up the message. The recipient needed to remove the wax to see the message. This was reportedly used by a Greek named Demaratus, who warned the Spartans of the impending invasion by Xerxes.

In the fourth century B.C.E., the Greek Aeneas Tacitus wrote about the art of war and is considered one of the first to provide a guide for secure military communications. Among his writings on secure military communications is this:

> Those who employ traitors must know how they should send in messages. Dispatch them, then, like this. Let a man be sent openly bearing some message about other matters. Let the letter be inserted without the knowledge of the bearer in the sole of his sandals and be sewed in, and, to guard against mud and water, have it written on beaten tin so that the writing will not be effaced by the water. And when he reaches the one intended and goes to rest for the night, this person should pull out the stitches of the sandals, take out and read the letter, and, writing another secretly, let him send the man back, having dispatched some reply and having given him something to carry openly. For in this way no one else, not even the messenger, will know the message.[1]

Among Aeneas's innovations was the astragal, a hollow sphere with holes representing letters. String was threaded through the holes, and the order of the strings that passed through various holes spelled out words.

In 1499, Johannes Trithemius (1462–1516) wrote a three-volume book entitled *Steganographia,* which included the first known use of the term "steganography." The book is about the occult, but hidden within the text is a message concerning cryptography and steganography.

Note   Trithemius was a Benedictine abbot, but also a cryptographer who was involved in the occult, particularly regarding contacting spirits to communicate over long distances. He wrote extensive histories, but it was later discovered that he had inserted several fictional portions into his historical works.

Another interesting form used to hide messages was the Cardan grille, invented by Girolamo Cardano (1501–1576). Essentially, after a message is written on paper, a grille containing strategically placed holes is laid over the paper, revealing certain letters that combine to form the hidden message. You can see an example of this technique in Figure 16-4.

This is a very simple message, nothing tantalizing at all. It can be used without anyone knowing there is another message hidden along with this message, within the letters and words, unseen.

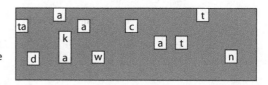

FIGURE 16-4   An example of a Cardan grille

Note Cardano was known for significant contributions to mathematics, especially for his contributions to algebra. He also wrote about physics, philosophy, medicine, and other topics and was well-known as both a gambler and chess player.

During WWII, the French Resistance sent messages written on the backs of couriers using invisible ink. If the courier was intercepted, even a strip search would not reveal the message. When the courier reached his or her destination, the message was retrieved.

Microdots, text or images reduced to the size of a typewriter period and embedded in innocuous documents, were said to be used by spies during the Cold War. A very close examination of a document using a magnifying class might reveal the microdot, but the detection process was so tedious that detection was highly unlikely. Also during the Cold War, the U.S. Central Intelligence Agency used various devices to hide messages. For example, they developed a working tobacco pipe that included a small space in which to hide microfilm.

Steganography Methods and Tools

As stated earlier, using the LSB is the most common method for performing steganography. However, it is not the only method. As you know, a number of steganography methods predate computers. Even in this digital age, there are alternative ways to hide data and different carrier files. Most books and tutorials focus on hiding data in an image, but you can also hide data in a sound file (Waveform Audio File Format, or .wav), a video file, or in any sort of digital file.

Whatever the technique used for steganography, issues of *capacity* (the amount of information that can be hidden) and *security* (how well the data is hidden) exist. Obviously, there is a relationship between the size of the carrier file and the size of data that can be hidden in that file. And security is measured by the ease with which the hidden message can be detected using steganalysis techniques, which we will examine later in this chapter.

A number of tools are available for implementing steganography. Many are free or at least offer a free trial version. The sections that follow examine a few such tools. As you will see, some tools do a better job of providing security than others. First, let's look at some of the classes of steganography.

Steganographic Methods

Although the LSB is the most common method used in steganography, it is one of three general classes of steganographic methods: injection-based methods, substitution-based methods, and generation-based methods.

- **Injection-based methods**   These methods hide data in sections of a file that are not processed by the processing applications—such as in comment blocks of an HTML file. Using this method changes the file size.[2]
- **Substitution-based methods**   These methods literally substitute some bits of the data to be hidden for some bits of the carrier file. This replaces bits in the carrier file and does not increase file size. The LSB method is the most obvious example of a substitution method.
- **Generation-based methods**   Using these methods, the file that is to be hidden is altered to create a new file. There is no carrier file. Obviously, there are limits to what one can do with generation-based techniques.

In addition to classifying steganography by the techniques used to hide data, we can categorize steganographic techniques based on the medium used. As stated earlier, hiding files within images is the most common technique, but literally any medium can be used.

Discrete Cosine Transform

The discrete cosine transform (DCT) is referenced throughout the literature on steganography. It has been applied to image steganography, audio steganography, and video steganography, so it is important that you be familiar with this technique.

A DCT expresses a finite sequence of data points in terms of the sum of cosine functions oscillating at different frequencies. It expresses a function or a signal in terms of a sum of *sinusoids* with different frequencies and amplitudes.

> **Note** A sinusoid is a curve similar to the sine function but possibly shifted in phase, period, amplitude, or any combination thereof.[3]

DCTs work on a function only at a finite number of discrete data points. They use only cosine functions. Variations of the DCT are simply termed DCT-I, DCT-II, DCT-III, DCT-IV, DCT-V, DCT-VI, DCT-VII, and DCT-VIII (that is, DCT 1 through 8).

> **Note** DCTs are a type of Fourier-related transform that are similar to the discrete Fourier transform (DFT). DFTs can use cosine or sine functions to convert a list of samples of a function that are equally spaced into a list of coefficients ordered by their frequencies. This is a somewhat simplified definition; a full explanation is beyond the scope of this text, but you can consult one of these resources for more information: www.dspguide.com/ch8.htm, www.robots.ox.ac.uk/~sjrob/Teaching/SP/l7.pdf, or http://mathworld.wolfram.com/DiscreteFourierTransform.html.

It is not imperative that you master DCTs to understand steganography. However, having a general understanding of the concept will be helpful, because DCTs are frequently used to implement steganography. If you aspire to develop your own steganographic tools or techniques, you'll need a deep understanding of DCTs.

Steganophony

In *steganophony*, messages are hidden in sound files. This can be done with the LSB method or using other methods, such as *echo hiding*, which adds extra sound to an echo inside an audio file, which conceals information.

Audio steganography can use the LSB method to encode hidden data. Usually, audio files such as MP3 or .wav files are large enough to hide data. MP3 files, which are often used with mobile music devices, are typically 4MB to 10MB and provide a large number of bytes wherein the LSB can be manipulated. For example, if you begin with a 6MB file and uses only 10 percent of the bytes in that file for storing data in the LSBs, that allows for approximately 600KB, or 75,000 bytes, of hidden data storage. To get some perspective on how much data this encompasses, a typical 20-plus–page Word document occupies far less space than 75,000 bytes!

Another method used with steganophony is *parity coding*, which divides the signal into separate samples and embeds the secret message into the parity bits. Phase coding can also be used to encode data, which is a bit more complex but very effective.

In their paper, "Information Hiding Using Audio Steganography–A Survey," Jayaram, Ranganatha, and Anupam describe this method as follows:

> The phase coding technique works by replacing the phase of an initial audio segment with a reference phase that represents the secret information. The remaining segments phase is adjusted in order to preserve the relative phase between segments. In terms of signal to noise ratio, Phase coding is one of the most effective coding methods. When there is a drastic change in the phase relation between each frequency component, noticeable phase dispersion will occur. However, as long as the modification of the phase is sufficiently small, an inaudible coding can be achieved. This method relies on the fact that the phase components of sound are not as perceptible to the human ear as noise is.

Phase coding is explained in the following procedure:

A. Divide an original sound signal into smaller segments such that lengths are of the same size as the size of the message to be encoded.
B. Matrix of the phases is created by applying Discrete Fourier Transform (DFT).
C. Calculate the Phase differences between adjacent segments.
D. Phase shifts between adjacent segments are easily detectable. It means, we can change the absolute phases of the segments but the relative phase differences between adjacent segments must be preserved. So the secret information is inserted only in the phase vector of the first signal segment.
E. Using the new phase of the first segment a new phase matrix is created and the original phase differences.
F. The sound signal is reconstructed by applying the inverse Discrete Fourier Transform using the new phase matrix and original magnitude matrix and then concatenating the sound segments back together.

The receiver must know the segment length to extract the secret information from the sound file. Then the receiver can use the DFT to get the phases and extract the secret information.[4]

Video Steganography

Information can also be hidden in video files using various methods, including LSB.[5] DCT is often used for video steganography; this method alters values of certain parts of the individual frames, usually by rounding up the values.

Steganographic Tools

A number of steganographic tools are available on the Internet, either for free or at very low cost. Following are some of those.

QuickCrypto

Formerly called QuickStego, this software has been available as a free download for many years (http://quickcrypto.com/download.html). Along with the name change to QuickCrypto, new features were added. The main screen is shown in Figure 16-5, with the steganography options highlighted.

After you click Hide at the top or click Stego at the bottom of the screen (both are highlighted in Figure 16-5), the original QuickStego screen is displayed, as shown in Figure 16-6.

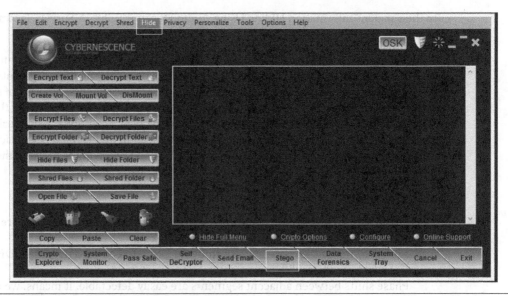

FIGURE 16-5 QuickCrypto main screen

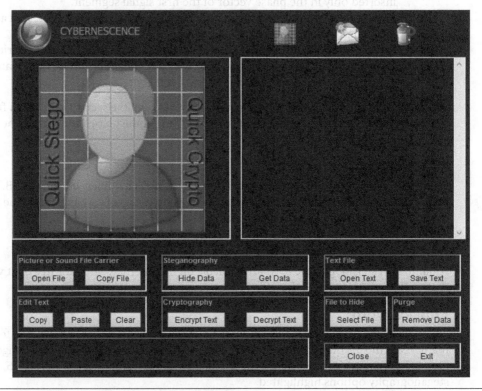

FIGURE 16-6 QuickStego original screen

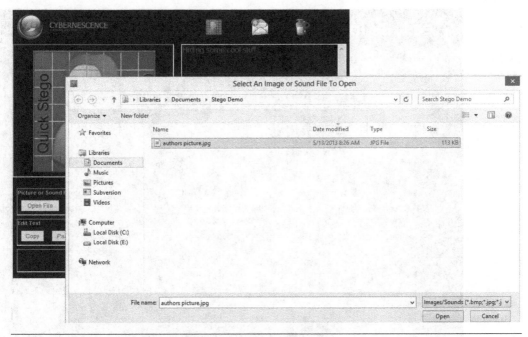

FIGURE 16-7 Selecting a carrier file with QuickStego

In this screen, you can either type in text you want to hide or open a text file to import the text to hide. For this demonstration, I'm assuming you've typed a message and then clicked Open File in the Picture Or Sound File Carrier section to select a carrier file from the window shown in Figure 16-7.

Next, you click the Hide Data button. In the folder with the carrier file is a new file, carrierfilename 2. If you open the original and the new file side-by-side, you won't be able to see any difference. The QuickStego tool works only with hiding text files and will not hide other images. Because of that limitation, the ratio of hidden data to carrier file is very large, making detection more difficult.

Invisible Secrets

You can download a trial version of the popular Invisible Secrets steganography tool at www .invisiblesecrets.com/download.html. This tool includes a number of capabilities, including encryption as well as steganography. The main screen is shown in Figure 16-8, with the steganography option highlighted.

Let's walk through the basic process of steganographically hiding data in an image using Invisible Secrets.

Click Hide Files in the area highlighted in Figure 16-8. That will take you to the screen shown in Figure 16-9, where you select the file or files you want to hide. Keep in mind that the

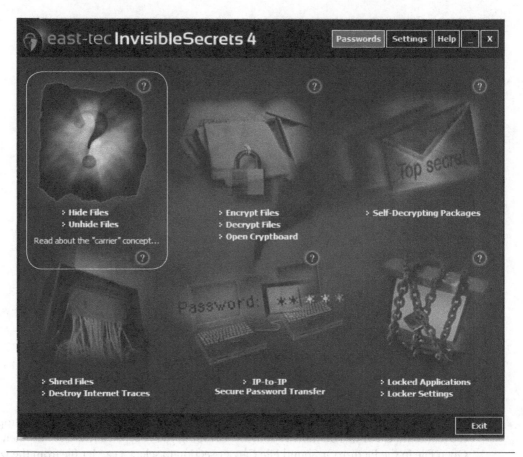

FIGURE 16-8   Invisible Secrets main screen

smaller the ratio of hidden files to carrier file, the easier it will be to detect. So, for example, if you choose to hide five JPEGs in one JPEG carrier file, it will most likely be detectable. This demonstration selects only one text file.

After clicking the Next button, you will be prompted to select a carrier file. One of the features that makes Invisible Secrets a preferable tool is that it gives you multiple options for a carrier file, including HTML or .wav (audio) files. You can see this in Figure 16-10, though for this demonstration, I've selected a JPEG image file.

After selecting the carrier file, you can enter a password that will be required to extract the hidden files. You can also choose to encrypt your hidden files with a number of symmetric algorithms, including AES and Blowfish; this is shown in Figure 16-11.

Finally, you must select the name of the resulting file (the carrier with hidden files). You cannot select a file type here, because the final file will be the same type of file as the carrier file you selected previously. You can see this in Figure 16-12.

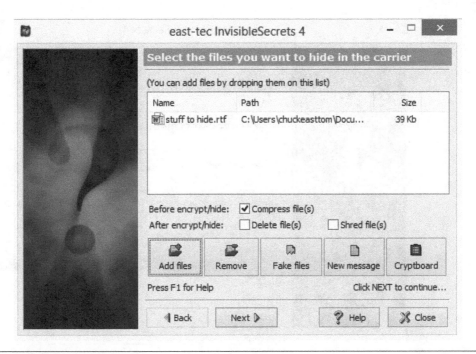

FIGURE 16-9   Selecting files to hide with Invisible Secrets

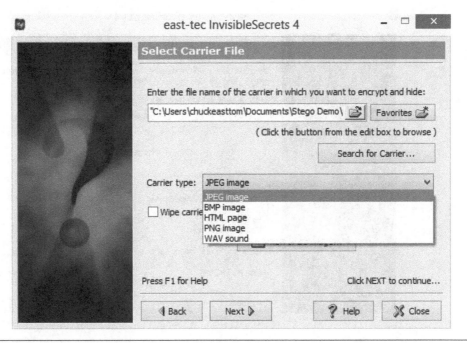

FIGURE 16-10   Selecting a carrier file with Invisible Secrets

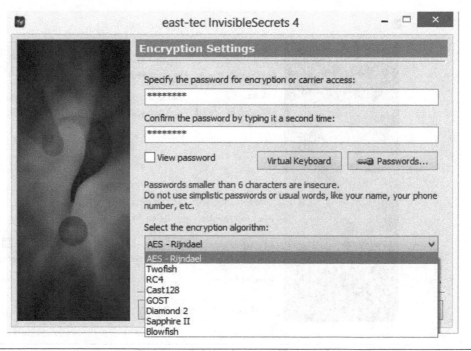

FIGURE 16-11   Password and encryption with Invisible Secrets

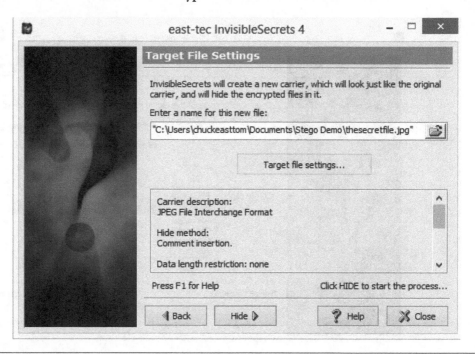

FIGURE 16-12   Naming the resulting file with Invisible Secrets

The Internet is replete with free or low-cost steganography tools. However, Invisible Secrets is relatively sophisticated, supports multiple carrier types, and integrates encryption, making it one of the better low-cost tools.

MP3stego

You can use MP3stego to hide data in MP3 files. Download it for free from www.petitcolas .net/steganography/mp3stego/. From the MP3stego readme file are the following instructions on how to encode or decode data into a .wav or .mp3 file:

- **encode -E data.txt -P pass sound.wav sound.mp3**   Compresses sound.wav (the carrier file) and hides data.txt. This produces the output called sound.mp3. The text in data.txt is encrypted using the password "pass".
- **decode -X -P pass sound.mp3**   Uncompresses sound.mp3 into sound.mp3.pcm and attempts to extract hidden information. The hidden message is decrypted, uncompressed, and saved into sound.mp3.

This is a very simple program to use. It is used entirely from the command line and works only with sound files as the carrier file. Given the ubiquitous nature of sound files, this tool is a good choice for hiding data in a secure manner.

OpenStego

OpenStego is a simple, easy-to-use tool that you can download for free from http://openstego .sourceforge.net/. On the main screen shown in Figure 16-13, you select the file to hide, the carrier file, the resulting file, and a password. Then click the Hide Data button.

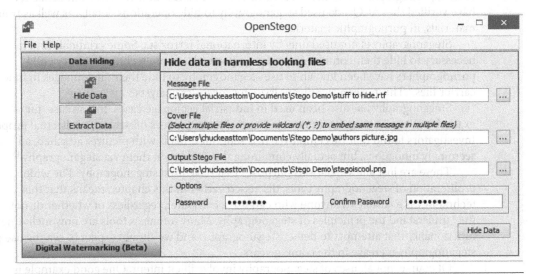

FIGURE 16-13   OpenStego

Other Tools

A simple Internet search will reveal a host of free or low-cost steganography tools. Some are general purpose tools, much like Invisible Secrets, while others have narrowly defined functionality. With so many easy-to-use tools available, you need not have an understanding of steganographic methods or of programming to use steganography.

A few other widely used tools include the following:

- **SNOW** (www.darkside.com.au/snow/) Hides data in the white space of a document.
- **Camouflage** (http://camouflage.unfiction.com/Download.html) Adds the option to hide a file to the context menu (the menu available by right-clicking) in Windows (though it does not work in Windows 8). Although Camouflage is no longer supported, you can still find the product on the Web and use it to increase your understanding of steganography.
- **BMP Secrets** (www.download32.com/bmp-secrets-software.html) Works primarily with BMP files.
- **Hide4PGP** (www.heinz-repp.onlinehome.de/Hide4PGP.htm) Hides data in BMP, WAV, or VOC files.

Current Uses of Steganography

Steganography is a powerful tool for hiding data. For this reason it is widely used today, both for innocuous as well as nefarious purposes. As early as 2001, there was speculation that terrorists were using steganography to communicate.[6] A 2015 paper from the SANS Institute has this to say about terrorists using steganography: "Using image files to transfer information is the method that first comes to mind."[7] Many newspapers have reported that some U.S. officials and foreign officials experts have claimed that terrorist groups are hiding maps and photographs of terrorist targets and posting instructions for terrorist activities on sports chat rooms, pornographic bulletin boards, and other web sites. Confessions from actual terrorists have verified that Al-Qaeda used steganography to hide operations details, as well as training materials, in pornographic material.[8]

Steganography is not used only by international terrorists. Some criminals find it necessary to hide their communications—in particular, more technically savvy child pornographers have been known to use steganography to hide their illicit images in innocuous carrier files.[9] This poses a significant issue for forensics analysts.

Steganography has also been used in industrial espionage cases. In one case, for example, an engineering firm suspected one of its employees of stealing intellectual property. Investigators found that this employee had sent out e-mails with pictures attached, all seemingly innocuous, but actually containing data hidden in them via steganography.[10]

These are just a few nefarious purposes that have used steganography. The wide proliferation of steganography tools, discussed earlier in this chapter, means that this technology is available to anyone who can use a computer, regardless of whether or not they understand the principles of steganography. Many forensics tools are now including functionality that attempts to detect steganography, and we should expect to see the use of steganography increase in the coming years.

Of course, not all uses of steganography involve illicit intent. One good example is watermarking, which embeds some identifying mark or text into a carrier file to identify copyright protected materials. For example, an artist who generates digital versions of his or her art may embed a watermark within the image to identify it should someone use that image without the artist's permission.

Steganalysis

If you can hide data in images or other carrier files, is there some way to detect it? Fortunately there is. *Steganalysis* is the attempt to detect steganographically hidden messages or files within carrier files. Note, however, that any attempt to detect steganography is simply a best effort, because there is no guarantee of success. One of the most common methods is to analyze close-color pairs. By analyzing changes in an image's close-color pairs, an analyst can determine whether it is likely that LSB steganography was used. Close-color pairs consist of two colors whose binary values differ only in their LSB. Of course, you would expect a certain number of pixels to vary only in the LSB, but if the number of pixels that meet this criteria is greater than the analyst expects, steganography may have been used to hide data.

A related method is the Raw Quick Pair (RQP) method, which is essentially an implementation of the close-color pair concept.[11] The RQP method is based on statistics of the numbers of unique colors and close-color pairs in a 24-bit image. RQP analyzes the pairs of colors created by LSB embedding.

Another option uses the chi-squared method from statistics. Chi-square analysis calculates the average LSB and builds a table of frequencies and a pair of values. Then it performs a chi-square test on these two tables. Essentially, it measures the theoretical versus calculated population difference.

Note	The details of chi-square analysis are beyond the scope of this text. However, any introductory university text on statistics should provide a good description of this and other statistical techniques.

In their paper "Practical Steganalysis of Digital Images – State of the Art," Fridrich and Goljan provide an overview of various steganalysis methods:

> Pfitzman and Westfeld introduced a powerful statistical attack that can be applied to any steganographic technique in which a fixed set of Pairs of Values (PoVs) are flipped into each other to embed message bits. For example, the PoVs can be formed by pixel values, quantized DCT coefficients, or palette indices that differ in the LSB. Before embedding, in the cover image the two values from each pair are distributed unevenly. After message embedding, the occurrences of the values in each pair will have a tendency to become equal (this depends on the message length). Since swapping one value into another does not change the sum of occurrences of both colors in the image, one can use this fact to design a statistical Chi-square test. We can test for the statistical significance of the fact that the occurrences of both values in each pair are the same. If, in addition to that, the stego-technique embeds message bits sequentially into subsequent pixels/indices/coefficients starting in the upper left corner, one will observe an abrupt change in our statistical evidence as we encounter the end of the message.[12]

More advanced statistical methods can also be used—for example, Markov chain analysis has been applied to steganalysis. A Markov chain is a collection of random variables {X_t} that transitions from one state to another, and the current state does not depend on the sequence of events that preceded it. This is sometimes referred to as a "memoryless state." It is named after famed Russian mathematician and statistician Andrey Markov (1856–1922). According to the article "Steganalysis for Markov Cover Data with Applications to Images" (Sullivan, et al.),

> In this paper, we take the logical next step toward computing a more accurate performance benchmark, modeling the cover data as a Markov chain (MC). The Markov model has the advantage of analytical tractability, in that performance benchmarks governing detection performance can be characterized and computed explicitly.[13]

Another steganalysis method compares similar files. If, for example, several MP3 files all came from the same CD, the analyst can look for inconsistencies in compression, statistical anomalies, and similar issues to see if one of the files is different from the others. That difference might indicate the presence of steganography.

Distributed Steganography

Various techniques have been used for distributing payload across multiple carrier files. My first patent, U.S. Patent No. 8,527,779 B1 "Method and apparatus of performing distributed steganography of a data message," was such a technique, so I will describe it in this section.

> **Note** This invention was designed specifically for covert communications for undercover law enforcement officers and intelligence agencies. Unfortunately, it can also be applied to nefarious communications, although the intent was a virtually undetectable communication channel for use with sensitive law enforcement and similar activities.

The purpose of steganography, regardless of the implementation, is to hide some underlying message so that an observer is not aware that the message is present. This is very useful in covert communications, particularly within the intelligence community. Most permutations of steganography deal with how to embed the message (text, image, video, or audio) into the carrier file. Some permutations, such as SNOW, even use blanks at the end of text files in which to hide messages. However, my invention is concerned with how to fragment the message and hide it in various carrier and cover files, making the detection of the entire message extremely difficult, approaching impossibility.

With distributed steganography, as described in U.S. Patent 8,527,779, the message is distributed across multiple carrier signals or sources in order to hide the message completely. For example, a single text message would be broken into blocks, with each block hidden in a different image. Note that the block size can vary, and the blocks are not necessarily stored in order; this means that permutation is applied to the blocks, and the first carrier file will not necessarily hold the first segment of the hidden message or file. Of course, the parties communicating would have to be able to reorder the blocks in their appropriate order.

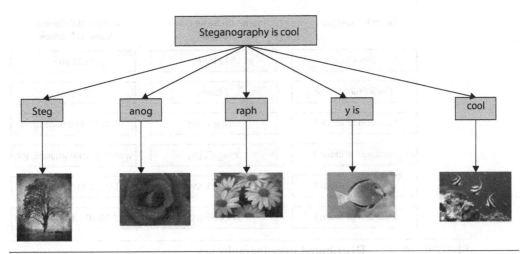

FIGURE 16-14   Distributing payload across multiple carrier files

Consider an example using 8-bit blocks for the message "Steganography is cool." Each character represents 8 bits, so every eight characters would be a separate block. Keep in mind that blanks are also represented by 8 bits, so this message would comprise five separate blocks stored in five separate images, as shown in Figure 16-14.

The next obvious issue is how to retrieve the blocks. This would involve knowing how many blocks total were to be retrieved, knowing the order of each block (for example, is this block 2 of 4, 3 of 7, and so on), and knowing the carrier or cover file to retrieve the blocks from. This invention deals with all three issues.

Total Blocks and Block Order

In this method, each block stored in an image would have an additional 2 bytes (16 bits) appended to the image. The first byte would contain information as to which block this was (such as block 3 of 9), and the second byte would store the total number of blocks the message contained (such as 9 blocks).

Because 8 bits can store decimal numbers between 0 and 255, this would necessitate breaking a message down into no more than 255 blocks. The size of the block would be determined by the size of the original message divided by 255.

It would also be possible to use additional bytes to store the block-numbering data. For example, you could use 2 bytes (16 bits) to store the value of the current block and an additional 2 bytes (16 bits) to store the total number of blocks. This would allow a message to be divided into 65,535 total blocks. Using up to 4 bytes (64 bits) for the value of the current block and 4 bytes (64 bits) for the total number of blocks would enable a message to be divided into 4,294,967,295 blocks. This would be appropriate for video or audio messages hidden in audio or video signals. These additional bytes indicating block number and total blocks are called *block pointers*.

The use of block numbering is similar to how TCP packets are sent over a network. Each packet has a number such as "packet 2 of 10." This same methodology is applied to hiding blocks of data in diverse images.

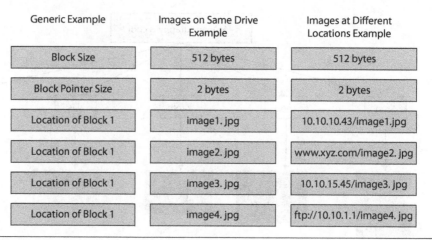

Generic Example	Images on Same Drive Example	Images at Different Locations Example
Block Size	512 bytes	512 bytes
Block Pointer Size	2 bytes	2 bytes
Location of Block 1	image1.jpg	10.10.10.43/image1.jpg
Location of Block 1	image2.jpg	www.xyz.com/image2.jpg
Location of Block 1	image3.jpg	10.10.15.45/image3.jpg
Location of Block 1	image4.jpg	ftp://10.10.1.1/image4.jpg

FIGURE 16-15 Distributed steganography key

This requires distributed steganography to have a key, much like the keys used in encryption. However, this key would contain the following information:

- Block size
- Size of block pointer (the bytes used to indicate block numbering)

The preferred way to find the location of the images containing secret messages would be to add that information to the key. This information could be an IP address or URL to find the image (if images are stored at different locations) or the image name (if all images are on a single storage device). You can see this in Figure 16-15.

Images can be stored on web pages, file servers, or FTP servers, which means that the actual message could be fragmented and stored across the Internet at various locations. In some cases, the message could be stored on third-party servers without their knowledge. It is also possible, and even recommended, that different carrier file types be used so that parts of the hidden message could be stored in images such as JPEGs, while other parts could be stored in audio or video files.

It would also be possible to implement distributed steganography in such a manner that the locations where data would be hidden could be predetermined. For example, messages could always be hidden in specific images at predetermined locations; thus the person who needs to receive those messages would simply check those images at regular intervals. This would, obviously, be less secure.

The message could be encoded with any standard steganography technique, such as using the LSBs or discrete cosine transform to store the hidden message. It is also advisable to encrypt the message using an encryption algorithm before hiding it using distributed steganography. It would also be advisable to at least encrypt the steganography key.

Note Combining encryption and steganography makes for a very powerful way to protect data. Some of the tools we examined in this chapter, such as Invisible Secrets, provide the option to encrypt the data as well as hide it in a carrier file.

Conclusions

In this chapter we have examined steganography, a fascinating area of data security. The most common way to perform steganography is via the LSB method. However, this chapter provided a brief overview of additional methods. You should be familiar with the concepts of steganography as well as at least one of the steganography tools mentioned in this chapter.

You were also introduced to steganalysis and were provided with a brief description of common methods for detecting steganography. The chapter concluded with a good description of a specific patented method for distributed steganography.

Test Your Knowledge

1. What is the most common method for doing steganography?
2. Where was the first known use of the word "steganography"?
3. What method uses a grill or mask to cover a paper to reveal only the hidden message?
4. _____ hide data in sections of file that are not processed by the processing applications.
5. _____ replace some bits of the carrier file with some bits of the data to be hidden.
6. _____ takes a finite sequence of data points and expresses them in terms of the sum of cosine functions oscillating at different frequencies.
7. Parity coding is often used with what type of steganography?
8. One of the most common methods of steganalysis is _____.
9. _____ is a statistical test that can be used to detect steganography.
10. The file in which data is hidden is called what?

Answers

1. LSB (least significant bit)
2. A book by Johannes Trithemius entitled *Steganographia*
3. Cardan grille
4. Injection-based techniques
5. Substitution-based techniques
6. Discrete cosine transform (DCT)
7. Steganophony
8. the close-color pair
9. The chi-squared test
10. The carrier file

Endnotes

1. The Siege Defense by Aeneas Tacitus, http://penelope.uchicago.edu/Thayer/E/Roman/Texts/Aeneas_Tacticus/Fragments*.html.
2. Mark Owens, "A Discussion of Covert Channels and Steganography," SANS Institute, 2002, www.gray-world.net/cn/papers/adiscussionofcc.pdf.

3. Wolfram MathWorld, definition of sinusoid, http://mathworld.wolfram.com/Sinusoid .html.

4. P. Jayaram, H. R. Ranganatha, and H. S. Anupama, "Information Hiding Using Audio Steganography–A Survey," *The International Journal of Multimedia & Its Applications (IJMA)*, vol. 3, no. 3 (August 2011).

5. A. Swathi and SAK Jilani, "Video Steganography by LSB Substitution Using Different Polynomial Equations," *International Journal of Computational Engineering Research* (ijceronline.com), vol. 2, no. 5 (2012).

6. Bruce Schneier, "Terrorists and Steganography," *ZD Net*, 2001, www.zdnet.com/article/ terrorists-and-steganography/.

7. Tom Kellen, "Hiding in Plain View: Could Steganography Be a Terrorist Tool?" SANS Institute InfoSec Reading Room, http://www.sans.org/reading-room/whitepapers/ stenganography/hiding-plain-view-steganography-terrorist-tool-551.

8. "Al Qaeda Uses Steganography – documents hidden in porn videos found on memory stick," *InfoSecurity Magazine*, 2002, www.infosecurity-magazine.com/news/al-qaeda-uses-steganography-documents-hidden-in/.

9. B. Astrowsky, "Steganography: Hidden Images, A New Challenge in the Fight Against Child Porn," www.antichildporn.org/steganog.html.

10. Deborah Radcliff, "Steganography: Hidden Data," *Computer World*, 2002, www .computerworld.com/article/2576708/security0/steganography--hidden-data.html.

11. C. Easttom, *System Forensics, Investigation and Response* (Jones & Bartlett Learning, 2013).

12. J. Fridrich and M. Goljan, "Practical Steganalysis of Digital Images – State of the Art," 2002, www.ws.binghamton.edu/fridrich/Research/steganalysis01.pdf.

13. K. Sullivan, U. Madhow, S. Chandrasekaran, and B. S. Manjunath, "Steganalysis for Markov Cover Data with Applications to Images," *IEEE Transactions on Information Forensics and Security*, vol. 1, no. 2 (2012), www.ece.ucsb.edu/~manj/ ManjBio2008/06_sullivan_TIFS06.pdf.

17 Cryptanalysis

In this chapter we will cover the following:

- Classic techniques of cryptanalysis
- Modern methods
- Rainbow tables
- The birthday paradox
- Other methods for breaching cryptography

What does it mean to "break" a cipher? It means finding a method to decrypt the message that is more efficient than using a brute-force attempt—simply trying every possible key. If the encryption algorithm uses a 128-bit key, for example, that means 2^{128} possible keys to try. In the decimal number system, that is $3.402 * 10^{38}$ possible keys. If you are able to attempt 1 million keys every second, it could still take as long as 10,790,283,070,806,014,188,970,529 years to break a cipher with a 128-bit key.

This brings us to cryptanalysis: what is it? *Cryptanalysis* involves using techniques (other than brute force) to attempt to derive the key. Keep in mind that any attempt to crack any non-trivial cryptographic algorithm is simply that—an attempt. There is no guarantee of any method working, and whether a method works or not, it will probably require a long and tedious process. This should make sense, because if cracking encryption were a trivial process, encryption would be useless.

In fact, cryptanalysis is a very tedious and at times frustrating endeavor. It is entirely possible to work for months, and your only result may be to have a little more information on the key that was used for encrypting a given message. What we see in movies, when encryption is broken in hours or even minutes, is simply not realistic.

Who needs to understand cryptanalysis? Obviously certain intelligence-gathering agencies and military personnel have a need for a strong working knowledge of cryptanalysis—beyond what this chapter will provide. In some cases, law enforcement officers and forensics analysts need to understand cryptanalysis at least well enough to know what is feasible and what is not. It is not uncommon for suspects to use encryption to hide evidence from authorities. Furthermore, cryptanalysis techniques are often used to test algorithms. If a new algorithm, or a variation of an old algorithm, is proposed, you can begin testing that algorithm by subjecting it to appropriate cryptanalysis techniques.

> **Note** Providing a thorough exploration of cryptanalysis would take more than a single chapter of a book. In fact, many introductory cryptography books ignore the topic altogether. The goal of this chapter is simply to acquaint you with the fundamentals of cryptanalysis. If you want to study this topic in more depth, this chapter should provide a solid foundation. You will also find links and suggestions for further study here. If you don't want to learn more about cryptanalysis, this chapter will provide more than enough information for most security professionals.

Classic Cryptanalysis Methods

Recall that this book began with a study of classic ciphers to help you become comfortable with the concepts of cryptography before delving into more modern algorithms. As with ciphers, it is often easier for a student of cryptography to understand classic cryptanalysis methods before attempting to study modern methods. This section will examine methods that are effective only against classic ciphers. These won't help you break RSA, AES, or similar ciphers, but they might help you more fully understand the concepts of cryptanalysis.

Frequency Analysis

Frequency analysis is the basic tool for breaking most classical ciphers. In natural languages, certain letters of the alphabet appear more frequently than others. By examining those frequencies, you can derive some information about the key that was used. This method is very effective against classic ciphers such as Caesar, Vigenère, and so on. It is far less effective against modern methods, however. In fact, with modern methods, the most likely result is that you will get some basic information about the key, but you will not get the key. Remember that in the English language, the two most common three-letter words are *the* and *and*. The most common single-letter words are *I* and *a*. And if you see double letters in a word, they are most likely *ee* or *oo*.

Here are a few general facts that will help you—at least with English as the plain text:

- *T* is the most common first letter of a word.
- *E* is the most common last letter of a word.
- *The* is the most common word.
- Very common two-letter combinations are *he*, *re*, *an*, *th*, *er*, and *in*.
- Very common three-letter combinations are *ent*, *ing*, *ion*, and *and*.

As mentioned, these methods are quite effective with any of the classic ciphers discussed in Chapters 1 and 2, but are not effective against more modern ciphers. When I'm teaching introductory cryptography courses, I often conduct a lab to illustrate this. In this lab, I ask each student to write a brief paragraph, select some substitution shift (such as +1, −2, +3, and so on), and then apply that single substitution cipher to their message. Essentially, they are applying a Caesar cipher to their messages. Then I ask the students to exchange the resulting cipher text with a classmate. Each student then applies frequency analysis to attempt to break the cipher. Having conducted this lab on numerous occasions for many years, I've typically found that about half the class can crack the cipher within 10 to 15 minutes, and these students usually have no prior background in cryptography or cryptanalysis. This lab serves multiple purposes: it introduces the students to primitive cryptanalysis, and it illustrates the fact that classic ciphers are no longer adequate for modern cryptographic purposes.

Let's try an example. Consider this cipher text that was created using a single substitution cipher:

```
Etarvqitcrja ku qpg qh vjg oquv kpvgtguvkpi cpf ejcnngpikpi vqrkeu K mpqy qh
```

Notice the three, two-letter words:

```
ku, qh, qh
```

Notice, too, that *qh* appears twice. There are quite a few two-letter words in English, but *an* and *of* are two of the most common. If you assume *of*, then that means *q* is *o* and *h* is *f*.

Now let's look at the three-letter words: *qpg* and *vig*. Continuing our assumption that *q* is *o* and *h* is *f*, that would mean that *qpg* is a word starting with *o*. How many three-letter words start with *o*? It turns out that there are quite a few: oil, oak, one, off, ohm, and so on. If you have some knowledge of the subject matter of the message, you might be able to determine if a less common word (such as oak or oil) is likely; if not, you can pick a very common word—either *off* or *one*. If you guess *one*, then that means *q* is *o*, *h* is *f*, *p* is *n*, and *g* is *e*. Can we determine anything from this? Let's take a look:

$$q \rightarrow o \quad +2$$
$$h \rightarrow f \quad +2$$
$$p \rightarrow n \quad +2$$
$$g \rightarrow e \quad +2$$

In every case, the cipher text is +2 from the plain text (if our guesses are right). If you apply this to the entire cipher text, and reduce each letter by two, you get this:

```
Cryptography is one of the most interesting and challenging topics I know of
```

You have just deciphered the message. If your guesses lead to different shifts (such as some are +2, some are +3), then either you are wrong or it is a multi-substitution cipher.

Kasiski Examination

The *Kasiski examination* (sometimes called *Kasiski's Test* or *Kasiski's Method*), developed by Friedrich Kasiski in 1863, is a method of attacking polyalphabetic substitution ciphers, such as the Vigenère cipher. You can use this method to deduce the length of the keyword used in the polyalphabetic substitution cipher. Once you discover the length of the keyword, you line up the cipher text in *n* columns, where *n* is the length of the keyword. Then each column can be treated as a mono-alphabetic substitution cipher and then cracked with simple frequency analysis. The method involves looking for repeated strings in the cipher text—the longer the cipher text, the more effective this method will be.

Friedrich Kasiski (1805–1881) was a German officer and cryptographer. He published a book on cryptography in 1863 entitled *Die Geheimschriften und die Dechiffrir-Kunst (Secret Writing and the Art of Deciphering)*.

Modern Methods

Of course, cracking modern cryptographic methods is no trivial task. In fact, the most likely outcome of any attempt is failure. But with enough time and resources (such as computational power, sample cipher texts and plain texts, and so on) it *is* possible.

Here are some attack techniques that can be used to try to crack modern ciphers:

- **Known plain-text attack** With this technique, the attacker obtains a number of plain-text/cipher-text pairs. Using this information, the attacker attempts to derive information about the key being used. Any chance of success requires that the attacker have many thousands of plain-text/cipher-text pairs.
- **Chosen plain-text attack** In this case, the attacker obtains the cipher texts corresponding to a set of plain texts of his own choosing. This enables the attacker to attempt to derive the key used and thus decrypt other messages encrypted with that key. This can be difficult, but it is not impossible.
- **Cipher text–only attack** Here, the attacker has access only to a collection of cipher texts. The attack is completely successful if the corresponding plain texts—or, even better, the key—can be deduced. The ability to obtain any information about the underlying plain text is considered a success. This method is far more likely than using known plain text, but it's also the most difficult method.
- **Related-key attack** This attack is similar to a chosen plain-text attack, except the attacker can obtain cipher texts encrypted under two different keys. This is a very useful attack if the attacker can obtain the plain text and matching cipher text.

The chosen plain-text and known plain-text attacks often puzzle students who are new to cryptanalysis. How, they ask, can you get samples of plain text and cipher text? You cannot simply ask the target to hand over such samples, can you? Actually, it is not that difficult. Consider, for example, that many people use signature blocks in their e-mails. If you send an e-mail to the target and get a response, the signature block is an example of plain text. If you later intercept an encrypted e-mail from that target, you already know to match the encrypted text with the plain-text signature block at the end of the e-mail. This is just one trivial example of how to get plain-text/cipher-text pairs.

More and different mathematically sophisticated methods can also be used, including linear, differential, integral, and mod n cryptanalysis. Some of these are applications of known plain-text or chosen plain-text attacks.

Linear Cryptanalysis

This technique, invented by Japanese cryptographer Mitsuru Matsui, is a known plain-text attack that uses a linear approximation to describe the behavior of the block cipher.

Given enough pairs of plain text and corresponding cipher text, you can obtain bits of information about the key. Obviously, the more pairs of plain text and cipher text you have, the greater the chance of success. Linear cryptanalysis is based on finding affine approximations to the action of a cipher. It is commonly used on block ciphers.

> **Note**
> Mitsuru Matsui is known not only for the discovery of linear cryptanalysis, but he has published extensively on other cryptanalysis issues.[1]

Remember that cryptanalysis is an attempt to crack cryptography. For example, with the 56-bit Data Encryption Standard (DES) key, a brute-force attack could take up to 2^{56} attempts. Linear cryptanalysis will take 2^{47} known plain texts.[2] This is better than brute force, but it is still impractical in most situations. Matsui first applied linear cryptanalysis to the FEAL (Fast Data Encipherment Algorithm) cipher and then later to DES. However, the DES application required 2^{47} known plain-text samples, making it impractical.

> **Note**
> FEAL was proposed as an alternative to DES, and there have been various revisions of the cipher. Unfortunately, it was susceptible to several types of cryptanalysis.

In linear cryptanalysis, a linear equation expresses the equality of two expressions that consist of binary variables that are XOR'd. For example, in Figure 17-1, the equation XORs the sum of the first and third plain-text bits, and the first cipher-text bit is equal to the second bit of the key.

You can use linear cryptanalysis to slowly re-create the key that was used. After doing this for each bit, you will have an equation of the form shown in Figure 17-2.

You can then use Matsui's Algorithm 2, using known plain-text/cipher-text pairs, to guess the values of the key bits involved in the approximation. The right side of the equation is the partial key (the object is to derive some bits for part of the key). Now count how many times the approximation holds true over all the known plain-text/cipher-text pairs. This count is called T. The partial key that has a T value and that has the greatest absolute difference from half the number of plain-text/cipher-text pairs is determined to be the most likely set of values for those key bits. In this way, you can derive a probable partial key.

Differential Cryptanalysis

Invented by Eli Biham and Adi Shamir, *differential cryptanalysis* is a form of cryptanalysis that is applicable to symmetric key algorithms. According to Christopher Swenson, "Differential cryptanalysis focuses on finding a relationship between the changes that occur in the output bits as a result of changing some of the input bits."[3] It originally worked only with chosen plain text. However, later research found it could also work with known plain text and cipher text only.

$$P1 \oplus P3 \oplus C1 = K2$$

FIGURE 17-1   The basics of linear cryptanalysis

$$P_{i1} \oplus P_{i2}\cdots \oplus C_{j1} \oplus C_{j2}\cdots = K_{k1} \oplus K_{k2}\cdots$$

FIGURE 17-2   The form of linear cryptanalysis

The differential cryptanalysis attacker examines pairs of plain-text inputs that are related by some constant difference. The usual way to define the differences is via an XOR operation, but other methods can also be used. The attacker computes the differences in the resulting cipher texts and looks for some statistical pattern. The resulting differences are called the *differential*. The basic idea is that by analyzing the changes in some chosen plain text, and noting the difference in the outputs resulting from encrypting each text, it is possible to recover some properties of the key.

Differential cryptanalysis measures the XOR difference between two values. Differentials are often denoted with the symbol Ω; for example, you might have a differential Ωa and another differential Ωb. A *characteristic* is composed of two matching differentials; for example, differential Ωa in the input produces differential Ωb in the output. The characteristic demonstrates that the specified differential in the input leads to a particular differential in the output. Differential cryptanalysis is also about probabilities. So the question being asked is, What is the probability that a given differential in the input Ωa will lead to a particular differential in the output Ωb?

In most cases, differential analysis starts with the substitution box (S-box). Because most symmetric ciphers use S-boxes, this is a natural and convenient place to start. If, for example, you assume an input of X1 that produces output of Y1 and an input of X2 that produces an output of Y2, this produces a differential (that is, the difference between X1 and X2 produces the difference between Y1 and Y2). This is expressed as follows:

$$\Omega i = X1 \oplus X2 \quad \text{this is the input differential}$$

$$\Omega o = Y1 \oplus Y2 \quad \text{this is the output differential}$$

Next you need to consider the relationship between input differentials and output differentials. To do this, you have to consider all possible values of Ωi and measure how this changes the values of Ωo. For each possible value of X1, X2, and Ωi, you measure the change in Y1, Y2, and Ωo, and then record that information.

 Even though differential cryptanalysis was publically discovered in the 1980s, DES is resistant to differential cryptanalysis based on the structure of the DES S-box. Since the DES S-box is the portion of DES that was constructed by the NSA, it stands to reason that the NSA was aware of differential cryptanalysis in the 1970s.

Higher-Order Differential Cryptanalysis

An improvement on differential cryptanalysis was developed by Lars Knudsen in 1994. *Higher-order differential cryptanalysis* focuses on the differences between differences that would be found with ordinary differential cryptanalysis. This technique has been shown to be more powerful than ordinary differential cryptanalysis. Specifically, it was applied to a symmetric algorithm known as the KN-cipher, which had previously been proven to be immune to standard differential cryptanalysis. Higher-order differential cryptanalysis has also been applied to a variety of other algorithms, including CAST.

Truncated Differential Cryptanalysis

Ordinary differential cryptanalysis focuses on the full difference between two texts and the resulting cipher text, but *truncated differentials cryptanalysis* analyzes only partial differences.[4] By taking partial differences into account, it is possible to use two or more differences within the same plain-text/cipher-text pair. As the name suggests, this technique is only interested in making predictions of some of the bits, instead of the entire block. It has been applied to Twofish, Camellia, Skipjack, IDEA, and other block ciphers.

Impossible Differential Cryptanalysis

Put another way, standard differential cryptanalysis is concerned with differences that propagate through the cipher with a greater probability than expected. *Impossible differential cryptanalysis* is looking for differences that have a probability of 0 at some point in the algorithm. This has been used against Camellia, ARIA, TEA, Rijndael, Twofish, Serpent, Skipjack, and other algorithms.

Integral Cryptanalysis

Integral cryptanalysis was first described by Lars Knudsen. This attack is particularly useful against block ciphers based on substitution-permutation networks. While differential analysis looks at pairs of inputs that differ by only 1 bit position, with all other bits identical, integral analysis, for block size b, holds $b - k$ bits constant and runs the other k bits through all $2k$ possibilities. So $k = 1$ is just differential cryptanalysis; $k > 1$ is a new technique: integral cryptanalysis.

Mod *n* Cryptanalysis

Mod n cryptanalysis can be used for either block or stream ciphers. This method was developed in 1999 by John Kelsey, Bruce Schneier, and David Wagner. This excerpt from a paper written by the inventors provides a good overview of the technique:

> Nearly all modern statistical attacks on product ciphers work by learning some way to distinguish the output of all but the last rounds from a random permutation. In a linear attack, there is a slight correlation between the plain text and the last-round input; in a differential attack, the relationship between a pair of inputs to the last round isn't quite random. Partitioning attacks, higher-order differential attacks, differential attacks, and related-key attacks all fit into this pattern.
>
> Mod *n* cryptanalysis is another attack along these lines. We show that, in some cases, the value of the last-round input modulo *n* is correlated to the value of the plain text modulo *n*. In this case, the attacker can use this correlation to collect information about the last-round subkey. Ciphers that sufficiently attenuate statistics based on other statistical effects (linear approximations, differential characteristics, etc.) are not necessarily safe from correlations modulo *n*.[5]

Asymmetric Cryptanalysis and RSA

So far, we have focused on symmetric ciphers, particularly block ciphers. However, there are also known weaknesses in asymmetric ciphers. Because RSA is the most widely used asymmetric cipher, I will focus on it here. This section will introduce you to several issues with RSA; for more information, refer to any of the other sources referenced in this section.

Recent studies have discovered potential flaws in RSA. Heninger and Shacham[6] found that RSA implementations that used a smaller modulus were susceptible to cryptanalysis attacks. In their study, they considered RSA implementations that used a small exponent in the algorithm. A smaller modulus is sometimes used to increase the efficiency of the RSA algorithm. However, the size of the modulus value also could be used to reduce the set of possible factors and thus decrease the time required to factor the public key. In fact, a great many RSA implementations use $e = 2^{16} + 1 = 65537$. So a cryptanalysis already has the public key and thus has e and n. And the n is relatively small, making it possible, with extensive computing power and time, to derive the private key. The authors of this study clearly showed that it is possible to derive the private RSA key, which would render that particular RSA encryption implementation useless.

In their methodology, Heninger and Shacham formulated a series of linear equations that would progressively approximate the RSA private key. The approximations were based on factoring the public key. This technique is very similar to the linear cryptanalysis method for cryptanalysis of symmetric key algorithms.[7, 8]

Zhao and Qi[9] also used implementations that have a smaller modulus operator. The authors of this study applied modular arithmetic, a subset of number theory, to analyze weaknesses in RSA. Many implementations of RSA use a shorter modulus operator to make the algorithm execute more quickly. Like Heninger and Shacham, Zhao and Qi showed that, based on the mathematical relationships between the elements of the RSA algorithm, increases in efficiency resulting from a smaller modulus will also render a decrease in the efficacy of that RSA implementation.

In their study, Zhao and Qi used a lattice matrix attack on the RSA implementation to attempt to factor the public key and derive the private key. The specifics of this mathematical methodology are not relevant to this discussion; what is significant, however, is that the researchers used an approach different from Heninger and Shacham and achieved the same results on RSA applications using a small modulus.

Aciiçmez and Schindler[10] examined the RSA cryptographic algorithm as implemented in Secure Sockets Layer (SSL). Given that RSA and SSL/TLS are used for online banking and e-commerce, the security of any implementation of the protocol is an important topic. Aciiçmez and Schindler wanted to determine whether there were flaws in the implementation that would allow an unintended third party to break the SSL implementation. The authors explained how a particular type of cryptanalysis can be used to break this specific implementation of RSA. This analysis was dependent upon essential elements of number theory.

In their study of SSL using RSA, Aciiçmez and Schindler examined the timing for modular arithmetic operations used in that specific implementation of RSA. This ultimately led to a method for factoring the public key, thus yielding the private key used in that RSA implementation. This methodology is important because normal approaches to factoring the public key are entirely too time consuming to be of practical use (Swenson, 2008). It is important to derive some additional information about the implementation of RSA in order to attempt a more practical approach to factoring. By using number theory, specifically with respect to the functionality of modular arithmetic, the researchers significantly decreased the time required for factoring the public key. Clearly these findings are significant and show an important problem with some implementations of RSA.

These studies are simply a sample of known attack vectors against RSA. Many of these attacks depend on a small modulus. And you have seen that many RSA implementations use the same small modulus ($e = 2^{16} + 1 = 65537$). It is also true that increases in computing power will make these attacks, as well as brute-force attempts to crack RSA, even more practical. So far, the cryptography community has reacted by simply using ever larger key sizes for RSA. It seems likely that an entirely new asymmetric algorithm will be needed. But in the meantime, when you implement RSA, make sure that you not only use a large key size, but that you be wary of using too small a modulus value.

General Rules for Cryptanalysis

Regardless of the technique used, three resources are required for all cryptanalysis:

- **Time**   The number of "primitive operations" that must be performed. This is quite loose; primitive operations could be basic computer instructions, such as addition, XOR, shift, and so forth, or entire encryption methods.
- **Memory**   The amount of storage required to perform the attack.
- **Data**   The *quantity* of plain texts and cipher texts required.

With infinite time, memory, and data, any cipher can be broken. Of course, nobody has infinite resources, and, in fact, resources are generally quite limited—particularly time. It would do no good to break the encryption of military communications and learn of an attack, if that break occurred several weeks *after* the attack. The information is useful only if it is timely.

Note   In general, the primary advantage that a government entity has in cryptanalysis is the resource of memory. A supercomputer, or even a cluster of high-end servers, can put far more resources to breaking a cipher than an individual with a single computer can. Even with those resources, however, breaking a modern cipher is far from trivial. It is still an onerous, resource-intensive task with no guarantee of success. And breaking a modern cipher with a PC is simply not feasible.

With any cryptanalysis attack, varying degrees of success are possible:

- **Total break**   The attacker deduces the secret key.
- **Global deduction**   The attacker discovers a functionally equivalent algorithm for encryption and decryption, but without learning the key.
- **Instance (local) deduction**   The attacker discovers additional plain texts (or cipher texts) not previously known.

- **Information deduction** The attacker gains some Shannon information about plain texts (or cipher texts) not previously known.
- **Distinguishing algorithm** The attacker can distinguish the cipher from a random permutation.

Consider this list carefully. A total break may be the only type of cryptanalysis success you've considered. However, that is only one possible definition of a successful cryptanalysis—and, in fact, it is the least likely outcome. In general, if your cryptanalysis produces more information about the key than was previously known, it is considered a success.

Rainbow Tables

Many passwords are stored with a cryptographic hash, which prevents the network or database administrator from reading the password. Recall from Chapter 9 that cryptographic hashes are not reversible—it is not merely computationally difficult, or impractical, to "unhash" something; it is mathematically impossible. It would seem, then, that breaking passwords protected by cryptographic hashes is impossible. However, that is not actually the case.

A *rainbow table* is a precomputed table of hashes. The most primitive way to create such a table would be to precompute hashes of all possible passwords of a given size. Assuming a standard English keyboard, there are 26 characters in uppercase and 26 in lowercase (52 possibilities), 10 digits, and about 8 special characters (#, !, $, and so on)—or about 70 possible values available for each character (the value 70 is just a rough estimate to illustrate this concept). A single character password could have 70 possible values, whereas a two-character password could have 70^2, or 4900 possible values. Even an 8-character password could have up to 576,480,100,000,000 possible values! So calculating tables that account for all passwords of any length from 5 to 10 characters would be computationally intensive and would require a great deal of storage.

Because this method for composing precomputed tables of hashes is very primitive, hash chains can be used instead to make this process efficient and to reduce the space needed to store the precomputed hashes. To create a hash chain, you use a reduction function, we will call R, that maps hash values back to plain-text values. This is not unhashing or reversing a hash; it is merely a method to precompute hashes more quickly.

Another, even more advanced, method is to replace the reduction function with a sequence of related reduction functions $R_1...R_k$. The issue then becomes how to implement this process. For example, Microsoft Windows stores password hashes in the Security Account Manager (SAM) file. To find a password, you would first obtain the SAM file for a target machine, and then search the contents through rainbow tables for matches.

The Windows password-cracker tool Ophcrack can automate this process for you. After loading a CD/DVD containing rainbow tables, Ophcrack boots to a live version of Linux. Then it launches a tool that copies the SAM file from the Windows machine and searches the rainbow tables on the CD/DVD for a match. Figure 17-3 shows the Ophcrack interface taken from an actual system, so some information has been redacted for security purposes.

Note Rainbow tables get very large. As of this writing, no portable rainbow tables can return passwords that are more than 12 to 14 characters in length. Therefore, longer passwords are useful for thwarting this attack.

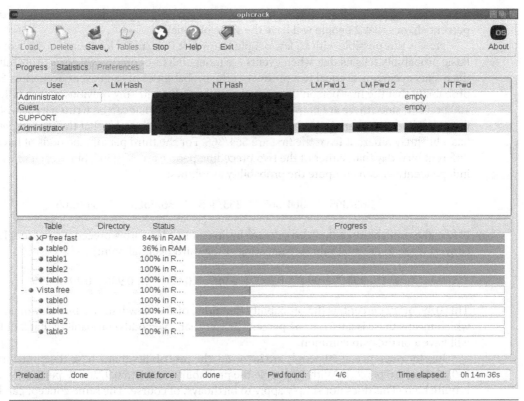

FIGURE 17-3   Ophcrack interface

The Birthday Paradox

If none of the previous methods works, and you are forced to rely on brute force, finding the key may not take as much time as you think. Consider DES, for example, with its 56-bit key. This means 2^{56} possible keys, or in decimal notation, 72,057,594,037,927,936 possible keys. Even if you could try 1 million keys per second, this would take 72,057,594,037 seconds, or about 2285 years—much too long. You should realize that you probably won't have to try every single key; you might get the right key just by chance in the first 100 you try, though the odds against that are beyond astronomical! Once you pass the first half the possible keys (at about the 1142-year mark) it gets increasingly likely that you will hit the key with your next attempt. That still is not helpful.

There is a mathematical puzzle that can help, however, called the *birthday paradox* (sometimes called the birthday problem). Here's the basic idea: How many people would you need to have in a room to have a strong likelihood that 2 would have the same birthday (month and day, not year)? Obviously, if you put 367 people in a room, at least 2 of them must have the same birthday, as there are only 365 days in a year (plus one more on a leap year). However, we are not asking how many people you need to *guarantee* a match, just how many you need to create a strong probability. It just so happens that with only 23 people in the room, there is a 50 percent chance that 2 people will have the same birthday.

How is this possible with so few people? How is it that such a low number can work? Basic probability tells us that when events are independent of one another, the probability of all the events occurring is equal to a product of the probabilities of each event occurring. So the probability that the first person does not share a birthday with any previous person is 1.0, or 100 percent, since there are no previous people in the set: That can be written as 365/365. For the second person, there is only one preceding person, and the odds that the second person has a birthday different from the first are 364/365. For the third person, the odds of having a different birthday than either of the two preceding people are 363/365. Since each of these is independent, we can compute the probability as follows:

$$365/365 \quad * \quad 364/365 \quad * \quad 363/365 \quad * \quad 362/365 \dots * \quad 342/365$$

(342 is the probability of the 23rd person sharing a birthday with a preceding person.) Let's convert these to decimal values (truncating at the third decimal point):

$$1 * 0.997 * 0.994 * 0.991 * 0.989 * 0.986 * \dots 0.936 = 0.49 \text{ or } 49\%$$

This 0.49, or 49 percent, is the probability that none of the 23 will have a birthday in common, which means there is a 0.51, or 51 percent (better than even odds) probability that 2 of the 23 will have a birthday in common.

Just for reference, if 30 people are involved, the probability that 2 have the same birthday is 0.706, or 70.6 percent. With 50 people the probability raises to 0.97, or 97 percent, which is quite high. This does not simply apply to birthdays, of course. The same concept can be applied to any set of data, and it is often used in cryptography and cryptanalysis.

In reference to cryptographic hash functions, the goal is to find two different inputs that produce the same output. When two inputs produce the same output from a cryptographic hash, this is referred to as a *collision*. It just so happens that from any set of n elements, the number of samples required to get a match or collision with a greater than 0.5, or 50 percent, probability is $1.174 \sqrt{n}$. Returning to the preceding birthday problem, $1.174 \sqrt{365} = 22.49$.

You can apply this to other cryptographic issues as well. Let's return to the DES algorithm. Recall that it has 72,057,594,037,927,936 possible keys. To guarantee that you find the correct key, you may need to check all 72,057,594,037,927,936 possibilities. However, if all you are seeking is a greater than 50 percent chance of finding the right key, you can try $1.774 \sqrt{72,057,594,037,927,936}$ possible keys—only 476,204,499 possible keys. This is far more manageable. In fact, again referring to our earlier scenario with DES, if you can attempt 1 million keys per second, you have a 50 percent chance of finding the right key in 7.9 minutes. Although 1 million keys per second is beyond the capability of your standard personal computer, it is well within the capabilities of supercomputers or even computing clusters.

The birthday paradox is one reason why larger key sizes are necessary for security. If we move our attention from DES to an AES 128-bit key, there are approximately $3.402 * 10^{38}$ possible keys. Applying the birthday paradox gives us $1.774 \sqrt{(3.402 * 10^{38})}$, or 32,724,523,986,760,744,567, keys that need to be attempted to have a 50 percent chance of finding a match. This number is large enough that it is computationally infeasible to break it through brute-force methods, even with the birthday paradox.

For more details on this mathematical problem and how it applies to cryptography, you can consult Chapter 2 of *Modern Cryptanalysis: Techniques for Advanced Code Breaking* (Wiley, 2008), which provides even more detailed coverage of the birthday paradox. Professor Dan Boneh also created a very good video on this topic at www.youtube.com/watch?v=ZZovSCFZffM.

Other Methods

Cryptanalysis is a formal process whereby one applies specific techniques in an attempt to crack cryptography. However, as you have seen in this chapter, one's ability to crack a cipher completely is quite limited. In many cases, the best one can hope to achieve is to derive some additional information about the target key. In many cases, breaking cryptography is so time consuming, and the probability of actually deriving the key is so small, that cryptanalysis provides no practical means of breaking ciphers. Put another way, cryptanalysis is an excellent tool for testing the security of a given cipher, but it is usually not efficient enough to make it a practical means for situations that require that the cipher be compromised in a short period of time. For example, a law enforcement agency that needs to break the encryption on a hard drive is unlikely to find cryptanalysis techniques of much use. However, using other methods for compromising ciphers might provide more immediate results. These methods all depend on some flaw in the implementation of the cryptography.

Other Passwords

Particularly with e-mail and hard drive encryption, a user is typically required to know some password in order to decrypt and access the information. Many hard drive encryption tools use very strong encryption. For example, Microsoft BitLocker, introduced with Windows 7, uses AES with a 128-bit key.

Several open source hard drive encryption tools use AES with a 256-bit key. It is simply not feasible to break this key. However, because it is possible that the user has used the same password (or a substantially similar permutation) somewhere else—such as with an e-mail account, or with a Windows password—you can check these sources for the key. You might even use Ophcrack on a Windows computer and use those passwords (and permutations of those passwords) to try and decrypt the encrypted partition or e-mail.

After the fact, many people are not even aware that their e-mail password has been cracked. Several web sites keep lists of e-mail accounts that have been breached, including haveibeenpwned.com and PwnedList.com.

If you are a law enforcement officer attempting to breach an encrypted drive belonging to a suspect, you can check these sites to see if the suspect's e-mail account has been breached. You can then use the e-mail password, and close permutations, to attempt to decrypt the hard drive.

Related Data

It is often the case that people choose passwords that have some meaning for them. This makes memorization much easier. I frequently advise forensic analysts to learn all they can about a suspect, and photographing or videotaping the area where the computer is seized can be quite valuable as well. If, for example, the suspect is an enthusiastic fan of a particular sports team, with memorabilia extensively displayed in his or her home or office, this type of information might aid in breaking encrypted drives, phones, and e-mails. It is at least reasonably likely that this individual's cryptography password is related to a beloved sports team.

Spyware

Of course, the easiest way to breach encryption is to see the password as the user types it in. This is often accomplished via spyware. For intelligence-gathering agencies, this is a viable option. For law enforcement, this can be done only with a warrant, and for civilians this is simply not an option.

Side-Channel Attack

Side-channel attacks are more difficult to accomplish. They are based on studying the physical components of a cryptographic system, seeking clues as to the cryptographic keys. For example, a gateway router that implements a virtual private network might be examined to study its power consumption or timing, or to see if there are electromagnetic leaks that provide cryptographic clues that can be used in cryptanalysis.

There are variations of this attack, including the following:

- **Timing attacks**   Attacks that measure how much time various computations take to perform.
- **Data remanence**   Attacks that gather sensitive data or portions thereof that remain in memory after having been deleted.
- **Electromagnetic attacks**   Attacks based on leaked electromagnetic radiation.

Electromagnetic emanations are particularly interesting with respect to the most common sort of network cable, unshielded twisted pair (UTP). You can attempt to detect the signal passing through UTP cable and derive information from it. As you might suspect, this is a non-trivial task. In fact, in response to this issue, the U.S. National Security Agency established the TEMPEST standard, which prohibits cables used to transmit classified data from being within a certain distance of cables transmitting unclassified data to prevent information "leakage."

Resources

As stated at the beginning of this chapter, the goal of this chapter is to get you familiar with the concepts of cryptanalysis. If you are seeking more specific information, perhaps even tutorials on cryptanalysis, I suggest you first master the information in this chapter, and then consider the following resources:

- "A Tutorial on Linear and Differential Cryptanalysis," by Howard M. Heys, Memorial University of Newfoundland, www.engr.mun.ca/~howard/PAPERS/ldc_tutorial.pdf.
- "Differential Cryptanalysis Tutorial," The Amazing King web site, www.theamazingking .com/crypto-diff.php. This source is not a typical scholarly resource and provides information in a way that is easy to understand.
- "Linear Cryptanalysis Tutorial," The Amazing King web site, www.theamazingking.com/ crypto-linear.php.
- "A Self-Study Course in Block-Cipher Cryptanalysis," by Bruce Schneier, www.schneier .com/paper-self-study.pdf.
- "A Tutorial on Linear and Differential Cryptanalysis," by Howard M. Heys. *Cryptologia* 26, 3 (July 2002), 189–221, http://dx.doi.org/10.1080/0161-110291890885.
- "Cryptography and Network Security" video, by Prof. D. Mukhopadhyay, www.youtube .com/watch?v=xcBqraHhcJU.

Conclusions

This chapter provided a broad general introduction to cryptanalysis. You should be very familiar with classic techniques such as frequency analysis, and you should understand the concept of the birthday paradox, as well as how it is applied to cryptographic problems.

For modern methods such as linear cryptanalysis and differential cryptanalysis, you should have a general understanding of the concepts and some grasp of the applications. It is not critical that you be able to apply these techniques. You should, however, have a working knowledge of rainbow tables.

Test Your Knowledge

1. What is brute-force cracking?
2. Applying the birthday paradox, how many keys would you need to try out of n possible keys to have a 50 percent chance of finding a match?
3. In the English language, _____ is the most common first letter of a word.
4. _____ is the most common word in the English language.
5. With a _____, the attacker obtains a number of plain-text/cipher-text pairs.
6. _____ is based on finding affine approximations to the action of a cipher.
7. Using _____, the attacker discovers additional plain texts (or cipher text) not previously known.
8. In _____, the attacker discovers a functionally equivalent algorithm for encryption and decryption, but without learning the key.
9. A _____ is essentially a precomputed table of hashes.
10. The concept of a hash-chain is to use a _____, we will call R, that _____.

Answers

1. Trying every possible key to guess the right one
2. $774\sqrt{n}$
3. T
4. the
5. known plain-text attack
6. Linear cryptanalysis
7. instance (local) deduction
8. global deduction
9. rainbow table
10. reduction function, maps hash values back to plain-text values

Endnotes

1. For a list of Mitsuru Matsui's publications, see www.cryptographersworld.com/a .php?a=64.
2. M. Matsui, "Linear Cryptanalysis Method for DES Cipher," 1999, www.cs.bgu .ac.il/~beimel/Courses/crypto2001/Matsui.pdf.
3. C. Swenson, *Modern Cryptanalysis: Techniques for Advanced Code Breaking* (Wiley, 2008).
4. J. Kelsey, B. Schneier, and D. Wagner, "Mod n Cryptanalysis, with Applications Against RC5P and M6," 1999, www.schneier.com/paper-mod3.pdf.
5. N. Heninger and H. Shacham, "Reconstructing RSA Private Keys from Random Key Bits," *Advances in Cryptology Lecture Notes in Computer Science*, 1 (1) (2009).
6. B. Su, W. Wu, and W. Zhang, "Security of the SMS4 Block Cipher Against Differential Cryptanalysis," *Journal of Computer Science and Technology*, 26(1), 130–138 (2011).
7. A. Alekseychuk, L. Kovalchuk, and S. Pal'chenko, "Cryptographic Parameters of s-Boxes that Characterize the Security of GOST-like Block Ciphers Against Linear and Differential Cryptanalysis," *Zakhist Inform*, 2, 12–23 (2007).
8. Y. Zhao and W. Qi, "Small Private-Exponent Attack on RSA with Primes Sharing Bits," *Lecture Notes in Computer Science*, 4779, 221–229 (2007).
9. O. Aciiçmez and W. Schindler, "A vulnerability in RSA implementations due to instruction cache analysis and its demonstration on OpenSSL," Proceedings of the 2008 Cryptographer's Track at the RSA conference on topics in cryptology, http:// portal.acm.org/citation.cfm?id=1791688.1791711&coll=DL&dl=GUIDE&CFID=96051 39&CFTOKEN=26457223.

18 Cryptographic Backdoors

In this chapter we will cover the following:

- What are cryptographic backdoors?
- General concepts of cryptographic backdoors
- Specific examples of cryptographic backdoors
- Prevalence of cryptographic backdoors
- Countermeasures

In 2013 Edward Snowden released classified documents that demonstrated that the U.S. National Security Agency (NSA) had placed a cryptographic backdoor into a particular pseudo-random-number generator (PRNG), the DUAL_EC_DRBG, or Dual Elliptic Curve Deterministic Random Bit Generator (some sources cite it as DUAL_ECC_DRBG, emphasizing the elliptic curve cryptography). This made quite a bit of news in the computer security world. Suddenly everyone was talking about cryptographic backdoors, but few people knew what such a backdoor was or what it meant. Did it mean the NSA could read your e-mail as easily as reading the *New York Times*? Did it mean you were vulnerable to hackers exploiting that backdoor? In this chapter we are going to address these questions.

This chapter provides a general overview of cryptographic backdoors, including how they function and the specific types. We will also discuss a few general countermeasures for defeating cryptographic backdoors. Although these details are quite interesting, the most important part of this chapter is the general concepts. By the end of this chapter, you should have a working understanding of what a cryptographic backdoor is and how it affects security.

What Are Cryptographic Backdoors?

The concept of a "backdoor" is borrowed from computer security and computer programming. In computer programming, a backdoor is a defect or feature of a computer system that provides a way for someone to bypass normal authentication. A backdoor is usually included in the application code by the programmer, often for benign purposes, such as the ability to circumvent the normal authentication process (which may be cumbersome) for testing purposes. It is important that these backdoors be removed from the code before the final product is distributed, however. In security, a backdoor can allow an attacker to circumvent the normal authentication for a target computer. An attacker might send a Trojan horse that contains some remote desktop software to a victim machine, such as Timbuktu, or he may use a tool such as Netcat to open a reverse command shell. Then the attacker could circumvent normal authentication methods and directly access the target computer.

> **Note**   Netcat is a popular tool with network administrators and with hackers that provides a robust set of networking tools. Most relevant to the current discussion is the fact that Netcat allows the administrator or hacker to set up remote command-line connections with a target computer.

The concept of a cryptographic backdoor is not exactly the same, but it is related. A software backdoor provides unfettered access to the intruder. A cryptographic backdoor makes the encrypted message more susceptible to cryptanalysis—in other words, some element of a cipher is susceptible to an attack. For example, if the PRNG used to generate a key for a symmetric cipher contains a backdoor, then that key is not really random.

Author Nick Sullivan describes the issue in the following way:

> TrueCrypt, like most cryptographic systems, uses the system's random number generator to create secret keys. If an attacker can control or predict the random numbers produced by a system, they can often break otherwise secure cryptographic algorithms. Any predictability in a system's random number generator can render it vulnerable to attacks. …It's absolutely essential to have an unpredictable source of random numbers in secure systems that rely on them.[1]

General Properties

A *kleptographic attack* occurs when an attacker uses cryptographic algorithms that resemble the original or actual algorithms to provide an advantage in cracking encrypted messages. In both cryptographic backdoors and kleptography, some basic properties are necessary for success:

- **Output indistinguishability**   If you compare the output of the standard algorithm without the backdoor to the output of the algorithm with the backdoor, no difference is discernible.[2] Without output indistinguishability, anyone with even moderate cryptographic skills could simply compare the output of your algorithm implementation with the backdoor to other algorithm implementations and discover the existence of the backdoor.
- **Confidentiality**   If a cryptographic algorithm has a backdoor, that backdoor should not generally reduce the security of the cipher. In other words, the vulnerability should be available only to the person who created the backdoor. A random attacker, unaware of the existence of the backdoor, should not have an increased chance to break the cipher.
- **Ability to compromise the backdoor**   Obviously, the backdoor must provide a means whereby the person who created the backdoor can compromise the cipher. This is, indeed, the entire purpose of having a cryptographic backdoor. As mentioned, however, that should not make the cipher more susceptible to general attacks.

Bruce Schneier described three other properties that he believed a successful cryptographic backdoor should possess:[3]

- **Low discoverability** The less the backdoor affects the normal operations of the program and the smaller the backdoor, the better. Ideally, the backdoor should not affect functionality and should just look like regular functional code. For example, an e-mail encryption backdoor that appends a plain-text copy to the encrypted copy is much less desirable than a backdoor that reuses most of the key bits in a public initialization vector.
- **High deniability** If the backdoor is discovered, it should look like a mistake—such as a change in the operation code, a "mistyped" constant, or an "accidental" reuse of a single-use key multiple times. According to Schneier, "This is the main reason I am skeptical about _NSAKEY as a deliberate backdoor, and why so many people don't believe the DUAL_EC_DRBG backdoor is real: they're both too obvious."
- **Minimal conspiracy** A good backdoor should be known to very few people. Says Schneier, "That's why the [2013] described potential vulnerability in Intel's random number generator worries me so much; one person could make this change during mask generation, and no one else would know."

In general, a cryptographic backdoor needs to, first and foremost, allow the attacker to subvert the security of the backdoored cipher.[4] It must also be relatively easy to use. Preferably, it would compromise a wide number of ciphers, giving the attacker the greatest range of potential access.

Examples of Backdoors

The following examples of specific cryptographic backdoors provide a practical illustration of the general principles. The RSA example is probably the easiest to understand. The Dual_EC_DRBG backdoor has received so much attention in the media that it would be impossible to have a discussion of backdoor and not discuss it.

Note	It is not critical that you memorize the backdoor techniques discussed in this section, but you should understand the general concepts.

Dual_EC_DRBG

The Dual Elliptic Curve Deterministic Random Bit Generator (Dual_EC_DRBG) was promoted as a cryptographically secure PRNG (CSPRNG) by the National Institute of Standards and Technology (NIST). This PRNG is based on the elliptic curve discrete logarithm problem (ECDLP) and is one of the four CSPRNGs standardized in NIST SP 800-90A. As early as 2006, cryptography researcher Gjøsteen suggested that the algorithm had significant security issues.[5] In 2007, researchers Brown and Gjøsteen discovered issues with the efficiency of Dual_EC_DRBG[6] and questioned why the government would endorse such an inefficient algorithm. Then, in 2007, Shumow and Ferguson published an informal presentation suggesting that Dual_EC_DRBG might have a cryptographic backdoor.[7]

In 2013, the *New York Times* reported that internal NSA memos leaked by Edward Snowden suggest that an RNG generated by the NSA that was used in the Dual_EC_DRBG standard does indeed contain a backdoor for the NSA.[8] Given that there had been discussions regarding the security of Dual_EC_DRBG for many years, this revelation was not a particular shock to the cryptographic community. However, it generated a great deal of surprise in the general security community.

> **Note** The following section is much easier to understand if you have a good understanding of elliptic curve cryptography in general. You might review Chapter 11 before proceeding.

Details The Dual_EC_DRBG algorithm specification specifies an elliptic curve, which is basically just a finite cyclic group G. The algorithm also specifies two group elements, P and Q. The NIST standard for Dual_EC_DRBG provides no insight into how P and Q are chosen. Normally you would expect these to be chosen randomly, but in the case of Dual_EC_DRBG, they were selected by the NSA. It is the choice of P and Q that forms the basis for the backdoor.

The following information provides insight into the backdoor within Dual_EC_DRBG.

In the simplified algorithm, the state of the PRNG at time t is some integer s. To run the PRNG forward one step, you would do the following:

1. Compute sP and produce the result as an integer labeled r.
2. Compute rP and produce the result as an integer s ′ (this will become the new state in the next step).
3. Compute rQ (remember we started with two points, P and Q) and output it as this step's output from the PRNG.

It should be obvious that $P = eQ$ for some integer e. Not knowing e makes it completely impractical to compute P from Q. However, since the NSA chose the values P and Q, it could have chosen them by picking Q randomly, picking e randomly, and setting $P = eQ$. In particular, the NSA could have chosen them so that they know e.

Thus, it is this number e that functions as a backdoor and facilitates someone breaking the PRNG. You can observe one output from the PRNG—namely, rQ. This can be multiplied by e, to get erQ. Note that $erQ = r(eQ) = rP = s ′$. So the attacker can infer what the next state of the PRNG will be and predict the state of the PRNG and thus the next random number produced by the PRNG. If this PRNG is being used to generate keys, the attacker could consider the first key generated and predict subsequent keys that would be generated by that PRNG.

Recall in Chapter 12 the discussion of German standards for a PRNG; one of the desirable properties for a PRNG is that no one should be able to predict future states of a PRNG from the current state. By placing a backdoor in Dual_EC_DRBG, this standard is violated.

RSA Backdoor

The RSA backdoor involves compromising the generation of keys for RSA. This example is based on an example by Yung & Young RSA labs.[9] The specific steps are similar to the usual method of generating RSA keys, but slightly modified.

Before we delve into the steps of the backdoor version of RSA, it might be useful for you to refresh your memory regarding the typical RSA process. RSA key generation is accomplished with the following steps:

1. Generate two large random primes, p and q, of approximately equal size such that their product n = pq is of the required bit length (such as 2048 bits, 4096 bits, and so on).
2. Let n = pq.
3. Let m = (p–1)(q–1).
4. Choose a small number e, co-prime to m. (Note: Two numbers are co-prime if they have no common factors.)
5. Find d, such that de % m = 1.
6. Publish e and n as the public key. Keep d and n as the secret key.

To encrypt with RSA,

$$C = M^e \% n$$

where M is the message and C is the cipher text.

To decrypt with RSA:

$$P = C^d \% n$$

Now the backdoor steps are as follows:

1. Choose a large value x randomly that is of the appropriate size for an RSA key (such as 2048 bits, 4096 bits, and so on).
2. Compute the cryptographic hash of this x value, denoted as H(x). We will call that hash value p.
3. If the cryptographic hash of x, the value p, is either a composite number or if p–1 is not relatively prime to e, then repeat step 1 until p is a prime. Then proceed to step 4. (Note that you may need to repeat this step several times to find a suitable H(x), so this entire process is not particularly efficient.)
4. Choose some large random number we will call R.
5. Encrypt the value of x with the attacker's own private key. Denote this value as c. Essentially c is the digital signature of x, signed by the attacker. (Note that this is yet another flaw in this particular approach. You have to ensure you generate a public/ private key pair just for this purpose. If you use a private/public key pair that you use for general communication, you will have just signed your backdoor.)
6. Now you solve for (q,r) in (c || R) = pq + r.
7. Much like computing H(x), if it turns out that q is composite or q–1 is not co-prime to e, then go back to step 1.
8. Next, output the public key (n = pq,e) and the private key p.

The victim's private key can then be recovered in the following manner:

1. The attacker obtains the public key (n,e) of the user. Let u be the 512 uppermost bits of n.

2. The attacker sets $c_1 = u$ and $c_2 = u + 1$. (c_2 accounts for a potential borrow bit having been taken from the computation.)

$$n = pq = (c \mid\mid R) - r$$

3. The attacker decrypts c_1 and c_2 to get s_1 and s_2, respectively
4. Either $p_1 = H(s_1)$ or $p_2 = H(s_2)$ will divide n.

Only the attacker can perform this operation since only the attacker knows the needed private decryption key.

Compromising a Hashing Algorithm

Some researchers have even been exploring methods for compromising cryptographic hashing algorithms. Several cryptographers created a cryptographic backdoor for SHA-1 and then wrote the following:

> SHA-1 as a target because it is (allegedly) the most deployed hash function and because of its background as an NSA/NIST design. We exploit the freedom of the four 32-bit round constants of SHA-1 to efficiently construct 1-block collisions such that two valid executables collide for this malicious SHA-1. Such a backdoor could be trivially added if a new constant is used in every step of the hash function. However, in SHA-1 only four different 32-bit round constants are used within its 80 steps, which significantly reduces the freedom of adding a backdoor. Actually our attack only modifies at most 80 (or, on average, 40) of the 128 bits of the constants.[10]

The details of their approach are not important to our current discussion. What is important is that this is one more avenue for compromising cryptographic algorithms—not only symmetric ciphers and asymmetric ciphers, but cryptographic hashes as well.

Other Ways to Compromise Cryptography

Cryptographic backdoors are an obvious way to compromise cryptography, and they are clearly of interest to anyone studying cryptography. However, other mechanisms could be used. Frequently, the implementation of cryptography is flawed, either intentionally or accidentally. This means that the algorithms have not been tampered with, but that the encryption is circumvented.

Heartbleed Bug

The Heartbleed Bug is an excellent example of such a vulnerability, which was discovered in the OpenSSL software in December 2011 and publically disclosed in April 2014. The issue involves the Heartbeat extension for TLS used by OpenSSL, which is a mechanism whereby a client and server using OpenSSL can verify that the other machine is still alive (or still has a heartbeat). To do this, the client sends a heartbeat request message with a 16-bit payload.

The server responds by sending back 16 bits from RAM. It is impossible for those 16 bits to provide any meaningful data to the client, other than that the server is still functioning. The bug involved a failure to check bounds, however, and the attacker could get up to 64 kilobytes of the server's memory.

This is a particularly critical issue because OpenSSL is widely used on e-commerce servers. So 64KB of data from an e-commerce server is likely to include cryptographic keys of other users, credit card information, and other sensitive data.

This is a classic example in which the cryptographic algorithm was not compromised and the key was not broken via cryptanalysis, but the data that was intended to be protected was exposed. What makes this especially pertinent to our discussions in this chapter is that it appears that the NSA and possibly other intelligence agencies were aware of this bug, but did not publically disclose it. Essentially, these intelligence agencies did not create this backdoor, but they found it and exploited it.

Key Escrow

Another vulnerability issue involves key escrows. To understand this vulnerability, you must first understand key escrows. Consider a company wherein all employees are issued digital certificates so they can exchange encrypted information as needed. Each employee has his or her private key on his or her own machine. Eventually someone's machine will crash and that user's private key will be lost. To prevent this situation, many companies create a key escrow server, which has a copy of everyone's private key. Clearly this is a security risk.

The correct way to set up a key escrow server involves several requirements:

- The server should have no other function than to store the keys.
- No one person should be able to access the keys. For example, one person can have access to the machine itself and another can have the password for the encrypted folder on that server that stores everyone else's key. These two individuals must collaborate to get a key out of escrow. That makes malicious activity more difficult.
- This server should not be networked. You must physically go to the server to retrieve a lost key.
- The server itself, and the room it is in, must be highly secured.

If all of these measures are not taken, someone could breach the security of the escrow server and get the private keys of all the individuals. Consider, for example, the ramifications if spyware was on that server. This is yet another example of circumventing cryptography without actually breaking any algorithm or keys.

The Prevalence of Backdoors

Although a cryptographic backdoor can be a significant security issue, the problem is not particularly prevalent. Consider the resources that are needed to implement a cryptographic backdoor. As you have seen in this chapter, the algorithms are not overly difficult, but how does an attacker get a target organization to use a cipher, PRNG, key generator, or hash that contains a backdoor? Clearly, there are two primary methods for doing this, a governmental method and a private method, and here we will look at both.

Governmental Approach

Government agencies either implement backdoors in standards, as with DUAL_EC_DRBG, or work with a company to include a backdoor in its product. This method always runs the risk of being discovered, however. Even the most secure intelligence agency, when working with outside vendors, runs a risk of operational security being compromised.

Let's look at an example. This example was not really a backdoor, so much as a method whereby law enforcement, with a warrant, could gain access to symmetric keys used in secure voice communications. The Skipjack symmetric cipher was implemented on the Clipper chip. However, negative reactions to the possibility of the federal government being able to listen in on secure communications prevented this project from moving forward.

According to Schneier,

> The FBI tried to get backdoor access embedded in an AT&T secure telephone
> system in the mid-1990s. The Clipper Chip included something called a LEAF: a Law
> Enforcement Access Field. It was the key used to encrypt the phone conversation,
> itself encrypted in a special key known to the FBI, and it was transmitted along with
> the phone conversation. An FBI eavesdropper could intercept the LEAF and decrypt
> it, then use the data to eavesdrop on the phone call.[11]

Snowden also alleged that Cisco cooperated with the NSA to introduce backdoors in Cisco products. Specifically, Snowden said that Cisco routers built for export (not for use in the United States) were equipped with surveillance tools. He further claimed that this was done without the knowledge of Cisco. According to an article in *InfoWorld*, "Routers, switches, and servers made by Cisco are booby-trapped with surveillance equipment that intercepts traffic handled by those devices and copies it to the NSA's network."[12]

In other cases, a government agency may gain the full cooperation of a technology company. Several sources claim that the computer security firm RSA took $10 million from the NSA to make the Dual_EC_DRBG the default for its BSAFE encryption toolkit.[13, 14]

Private Citizen/Group Approach

It may seem like cryptographic backdoors are a tool that only government agencies—generally intelligence gathering agencies—can use, but that is not the case. A small group, or even an individual, might also introduce a cryptographic backdoor, and although I am not aware of any real-world cases of this occurring, it is certainly possible. Following are three ways that an individual or small group might implement a cryptographic backdoor. Clearly this makes such backdoors a serious concern.

- **PRNG**   People often select third-party products to generate random numbers for cryptographic keys. Any competent programmer with a working knowledge of cryptographic backdoors could create a product that generated random numbers/keys with a backdoor. Such a product could then be released as freeware, or via a web site, guaranteeing a significant number of people might use the PRNG.

- **Product tampering** Any individual working in a technology company, if that individual works in the appropriate section of the company, could potentially introduce a backdoor without the company being aware of it.
- **Hacking** Although this is more difficult and thus less likely to occur, there is always the potential of someone hacking into a device and compromising its cryptography. For example, a router with VPN capabilities must generate new keys for each VPN session. Theoretically, someone could hack that router and alter its key generation. Such a task would be difficult, however.

> **Note** Although I indicate that I have not yet heard of individuals or small groups creating cryptographic backdoors, that may be due simply to a lack of skills on their part. The primary purpose in my writing this book was to provide a real understanding of cryptography. The same lack of knowledge about the details of cryptography also permeates the hacking community.

Countermeasures

Detecting cryptographic backdoors is a very difficult task. As you have seen earlier in this chapter, one of the goals of a cryptographic backdoor is to be undetectable. You could, of course, subject any random number generator or cipher to extensive cryptanalysis to determine if a backdoor is likely, but that process is very time-consuming and beyond the capabilities of most organizations. And waiting until some researcher discovers a likely backdoor is inefficient. You could be using that backdoor cipher for quite a few years before some researcher discovers the backdoor.

The first issue is key generation. There is always a risk when you rely on a third party for key generation. The best solution, assuming you have the necessary skills in programming and basic mathematics, is to write code for your own key generation. For symmetric keys, I recommend implementing Blum, Blum, Shub, Yarrow, or Fortuna. Crépeau and Slakmon state the following: "This suggests that nobody should rely on RSA key generation schemes provided by a third party. This is most striking in the smartcard model, unless some guarantees are provided that all such attacks to key generation cannot have been embedded."[15]

For many, writing code for key generation is not a viable option. For example, many programmers who write applications for Microsoft Windows rely on the Microsoft CryptoAPI for key generation. A simple mechanism, at least for generating symmetric keys, would be to take that API (or any other) and subject it to a cryptographic hash that has the appropriate sized output, and then use that output as the key. An even simpler approach would be to generate two random numbers, and then XOR them together using the resulting number as the key. Either technique will essentially bury the cryptographic backdoor in another operation. The cryptographic hashing technique is the more secure and reliable of the two methods.

There have been some attempts in the industry to address this issue as well. The Open Crypto Audit Project is an attempt to detect cryptographic flaws, including backdoors, in open source software. The group includes a number of respected cryptographers. Its web site (https://opencryptoaudit.org/) lists the organization's charter:

- Provide technical assistance to free open source software ("FOSS") projects in the public interest

- Coordinate volunteer technical experts in security, software engineering, and cryptography
- Conduct analysis and research on FOSS and other widely used software in the public interest
- Contract with professional security researchers and information security firms to provide highly specialized technical assistance, analysis, and research on FOSS and other widely used software in the public interest

Conclusions

This chapter provided an introduction to cryptographic backdoors. Since the Snowden revelations of 2013, this topic has become very widely discussed in the security community. Cryptographic researchers have been exploring backdoors for many years before those revelations, however.

You need not know the details of the specific implementations discussed in this chapter; however, the general concepts of output indistinguishability, confidentiality, and so on, are critical, and you should have a solid working knowledge of these topics. It is also important that you have some knowledge of the countermeasures discussed in this chapter.

Test Your Knowledge

1. With regard to cryptographic backdoors, what is output indistinguishability?
2. With regard to cryptographic backdoors, what is confidentiality?
3. What made the Clipper chip relevant to backdoors?
4. _____ is a colloquial term for creating cryptographic algorithms that resemble the original/actual algorithms, but provide the creator an advantage in cracking encrypted messages.
5. In simple terms, the backdoor in Dual_EC_DRBG is based on what?

Answers

1. With output indistinguishability, you cannot distinguish the backdoor version of a cipher from the traditional version of the cipher.
2. The cipher with the backdoor should still be secure from attackers who don't know about the backdoor.
3. It was designed so that all cryptographic keys would be kept in an escrow that would be available to law enforcement.
4. Kleptography
5. The selection of P and Q

Endnotes

1. N. Sullivan, "How the NSA (may have) put a backdoor in RSA's cryptography: A technical primer," 2014, http://arstechnica.com/security/2014/01/how-the-nsa-may-have-put-a-backdoor-in-rsas-cryptography-a-technical-primer/.

2. A. Young and M. Yung, "Kleptography: Using Cryptography Against Cryptography," 2002, http://cryptome.org/2013/09/klepto-crypto.pdf.

3. B. Schneier, "Defending Against Crypto Backdoors," 2013, www.schneier.com/blog/archives/2013/10/defending_again_1.html.

4. B. Schneier, M. Fredrikson, T. Kohno, and T. Ristenpart, "Surreptitiously Weakening Cryptographic Systems," 2015, https://eprint.iacr.org/2015/097.pdf.

5. K. Gjøsteen, "Comments on Dual-EC-DRBG/NIST SP 800-90, Draft December 2005," 2006, www.math.ntnu.no/~kristiag/drafts/dual-ec-drbg-comments.pdf.

6. D. Brown and K. Gjøsteen, "A Security Analysis of the NIST SP 800-90 Elliptic Curve Random Number Generator," 2007, http://eprint.iacr.org/2007/048.pdf.

7. D. Shumow and N. Ferguson, "On the Possibility of a Back Door in the NIST SP800-90 Dual Ec Prng," 2007, http://rump2007.cr.yp.to/15-shumow.pdf.

8. M. Scott, "Backdoors in NIST elliptic curves," 2013, www.certivox.com/blog/bid/344797/Backdoors-in-NIST-elliptic-curves.

9. A. Young and M. Yung, "Malicious Cryptography: Kleptographic Aspects," 2005, http://citeseerx.ist.psu.edu/viewdoc/download?doi=10.1.1.120.6265&rep=rep1&type=pdf.

10. A. Albertini, J. Aumasson, M. Eichlseder, F. Mendel, and M. Schläffer, "Malicious Hashing: Eve's Variant of SHA-1," 2014, https://malicioussha1.github.io/doc/malsha1.pdf.

11. Schneier, 2013.

12. B. Snyder, "Snowden: The NSA planted backdoors in Cisco products," *InfoWorld*, 2014, www.infoworld.com/article/2608141/internet-privacy/snowden--the-nsa-planted-backdoors-in-cisco-products.html.

13. J. Menn, "Exclusive: Secret contract tied NSA and security industry pioneer," 2013, www.reuters.com/article/2013/12/20/us-usa-security-rsa-idUSBRE9BJ1C220131220.

14. A. Glaser, "After NSA Backdoors, Security Experts Leave RSA for a Conference They Can Trust," 2014, www.eff.org/deeplinks/2014/01/after-nsa-backdoors-security-experts-leave-rsa-conference-they-can-trust.

15. C. Crépeau and A. Slakmon, "Simple Backdoors for RSA Key Generation," 2003, http://link.springer.com/chapter/10.1007%2F3-540-36563-X_28#page-2.

19 The Future of Cryptography

In this chapter we will cover the following:

- Cryptography and the cloud
- Homomorphic cryptography
- Quantum cryptography

In the preceding 18 chapters, you have learned about the development of cryptography from ancient times (Scytale, Caesar, Atbash, and so on) through modern times (AES, Serpent, RSA, ECC, and so on). But what does the future hold for cryptography? It is always difficult to predict the future trends in any scientific or technological discipline. However, several emerging issues today can offer a glimpse at what is likely to be occurring in the next few decades. In this chapter we will explore these issues.

Cryptography and the Cloud

It is impossible today to avoid discussions of the cloud. Although most people misunderstand what the cloud is, that does not impede conversations about it. Clearly, a great deal of data is being stored in the cloud, and that means that data must be secured. In some cases, the traditional encryption methods that you have read about in previous chapters are adequate for security, but in other cases they may not be. Here we will explore cryptographic solutions that are uniquely suited for the cloud.

What Is the Cloud?

Before we can meaningfully explore cryptographic solutions in the cloud, you need to have a firm understanding of what "the cloud" is. To begin with, there really is no such thing as "the cloud"; there are, in fact, many clouds. A brief discussion of the evolution of data storage that has culminated in cloud storage might help explain this.

When most of us think of data storage, a simple server comes immediately to mind. And for many years, this was the primary storage modality (and still is for very small organizations). However, this modality eventually became impractical for larger data storage needs: the first problem was the need for more storage capacity than a single server could provide, and second was the need to maintain data access, even if a server was offline. So two different, but quite similar and overlapping, approaches were developed.

The first approach was the *storage area network* (SAN), which connects multiple servers and network storage devices via high-speed connections such as fiber-optics. In a SAN, there is redundancy—so, for example, three servers might store data, but each server has a duplicate server on the SAN. In this way, should a server go down, data access is not interrupted. The SAN is presented to the primary network as a single, monolithic storage device—but, in fact, it is an entirely separate network of servers, as shown in Figure 19-1.

A SAN provides a very resilient, high capacity storage solution. The failure of one or more servers does not render the data inaccessible; in fact, such a failure would not even be noticed by the end users.

Closely related to the SAN is the *cluster*, a grouping of servers that includes redundant copies of other servers that can be accessed either locally or over the Internet.

Both the SAN and the cluster solutions provide a high degree of resiliency, along with easily expandable storage capacity. A weakness with both solutions, however, can be seen if a problem occurs at the location where the SAN or cluster is stored—something as simple as interrupted connectivity to that location or as disastrous as a fire, earthquake, hurricane, or other natural disaster can render the network inoperable.

This brings us to *cloud storage*, which spreads the concepts of clustering and SAN over a diverse geographic area. If, for example, one cluster (or SAN) exists in Paris and a duplicate cluster (or SAN) is located in London, and both appear as a single storage area to end users, this is a cloud. You can see this in Figure 19-2.

The cloud concept is actually rather simple. By having data replicated across diverse geographical areas, the only disaster that would wipe out all the data would be of such an enormous magnitude as to make accessing data an irrelevant issue. Essentially, as long as modern civilization is intact, the data will be accessible in the cloud.

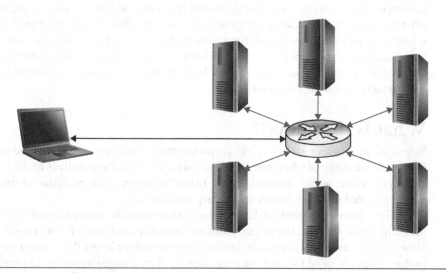

FIGURE 19-1   The SAN

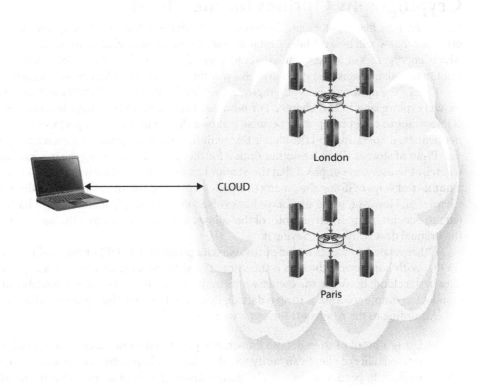

FIGURE 19-2   Basic cloud

In addition to there being numerous clouds, there are different types of clouds. There are actually three types of clouds: public, private, and community.

- *Public clouds* are defined by the National Institute of Standards and Technology (NIST) as clouds that offer their infrastructure or services to either the general public or a large industry group.
- *Private clouds* are used specifically by a single organization without offering the services to an outside party. Hybrid clouds combine the elements of a private and public cloud, but these are essentially private clouds that have some limited public access.
- *Community clouds* are a midway point between private and public. These are systems wherein several organizations share a cloud for specific community needs. For example, several computer companies might join to create a cloud devoted to common security issues.

Regardless of the type of cloud, the structure is the same: geographically dispersed, replicated data. And the issues of securing that data are the same.

Cryptography Options for the Cloud

You might think that cryptography in the cloud is no different from encrypting any file or hard drive, but that would be a mistake. Certainly you can use traditional algorithms such as Blowfish or AES to encrypt files or folders that are stored in the cloud. The issue arises when cloud customers want to have data that is encrypted in such a way that the cloud vendor cannot access it.

One of the options for cryptography in the cloud is *homomorphic cryptography*, which we will explore later in this chapter. For now, just keep in mind that homomorphic encryption is important to cloud computing because it allows the cloud vendor to perform some limited mathematical operations on the cipher text without first decrypting it or even having the key.

Proof of storage (PoS) is another option for the cloud. Proof of storage is a mechanism whereby the user can get proof that the vendor has not tampered with the data. There are a number of ways of doing this, many of which involve the use of hashing algorithms (see Chapter 9). However, proof of storage has evolved beyond simply maintaining a hash of your data to become an interactive protocol that allows a client to verify that the server possesses the original data without retrieving it.

Other related concepts include provable data possession (PDP) or proof of retrievability (POR). With both terms, the idea is the same: The data owner does not have a copy of all the data in the cloud; however, the owner wants to make sure their data is still available in the cloud. One simple solution is to sign data digitally and to check the signature when needed.

According to the Microsoft Research web site,

> Using a proof of storage (also known as a proof of data possession or a proof of retrievability) a client can verify whether the cloud operator has tampered with its data. In particular, this can be done without the client storing a local copy of the data and without it having to retrieve any of the data. In fact, the work for the client is negligible no matter how large the data is.[1]

Of course, there is a simpler option. Each customer keeps its own cryptographic keys in its own network and is responsible for key management. The problem with this approach, however, is that it leads to a wide range of different levels of security within the same cloud, because customers may be adept or not so adept at key management. Invariably, some end user may lose his or her key and expect the cloud vendor to be able to recover it. But if each customer is responsible for its own key management, there is nothing the vendor can do. Also, the vendor is unable to perform any operations with the encrypted data (see the next section, "Homomorphic Cryptography").

Homomorphic Cryptography

Homomorphic encryption is a fascinating branch of cryptography that enables someone to carry out computations on cipher text without first decrypting the message. In other words, you can perform math on the encrypted data without actually decrypting the data. It must be stressed, however, that the entity performing the operation on the encrypted data has no idea what the actual data is. The entity cannot see the plain text, since it doesn't have access to the encryption key. This is particularly interesting in cloud environments because it allows the cloud vendor to perform some operations on the encrypted data without having access to the encryption key.

In *Wired* magazine, Andy Greenberg described homomorphic encryption, as well as its uses, as follows:

> A homomorphic encryption scheme is a crypto system that allows computations to be performed on data without decrypting it. A homomorphically encrypted search engine, for instance, could take in encrypted search terms and compare them with an encrypted index of the web. Or a homomorphically encrypted financial database stored in the cloud would allow users to ask how much money an employee earned in the second quarter of 2013. But it would accept an encrypted employee name and output an encrypted answer, avoiding the privacy problems that usually plague online services that deal with such sensitive data.[2]

Craig Gentry described the first plausible homomorphic encryption process, which supported both addition and multiplication on cipher text, without first decrypting the cipher text. Several algorithms are either partially homomorphic (that is, they allow one operation to be done homomorphically) or fully homomorphic (they allow addition and multiplication).

Note Craig Gentry is an American computer scientist who won a MacArthur Fellowship in 2014. He also invented the first plausible construction for a fully homomorphic encryption scheme. The MacArthur Fellowship, often referred to as the "Genius Grant," is awarded each year to several individuals who show exceptionally creative work. The prize is currently $625,000 awarded over five years in quarterly installments. An anonymous group nominates potential MacArthur Fellows; there are no applications.

Although homomorphic encryption has uses beyond the cloud, it has been specifically lauded as a solution to cloud issues. In a 2011 *MIT Technology Review* article, author Erica Neone specifically described Gentry's innovations as follows: "Craig Gentry is creating an encryption system that could solve the problem keeping many organizations from using cloud computing to analyze and mine data: it's too much of a security risk to give a public cloud provider such as Amazon or Google access to unencrypted data."[3]

Note When the first papers on homomorphic encryption were published, it was an impractical, theoretical technology. However, in the past several years it has moved from the theoretical to the practical and applied. For example, as early as 2011, researchers at Microsoft developed a practical, applicable homomorphic approach.[4] In 2011, Gentry and Shai Halevi published a methodology for implementing Gentry's original homomorphic process.[5]

RSA

RSA in textbook format (that is, not modified) can be used homomorphically. Here's an example. Assume that the public key is modulus m and exponent e. You encrypt any message by $x^e \bmod m$. You can certainly perform some mathematical operations on the encrypted data by simply encrypting that data and applying the operation to the two encrypted texts. For example, let's use E to represent the encryption operation of RSA: $E(x_1) * e(x_2) = x_1^e x_2^e \bmod m$, which is, in turn, equal to $E(x_1 * x_2)$. Basically multiplying two cipher texts together is the same as multiplying two plain texts and then encrypting them. Not all ciphers lend themselves to this sort of operation, but RSA does. ElGamal can also be used in a homomorphic manner.

Goldwasser–Micali

Goldwasser–Micali is an asymmetric cipher developed by Shafi Goldwasser and Silvio Micali in 1982. It was the first probabilistic public key algorithm that is provably secure. This algorithm has not gained wide use because the cipher texts are far larger than the initial plain text—as much as several hundred times larger. However, this algorithm supports homomorphic properties.

> **Note** Shafi Goldwasser is an Israeli computer scientist born in New York City. She has held professorships at MIT and the Weizmann Institute of Science in Israel. Silvio Micali is a professor of computer science at MIT and has done extensive research in cryptography.

The Benaloh cipher is an extension of the Goldwasser–Micali cipher that was created by Josh Benaloh in 1994. It allows for longer segments of plain text to be encrypted at a single time. Since it is an extension of Goldwasser–Micali, Benoloh also has homomorphic properties.

> **Note** Josh Benaloh has a Ph.D. in computer science from Yale University and works for Microsoft.

Paillier

Perhaps the most widely known homomorphic system is the Paillier system. This probabilistic asymmetric algorithm was invented by Pascal Paillier in 1999. The math is a bit more complex than some of the other algorithms we have studied in this book.

> **Note** Pascal Paillier is a French mathematician who has published extensively on cryptography and has a number of patents in cryptography.

The entire algorithm is presented here, but if you do not fully understand it, it is enough that you have a good understanding of the general concepts:

1. The algorithm begins much like RSA, in that you select two large prime numbers p and q. The values p and q should have the property that the greatest common denominator $(pq, (p-1)(q-1)) = 1$.

2. Next you compute p * q. Usually this is denoted as n = pq.
3. You also need to compute the least common multiple of p–1 and q–1. This is often denoted as λ (lambda) so that:

$$\lambda = \text{lcm}(p-1, q-1)$$

Note this is also referred to as the Carmichael function. (Robert Carmichael was an American mathematician known for his research in what are now called the Carmichael numbers, a subset of Fermat pseudoprime numbers.)
4. Select a random integer g that is where $g \in \mathbb{Z}^*_{n^2}$.
   Note that a number is said to be $\in \mathbb{Z}^*_{n^2}$ an n-th residue modulo n^2 if there exists any number $g \in \mathbb{Z}^*_{n^2}$ such that $z = g^n \bmod n^2$.
5. Ensure that n divides the order of g by checking the existence of the following modular multiplicative inverse. That equation is given here:

$$\mu = (L(g^{\lambda} \bmod n^2))^{-1} \bmod n$$

The L in the above equation is itself an equation, shown here:

$$L(u) = (u - 1)/n$$

The public key, used for encryption, is (n, g); the private key, used for decryption, is (λ, μ).
  After the key is generated, you can encrypt with the following steps:

1. Let m be the plain-text message.
2. Select random r where $r \in \mathbb{Z}^*_n$.
3. The cipher text c is computed with the following formula: $c = g^m \cdot r^n \bmod n^2$.

Decryption is accomplished via this formula:

1. Let c be the cipher text you wish to decrypt.
2. Compute the plain-text message as $m = L\ (c^{\lambda} \bmod n^2) \cdot \mu \bmod n$.

Encryption in Paillier is additively homomorphic. That means you can add data without first decrypting the cipher text.

Note As I stated at the beginning of our discussion of the Paillier crypto system, the mathematics for this particular algorithm is a bit more complex than the math used in other algorithms we have studied in this text. If you have trouble with the math shown here, don't be overly concerned. It is not critical that you have a detailed understanding of this algorithm.

If you have a programming background, it might be helpful for you to see the Paillier system in code. The University of Maryland offers the following code as open source, free to use.[6] This is a complete code example that would allow a programmer to implement a homomorphic system.

```java
import java.math.*;
import java.util.*;


/**
* Paillier Cryptosystem <br><br>
* References: <br>
* [1] Pascal Paillier, "Public-Key Cryptosystems Based on Composite Degree
Residuosity Classes," EUROCRYPT'99.
* URL: <a href="http://www.gemplus.com/smart/rd/publications/pdf/Pai99pai.
pdf">http://www.gemplus.com/smart/rd/publications/pdf/Pai99pai.pdf</a><br>
*
* [2] Paillier cryptosystem from Wikipedia.
* URL: <a href="http://en.wikipedia.org/wiki/Paillier_
cryptosystem">http://en.wikipedia.org/wiki/Paillier_cryptosystem</a>
* @author Kun Liu (kunliu1@cs.umbc.edu)
* @version 1.0
*/
public class Paillier {
    /**
    * p and q are two large primes.
    * lambda = lcm(p-1, q-1) = (p-1)*(q-1)/gcd(p-1, q-1).
    */
    private BigInteger p, q, lambda;
    /**
    * n = p*q, where p and q are two large primes.
    */
    public BigInteger n;
    /**
    * nsquare = n*n
    */
    public BigInteger nsquare;
    /**
    * a random integer in Z*_{n^2} where gcd (L(g^lambda mod n^2), n) = 1.
    */
    private BigInteger g;
    /**
    * number of bits of modulus
    */
    private int bitLength;

    /**
    * Constructs an instance of the Paillier cryptosystem.
```

```
* @param bitLengthVal number of bits of modulus
* @param certainty The probability that the new BigInteger represents a
prime number will exceed (1 - 2^(-certainty)). The execution time of this
constructor is proportional to the value of this parameter.
*/
public Paillier(int bitLengthVal, int certainty) {
KeyGeneration(bitLengthVal, certainty);
}


/**
* Constructs an instance of the Paillier cryptosystem with 512 bits of
modulus and at least 1-2^(-64) certainty of primes generation.
*/
public Paillier() {
KeyGeneration(512, 64);
}


/**
* Sets up the public key and private key.
* @param bitLengthVal number of bits of modulus.
* @param certainty The probability that the new BigInteger represents a
prime number will exceed (1 - 2^(-certainty)). The execution time of this
constructor is proportional to the value of this parameter.
*/
public void KeyGeneration(int bitLengthVal, int certainty) {
bitLength = bitLengthVal;
/*Constructs two randomly generated positive BigIntegers that are probably
prime, with the specified bitLength and certainty.*/
p = new BigInteger(bitLength / 2, certainty, new Random());
q = new BigInteger(bitLength / 2, certainty, new Random());

n = p.multiply(q);
nsquare = n.multiply(n);

g = new BigInteger("2");
lambda = p.subtract(BigInteger.ONE).multiply(q.subtract(BigInteger.ONE)).
divide(
p.subtract(BigInteger.ONE).gcd(q.subtract(BigInteger.ONE)));
/* check whether g is good.*/
if (g.modPow(lambda, nsquare).subtract(BigInteger.ONE).divide(n).gcd(n).
intValue() != 1) {
System.out.println("g is not good. Choose g again.");
System.exit(1);
}
}
```

```
/**
* Encrypts plaintext m. ciphertext c = g^m * r^n mod n^2. This function
explicitly requires random input r to help with encryption.
* @param m plaintext as a BigInteger
* @param r random plaintext to help with encryption
* @return ciphertext as a BigInteger
*/
public BigInteger Encryption(BigInteger m, BigInteger r) {
return g.modPow(m, nsquare).multiply(r.modPow(n, nsquare)).mod(nsquare);
}

/**
* Encrypts plaintext m. ciphertext c = g^m * r^n mod n^2. This function
automatically generates random input r (to help with encryption).
* @param m plaintext as a BigInteger
* @return ciphertext as a BigInteger
*/
public BigInteger Encryption(BigInteger m) {
BigInteger r = new BigInteger(bitLength, new Random());
return g.modPow(m, nsquare).multiply(r.modPow(n, nsquare)).mod(nsquare);

}

/**
* Decrypts ciphertext c. plaintext m = L(c^lambda mod n^2) * u mod n,
where u = (L(g^lambda mod n^2))^(-1) mod n.
* @param c ciphertext as a BigInteger
* @return plaintext as a BigInteger
*/
public BigInteger Decryption(BigInteger c) {
BigInteger u = g.modPow(lambda, nsquare).subtract(BigInteger.ONE).
divide(n).modInverse(n);
return c.modPow(lambda, nsquare).subtract(BigInteger.ONE).divide(n).
multiply(u).mod(n);
}

/**
* main function
* @param str intput string
*/
public static void main(String[] str) {
/* instantiating an object of Paillier cryptosystem*/
Paillier paillier = new Paillier();
/* instantiating two plaintext msgs*/
```

```
BigInteger m1 = new BigInteger("20");
BigInteger m2 = new BigInteger("60");
/* encryption*/
BigInteger em1 = paillier.Encryption(m1);
BigInteger em2 = paillier.Encryption(m2);
/* printout encrypted text*/
System.out.println(em1);
System.out.println(em2);
/* printout decrypted text */
System.out.println(paillier.Decryption(em1).toString());
System.out.println(paillier.Decryption(em2).toString());

/* test homomorphic properties -> D(E(m1)*E(m2) mod n^2) = (m1 + m2) mod n
*/
BigInteger product_em1em2 = em1.multiply(em2).mod(paillier.nsquare);
BigInteger sum_m1m2 = m1.add(m2).mod(paillier.n);
System.out.println("original sum: " + sum_m1m2.toString());
System.out.println("decrypted sum: " + paillier.Decryption(product_
em1em2).toString());

/* test homomorphic properties -> D(E(m1)^m2 mod n^2) = (m1*m2) mod n */
BigInteger expo_em1m2 = em1.modPow(m2, paillier.nsquare);
BigInteger prod_m1m2 = m1.multiply(m2).mod(paillier.n);
System.out.println("original product: " + prod_m1m2.toString());
System.out.println("decrypted product: " + paillier.Decryption(expo_
em1m2).toString());


}
}
```

You may also find the following sources useful:

- The Google Homomorphic Code Project: http://code.google.com/p/thep/.
- IBM Homomorphic research: http://researcher.watson.ibm.com/researcher/view_group
  .php?id=1548.

Quantum Cryptography

Quantum cryptography is clearly the next innovation in cryptography, but what exactly does it mean? There are several ways to apply quantum mechanics to cryptography. Two of the most obvious are quantum key distribution and using quantum computing to break cryptographic implementations. Before we can examine these issues, however, let's briefly review the essentials of quantum mechanics.

What Is Quantum Mechanics?

Quantum mechanics deals with the physics that occurs at the subatomic level. At this level, things behave very differently from their behavior in our ordinary world. The term *quantum* comes from the fact that at the subatomic level things change by discrete amounts, rather than across a continuum. A classic example often encountered in university freshman and sophomore chemistry is the orbit of electrons around the nucleus of an atom. Electrons appear at discrete energy states and do not appear at intermediate states. In other words, they are in specific quantum states.

Note	Obviously a single section in one chapter of a book cannot provide thorough coverage of such a complex topic. But you need to have only a broad outline of quantum mechanics to understand quantum cryptography.

Another fascinating, and counter-intuitive, aspect of quantum mechanics is the *wave-particle duality*. In fact, this was one of the issues that led to the discovery of quantum mechanics. At the end of the 19th century and the beginning of the 20th, there was a debate in physics as to whether or not light behaved as a particle or a wave. It turns out that it behaves in both ways, depending on circumstances, and it turns out that all particles are both a wave and a particle.

Two aspects of quantum mechanics are particularly relevant to quantum cryptography. The first is *quantum entanglement*, a process that occurs when two particles (or two groups of particles) are generated together or interact so that they become entangled. Even if you separate the particles (or groups of particles), any changes to one will immediately be correlated on the other. So, for example, if one particle is given a clockwise spin, the other will have a counterclockwise spin. The distance between the particles doesn't matter, and there is no known transformation of information—the two entangled particles just somehow "know" each other's state and correlate their states to match. If this seems remarkable to you, even hard to believe, you are in good company. Albert Einstein referred to this as "spooky action at a distance," and it is one reason he died believing quantum mechanics was flawed.

The other aspect of quantum mechanics that is of use in cryptography is the *Heisenberg uncertainty principle*, which states that the more precisely the position of some particle is determined, the less precisely its momentum can be known—and vice versa. In essence, attempting to measure a particle changes properties of that particle. We will examine some cryptographic implications for this principle later in this chapter.

Quantum Key Distribution

The most practical use of quantum cryptography, and the one most likely to be implemented in the foreseeable future, is *quantum key distribution*. The issue of key distribution is at the heart of many algorithms such as Diffie-Hellman and Menezes–Qu–Vanstone, or MQV (recall both algorithms were discussed in Chapter 10). How do two parties exchange a key in such a way that a third party cannot intercept it? If the key is encoded as quantum bits, then the Heisenberg uncertainty principle provides security for key transmission. Any attempt to read the key will in fact alter the key.[7]

It is also possible to use quantum entanglement for key exchange. If a set of particles is entangled and then separated, the party on one end can encode bits as properties (such as spin) on the particles. By changing the property on the sender's side, the bits of the key are instantly transmitted to the receiving side. Because there is no known communication medium, it is impossible for someone to intercept the key transmission.

Breaking Quantum Code

Quantum computing is still in a nascent stage, a very long way from practical implementation. But the possibilities could radically change cryptography. Current digital computers maintain data in states of bits, a 1 or 0. A quantum computer maintains data in qubits. These qubits can use a 1, a 0, or a superposition of these states. This allows quantum computers to store much more data and to process data much faster.

What this means in practical terms is that a quantum computer would have immensely more computational power than any digital computer. Consider the asymmetric algorithms you've studied in this book. They were all based on some problem being infeasible to solve, such as factoring a composite number into its prime factors (as seen in RSA), or solving a discrete logarithm problem (as in elliptic curve cryptography). If quantum computers become a practical reality, these problems will no longer be impractical to solve. In fact, they will be solvable in a reasonably short period of time, thus undermining the basis for all asymmetric algorithms.

Symmetric cryptography will not be safe from the onslaught of quantum computing either. Consider that keys such as the AES 256-bit key are essentially immune from brute-force attacks using current methods; a quantum computer could try far more keys in a shorter period of time, making brute-force attacks far more practical.

Currently there are no working quantum computers, so these issues are only hypothetical at this point. But given the attention and resources committed to quantum computing, it seems likely that we will eventually face these problems. Right now, the only solution is to use much larger keys, but this is only a stopgap solution, not a permanent one. Quantum computing will require an entirely new approach to cryptography—one that has not yet been developed.

Conclusions

Cryptography is evolving, and new issues are on the horizon. Currently one of the more immediate issues in cryptography is that of homomorphic encryption, which allows an entity to perform operations on encrypted data without first decrypting the data, and indeed without even having the capability to decrypt the data. Homomorphic encryption has applications in electronic voting, e-commerce, and cloud computing. Cloud computing itself poses cryptographic challenges, and homomorphic cryptography is one of the primary solutions to those challenges.

Quantum mechanics has not only revolutionized physics, but it could revolutionize computing and cryptography as well. Quantum key exchanges is perhaps the most immediate issue in cryptography and could solve secure key exchange issues. Code-breaking could also be enhanced dramatically by quantum computing.

Test Your Knowledge

1. _____ is a mechanism whereby the user can get proof that the vendor has not tampered with the data.
2. Briefly describe homomorphic encryption.
3. Who invented the first plausible construction for a fully homomorphic encryption scheme?
4. _____ was the first probabilistic public key algorithm that is provably secure.
5. What is the most widely known homomorphic system?
6. What is (currently) the most practical application of quantum mechanics to cryptography?
7. What property of quantum mechanics makes it impossible to tamper with a key being transmitted with quantum bits?

Answers

1. Proof of storage
2. Homomorphic encryption allows an entity to carry out computations on cipher text, without first decrypting the message.
3. Craig Gentry
4. Goldwasser–Micali
5. Paillier system
6. Quantum key distribution
7. The Heisenberg uncertainty principle

Endnotes

1. "Cloud Security & Cryptography," http://research.microsoft.com/en-us/projects/cryptocloud/.
2. A. Greenberg, "Hacker Lexicon: What is Homomorphic Encryption?" *Wired*, 2014, www.wired.com/2014/11/hacker-lexicon-homomorphic-encryption/.
3. E. Naone, "Homomorphic Encryption: Making Cloud Computing More Secure," *MIT Technology Review*, 2011, www2.technologyreview.com/article/423683/homomorphic-encryption/.
4. K. Lauter, M. Naehrig, and V. Vaikuntanathan, "Can Homomorphic Encryption be Practical?" Microsoft Research, 2011, www.msr-waypoint.com/pubs/148825/ccs2011_submission_412.pdf.
5. C. Gentry and S. Halevi, "Implementing Gentry's Fully-Homomorphic Encryption Scheme," in *Advances in Cryptology – EUROCRYPT 2011 Lecture Notes in Computer Science*, vol. 6632, 2011, 129–148, http://link.springer.com/chapter/10.1007%2F978-3-642-20465-4_9#page-2.
6. You can download the Paillier code from www.csee.umbc.edu/~kunliu1/research/Paillier.html.
7. S. Selvan, R. Rajan, and S. Tamilenthi, "An overview of new trends in cryptography," *Recent Research in Science and Technology* 2012, 4(6), 38–42.

A Implementing Cryptography

This appendix provides brief tutorials for several cryptography products, including those for file/drive and e-mail encryption. It also includes tools to aid in learning cryptography that can provide you with options for implementing cryptography to secure your data. If this book is used as a textbook, the tutorials can be used as labs for the class.

Hard Drive/File Encryption

This section includes tutorials regarding how to use some common tools for encrypting hard drives or individual files. Clearly, government agencies and many businesses store confidential data on computers. The need to encrypt data is not limited to large corporations and government entities, however. Most computer users have some data on their computer that they want to keep confidential, such as financial records or tax returns. Using the following tools, you'll find that encrypting a file or an entire partition is a very easy task. A variety of drive/file encryption solutions are available, including many free and open source tools.

VeraCrypt

VeraCrypt has the advantage of being available for Macintosh, Linux, and Windows. It is based on the earlier product, TrueCrypt 7.1a. VeraCrypt is open source, and you can download the source code from https://veracrypt.codeplex.com/. VeraCrypt can use AES, Serpent, Twofish, or cascade cryptographic algorithms. For hashing, it can use SHA-256, SHA-512, RIPEMD-160, or Whirlpool.

 Note TrueCrypt was once one of the most widely used open source drive/letter encryption tools available. However, it is no longer supported, so any new security issues are not being patched. VeraCrypt works exactly like TrueCrypt, however, and it can even mount TrueCrypt-encrypted drives.

VeraCrypt has an easy graphical user interface that enables you to create an entire encrypted volume or a specific file. The initial interface is shown in Figure A-1.

To create a volume, click the Create Volume button to launch the Select A VeraCrypt Volume screen, shown in Figure A-2.

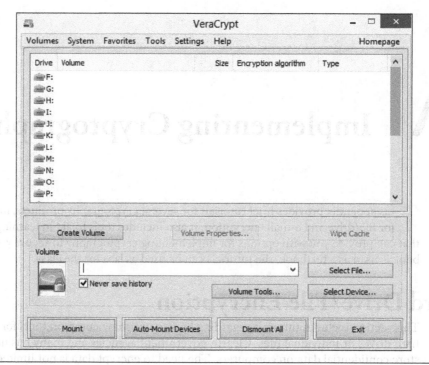

FIGURE A-1   VeraCrypt main screen

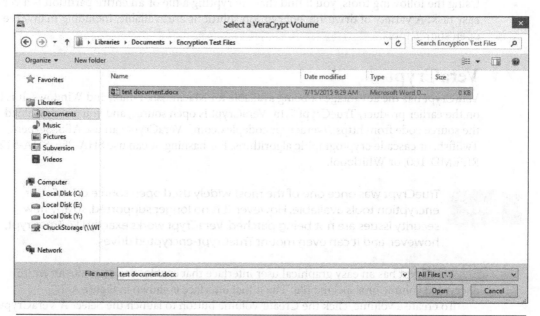

FIGURE A-2   Select a VeraCrypt volume from this screen.

As you go through the process, you will be presented with three options regarding what you wish to create:

- *Create an encrypted file container.* This is recommended for new users.
- *Encrypt a non-system drive.* This is a very common option if you want to encrypt a USB external drive.
- *Encrypt the system partition.* This is not recommended for new users. If an error is encountered, the system drive could be rendered unusable.

Select the first option. Then, in the Volume Type screen, choose to create a standard volume or a hidden volume, as shown in Figure A-3. Then click Next.

Next, in the Volume Location screen, select a file for the encrypted volume, as shown in Figure A-4. Notice that each screen of the encryption wizard includes instructions detailing what a specific step entails. Then click Next.

In the next screen of the wizard, the Encryption Options screen, shown in Figure A-5, select the specific cryptographic algorithms you want to use. Then click Next.

Next, in the Volume Size screen shown in Figure A-6, select the size of the partition you want to create. The amount of free space on the existing partition is displayed to help you choose an appropriate-sized encrypted partition. Then click Next.

The final step is to type in a password, as shown in Figure A-7.

The last step is the most critical step in any drive or file encryption, because this is the weakest point in your drive/file encryption. No matter how secure the cryptographic algorithm, or how robust the pseudo-random-number generator (PRNG) used to generate cryptographic keys, if the password you select is easily bypassed, the rest of the security measures become moot points.

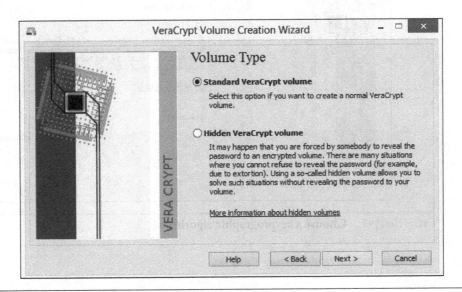

FIGURE A-3   Choose a hidden or standard volume.

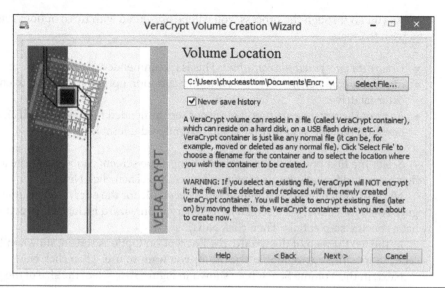

FIGURE A-4 Select a volume file.

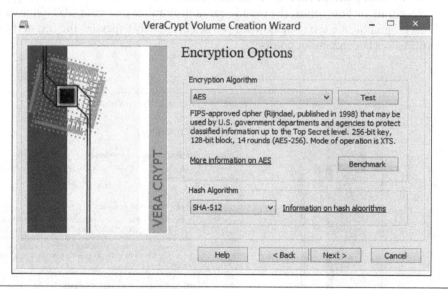

FIGURE A-5 Choose a cryptographic algorithm.

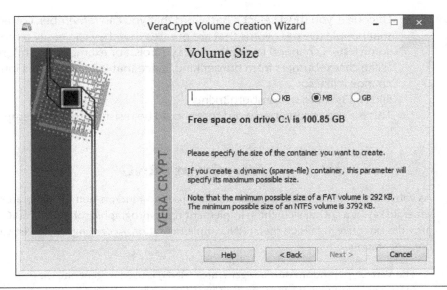

FIGURE A-6   Choose a volume size.

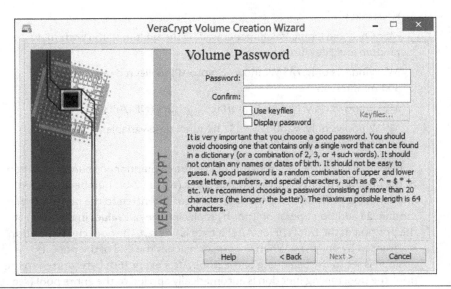

FIGURE A-7   Type a password.

> **Note** Of course, you must select a password that you can remember. I often suggest that people use passwords that are phrases that they can easily remember, with some letters changed to numbers or symbols. For example, you might select "I like cheeseburgers from burger king," since that is 32 characters long, but change it like so:
> !!!k3ch33s3burg3rsfromburg3rk!ng
> This is a very strong password that should be resistant to any attempts to break it.

VeraCrypt PRNG

As you know from this book, the selection of a pseudo-random-number generator to generate keys is a critical element in implementing cryptographic solutions. VeraCrypt provides extensive details on their PRNG implementation. According to the VeraCrypt documentation:

> The VeraCrypt random number generator (RNG) is used to generate the master encryption key, the secondary key (XTS mode), salt, and keyfiles. It creates a pool of random values in RAM (memory). The pool, which is 320 bytes long, is filled with data from the following sources:
>
> Mouse movements
>
> Keystrokes
>
> Mac OS X and Linux: Values generated by the built-in RNG (both /dev/random and /dev/urandom)
>
> MS Windows only: MS Windows CryptoAPI (collected regularly at 500-ms interval)
>
> MS Windows only: Network interface statistics (NETAPI32)
>
> MS Windows only: Various Win32 handles, time variables, and counters (collected regularly at 500-ms interval)
>
> Before a value obtained from any of the above-mentioned sources is written to the pool, it is divided into individual bytes (e.g., a 32-bit number is divided into four bytes). These bytes are then individually written to the pool with the modulo 28 addition operation (not by replacing the old values in the pool) at the position of the pool cursor. After a byte is written, the pool cursor position is advanced by one byte. When the cursor reaches the end of the pool, its position is set to the beginning of the pool. After every 16th byte written to the pool, the pool mixing function is automatically applied to the entire pool (see below).

Pool Mixing Function

The purpose of this function is to perform diffusion.[2] Diffusion spreads the influence of individual "raw" input bits over as much of the pool state as possible, which also hides statistical relationships. After every 16th byte written to the pool, this function is applied to the entire pool.

Description of the pool mixing function:
1. Let R be the randomness pool.
2. Let H be the hash function selected by the user (SHA-512, RIPEMD-160, or Whirlpool).
3. l = byte size of the output of the hash function H (i.e., if H is RIPEMD-160, then l = 20; if H is SHA-512, l = 64)
4. z = byte size of the randomness pool R (320 bytes)
5. q = z / l – 1 (e.g., if H is Whirlpool, then q = 4)
6. R is divided into l-byte blocks B0...Bq.

For $0 \leq i \leq q$ (i.e., for each block B) the following steps are performed:

1. M = H (B0 || B1 || ... || Bq) [i.e., the randomness pool is hashed using the hash function H, which produces a hash M]
2. Bi = Bi ^ M
3. R = B0 || B1 || ... || Bq

For example, if q = 1, the randomness pool would be mixed as follows:

1. (B0 || B1) = R
2. B0 = B0 ^ H(B0 || B1)
3. B1 = B1 ^ H(B0 || B1)
4. R = B0 || B1

Generated Values

The content of the RNG pool is never directly exported (even when VeraCrypt instructs the RNG to generate and export a value). Thus, even if the attacker obtains a value generated by the RNG, it is infeasible for him to determine or predict (using the obtained value) any other values generated by the RNG during the session (it is infeasible to determine the content of the pool from a value generated by the RNG).[1]

This detailed description of the PRNG provides you with enough information to evaluate whether or not the PRNG is sufficiently random for your security needs. The online documentation provided by VeraCrypt has even more details.

Windows EFS

Because Windows is such a common operating system, it is appropriate to examine the Encrypted File System (EFS), which was introduced in Windows 2000. At that time it was present in all Windows editions. Since Windows XP, EFS has been available only in Windows Professional or better editions of the operating system.

The original (Windows 2000) process of EFS is described by Howard Wright in a SANS Institute research document:

> The first time a file is encrypted, EFS assigns the user a public key/private key pair for the account. If a certificate service is available, it will generate the keys. For standalone systems, EFS will generate a self-signed certificate. When a file is encrypted, EFS generates a random number for that file called a file encryption key (FEK). The FEK is used to encrypt the file contents using data encryption standard (DESX). DESX is an enhanced version DES. Basically, DESX processes the data three times with three different keys. The FEK is stored on the system and is encrypted using the user's public key with the RSA public key encryption algorithm.[2]

The encrypted FEK is stored in the $EFS alternate data stream of the encrypted file. To decrypt the file, EFS uses the private key that matches the EFS digital certificate (used to encrypt the file) to decrypt the symmetric key that is stored in the $EFS stream. The process is actually very simple:

1. Right-click the file or folder you want to encrypt, and then select properties to open the Properties dialog shown in Figure A-8.

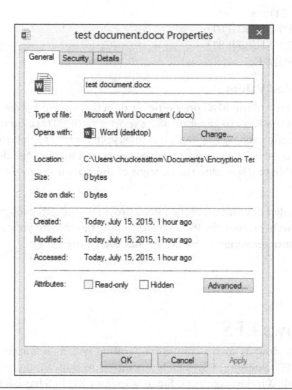

FIGURE A-8   **EFS File Properties dialog**

FIGURE A-9   Encrypting the EFS file

2. Click the Advanced button, and on the Advanced Attributes screen, select the Encrypt Contents To Secure Data check box, as shown in Figure A-9. Then click OK.

The filename will then appear in green in Windows Explorer.

> **Note** It is important that you back up the EFS key. If you do not, and the system crashes, you will have no way to recover the key and decrypt the files, and the data that was encrypted will be permanently lost. Fortunately, Microsoft provides easy-to-follow instructions on how to back up the key at http://windows.microsoft.com/en-us/windows/back-up-efs-certificate#1TC=windows-7.

BitLocker

Microsoft expanded on the concept of EFS with Windows 7 and included BitLocker, which can encrypt the entire drive. It is available only in Windows Professional Edition or better versions. It uses AES in cipher block chaining mode, and the user can select either a 128- or 256-bit key. You'll find BitLocker in the Control Panel, under System and Security, as shown in Figure A-10.

The process of encrypting the drive is very simple: The user selects the option to Turn On BitLocker, as shown in Figure A-11.

> **Note** As with EFS, it is important that you back up the BitLocker key and keep that backup in a secure location. Microsoft details several options for backing up this key at https://technet.microsoft.com/en-us/library/dd875529(v=ws.10).aspx.

FIGURE A-10 Windows BitLocker

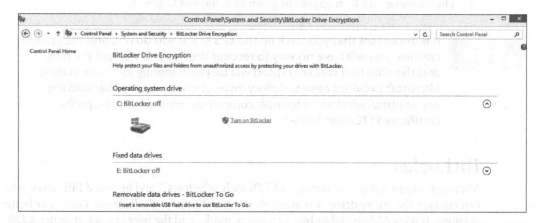

FIGURE A-11 Turning on BitLocker

AxCrypt

AxCrypt is for Windows only, but it is an open source product available at www.axantum.com. It has some similarities to EFS, but it contains some features that are not included with EFS. For example, AxCrypt allows the user to create self-decrypting files that decrypt based on the password only. AxCrypt supports the use of AES 128-bit for encryption and SHA1 128-bit for cryptographic hashes.

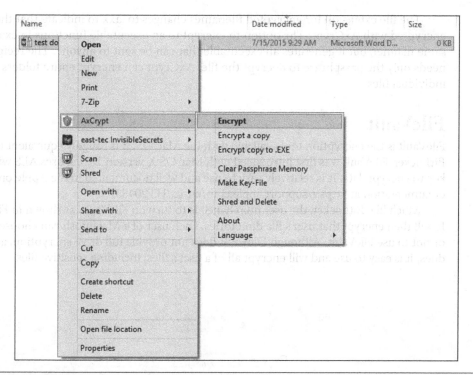

FIGURE A-12   AxCrypt menu options

After AxCrypt is installed on the computer, you can right-click any file or folder, and the AxCrypt menu will provide several options, as shown in Figure A-12.

If you select the Encrypt option, you will be prompted to select a passphrase for decrypting the file. It is important that this passphrase be long enough and complex enough to deter attempts to break or guess it—but also something you can remember. The passphrase dialog is shown in Figure A-13.

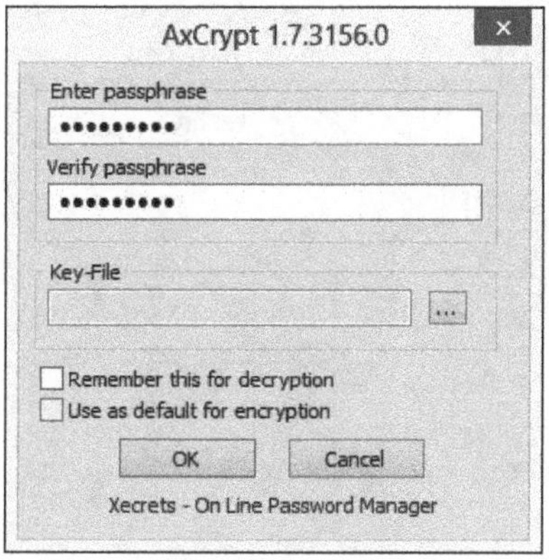

FIGURE A-13   AxCrypt encryption passphrase dialog

The file extension for encrypted filenames changes to .axx to indicate that they are encrypted with AxCrypt. The option to encrypt to an executable functions in exactly the same manner, but it generates an executable that can be sent to anyone. The recipient then needs only the passphrase to decrypt the file. AxCrypt can encrypt entire folders as well as individual files.

FileVault

FileVault is the encryption tool available with the Mac OS. It is roughly equivalent to Microsoft BitLocker. FileVault was first introduced with Mac OS X version 10.3. It uses AES with a 256-bit key to encrypt data. It is relatively easy to use and well documented in the Apple online documentation at https://support.apple.com/en-us/HT204837.

Much like BitLocker, the user merely needs to turn on FileVault, as shown in Figure A-14. It will then encrypt that user's file directories. Each user of a Macintosh can choose whether or not to use FileVault. Although FileVault does not provide full drive encryption, as BitLocker does, it is easy to use and will encrypt all of a user's files, including sensitive files.

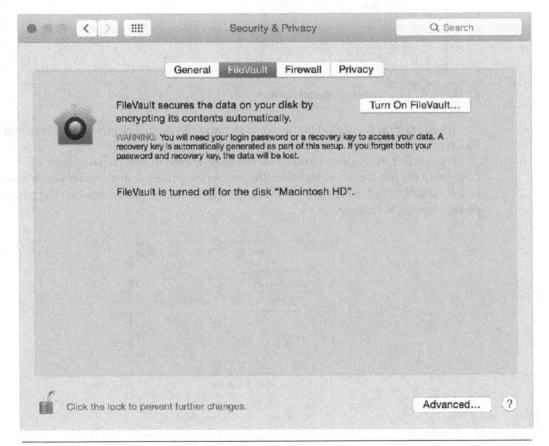

FIGURE A-14 **Turning on FileVault**

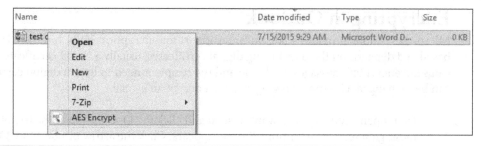

FIGURE A-15   AES Crypt options

FIGURE A-16   AES Crypt Password dialog

AES Crypt

AES Crypt is free and open source and can run on Windows, Linux, Macintosh, and even some mobile device operating systems. Java and C# libraries enable programmers to integrate AES Crypt into programs. AES Crypt uses 256-bit AES to encrypt files.

Once you've installed AES Crypt, you can right-click any file and AES Encrypt will be displayed as an option, as shown in Figure A-15.

After choosing AES Crypt, you'll be prompted to select a password for the file, as shown in Figure A-16. As with other drive/file encryption tools, the selection of a password is important because this can be the weakest link in cryptographic security.

AES Crypt has two issues: it encrypts only files, not folders; and it actually makes a copy of the file and encrypts that. You then need to delete the unencrypted original.

E-mail Encryption

Most of us occasionally need to send e-mails that contain confidential information. If the only issue is a confidential attachment, then you can use one of the previously described file encryption tools to encrypt the file before attaching it. However, if the e-mail itself needs to be encrypted, that presents a different challenge. In this section you will learn about several different options for encrypting e-mail.

In general, most e-mail options center around PGP (Pretty Good Privacy), which was described in detail earlier in this book. If you use a different e-mail client and find that none of the solutions discussed in this section work for you, you can simply perform an Internet search for "PGP" and the name of your e-mail client. It is virtually certain that there will be a PGP solution for your e-mail software.

Encrypting in Outlook

Microsoft Outlook provides some built-in support for encryption. This, however, is not PGP-based and depends on the user having digital certificates, usually a X.509 certificate. Before you can send encrypted messages, both you and the recipient need to have a digital certificate that can be exchanged. Use the following steps to encrypt an e-mail.

1. First, open a message you want to send and click the Options tab at the top of the message screen. The Options Ribbon appears. Click the arrow beside More Options, as shown next:

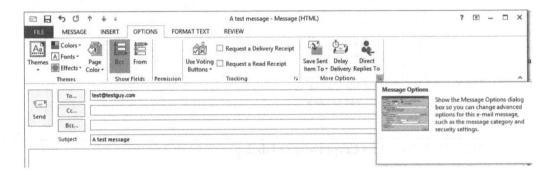

2. In the Properties dialog, click the Security Settings button, as shown next:

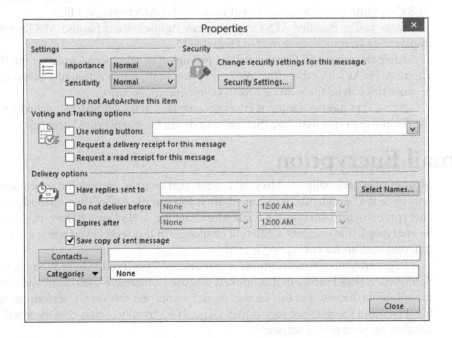

3. In the Security Properties dialog, select the Encrypt Message Contents And Attachments check box and click OK. This opens the Signing Data With The Your Private Exchange Key dialog. After you click Close, and the message is encrypted, digitally signed, and ready to send.

Encrypting with gpg4o

gpg4o is an e-mail add-in that provides PGP encryption for Microsoft Outlook. You can get a free trial or purchase the product at www.giepa.de/products/gpg4o/?lang=en. During the installation, you will be prompted either to use a current key pair (asymmetric cryptography) on your machine or to generate a new key pair, as shown in Figure A-17.

Note you can have many different key pairs if you want. For example, if you have multiple e-mail accounts, you might want to use a different key pair with each account. During the configuration process, a test e-mail will be sent to yourself. Once you've installed gpg4o, an additional option will be provided in Outlook that enables you to configure gpg4o, including generating and managing keys, as shown in Figure A-18.

When you're creating key pairs, gpg4o asks you to create a password/passphrase to access encrypted messages. It then evaluates the strength and security of your password/passphrase, as shown in Figure A-19.

You can use the default settings, which are currently RSA with a 4096-bit key, or you can configure the settings yourself, as shown in Figure A-20.

FIGURE A-17 gpg4o configuration

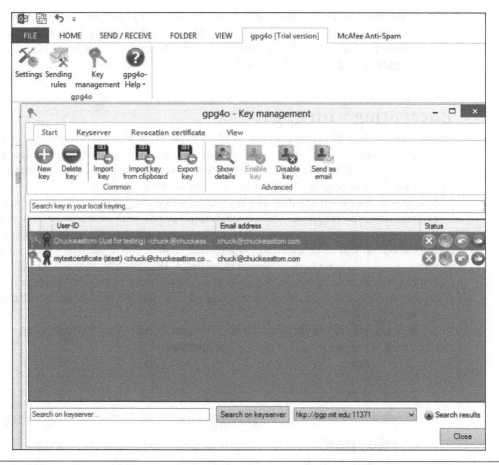

FIGURE A-18   gpg4o Key Management

FIGURE A-19   gpg4o password/passphrase strength

FIGURE A-20   gpg4o cryptography settings

After gpg4o is installed and configured, when you create a new e-mail message you are provided with several options: You can choose not to encrypt the e-mail, encrypt just the attachment, or encrypt the entire e-mail. You can also choose whether or not to digitally sign the e-mail, and whether or not to send your public key along to the recipient in the screen shown in Figure A-21.

FIGURE A-21   gpg4o e-mail options

FIGURE A-22 gpg4o encrypted text

The e-mail will then be encrypted and unreadable to anyone who does not have access to the encryption keys needed to decrypt, as shown in Figure A-22.

Usually, you will want to import the recipient's public key in order to encrypt messages to that recipient. gpg4o gives you the option of sending your public key to whomever you want. The product is not free, so after the trial period is over you must purchase the product to continue using it. It is relatively inexpensive and, as you have seen, easy to use.

CrypTool

Some software tools can assist you in learning more about cryptography, and perhaps the most widely known of these tools is CrypTool, which was briefly introduced earlier in this book.

The main screen of CrypTool provides a number of options. The text message shown in Figure A-23 will be used throughout this tutorial.

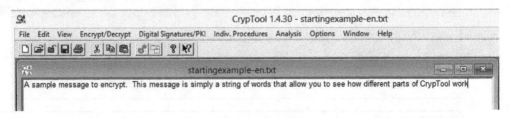

FIGURE A-23   CrypTool main screen and sample text

From the Encrypt/Decrypt menu, you can select from a wide range of classic ciphers, modern symmetric ciphers, and modern asymmetric ciphers, as shown next:

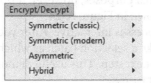

Regardless of the type of cipher you select, you can experiment with cryptographic algorithms and look at the output produced. For example, if you select Encrypt/Decrypt | Symmetric (Classic) | Playfair, the cipher text produced is shown next:

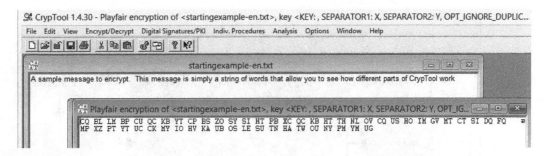

If you select Encrypt/Decrypt | Symmetric (Modern), regardless of which algorithm is selected, you need to supply a key in hexadecimal format, as shown next:

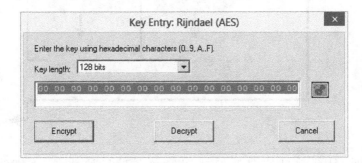

For testing and learning purposes, the randomness of the key is not critical, and you can type in any key you want, simply creating one as needed to see how the encrypted text is produced.

The next menu, Digital Signatures/PKI, and its options are shown here:

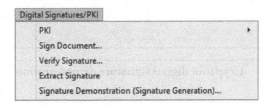

Most of the options in this menu demonstrate a specific function, but they are not very useful as learning tools. The last option, Signature Demonstration (Signature Generation), is very useful for educational purposes, however. It provides an interactive demo of the digital signature process, as shown in Figure A-24.

Each step in the process is interactive. After you click a step, you are prompted to enter the required data or make a selection (such as which hashing algorithm to use), and then the process proceeds to the next step. This useful demonstration gives you a step-by-step tutorial on the digital signature process.

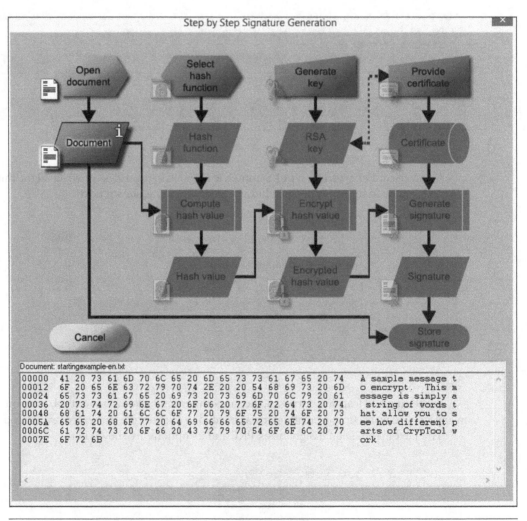

FIGURE A-24   CrypTool digital signature demonstration

The next menu option, Indiv. Procedures, includes several sub-options, described briefly here:

- **Hash** Provides a tool that will compute a hash using one of several algorithms including MD4, SHA1, SHA2, and RIPEMD.
- **RSA** In addition to providing tools to generate RSA keys and prime numbers, this interesting option includes an RSA demonstration, which enables you to provide or generate the prime numbers for RSA, then generate keys, and then encrypt a text using RSA.
- **Protocols** Allows you to experiment with demonstrations of various protocols, such as Diffie-Hellman. The Diffie-Hellman demonstration is also an interactive process, as shown in Figure A-25.
- **The Chinese Remainder Theorem** This is of interest in factoring numbers. This mathematical process is demonstrated with three separate demonstration options.
- **Visualization of Algorithms** This option is very important for learning cryptographic algorithms. It contains visual demonstrations of several algorithms including DES,

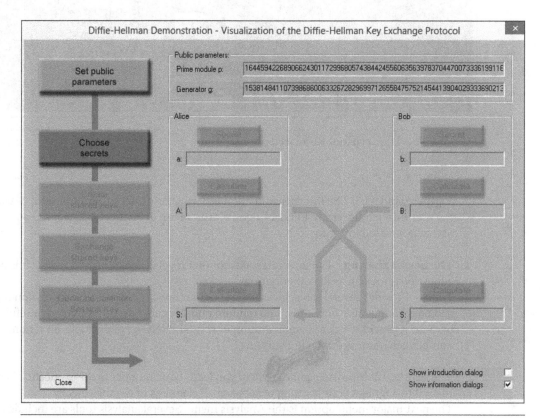

FIGURE A-25 CrypTool Diffie-Hellman demonstration

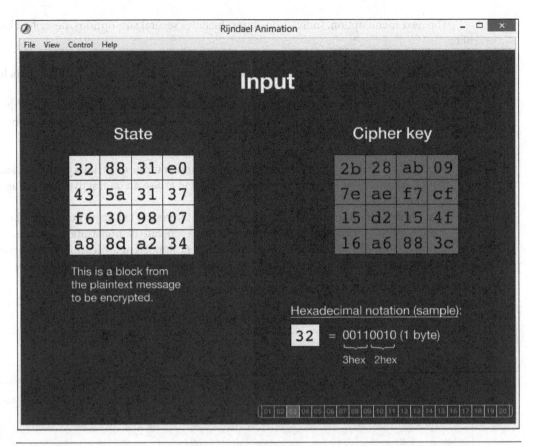

FIGURE A-26 CrypTool Rijndael demonstration

Vigenère, and AES. The Rijndael animation is particularly interesting and useful. It walks the user through the entire Rijndael algorithm as a flash animation. You can see one screen of that animation in Figure A-26.

- **The Secret Sharing** Demonstrates one option for generating a shared secret. It is not as educationally useful as the other options.
- **Tools** Provides several tools, including random number generation, compression tools, and password quality measures. The random number generator is particularly useful because it provides a clear demonstration of several PRNGs. For example, a random number generator is shown in Figure A-27.

The last two tools provide games to help you learn basic number theory concepts. Each can be used to augment your learning of some small elements of number theory.

The next major menu option is the Analysis menu. Several analysis tools are included here. I will introduce you to a few that are the most educational.

Generation of Random Numbers ☒

Random data is generated with the aid of so-called "pseudorandom number generators". This is a selection of both "cryptographically strong" and also insecure pseudorandom number generators.

Algorithm selection

○ Secude Library random number generator

○ X^2 (mod N) random number generator

◉ Linear Congruence Generator (LCG)

○ Inverse Congruence Generator (ICG)

Parameters

Seed: 314159

[Choose generator-specific parameters ...]

Output options

Length of output in bytes: 12000

☐ Print out internal random number states (only for X^2 mod N, ICG and LCG).

[Generate output]   [Cancel]

FIGURE A-27   CrypTool random number generator

Begin by encrypting the sample text shown in Figure A-23 with the Caesar cipher. Then proceed by choosing Encrypt/Decrypt | Symmetric (Classic) | Cipher Text Only | Caesar. You will notice that several screens show up, each providing a different analysis. The final screen provides the tool's best guess at the key, and will then decrypt the message for you. With ciphers such as Caesar, the decrypting is always quite fast and very accurate.

Another useful analysis tool is the Analyze Randomness tool, which offers a number of randomness tests, many of which were described earlier in this book. You can see these options next:

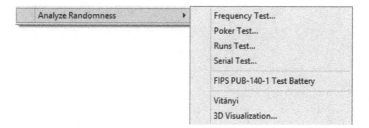

As you can see, CrypTool is an excellent resource for those who are learning cryptography. It includes several demonstration tools that can help you visualize algorithms, digital signatures, and more. The various tools for analyzing randomness are quite useful when you're evaluating a PRNG.

Endnotes

1. VeraCrypt, "Random Number Generator," https://veracrypt.codeplex.com/wikipage?title=Random%20Number%20Generator.
2. H. Wright, "The Encrypting File System: How Secure Is It?" 2001, www.sans.org/reading-room/whitepapers/win2k/encrypting-file-system-secure-it-211.

Index

Symbols

≡ (congruence) symbol, 72
mod (modulus operator), 72–73
Σ (sigma) symbol, 71

A

A5/1, 158
abelian group, 94, 213
abstract algebra. *See* algebra
Aciiçmez, O., 320
ACM (Association for Computing Machinery), 198
Adams, Carlisle, 135
addends, 70
addition of matrices, 97
addition rule, 84
ADFGX and ADFGVX ciphers, 29–31
Adleman, Leonard, 195
Advanced Encryption Standard. *See* AES
AES (Advanced Encryption Standard). *See also* Rijndael
S-box
    considerations about, 2
    development of, 144
    implementing LCGs in, 230
    military use of, 277
    Rijndael steps for, 144–145
    rounds for, 145–146
    Serpent vs., 149
    as Suite B algorithm, 282
AES Crypt, 367
affine ciphers, 7–8
affine transformation, 150, 172–173
Al-Karaji, 111
Al-Khwarizmi, Mohammed ibn-Musa, 63, 110
Alberti cipher disk, 14, 15
Alberti, Leon Battista, 14
Alexander's Weekly Messenger (Poe), 33
algebra, 91–115. *See also* algorithms
    algorithms, 102–109
    ancient Arabic, 111
    ancient Chinese, 111
    ancient Mediterranean, 110–111
    applying in cryptography, 91
    concepts of abstract, 92–93

    contributors to, 111–113
    developmental stages of, 109–110
    Diophantine equations, 96
    fields, 95–96
    finite or Galois fields m, 212
    groups, 93–94, 213
    historical highlights of, 109–113
    matrix math, 97–101
    origin of name, 63, 110
    Rhind Papyrus, 110
    rings, 94–95
algorithmic generators, 221
algorithms, 102–109. *See also specific algorithms by name*
    about, 102–103, 113
    based on discrete logarithm problem, 71, 215
    creating cryptographic hashes, 181–189
    designing, 106–107
    developing for Caesar cipher, 5–6
    Euclidean, 105–106
    finding DES replacement, 143–144
    finding prime numbers, 65–68
    mathematics for Paillier system, 347
    NSA organization of, 51
    P vs. NP, 107–109
    probabilistic and deterministic, 68
    quick sort, 104
    salt, 90
    self-test and answers, 114–115
    sorting, 103–104
    suites used by NSA, 279, 281–282
    used by block ciphers, 118–119
    using pseudo-random-number generators, 221
    visualizing, 375–376
Analytische Zahlentheorie (Bachmann), 103
ancient Arabic algebra, 111
ancient Chinese algebra, 111
ancient Mediterranean algebra, 110–111
AND operations, 57
Anderson, Ross, 148, 156, 157, 187–188
answers to tests. *See* self-test and answers
Anupam, H.S., 299
Apache web servers, 253–254
applications. *See* military applications; steganography tools;
  software applications

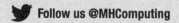